FUSHIGI YÛGI
GENBU KAIDEN™

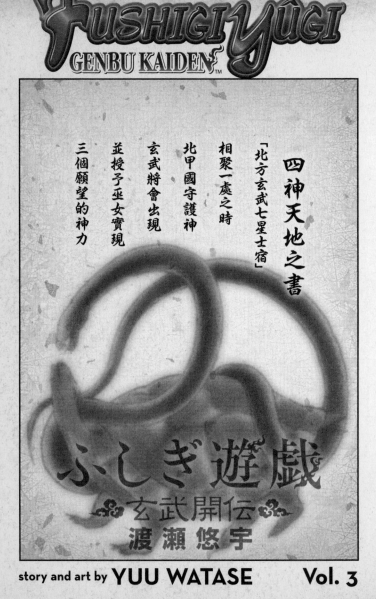

四神天地之書

「北方玄武七星士宿」

相聚一處之時

北甲國守護神

玄武將會出現

並授予巫女實現

三個願望的神力

ふしぎ遊戯

玄武開伝

渡瀬悠宇

story and art by YUU WATASE　　**Vol. 3**

CONTENTS

TRANSLATION OF "THE UNIVERSE OF THE FOUR GODS"

When all seven Celestial Warriors of Genbu are together, Genbu, the guardian god of Bêi-jîa, will appear and give the Priestess three uses of its holy powers.

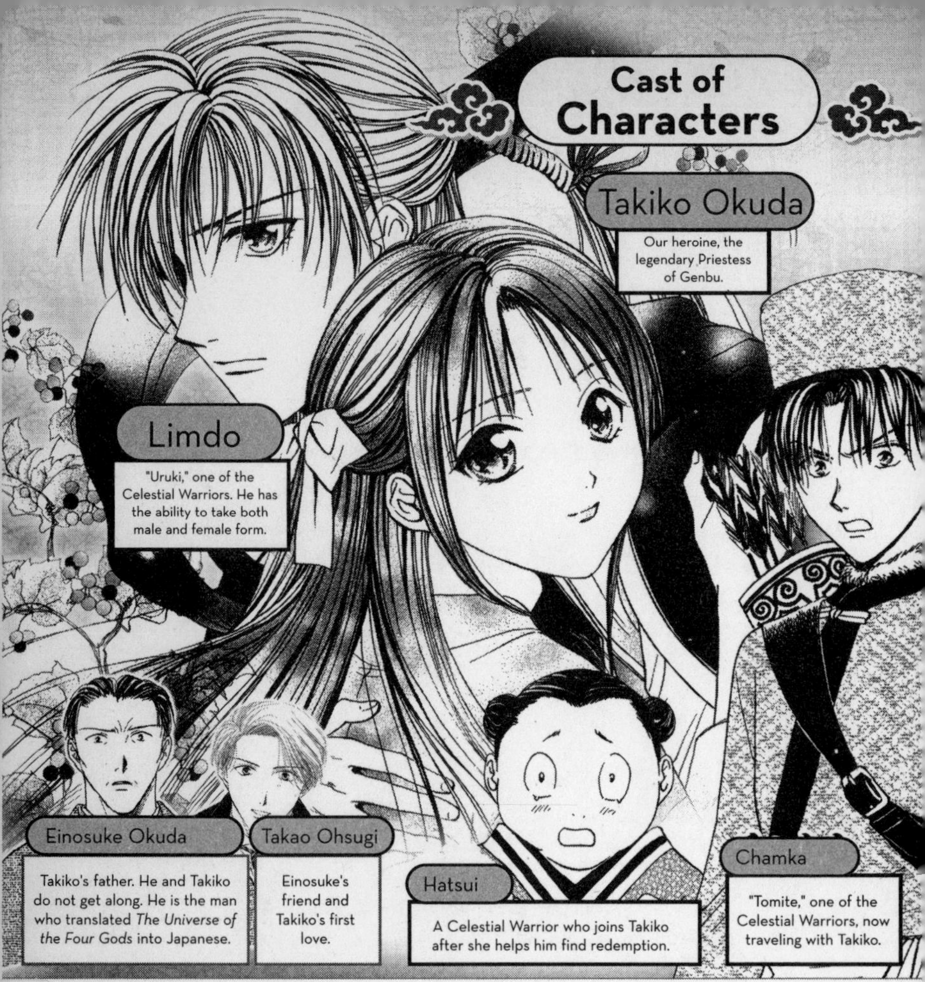
Cast of Characters
Takiko Okuda
Our heroine, the legendary Priestess of Genbu.
Limdo
"Uruki," one of the Celestial Warriors. He has the ability to take both male and female form.
Einosuke Okuda
Takiko's father. He and Takiko do not get along. He is the man who translated *The Universe of the Four Gods* into Japanese.
Takao Ohsugi
Einosuke's friend and Takiko's first love.
Hatsui
A Celestial Warrior who joins Takiko after she helps him find redemption.
Chamka
"Tomite," one of the Celestial Warriors, now traveling with Takiko.

The Story Thus Far

The year is 1923. Takiko is drawn into the pages of *The Universe of the Four Gods*, a book her father has translated from Chinese. There, she is told that she is the legendary Priestess of Genbu, destined to save the country of Bêi-jîa. She must find the seven Celestial Warriors who will help her on her quest. In Bêi-jîa, however, the Priestess and the Celestial Warriors are seen as ill omens.

Takiko sets out with Chamka (Tomite) to find the Celestial Warriors. They locate Hatsui, a boy who withdrew into his shell after unintentionally hurting others with his celestial powers. Meanwhile, Limdo (Uruki) sets out on his own. Although he is a prince of Bêi-jîa, he is hunted down by his own father. Their journey has only begun!

FUSHIGI YÛGI:
GENBU KAIDEN

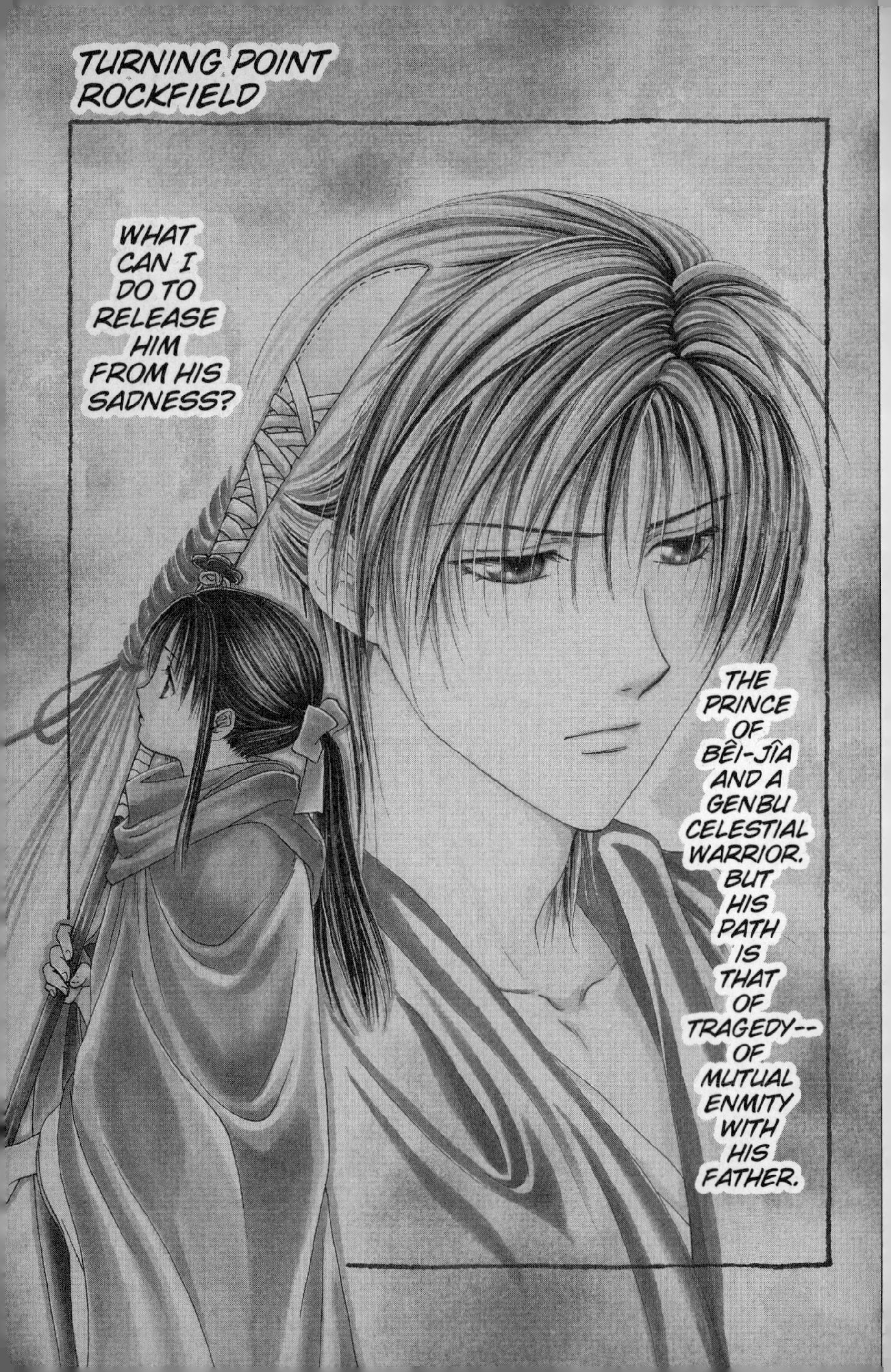
TURNING POINT ROCKFIELD
THE PRINCE OF BÊI-JÎA AND A GENBU CELESTIAL WARRIOR. BUT HIS PATH IS THAT OF TRAGEDY--OF MUTUAL ENMITY WITH HIS FATHER.
WHAT CAN I DO TO RELEASE HIM FROM HIS SADNESS?

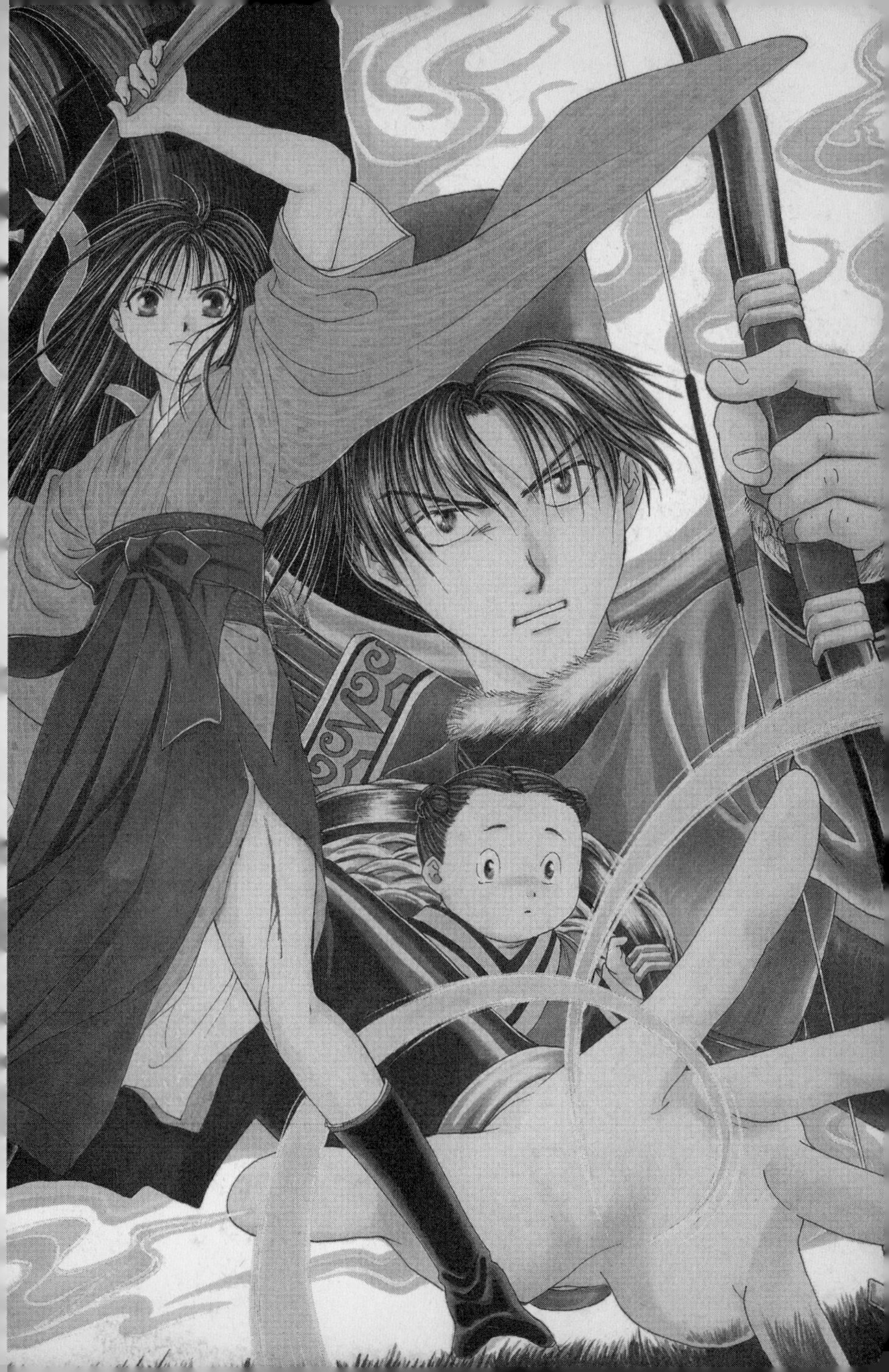

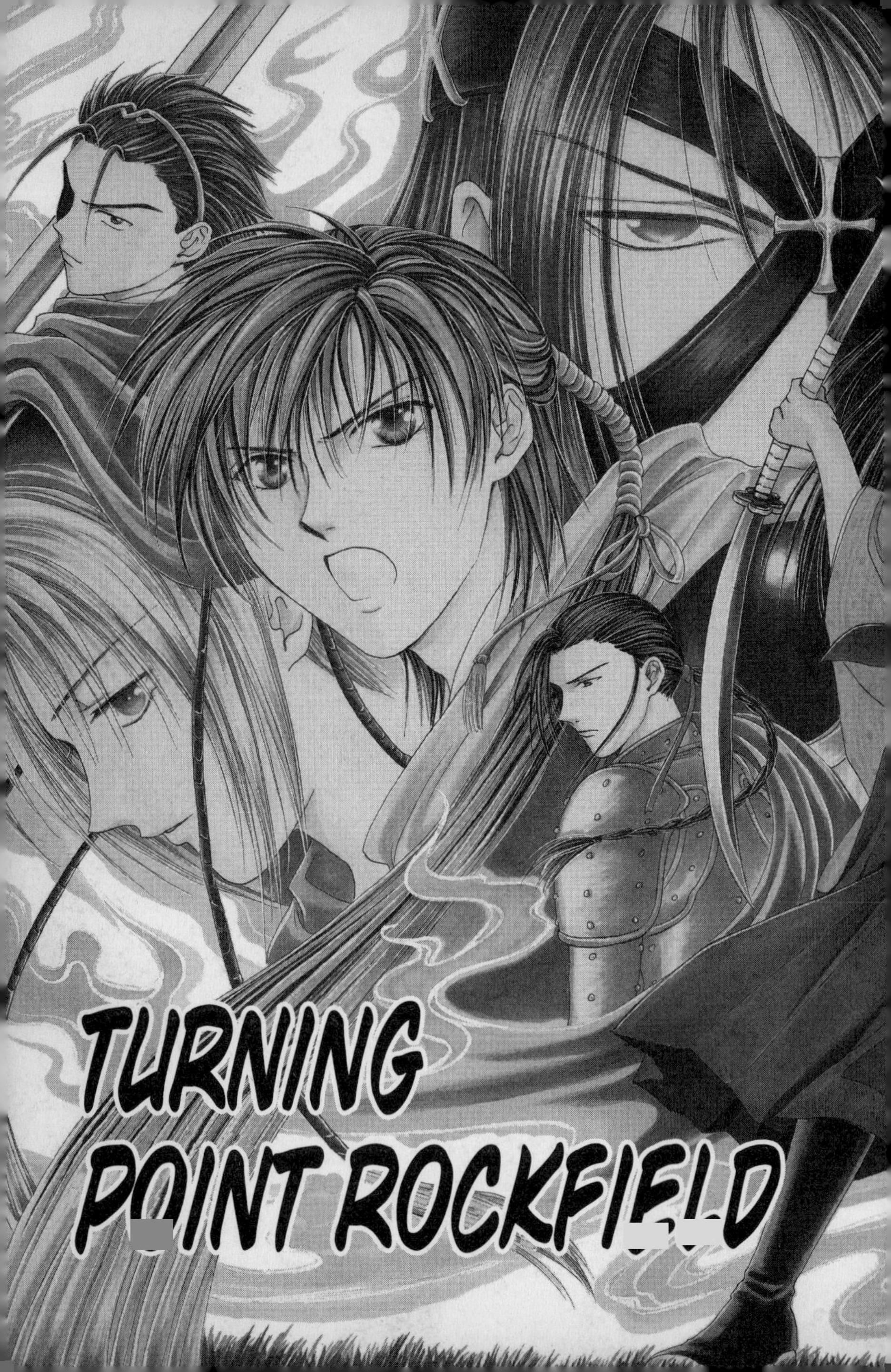
TURNING
POINT ROCKFIELD

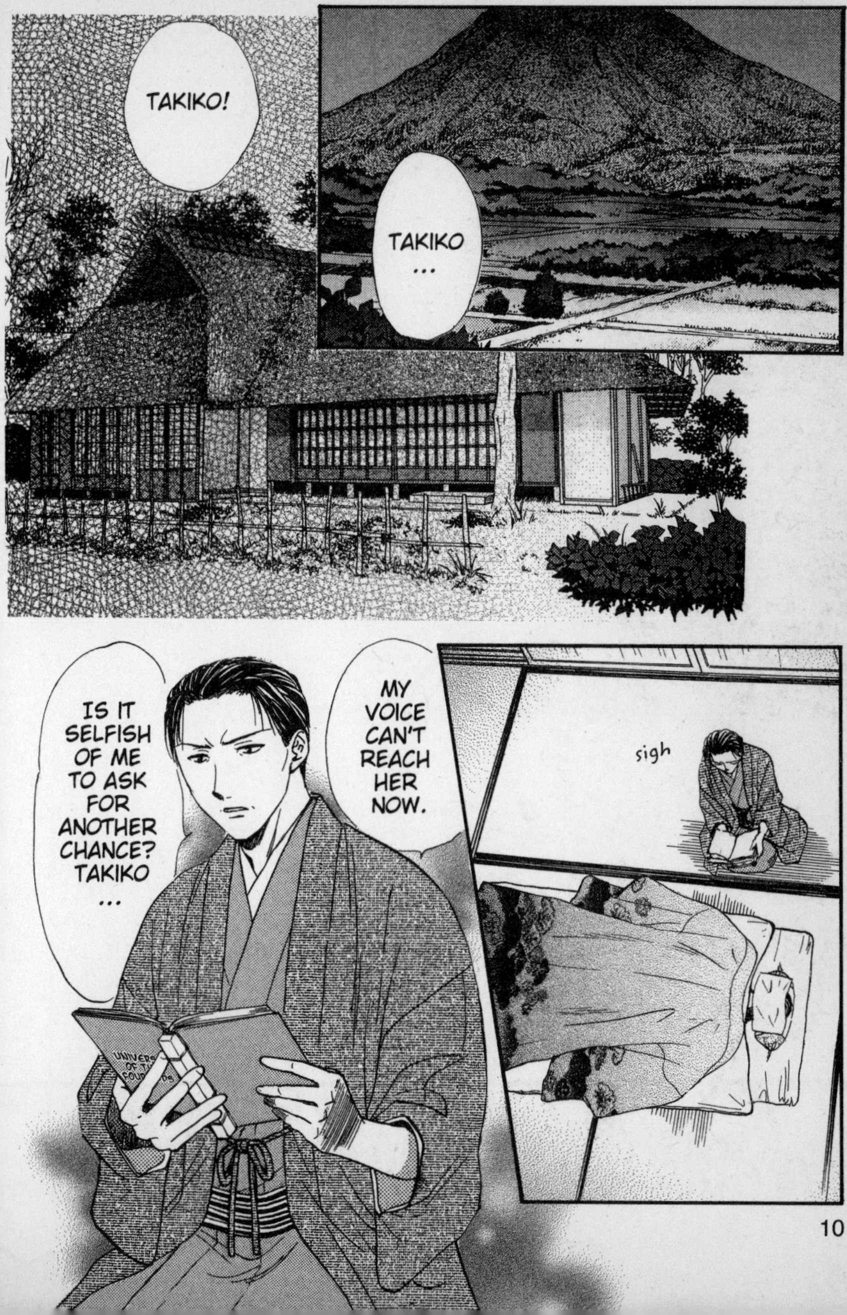
TAKIKO ...
TAKIKO!
sigh
MY VOICE CAN'T REACH HER NOW.
IS IT SELFISH OF ME TO ASK FOR ANOTHER CHANCE? TAKIKO ...

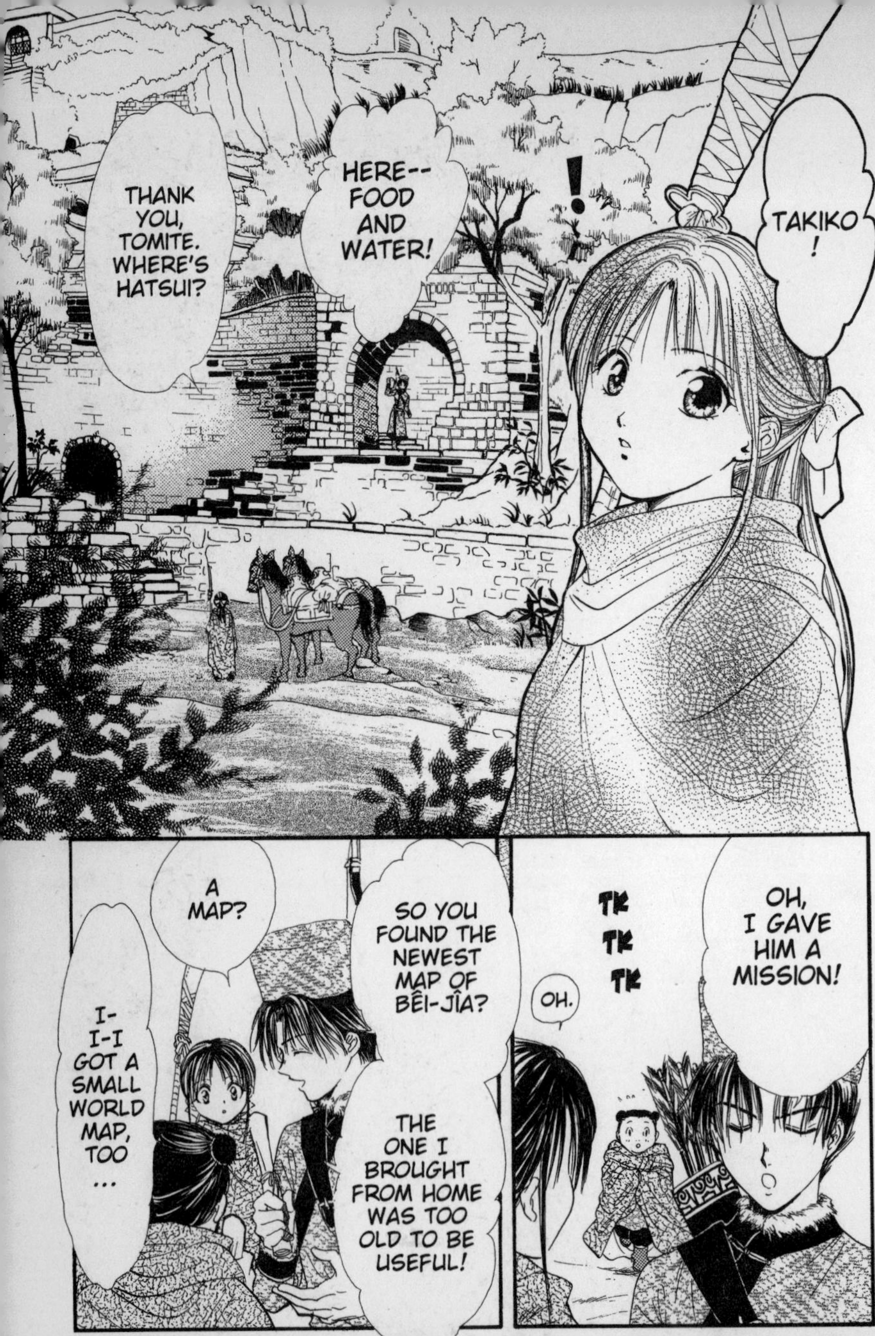
TAKIKO!
!
HERE-- FOOD AND WATER!
THANK YOU, TOMITE. WHERE'S HATSUI?
OH, I GAVE HIM A MISSION!
TK TK TK
OH.
SO YOU FOUND THE NEWEST MAP OF BÊI-JÎA?
THE ONE I BROUGHT FROM HOME WAS TOO OLD TO BE USEFUL!
A MAP?
I- I-I GOT A SMALL WORLD MAP, TOO...

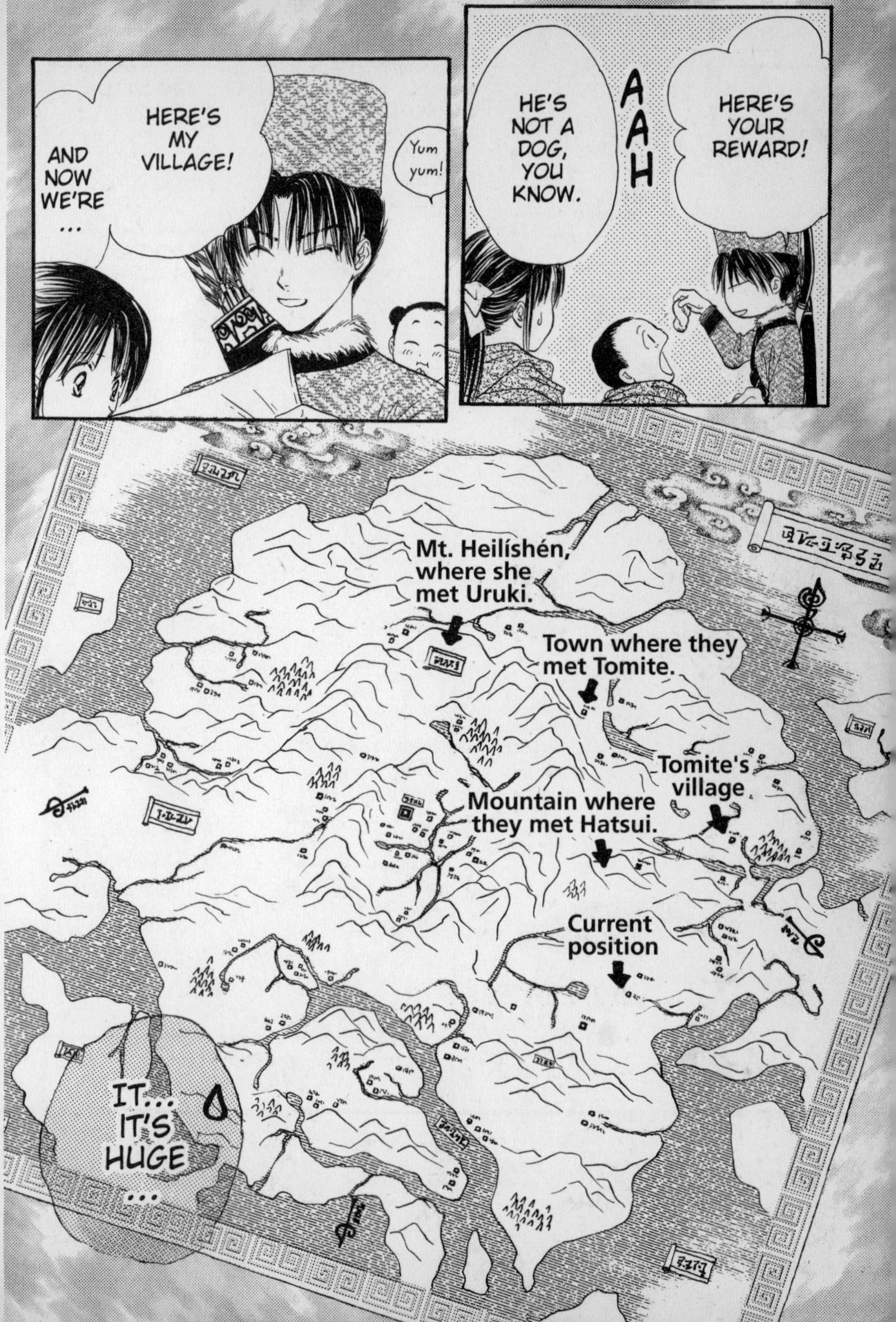
HERE'S YOUR REWARD!
AAH
HE'S NOT A DOG, YOU KNOW.
HERE'S MY VILLAGE!
Yum yum!
AND NOW WE'RE ...
Mt. Heilíshén, where she met Uruki.
Town where they met Tomite.
Tomite's village
Mountain where they met Hatsui.
Current position
IT... IT'S HUGE ...

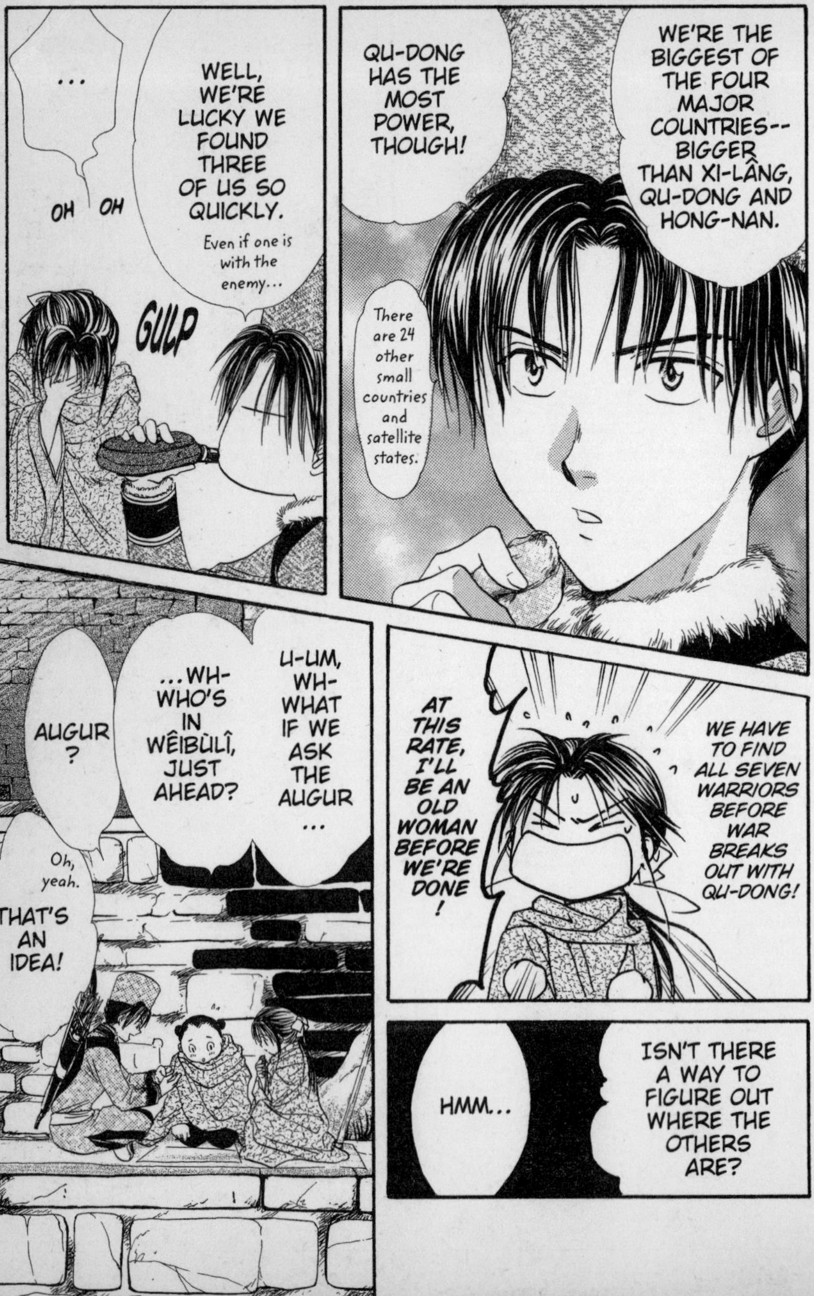
WE'RE THE BIGGEST OF THE FOUR MAJOR COUNTRIES-- BIGGER THAN XI-LÂNG, QU-DONG AND HONG-NAN.
There are 24 other small countries and satellite states.
QU-DONG HAS THE MOST POWER, THOUGH!
WELL, WE'RE LUCKY WE FOUND THREE OF US SO QUICKLY.
Even if one is with the enemy...
...
OH OH
GULP
WE HAVE TO FIND ALL SEVEN WARRIORS BEFORE WAR BREAKS OUT WITH QU-DONG!
AT THIS RATE, I'LL BE AN OLD WOMAN BEFORE WE'RE DONE!
ISN'T THERE A WAY TO FIGURE OUT WHERE THE OTHERS ARE?
HMM...
U-UM, WH-WHAT IF WE ASK THE AUGUR...
...WH-WHO'S IN WÊIBÙLÎ, JUST AHEAD?
AUGUR?
Oh, yeah.
THAT'S AN IDEA!

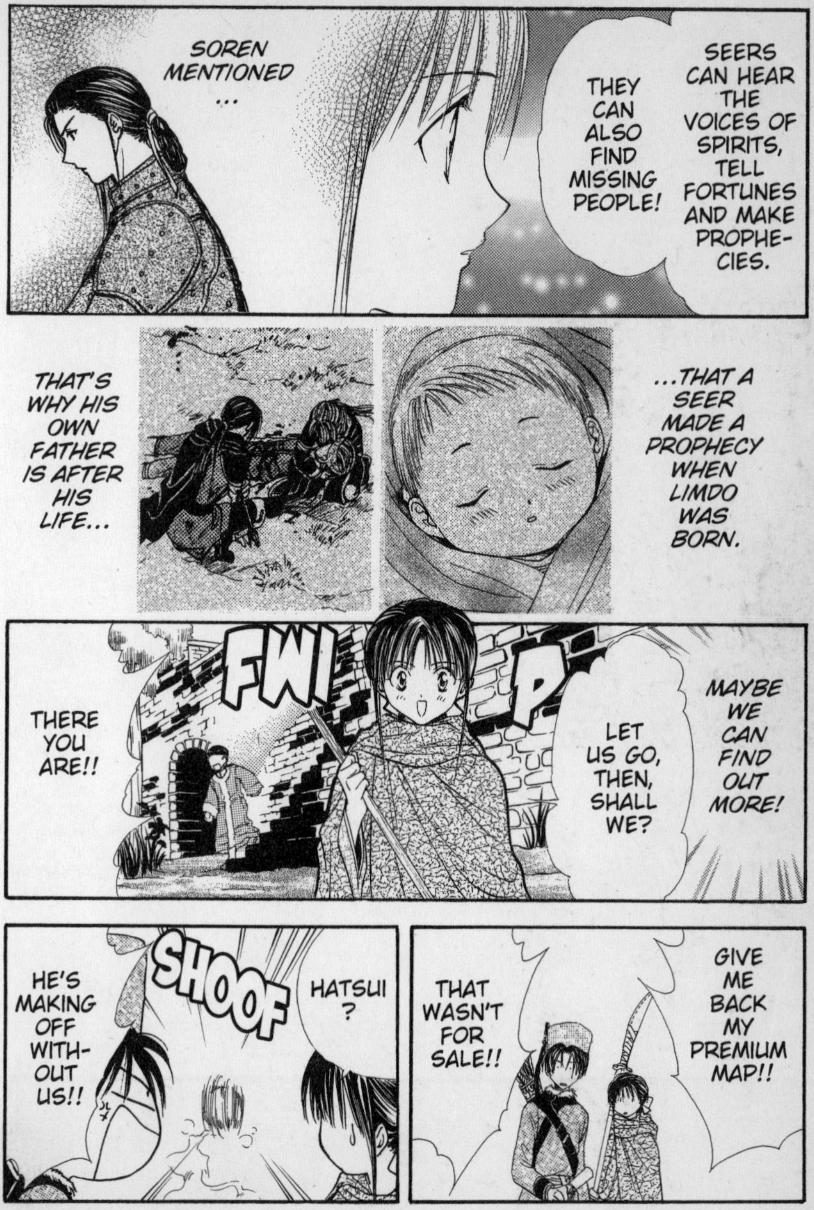
SEERS CAN HEAR THE VOICES OF SPIRITS, TELL FORTUNES AND MAKE PROPHE-CIES.
THEY CAN ALSO FIND MISSING PEOPLE!
SOREN MENTIONED ...
...THAT A SEER MADE A PROPHECY WHEN LIMDO WAS BORN.
THAT'S WHY HIS OWN FATHER IS AFTER HIS LIFE...
MAYBE WE CAN FIND OUT MORE!
LET US GO, THEN, SHALL WE?
FWIP
THERE YOU ARE!!
GIVE ME BACK MY PREMIUM MAP!!
THAT WASN'T FOR SALE!!
HATSUI ?
SHOOF
HE'S MAKING OFF WITH-OUT US!!

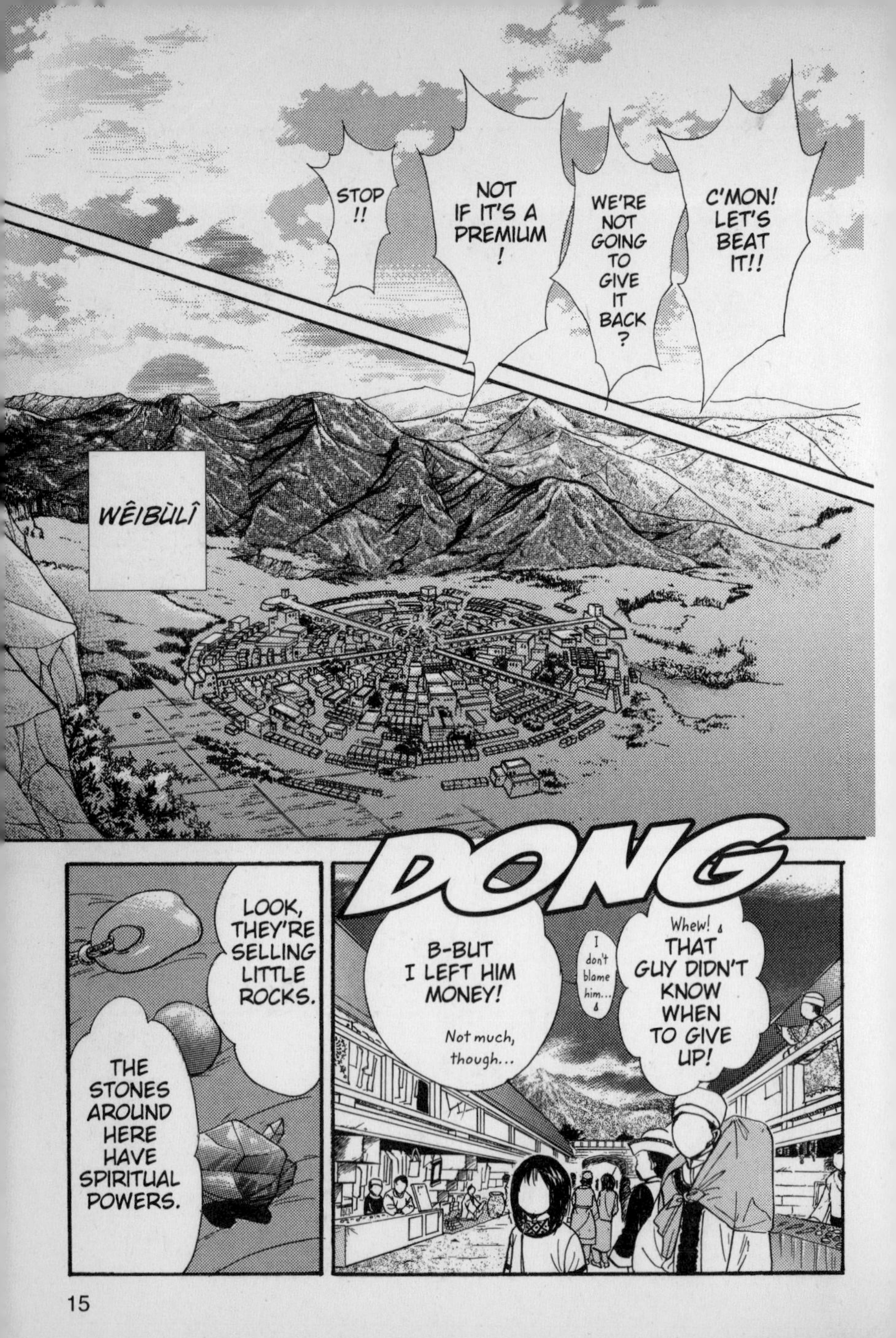

C'MON! LET'S BEAT IT!!
WE'RE NOT GOING TO GIVE IT BACK?
NOT IF IT'S A PREMIUM!
STOP!!
WÊIBÙLÎ
DONG
Whew! THAT GUY DIDN'T KNOW WHEN TO GIVE UP!
I don't blame him...
B-BUT I LEFT HIM MONEY!
Not much, though...
LOOK, THEY'RE SELLING LITTLE ROCKS.
THE STONES AROUND HERE HAVE SPIRITUAL POWERS.

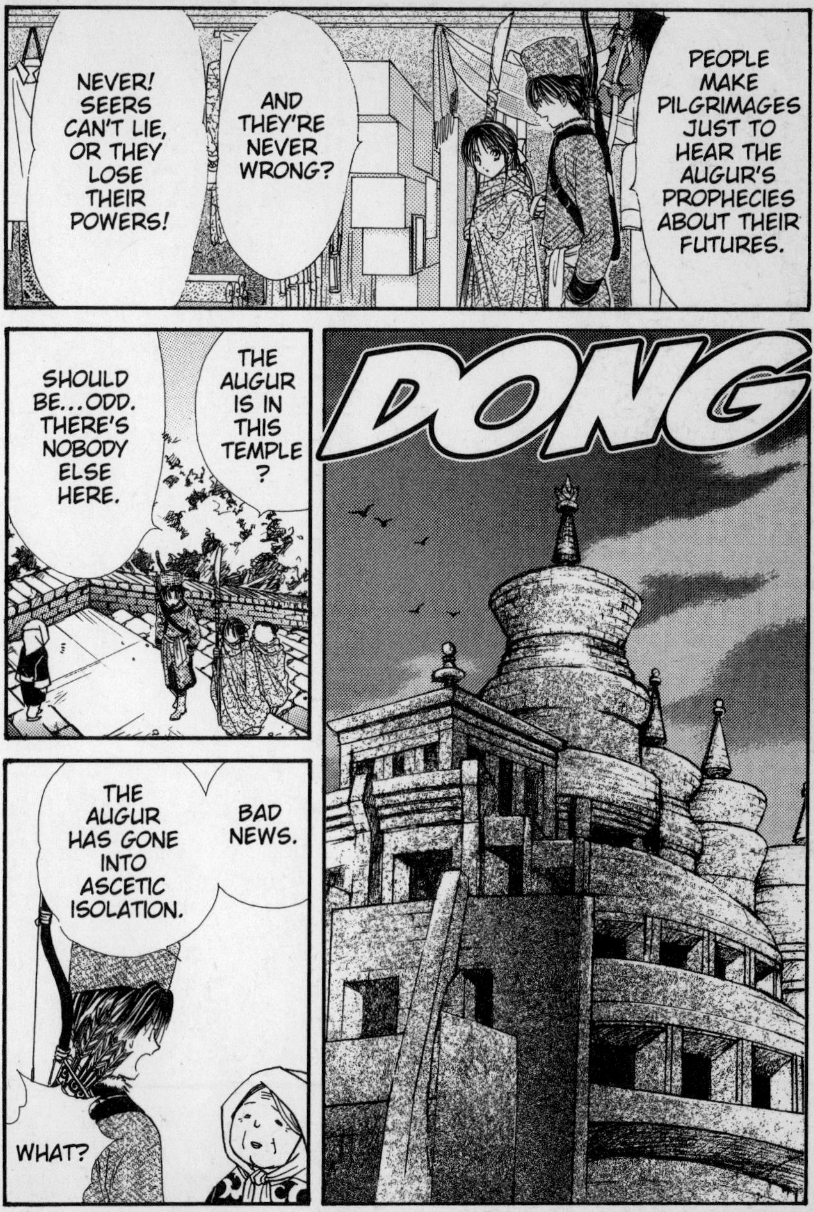
PEOPLE MAKE PILGRIMAGES JUST TO HEAR THE AUGUR'S PROPHECIES ABOUT THEIR FUTURES.
AND THEY'RE NEVER WRONG?
NEVER! SEERS CAN'T LIE, OR THEY LOSE THEIR POWERS!
DONG
THE AUGUR IS IN THIS TEMPLE?
SHOULD BE...ODD. THERE'S NOBODY ELSE HERE.
BAD NEWS.
THE AUGUR HAS GONE INTO ASCETIC ISOLATION.
WHAT?

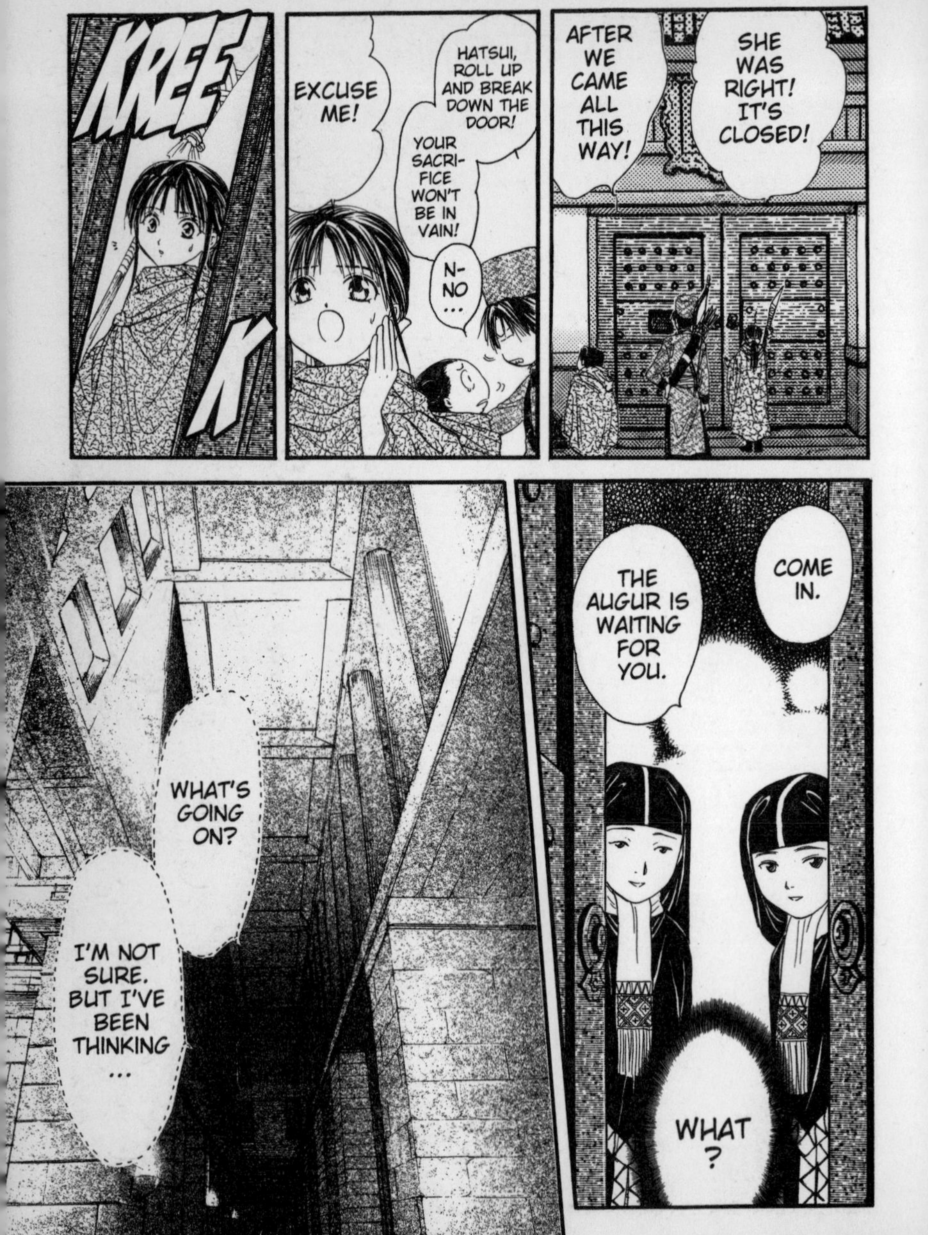
SHE WAS RIGHT! IT'S CLOSED!
AFTER WE CAME ALL THIS WAY!
HATSUI, ROLL UP AND BREAK DOWN THE DOOR!
EXCUSE ME!
YOUR SACRIFICE WON'T BE IN VAIN!
N-NO...
KREEK
COME IN.
THE AUGUR IS WAITING FOR YOU.
WHAT?
WHAT'S GOING ON?
I'M NOT SURE. BUT I'VE BEEN THINKING...

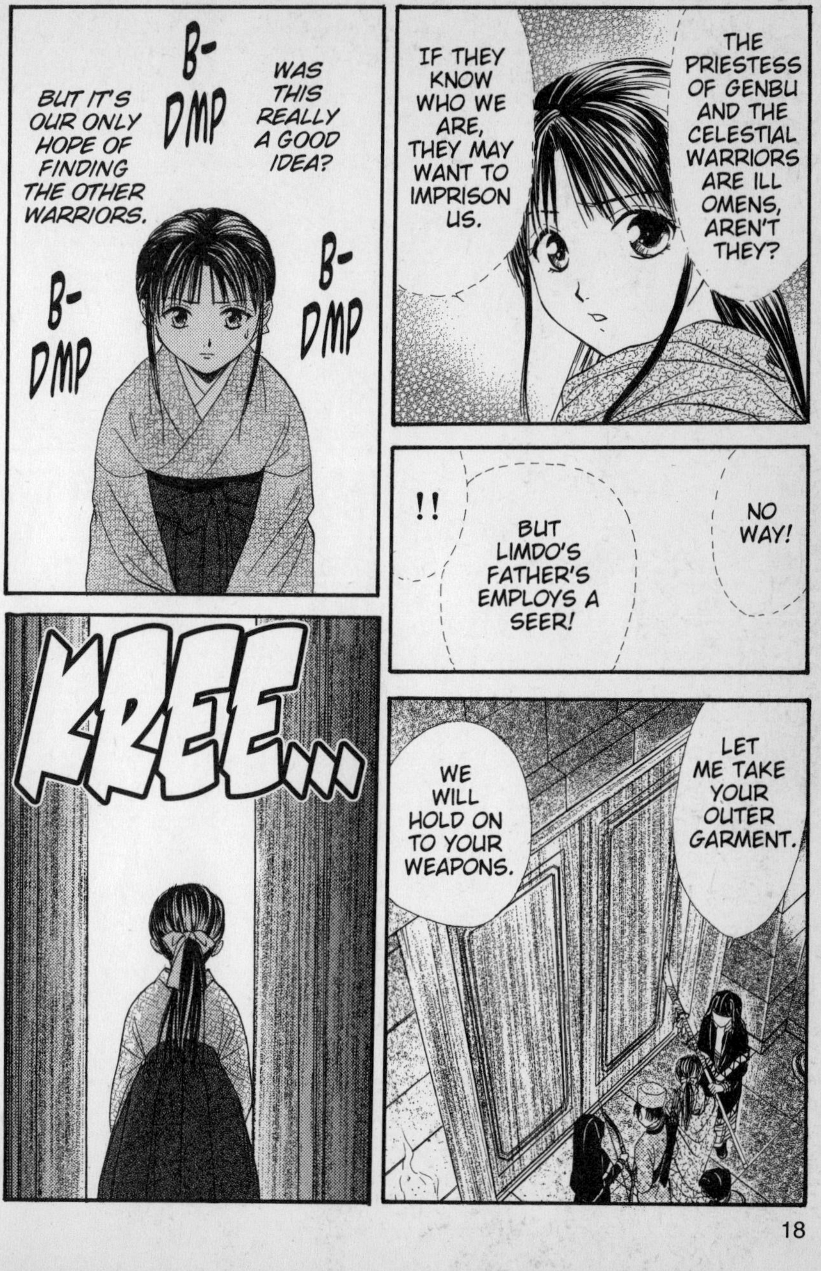
THE PRIESTESS OF GENBU AND THE CELESTIAL WARRIORS ARE ILL OMENS, AREN'T THEY?
IF THEY KNOW WHO WE ARE, THEY MAY WANT TO IMPRISON US.
NO WAY!
BUT LIMDO'S FATHER'S EMPLOYS A SEER!
!!
WAS THIS REALLY A GOOD IDEA?
B-DMP
BUT IT'S OUR ONLY HOPE OF FINDING THE OTHER WARRIORS.
B-DMP
B-DMP
LET ME TAKE YOUR OUTER GARMENT.
WE WILL HOLD ON TO YOUR WEAPONS.
KREE...

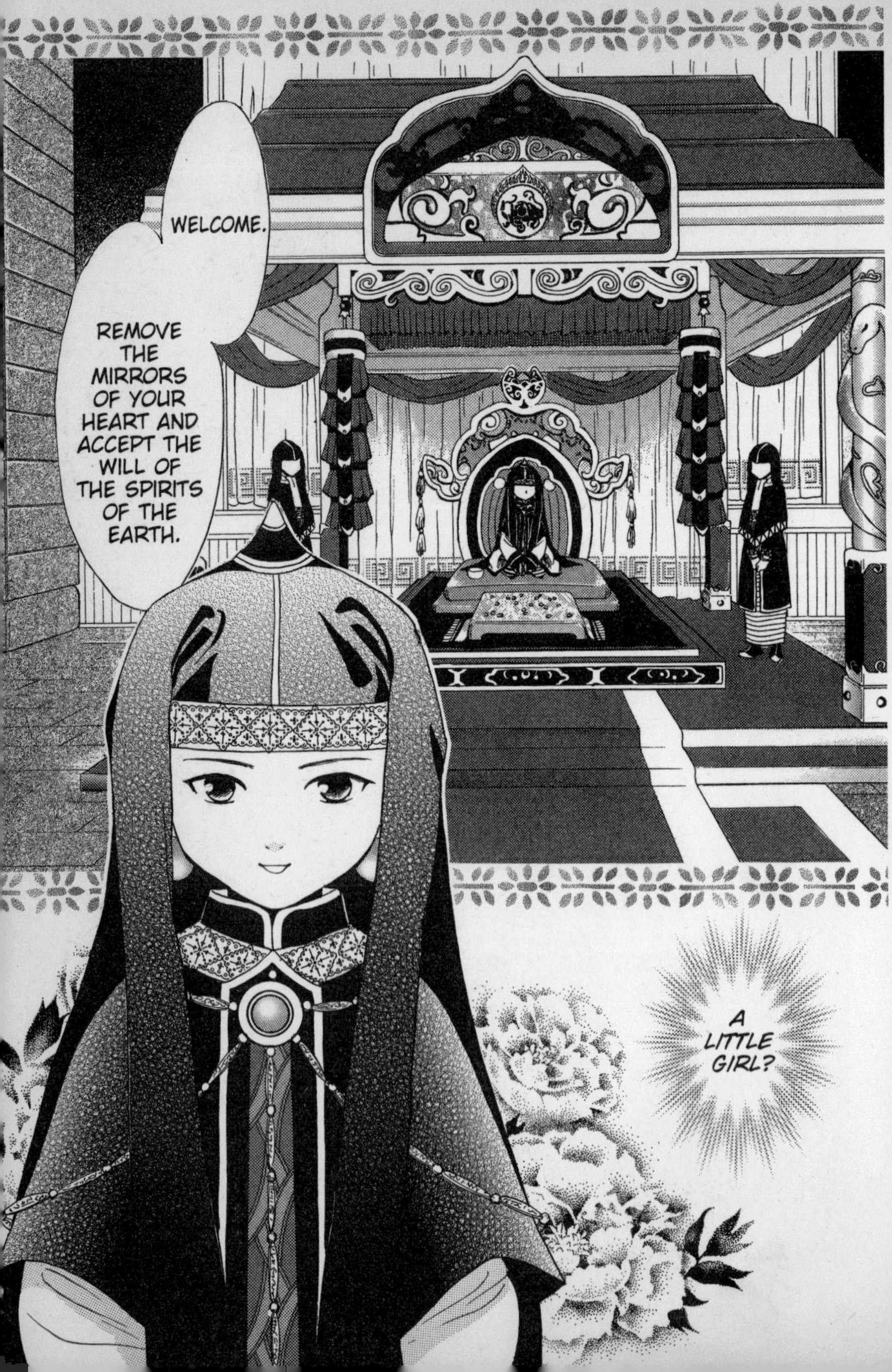
WELCOME.
REMOVE THE MIRRORS OF YOUR HEART AND ACCEPT THE WILL OF THE SPIRITS OF THE EARTH.
A LITTLE GIRL?

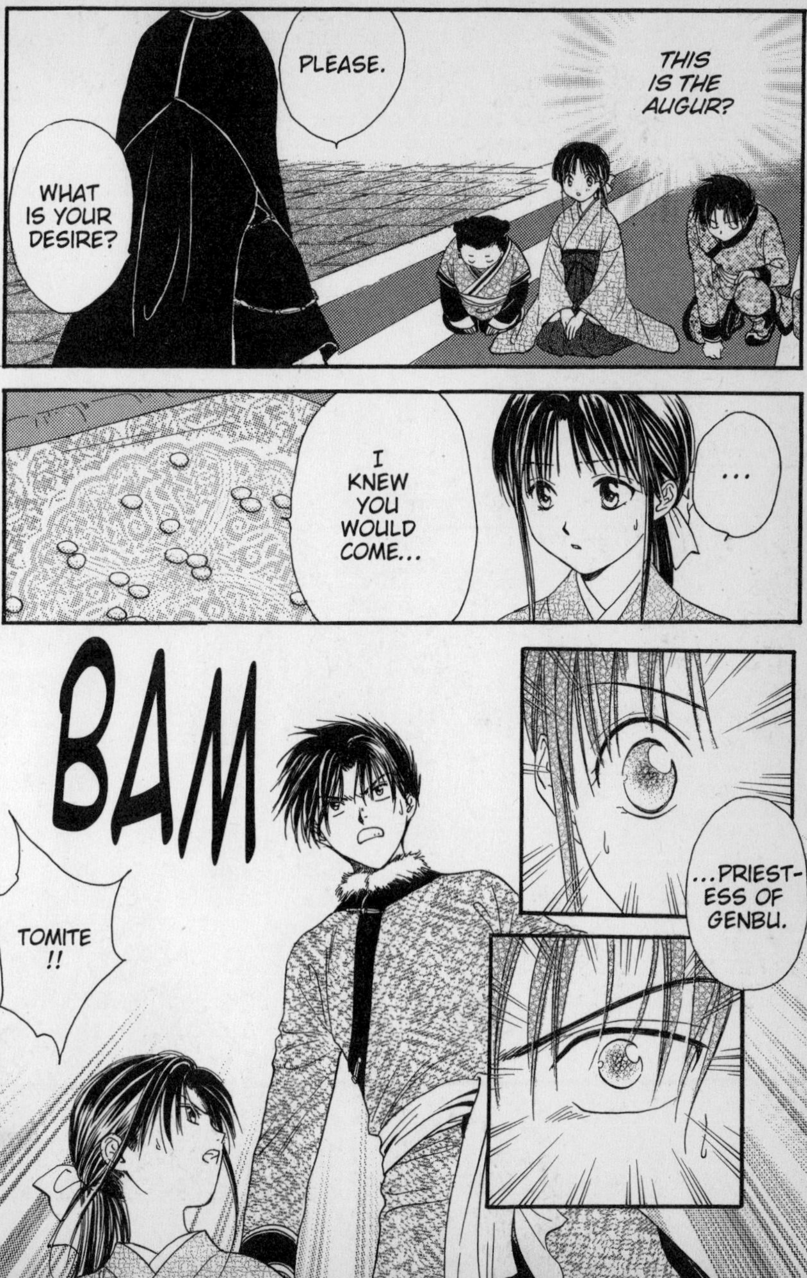
THIS IS THE AUGUR?
PLEASE.
WHAT IS YOUR DESIRE?
...
I KNEW YOU WOULD COME...
...PRIEST-ESS OF GENBU.
BAM
TOMITE !!

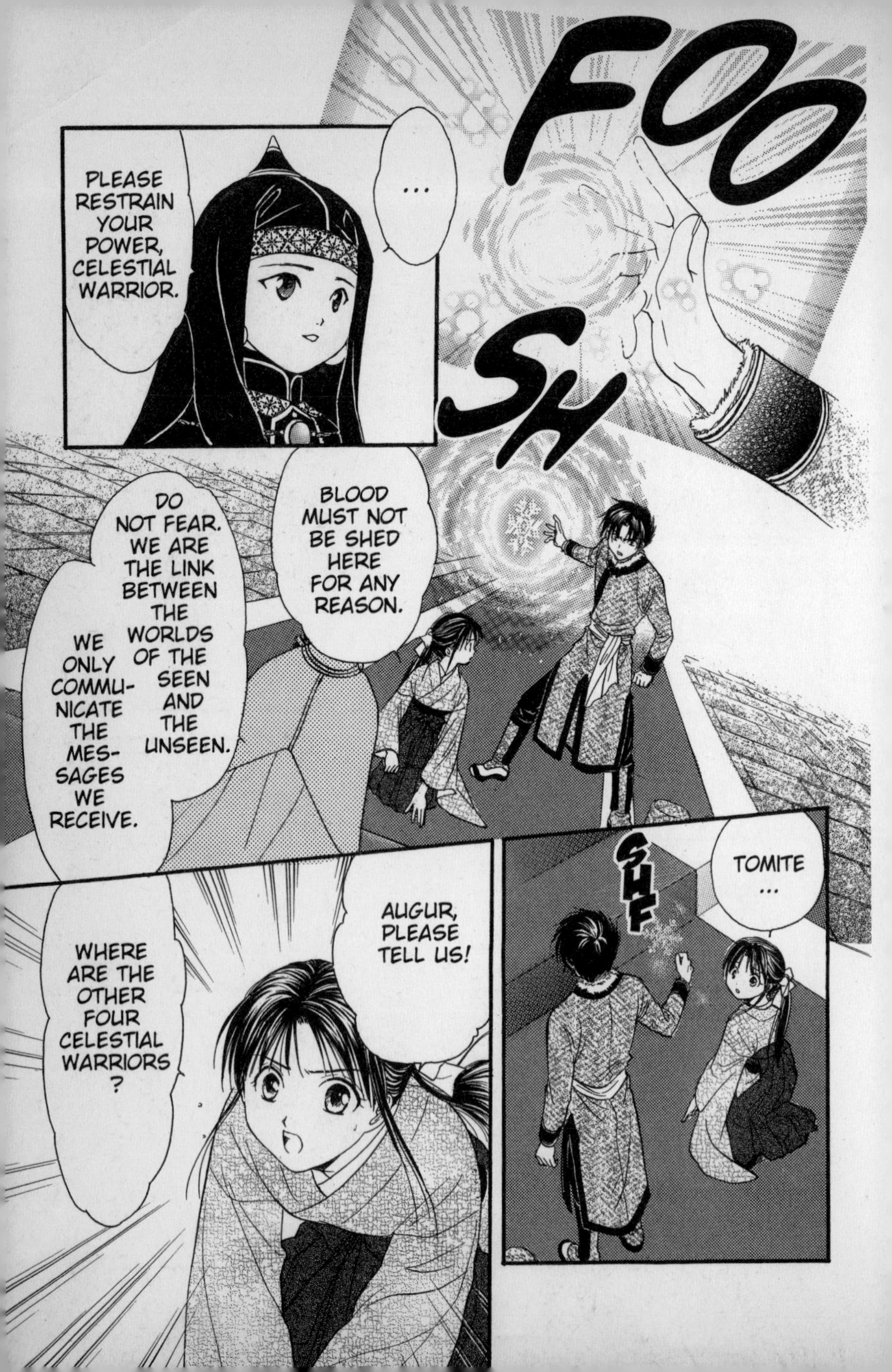
FOOSH
...
PLEASE RESTRAIN YOUR POWER, CELESTIAL WARRIOR.
BLOOD MUST NOT BE SHED HERE FOR ANY REASON.
DO NOT FEAR. WE ARE THE LINK BETWEEN THE WORLDS OF THE SEEN AND THE UNSEEN.
WE ONLY COMMUNICATE THE MESSAGES WE RECEIVE.
SHF
TOMITE ...
AUGUR, PLEASE TELL US!
WHERE ARE THE OTHER FOUR CELESTIAL WARRIORS ?

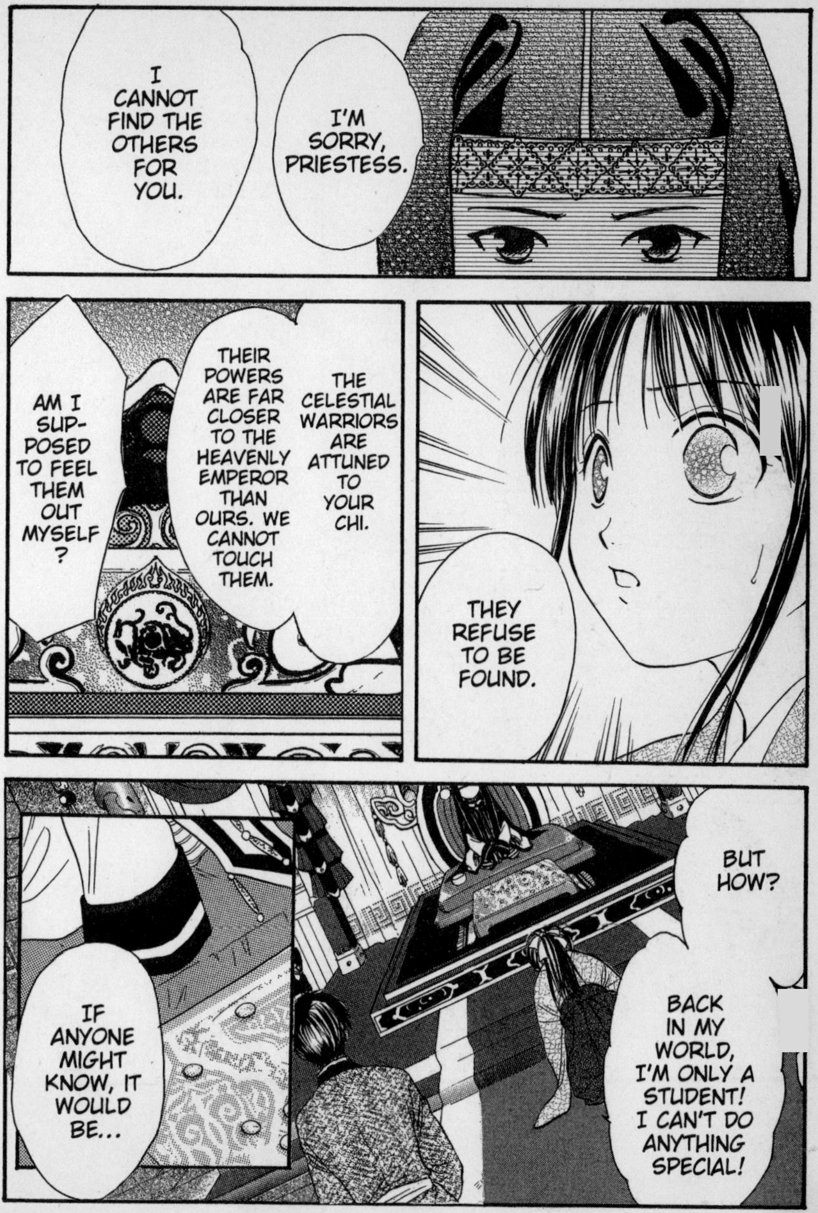
I'M SORRY, PRIESTESS.
I CANNOT FIND THE OTHERS FOR YOU.
THEY REFUSE TO BE FOUND.
THE CELESTIAL WARRIORS ARE ATTUNED TO YOUR CHI.
THEIR POWERS ARE FAR CLOSER TO THE HEAVENLY EMPEROR THAN OURS. WE CANNOT TOUCH THEM.
AM I SUPPOSED TO FEEL THEM OUT MYSELF?
BUT HOW?
BACK IN MY WORLD, I'M ONLY A STUDENT! I CAN'T DO ANYTHING SPECIAL!
IF ANYONE MIGHT KNOW, IT WOULD BE...

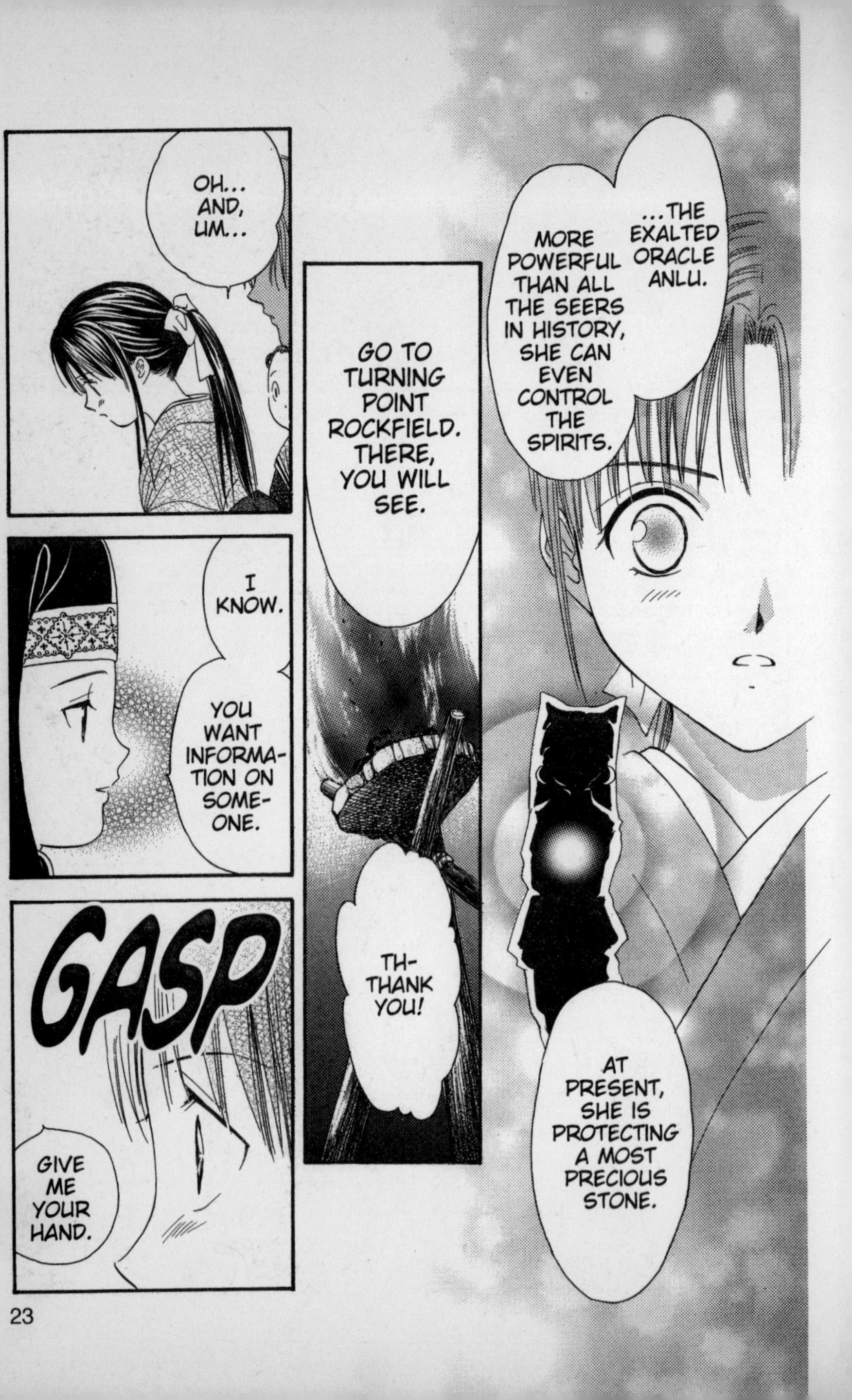
...THE EXALTED ORACLE ANLU.
MORE POWERFUL THAN ALL THE SEERS IN HISTORY, SHE CAN EVEN CONTROL THE SPIRITS.
AT PRESENT, SHE IS PROTECTING A MOST PRECIOUS STONE.
GO TO TURNING POINT ROCKFIELD. THERE, YOU WILL SEE.
TH-THANK YOU!
OH... AND, UM...
I KNOW.
YOU WANT INFORMATION ON SOME-ONE.
GASP
GIVE ME YOUR HAND.

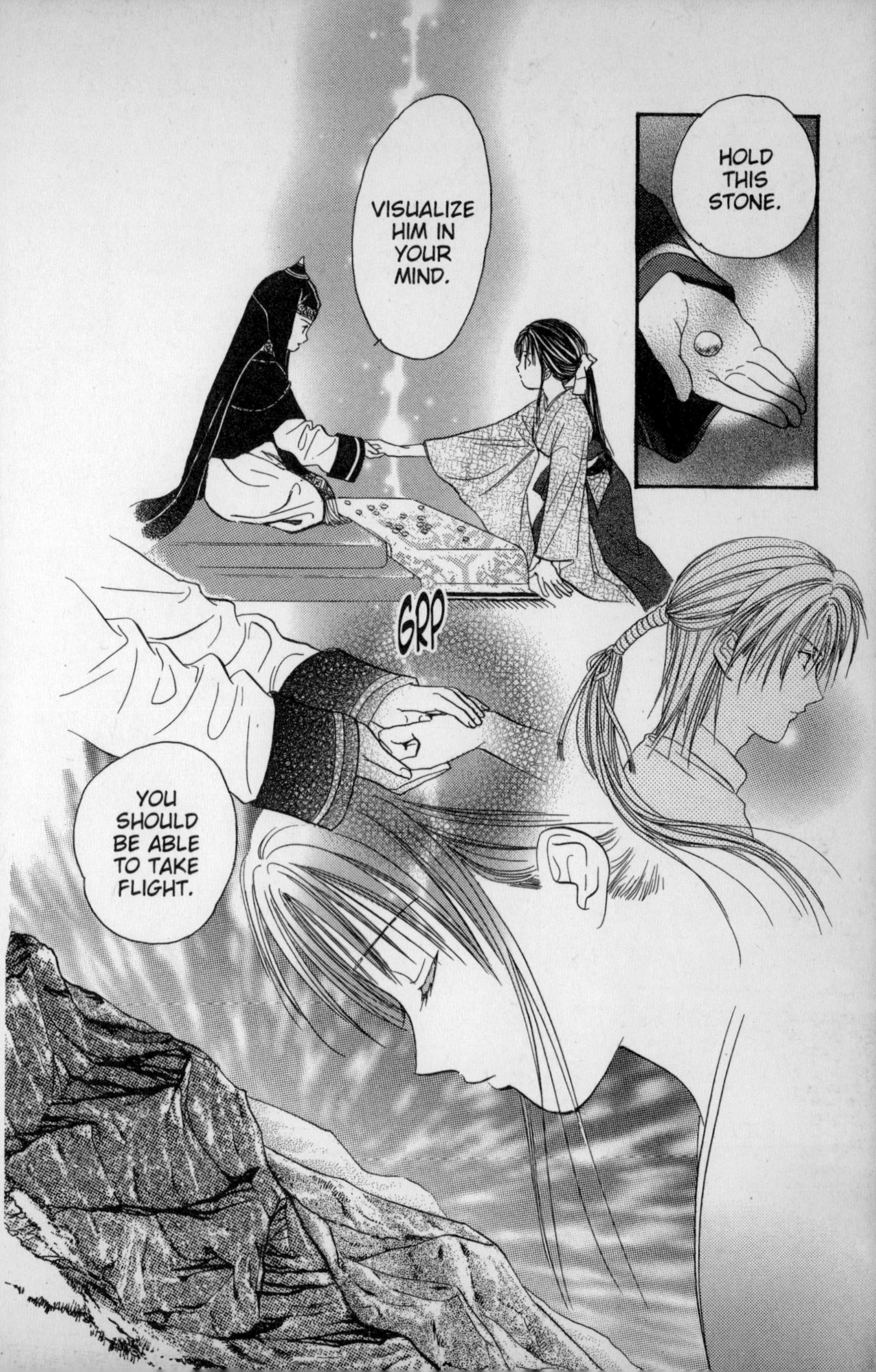
HOLD THIS STONE.
VISUALIZE HIM IN YOUR MIND.
GRP
YOU SHOULD BE ABLE TO TAKE FLIGHT.

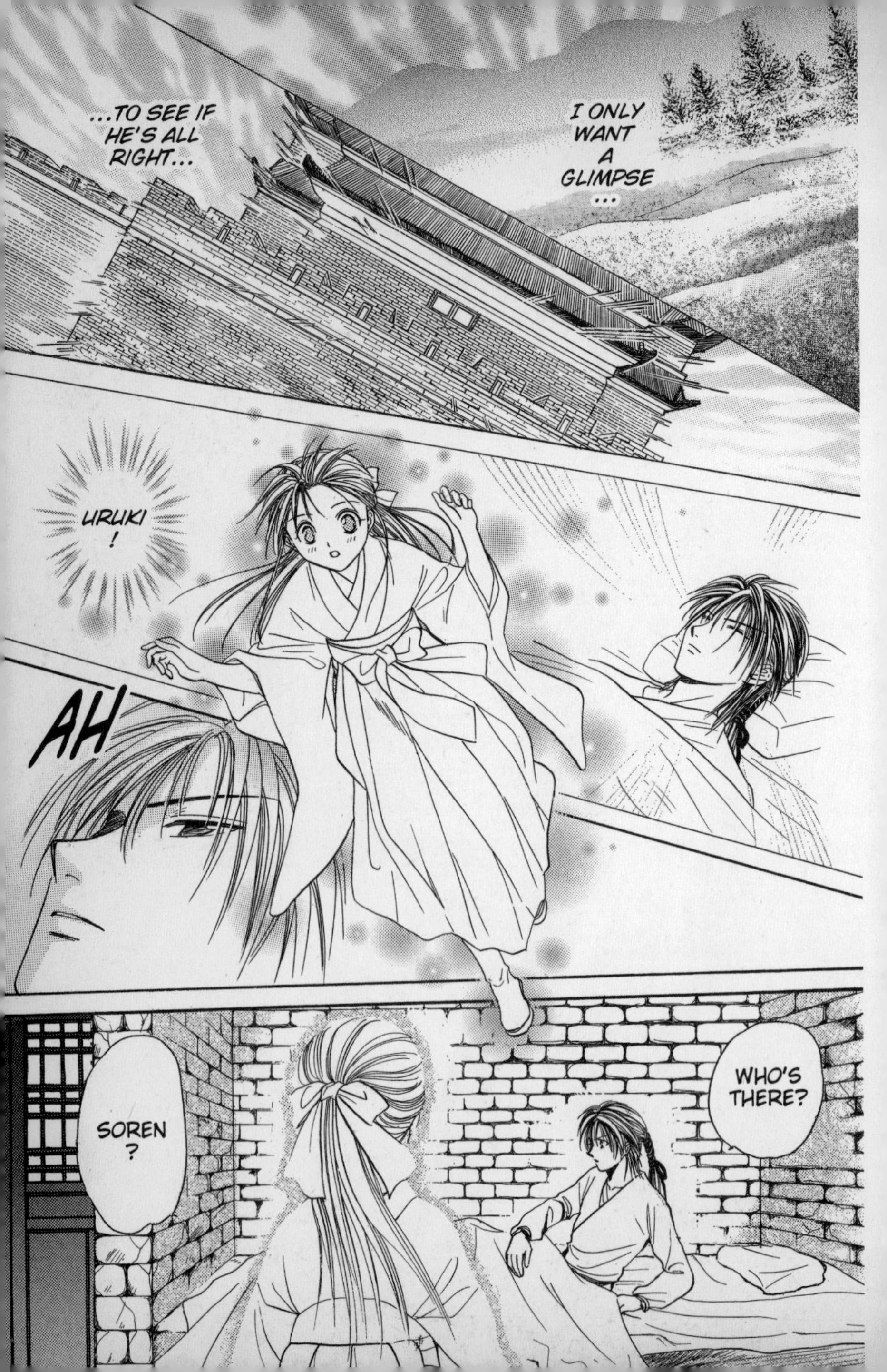

I ONLY WANT A GLIMPSE ...
...TO SEE IF HE'S ALL RIGHT...
URUKI!
AH
WHO'S THERE?
SOREN?

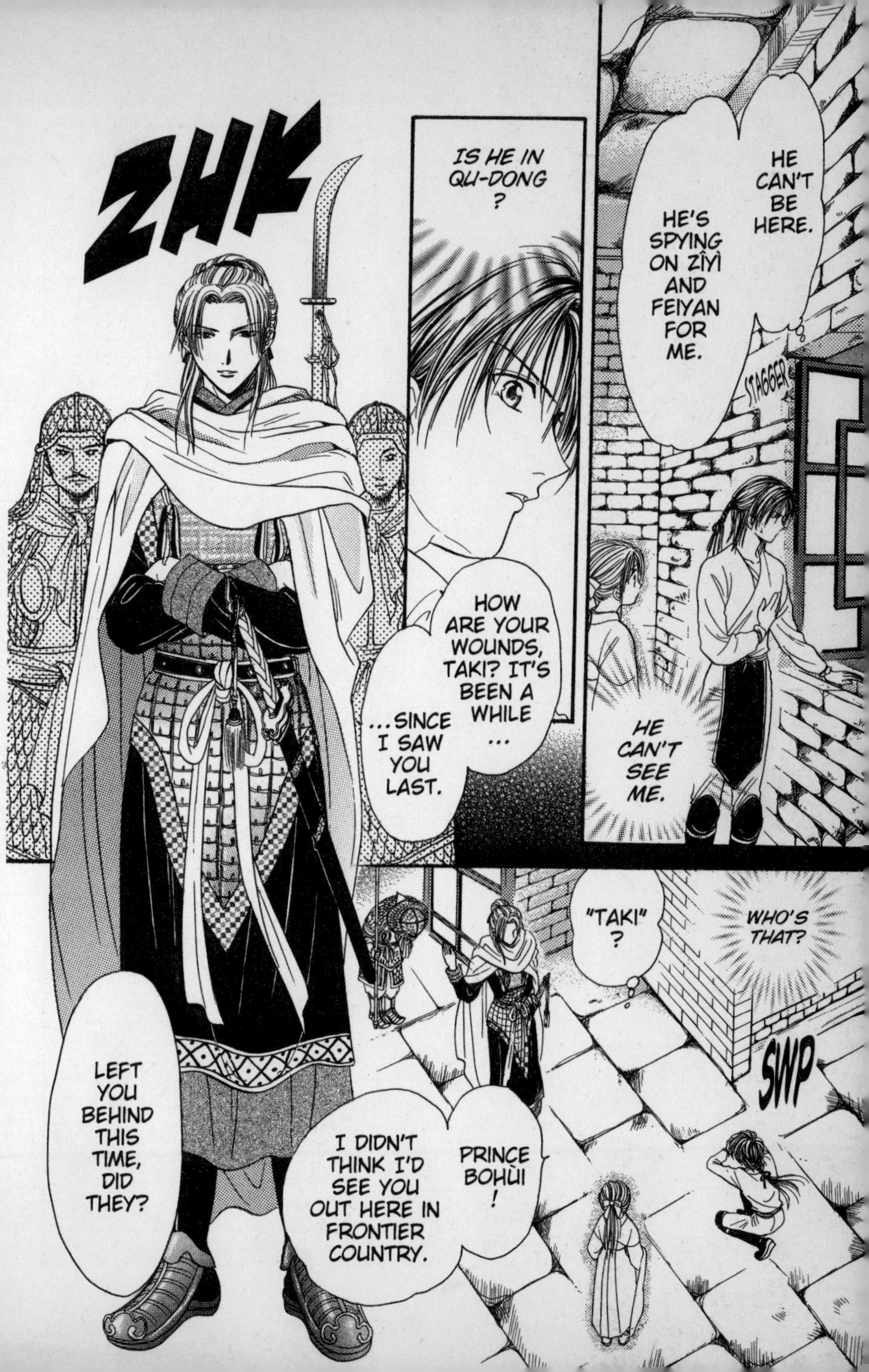
HE CAN'T BE HERE.
HE'S SPYING ON ZÎYÌ AND FEIYAN FOR ME.
STAGGER
HE CAN'T SEE ME.
IS HE IN QU-DONG?
WHO'S THAT?
"TAKI"?
SWP
PRINCE BOHÙI!
I DIDN'T THINK I'D SEE YOU OUT HERE IN FRONTIER COUNTRY.
ZHK
HOW ARE YOUR WOUNDS, TAKI? IT'S BEEN A WHILE...
...SINCE I SAW YOU LAST.
LEFT YOU BEHIND THIS TIME, DID THEY?

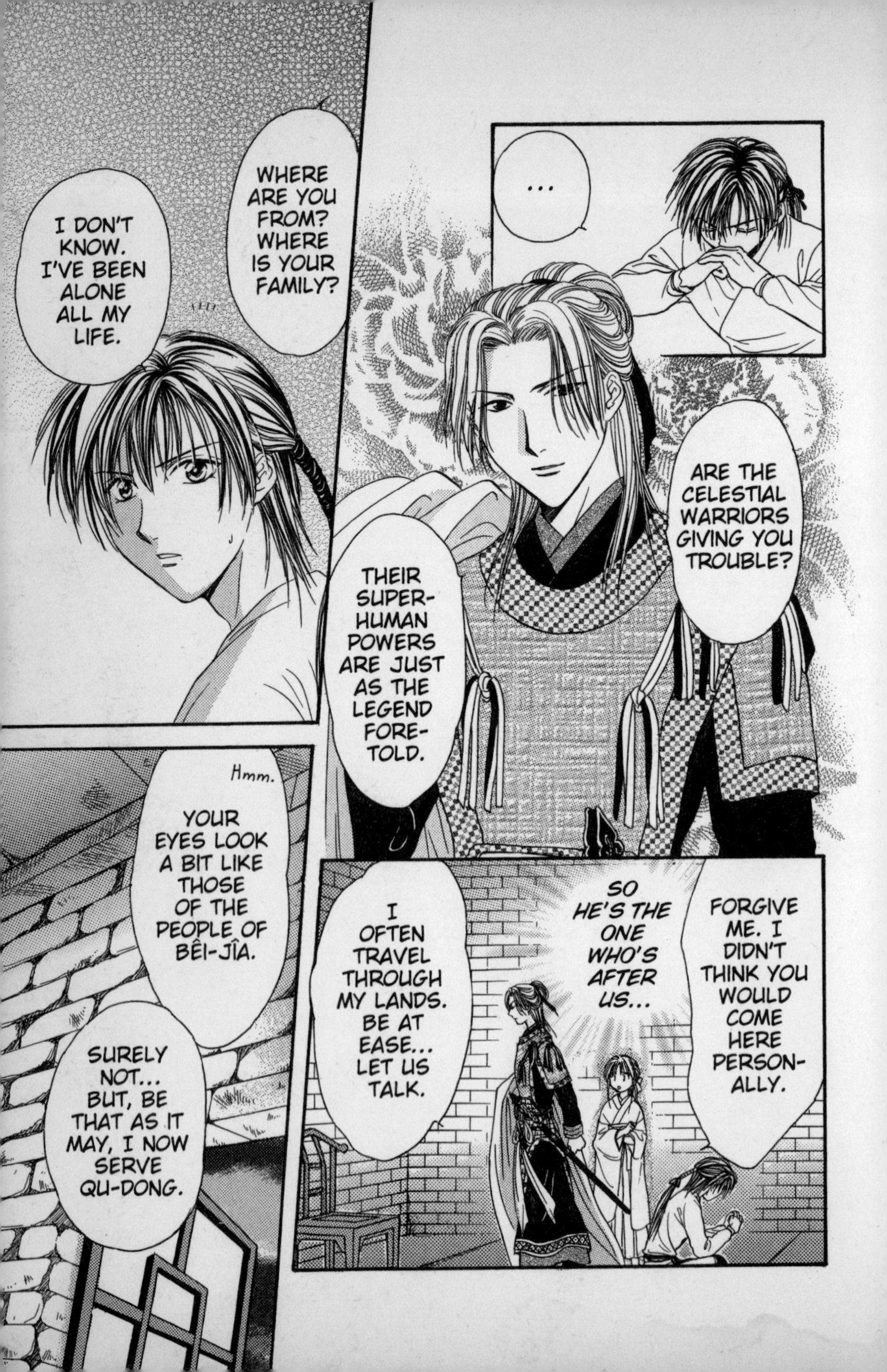
...
ARE THE CELESTIAL WARRIORS GIVING YOU TROUBLE?
THEIR SUPER-HUMAN POWERS ARE JUST AS THE LEGEND FORE-TOLD.
WHERE ARE YOU FROM? WHERE IS YOUR FAMILY?
I DON'T KNOW. I'VE BEEN ALONE ALL MY LIFE.
FORGIVE ME. I DIDN'T THINK YOU WOULD COME HERE PERSON-ALLY.
SO HE'S THE ONE WHO'S AFTER US...
I OFTEN TRAVEL THROUGH MY LANDS. BE AT EASE... LET US TALK.
Hmm.
YOUR EYES LOOK A BIT LIKE THOSE OF THE PEOPLE OF BÊI-JÎA.
SURELY NOT... BUT, BE THAT AS IT MAY, I NOW SERVE QU-DONG.

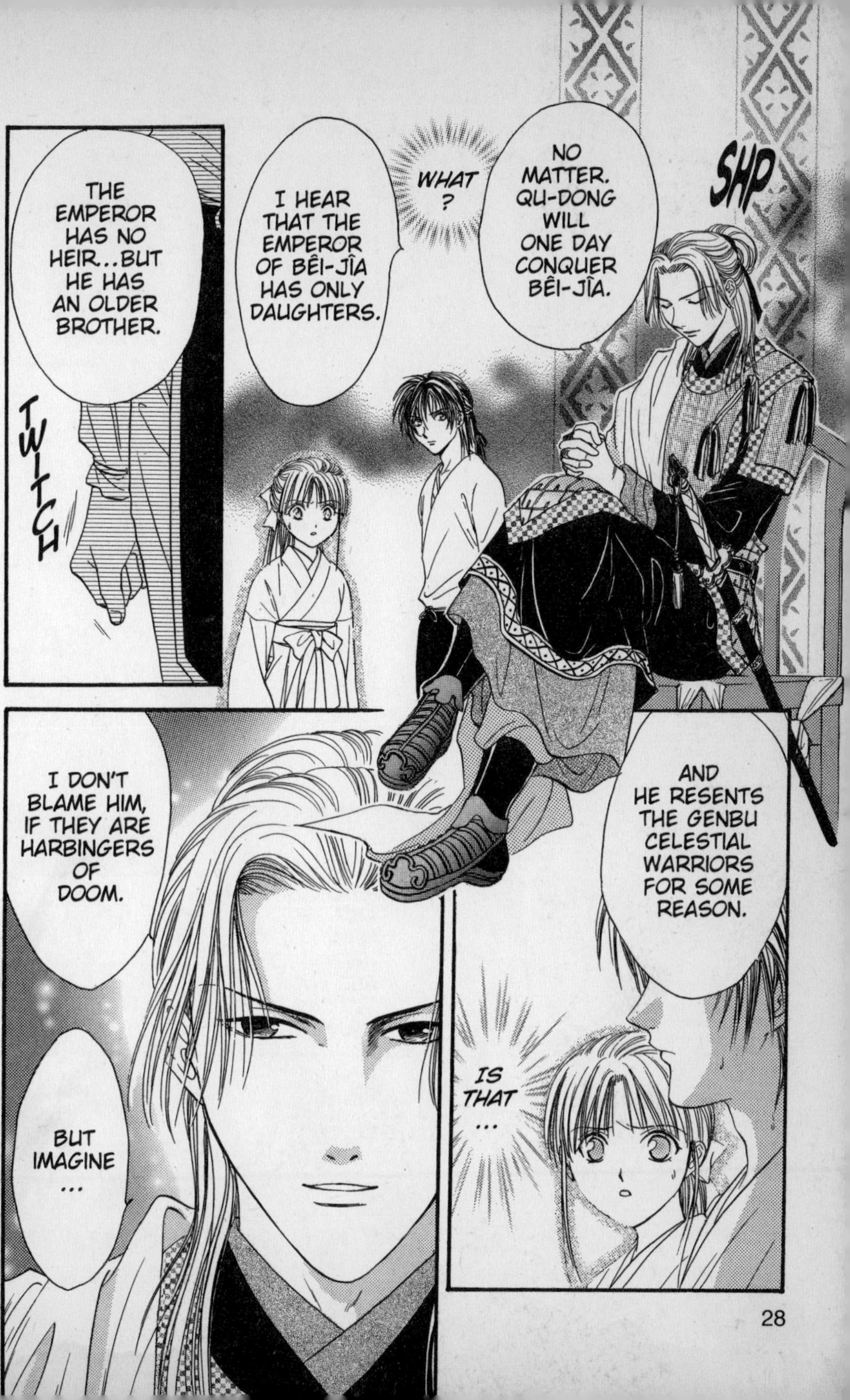
SHP
NO MATTER. QU-DONG WILL ONE DAY CONQUER BÊI-JÎA.
WHAT?
I HEAR THAT THE EMPEROR OF BÊI-JÎA HAS ONLY DAUGHTERS.
THE EMPEROR HAS NO HEIR...BUT HE HAS AN OLDER BROTHER.
TWITCH
AND HE RESENTS THE GENBU CELESTIAL WARRIORS FOR SOME REASON.
IS THAT...
I DON'T BLAME HIM, IF THEY ARE HARBINGERS OF DOOM.
BUT IMAGINE...

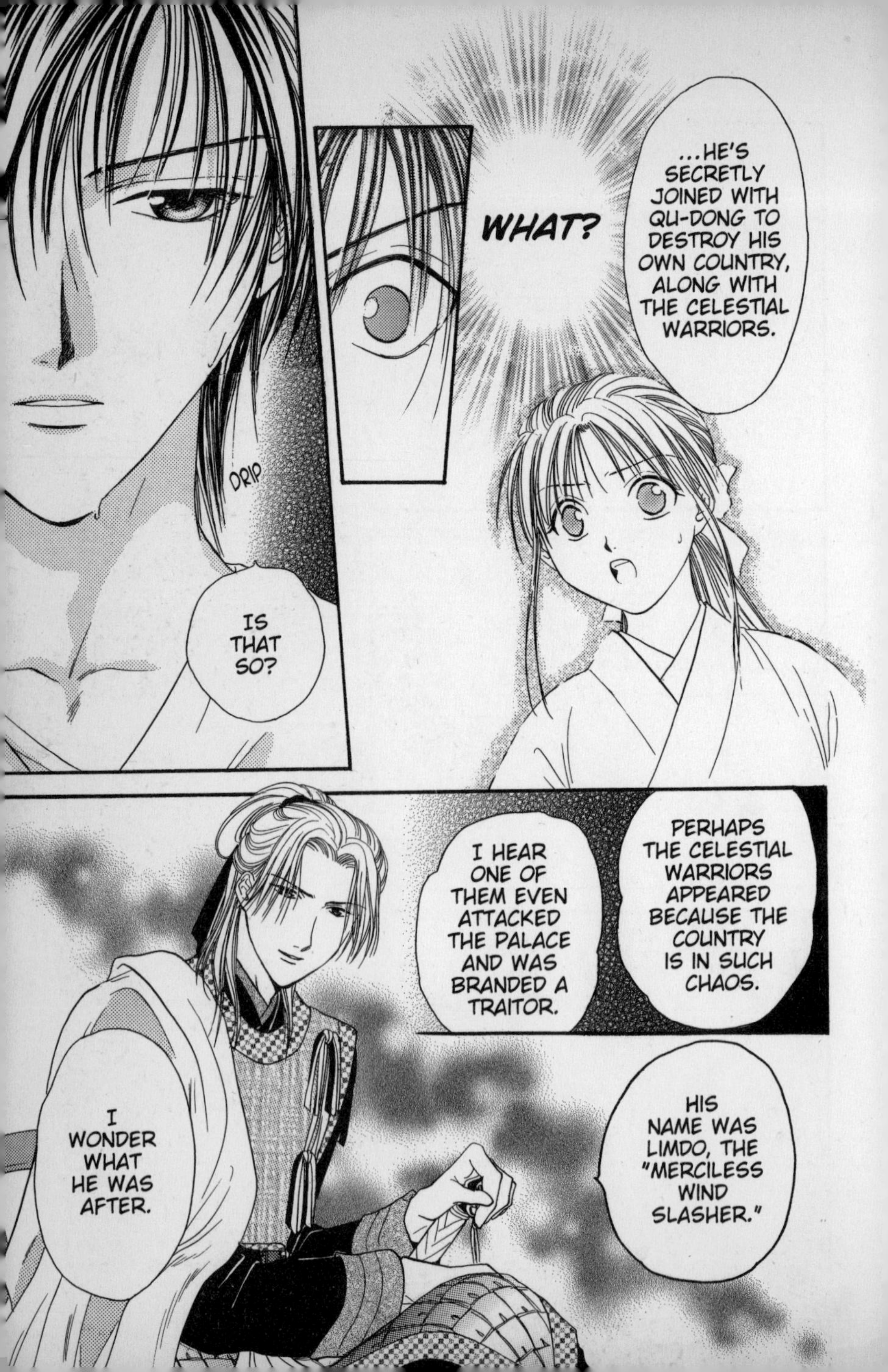
...HE'S SECRETLY JOINED WITH QU-DONG TO DESTROY HIS OWN COUNTRY, ALONG WITH THE CELESTIAL WARRIORS.
WHAT?
DRIP
IS THAT SO?
PERHAPS THE CELESTIAL WARRIORS APPEARED BECAUSE THE COUNTRY IS IN SUCH CHAOS.
I HEAR ONE OF THEM EVEN ATTACKED THE PALACE AND WAS BRANDED A TRAITOR.
HIS NAME WAS LIMDO, THE "MERCILESS WIND SLASHER."
I WONDER WHAT HE WAS AFTER.

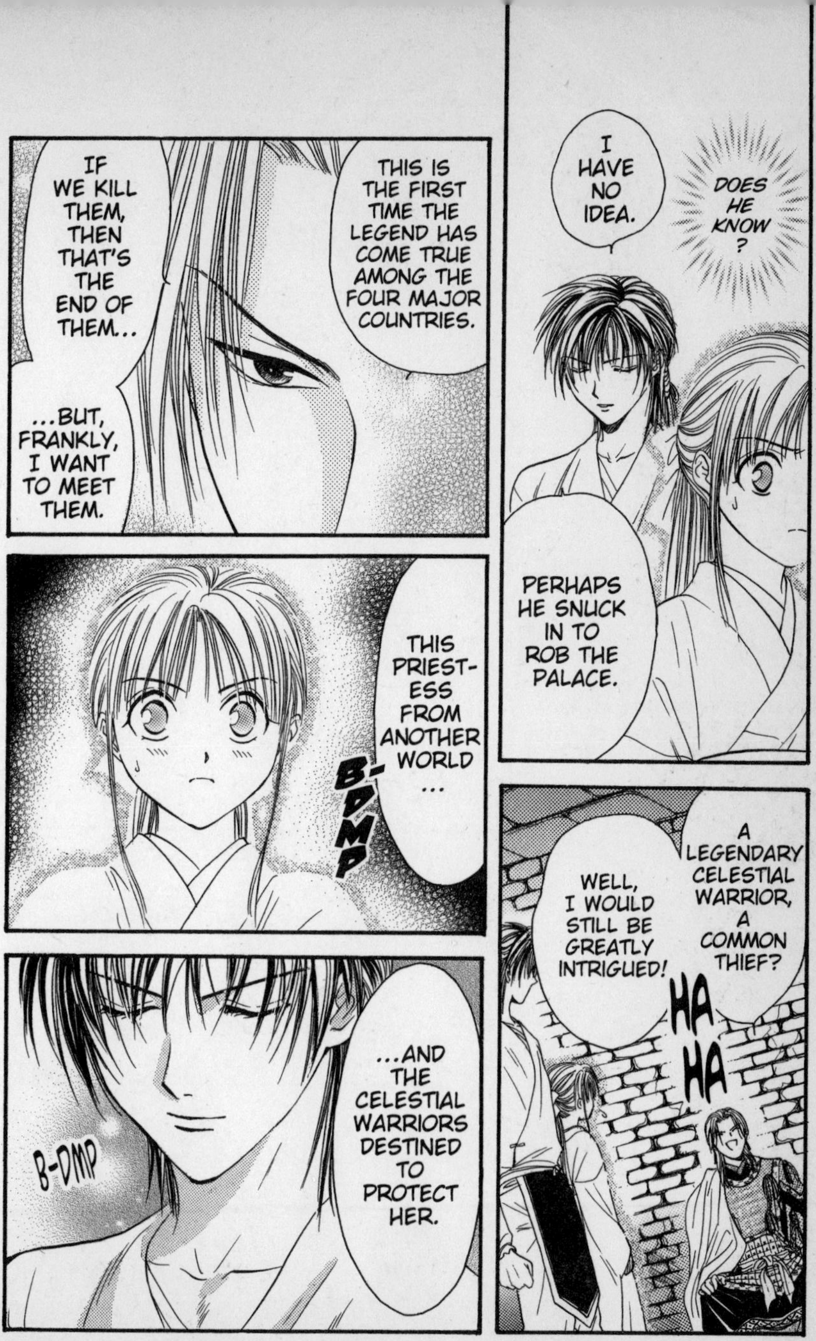
DOES HE KNOW?
I HAVE NO IDEA.
PERHAPS HE SNUCK IN TO ROB THE PALACE.
A LEGENDARY CELESTIAL WARRIOR, A COMMON THIEF?
WELL, I WOULD STILL BE GREATLY INTRIGUED!
HA HA
THIS IS THE FIRST TIME THE LEGEND HAS COME TRUE AMONG THE FOUR MAJOR COUNTRIES.
IF WE KILL THEM, THEN THAT'S THE END OF THEM...
...BUT, FRANKLY, I WANT TO MEET THEM.
THIS PRIESTESS FROM ANOTHER WORLD...
B-DMP
...AND THE CELESTIAL WARRIORS DESTINED TO PROTECT HER.
B-DMP

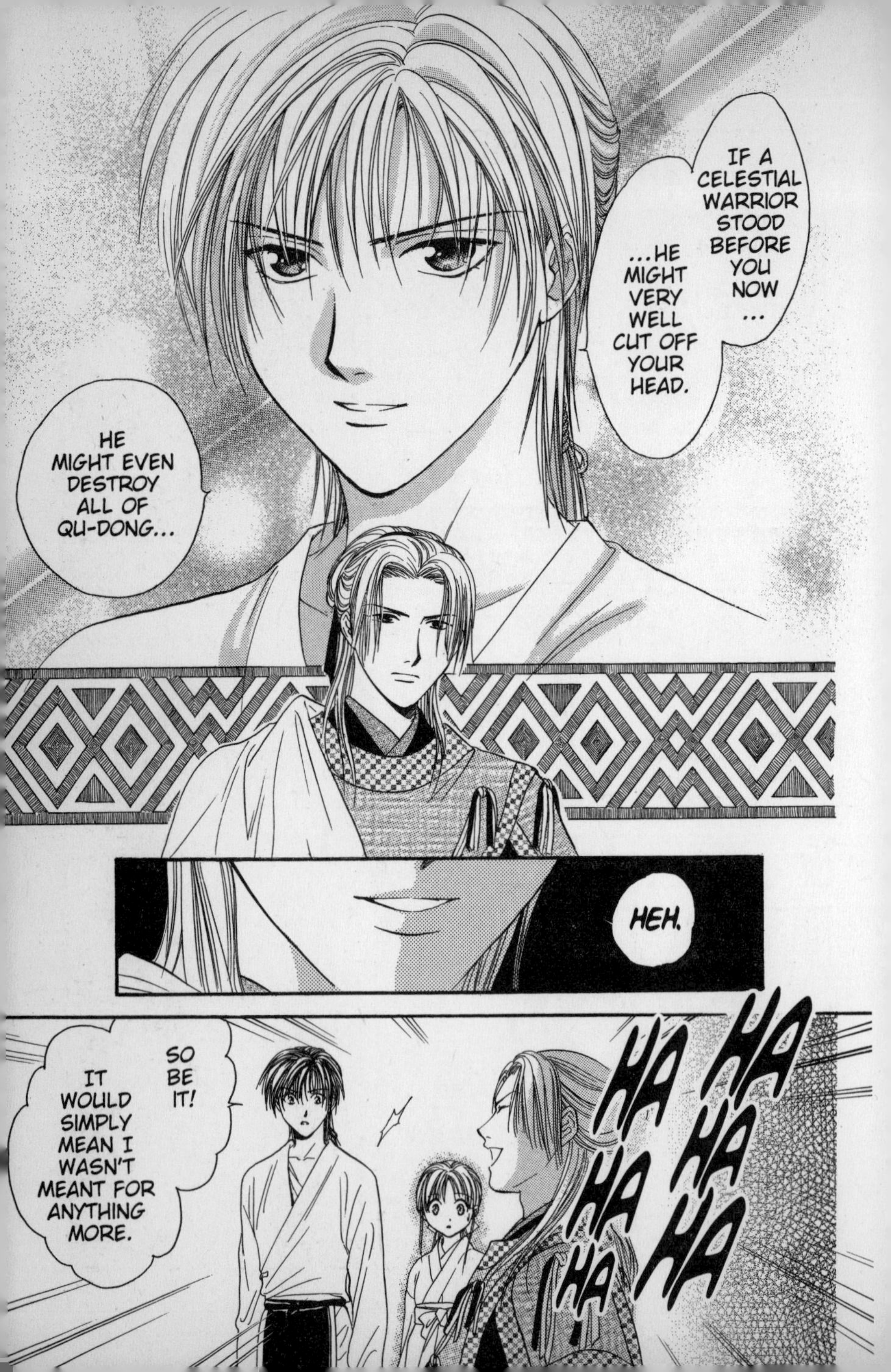

IF A CELESTIAL WARRIOR STOOD BEFORE YOU NOW ...
...HE MIGHT VERY WELL CUT OFF YOUR HEAD.
HE MIGHT EVEN DESTROY ALL OF QU-DONG...
HEH.
HA HA HA HA
HA HA HA HA
SO BE IT!
IT WOULD SIMPLY MEAN I WASN'T MEANT FOR ANYTHING MORE.

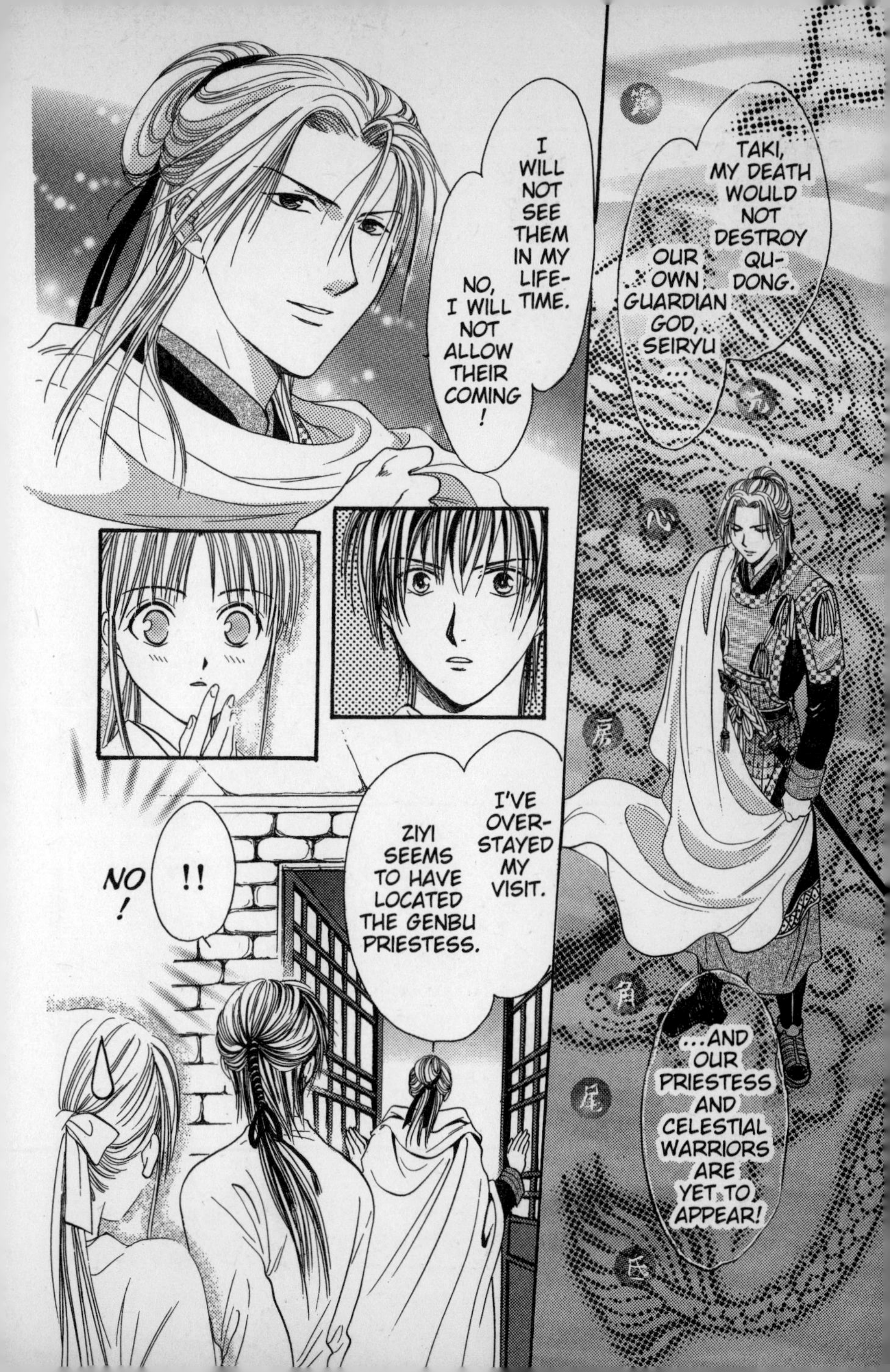
TAKI, MY DEATH WOULD NOT DESTROY QU-DONG.
OUR OWN GUARDIAN GOD, SEIRYU...
...AND OUR PRIESTESS AND CELESTIAL WARRIORS ARE YET TO APPEAR!
I WILL NOT SEE THEM IN MY LIFE-TIME.
NO, I WILL NOT ALLOW THEIR COMING!
I'VE OVER-STAYED MY VISIT.
ZIYI SEEMS TO HAVE LOCATED THE GENBU PRIESTESS.
!!
NO!

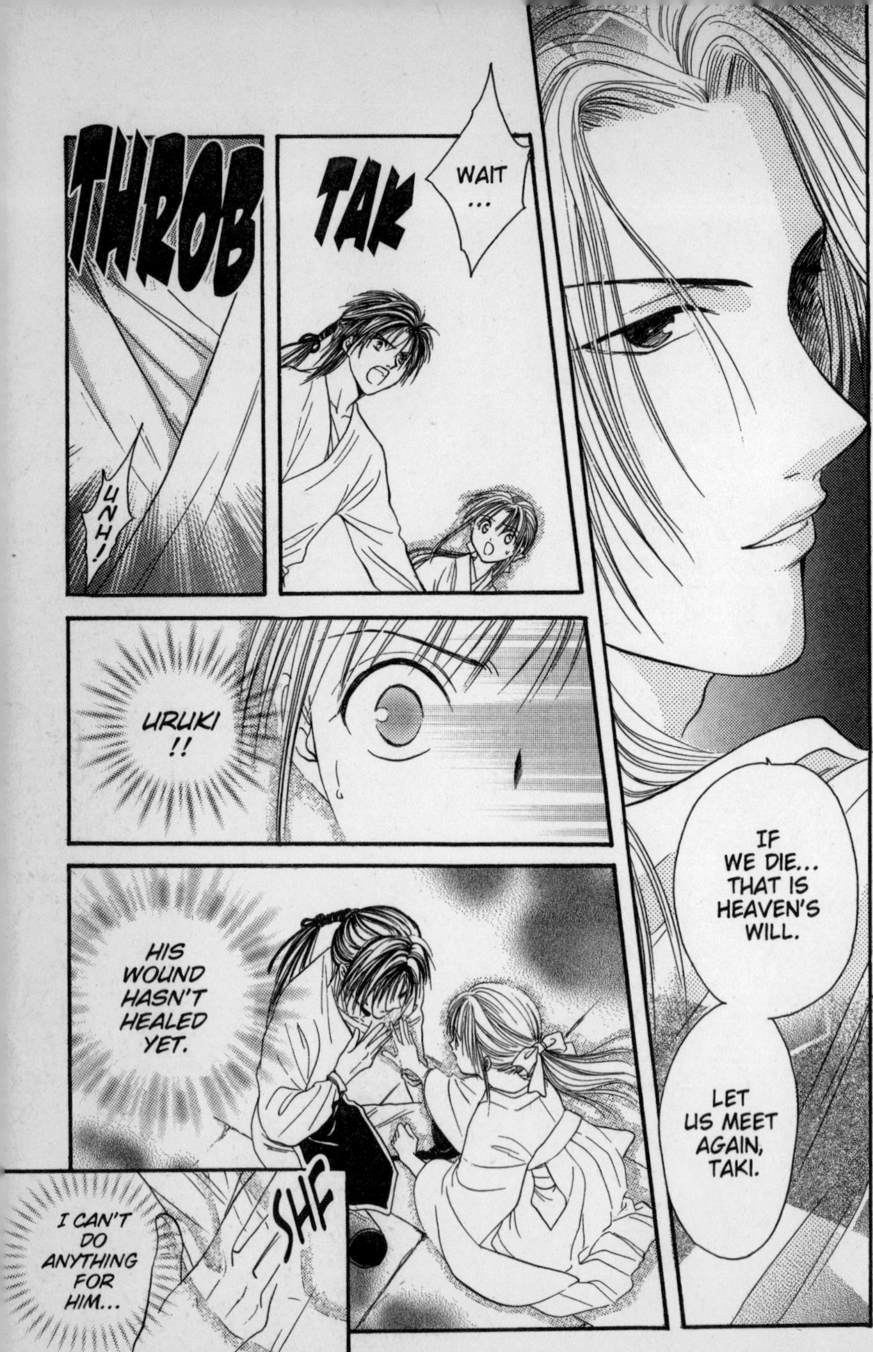
IF WE DIE... THAT IS HEAVEN'S WILL.
LET US MEET AGAIN, TAKI.
WAIT ...
TAK
THROB
UNH!
URUKI !!
HIS WOUND HASN'T HEALED YET.
SHF
I CAN'T DO ANYTHING FOR HIM...

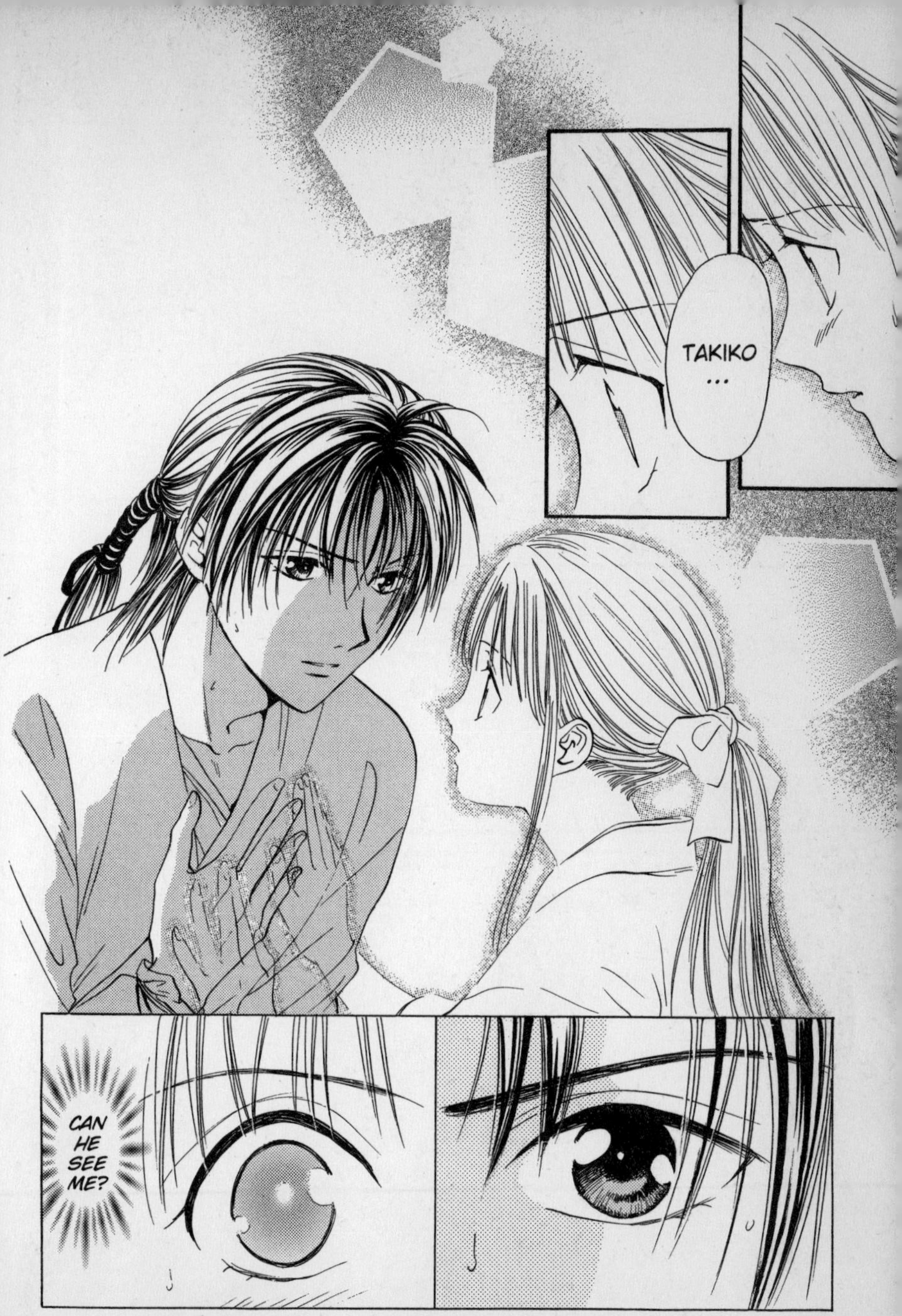
TAKIKO ...
CAN HE SEE ME?

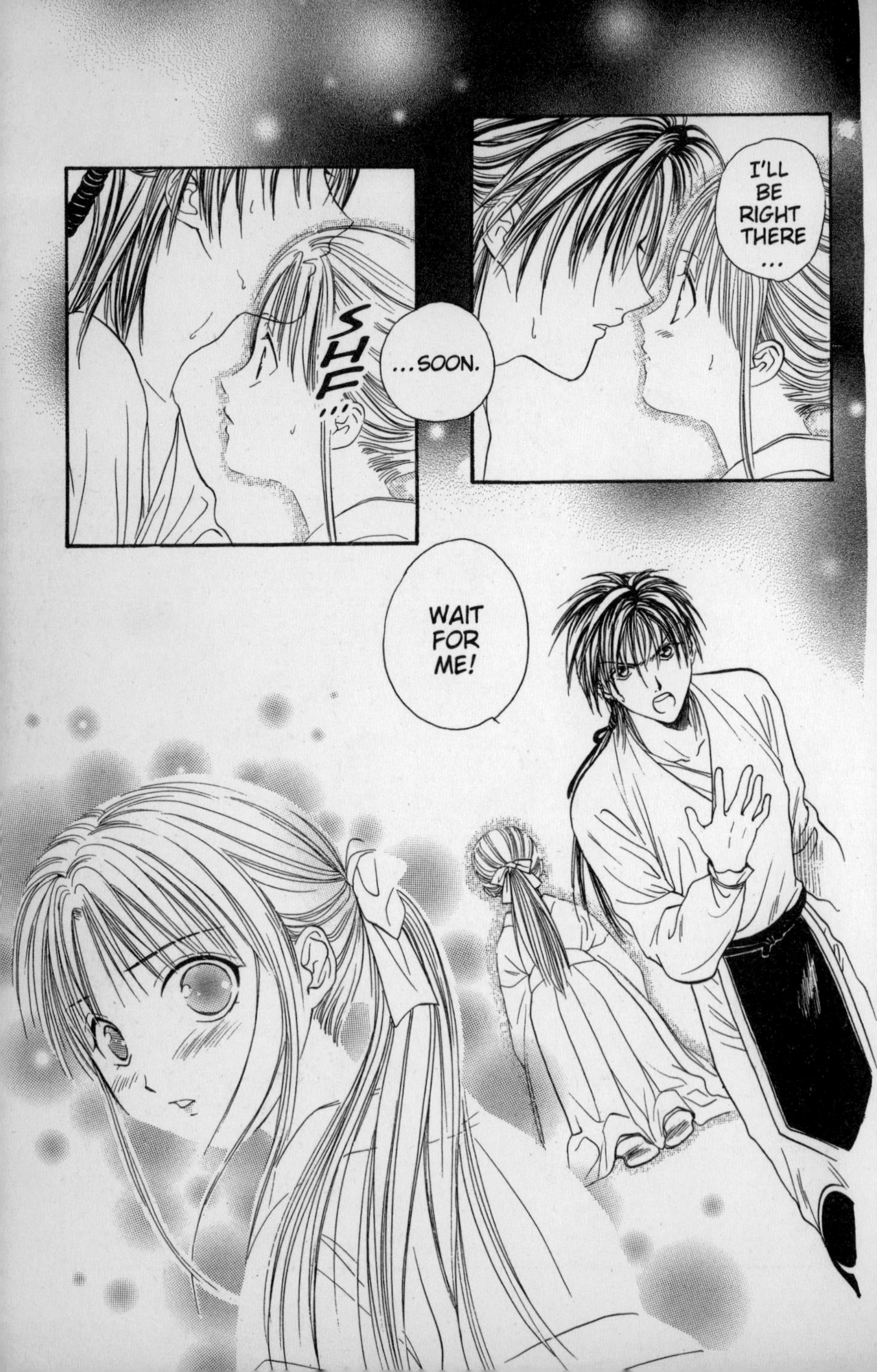
I'LL BE RIGHT THERE ...
...SOON.
SHF...
WAIT FOR ME!

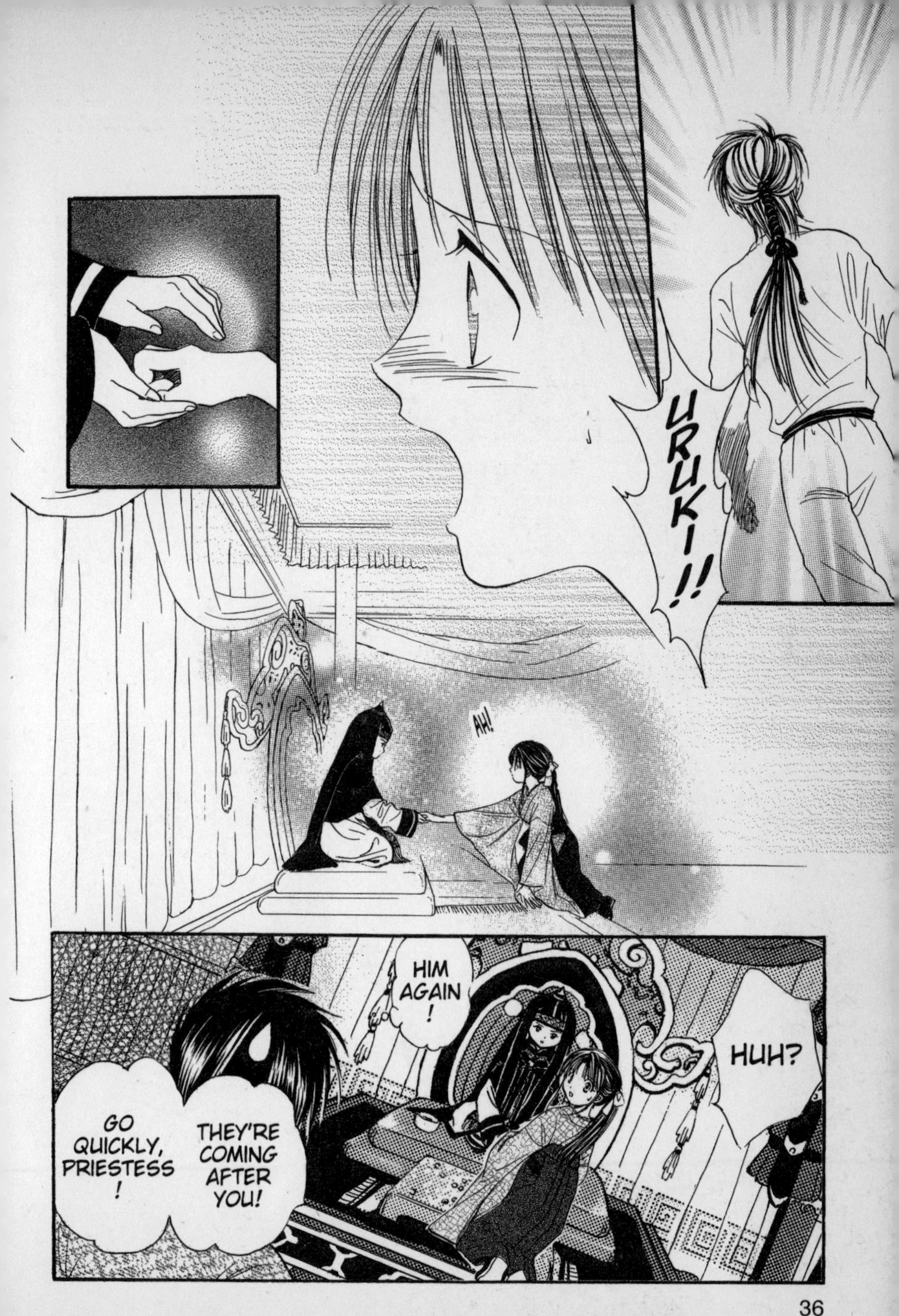
URUKI!!
AH!
HUH?
HIM AGAIN!
THEY'RE COMING AFTER YOU!
GO QUICKLY, PRIESTESS!

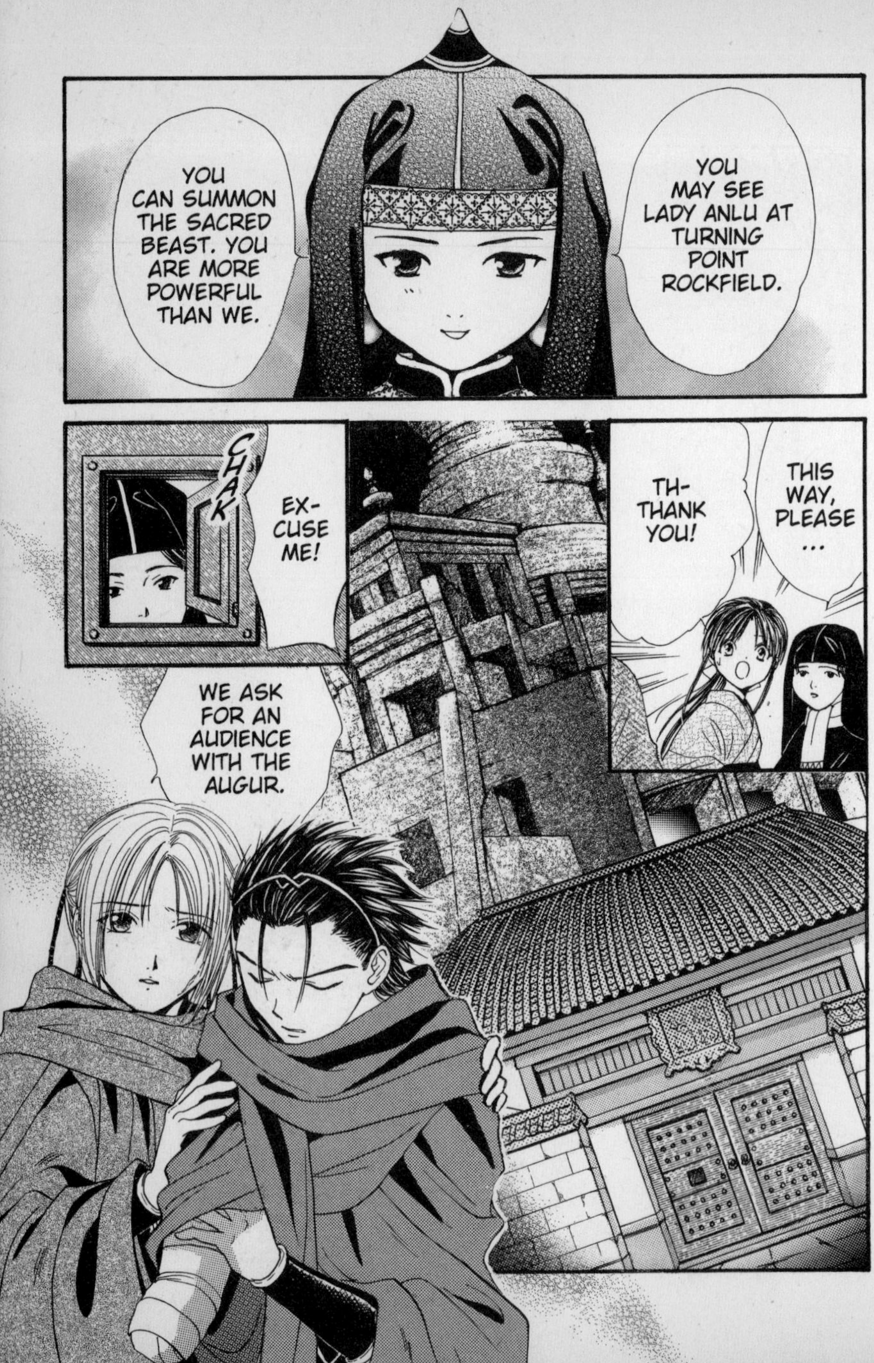
YOU MAY SEE LADY ANLU AT TURNING POINT ROCKFIELD.
YOU CAN SUMMON THE SACRED BEAST. YOU ARE MORE POWERFUL THAN WE.
THIS WAY, PLEASE ...
TH-THANK YOU!
CHAK
EX-CUSE ME!
WE ASK FOR AN AUDIENCE WITH THE AUGUR.

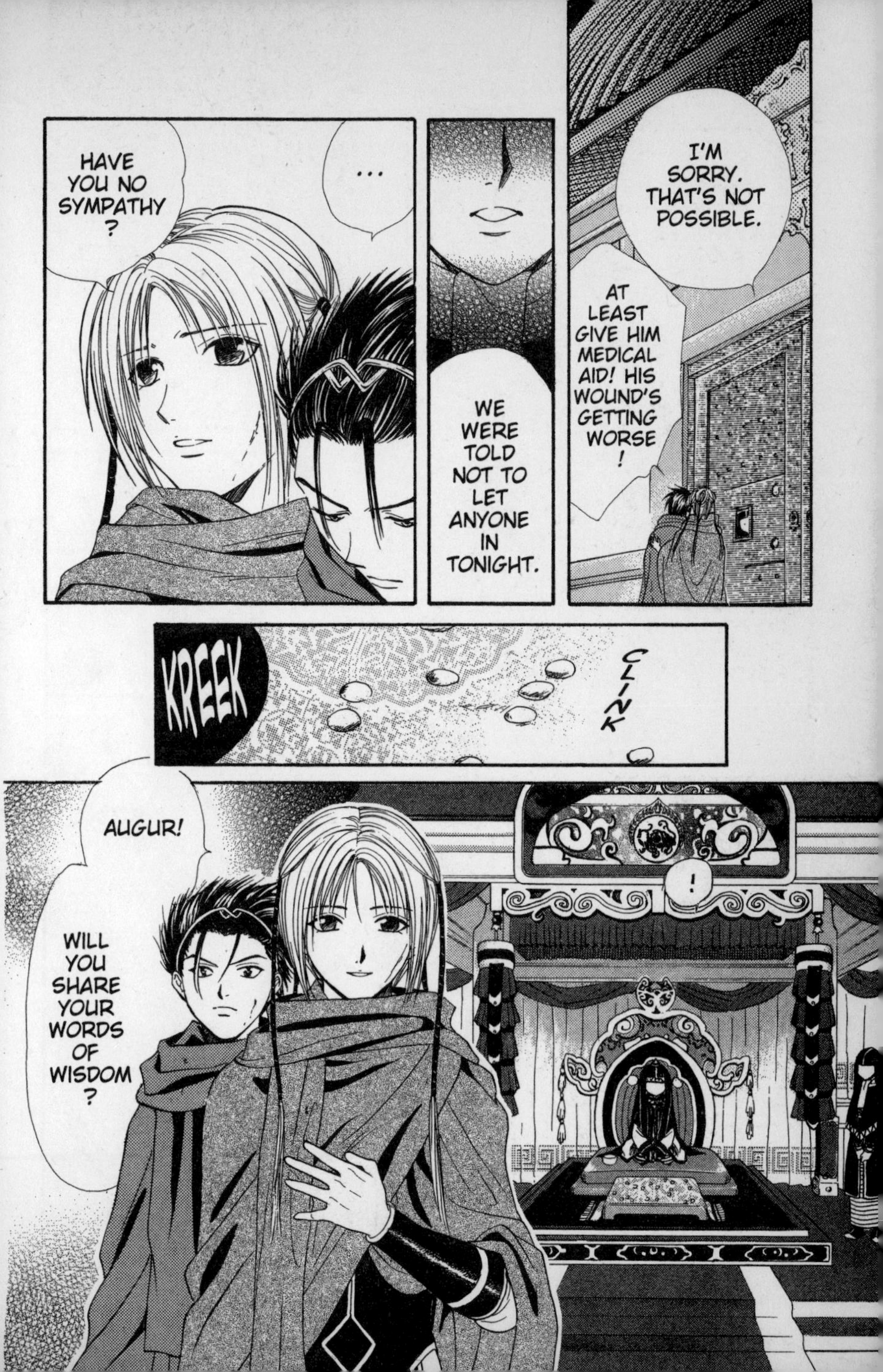
I'M SORRY. THAT'S NOT POSSIBLE.
AT LEAST GIVE HIM MEDICAL AID! HIS WOUND'S GETTING WORSE!
WE WERE TOLD NOT TO LET ANYONE IN TONIGHT.
...
HAVE YOU NO SYMPATHY?
CLINK
KREEK
!
AUGUR!
WILL YOU SHARE YOUR WORDS OF WISDOM?

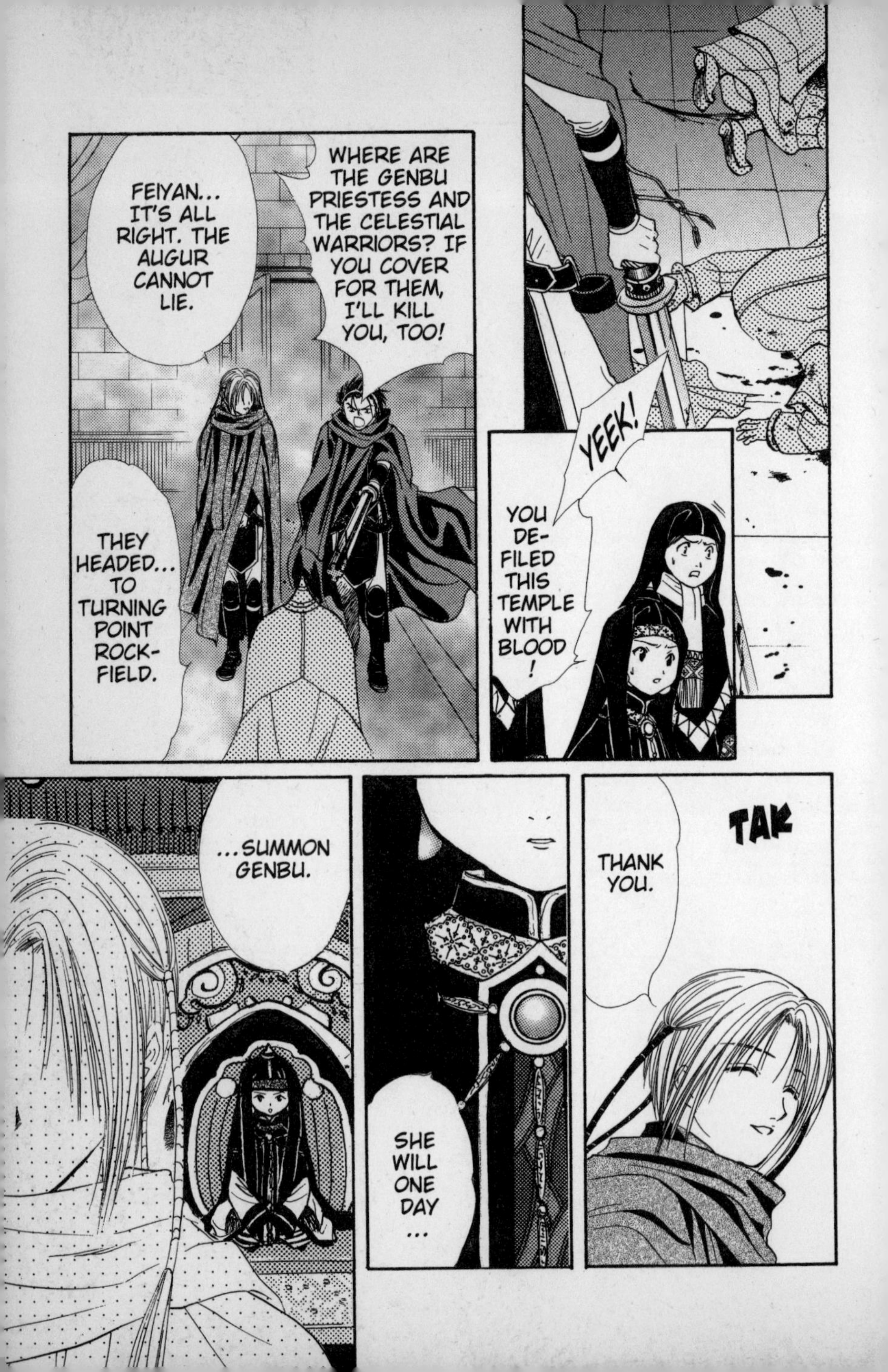
YEEK!
YOU DEFILED THIS TEMPLE WITH BLOOD!
WHERE ARE THE GENBU PRIESTESS AND THE CELESTIAL WARRIORS? IF YOU COVER FOR THEM, I'LL KILL YOU, TOO!
FEIYAN... IT'S ALL RIGHT. THE AUGUR CANNOT LIE.
THEY HEADED... TO TURNING POINT ROCKFIELD.
TAK
THANK YOU.
SHE WILL ONE DAY...
...SUMMON GENBU.

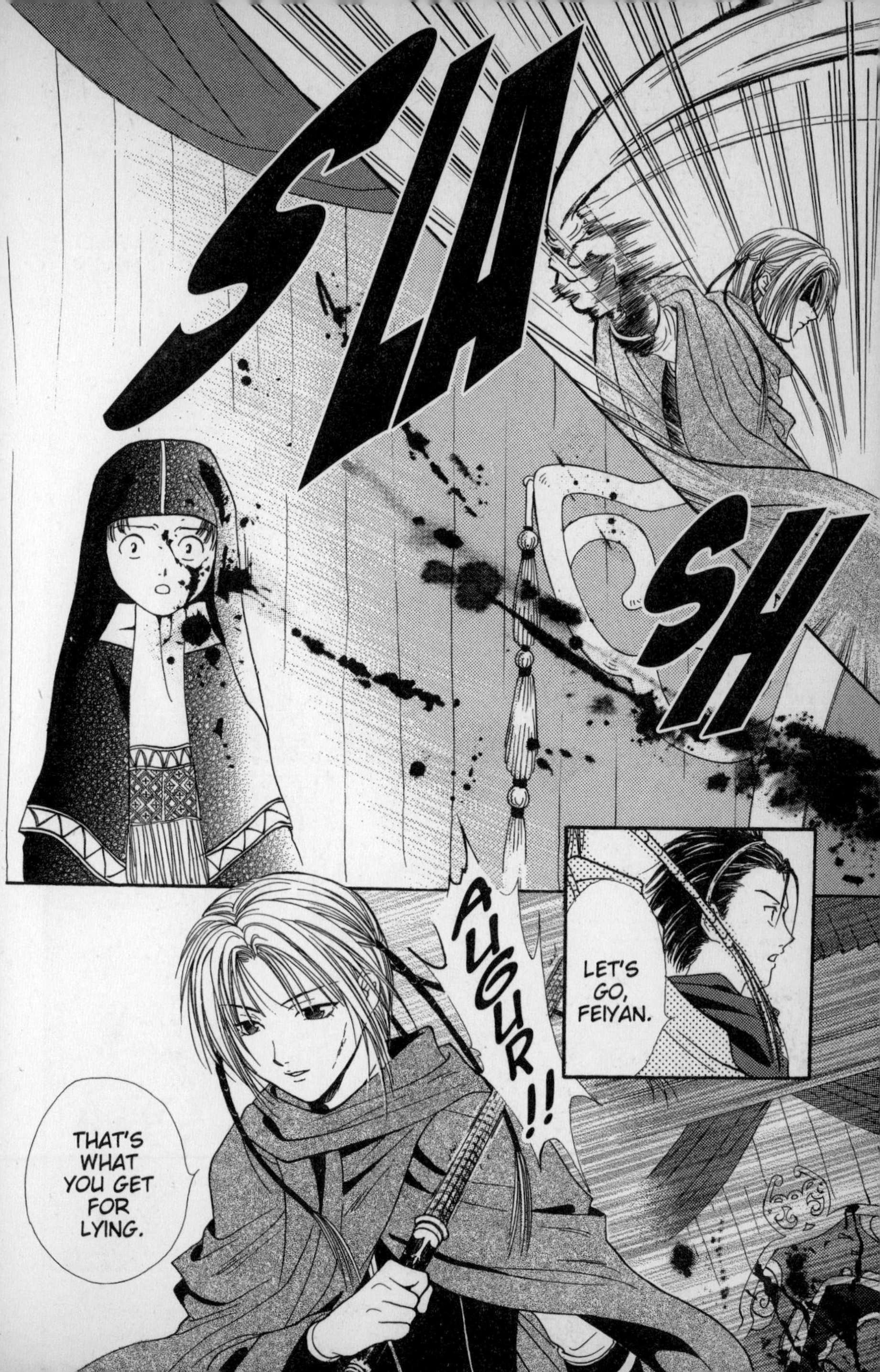
SLASH
LET'S GO, FEIYAN.
AUGUR!!
THAT'S WHAT YOU GET FOR LYING.

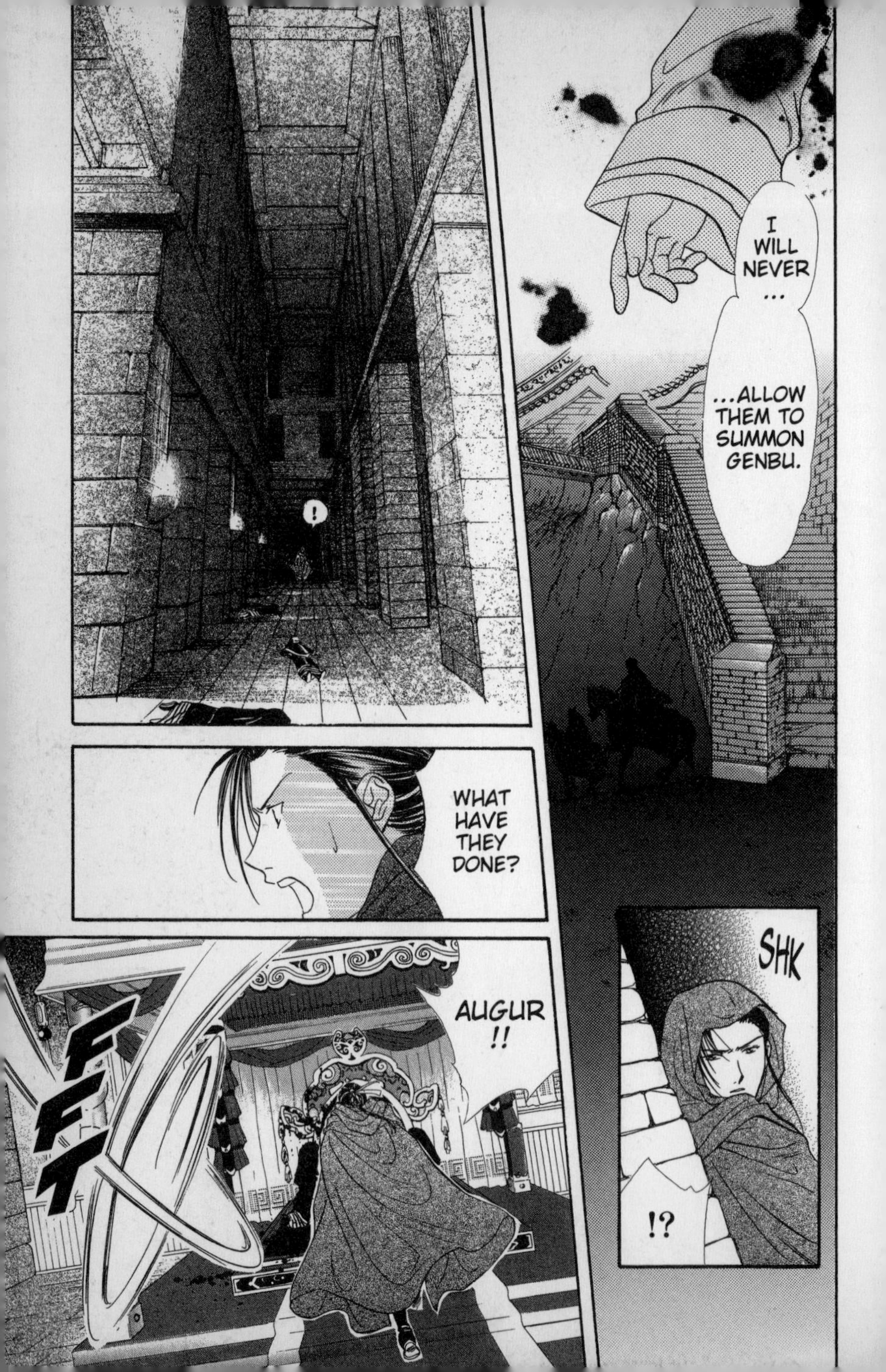
I WILL NEVER ...
...ALLOW THEM TO SUMMON GENBU.
!
WHAT HAVE THEY DONE?
SHK
!?
AUGUR !!

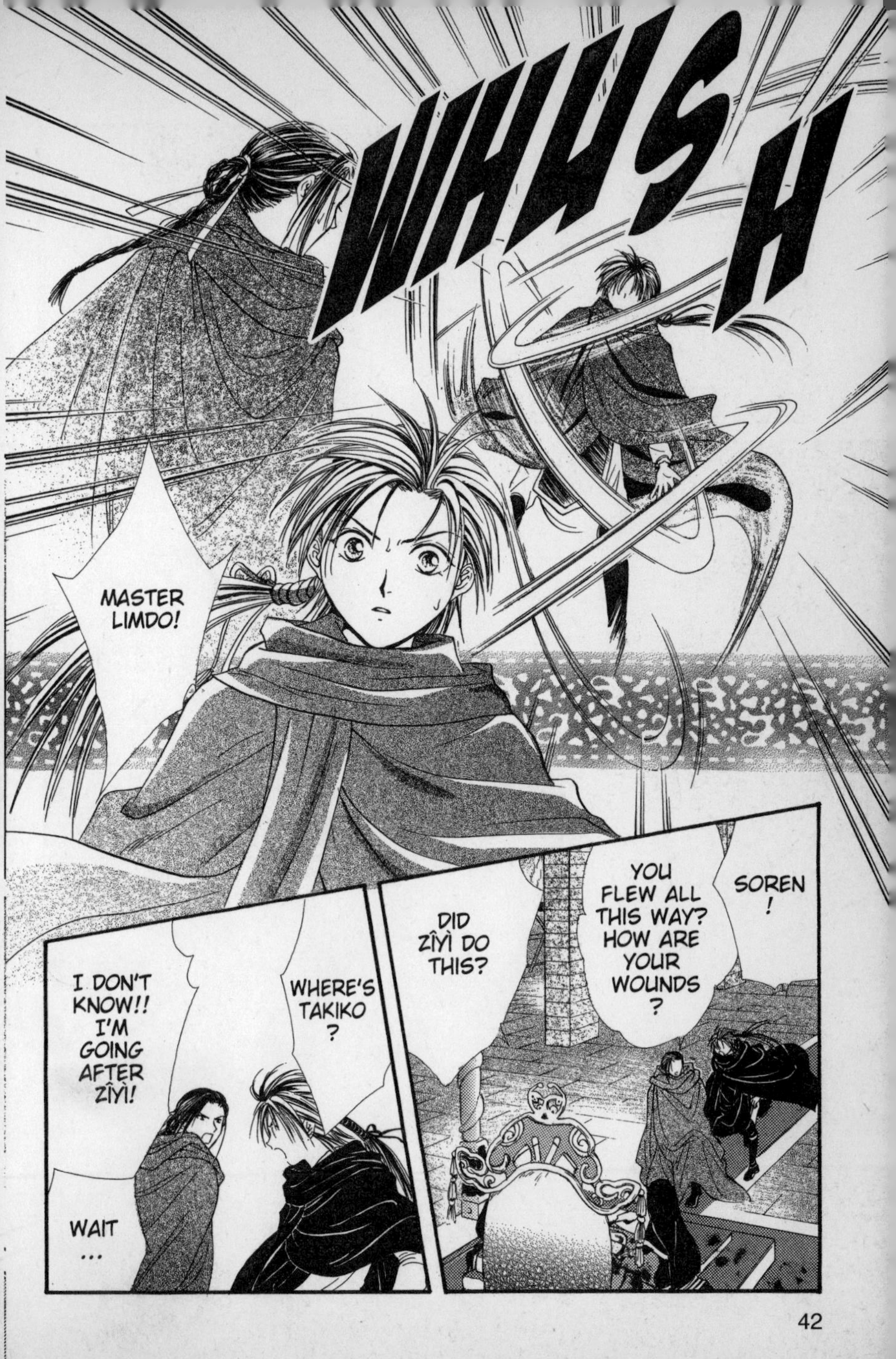
WHHSH
MASTER LIMDO!
SOREN!
YOU FLEW ALL THIS WAY? HOW ARE YOUR WOUNDS?
DID ZÎYÌ DO THIS?
WHERE'S TAKIKO?
I DON'T KNOW!! I'M GOING AFTER ZÎYÌ!
WAIT...

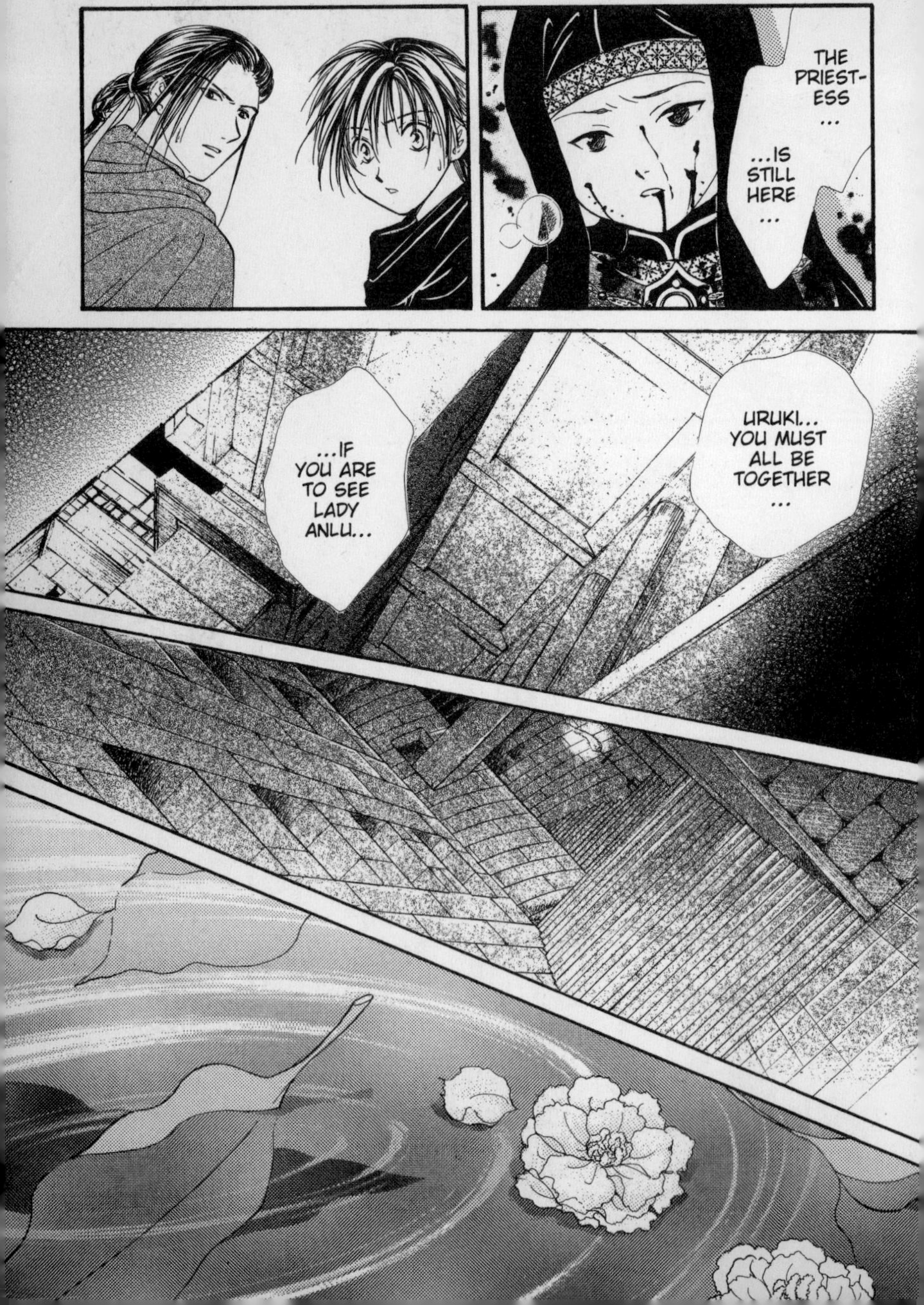

THE PRIEST-ESS...
...IS STILL HERE...
URUKI... YOU MUST ALL BE TOGETHER...
...IF YOU ARE TO SEE LADY ANLU...

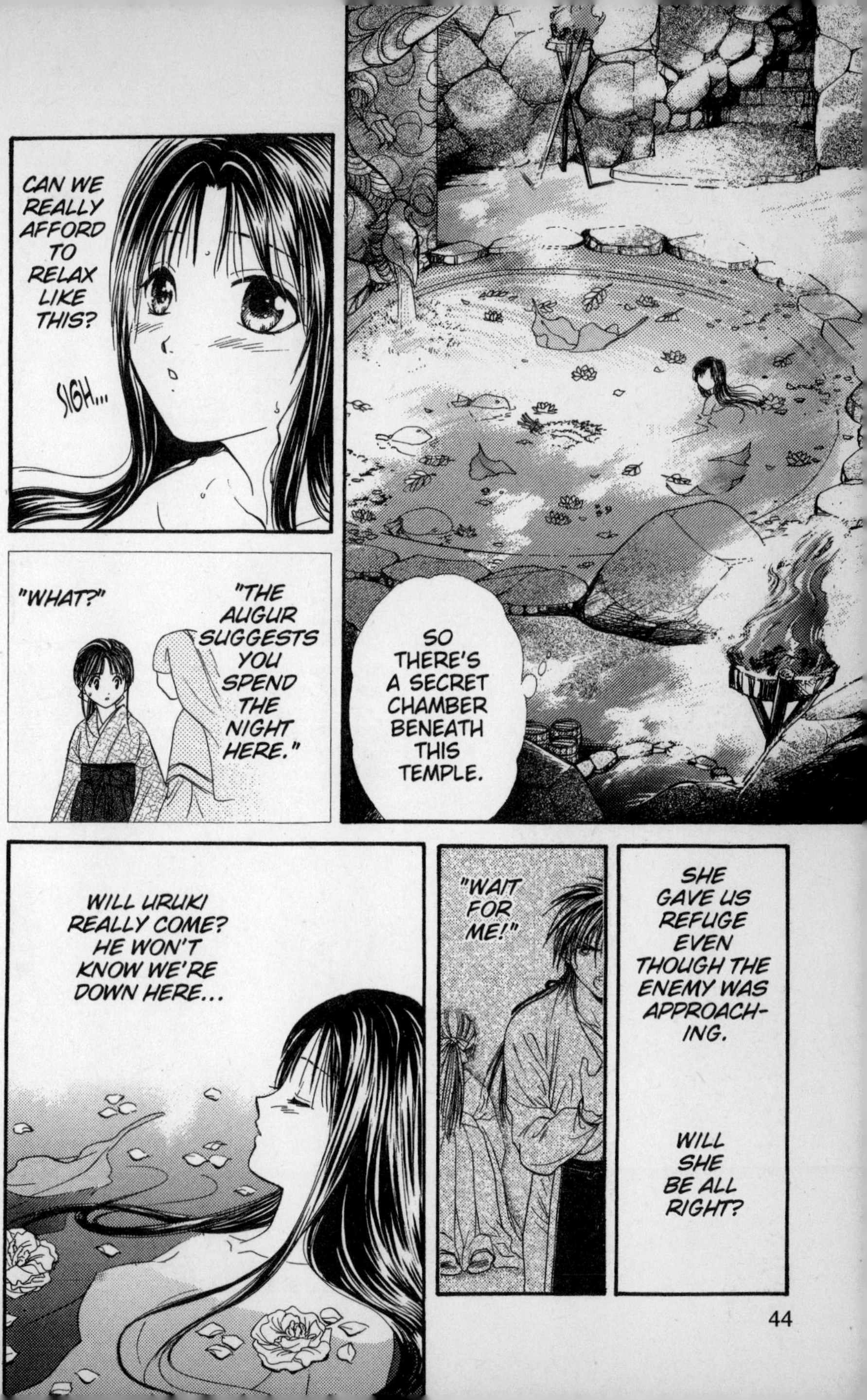
SO THERE'S A SECRET CHAMBER BENEATH THIS TEMPLE.
CAN WE REALLY AFFORD TO RELAX LIKE THIS?
SIGH...
"THE AUGUR SUGGESTS YOU SPEND THE NIGHT HERE."
"WHAT?"
SHE GAVE US REFUGE EVEN THOUGH THE ENEMY WAS APPROACH-ING.
WILL SHE BE ALL RIGHT?
"WAIT FOR ME!"
WILL URUKI REALLY COME? HE WON'T KNOW WE'RE DOWN HERE...

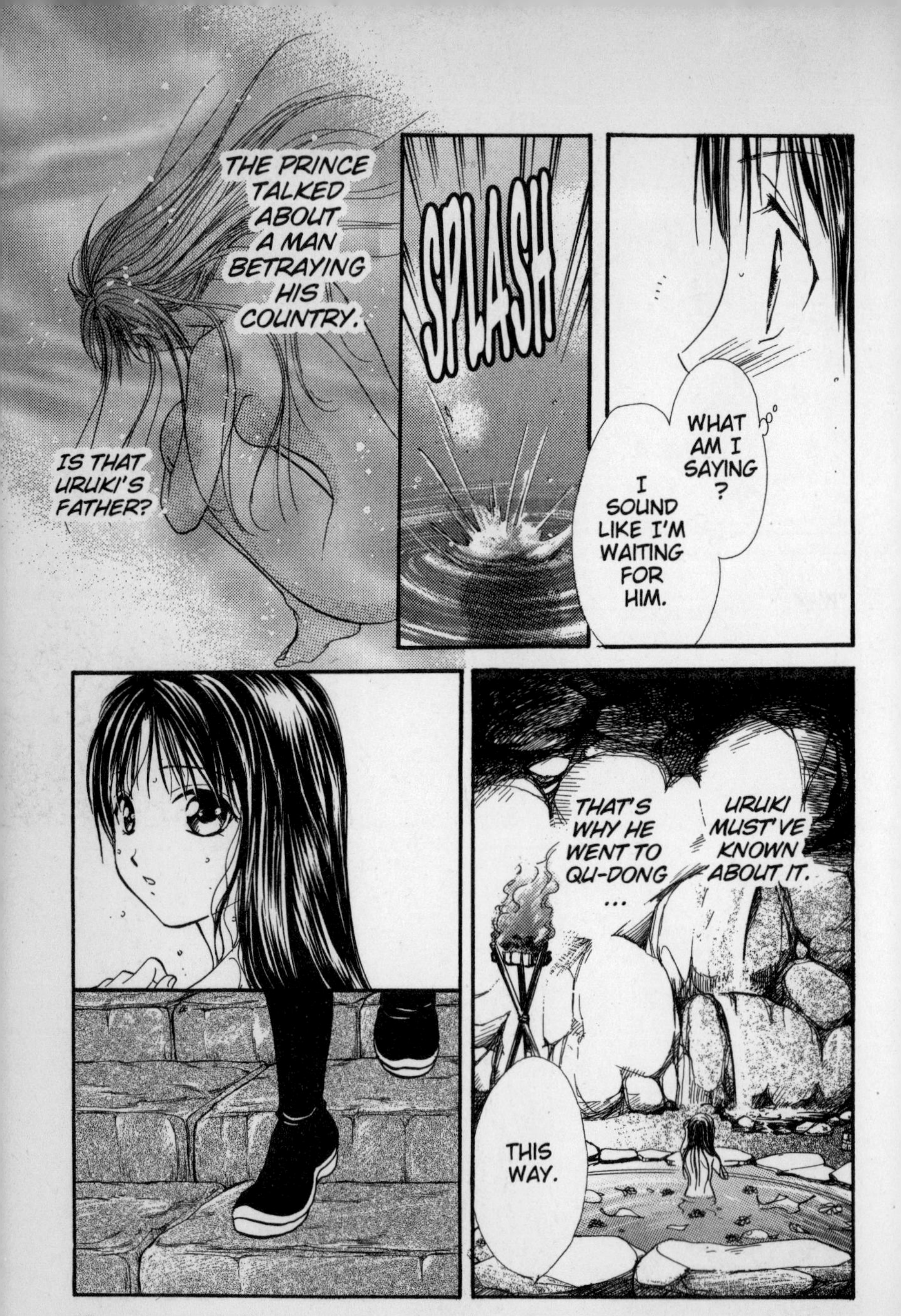
WHAT AM I SAYING?
I SOUND LIKE I'M WAITING FOR HIM.
SPLASH
THE PRINCE TALKED ABOUT A MAN BETRAYING HIS COUNTRY.
IS THAT URUKI'S FATHER?
URUKI MUST'VE KNOWN ABOUT IT.
THAT'S WHY HE WENT TO QU-DONG...
THIS WAY.

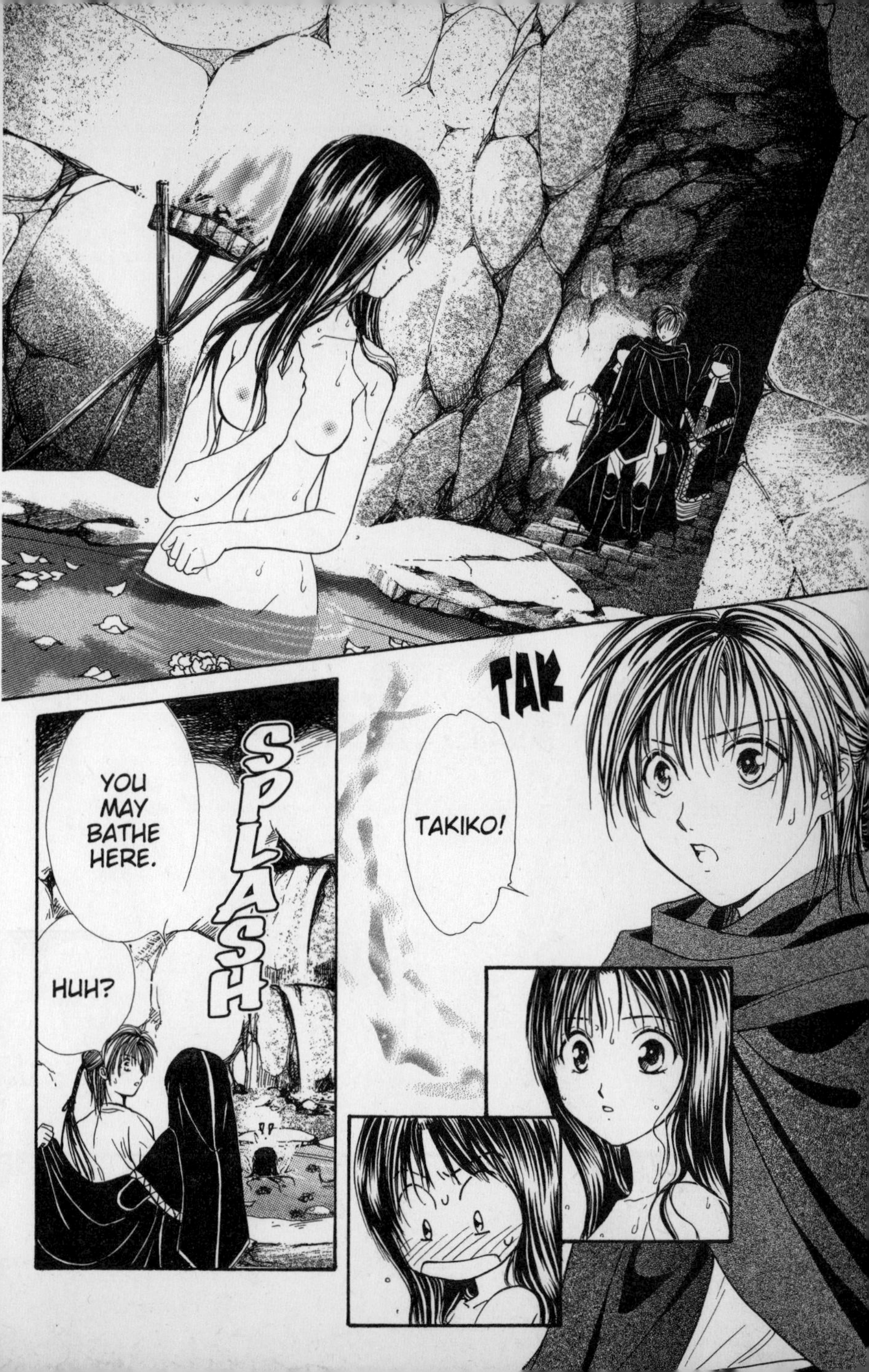
TAK
TAKIKO!
YOU MAY BATHE HERE.
SPLASH
HUH?

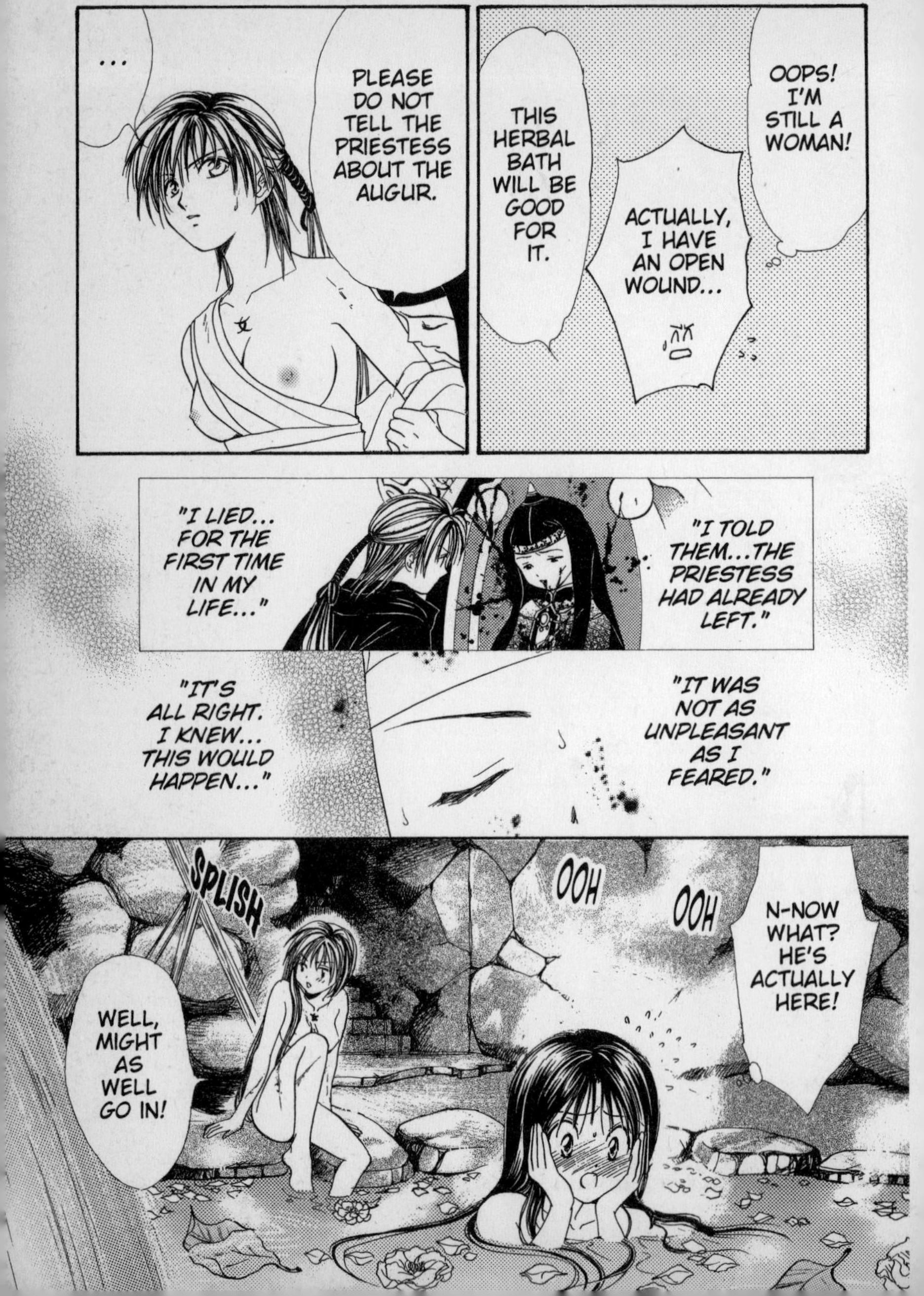
OOPS! I'M STILL A WOMAN!
ACTUALLY, I HAVE AN OPEN WOUND...
THIS HERBAL BATH WILL BE GOOD FOR IT.
PLEASE DO NOT TELL THE PRIESTESS ABOUT THE AUGUR.
...
"I TOLD THEM...THE PRIESTESS HAD ALREADY LEFT."
"I LIED... FOR THE FIRST TIME IN MY LIFE..."
"IT WAS NOT AS UNPLEASANT AS I FEARED."
"IT'S ALL RIGHT. I KNEW... THIS WOULD HAPPEN..."
N-NOW WHAT? HE'S ACTUALLY HERE!
OOH
OOH
SPLISH
WELL, MIGHT AS WELL GO IN!

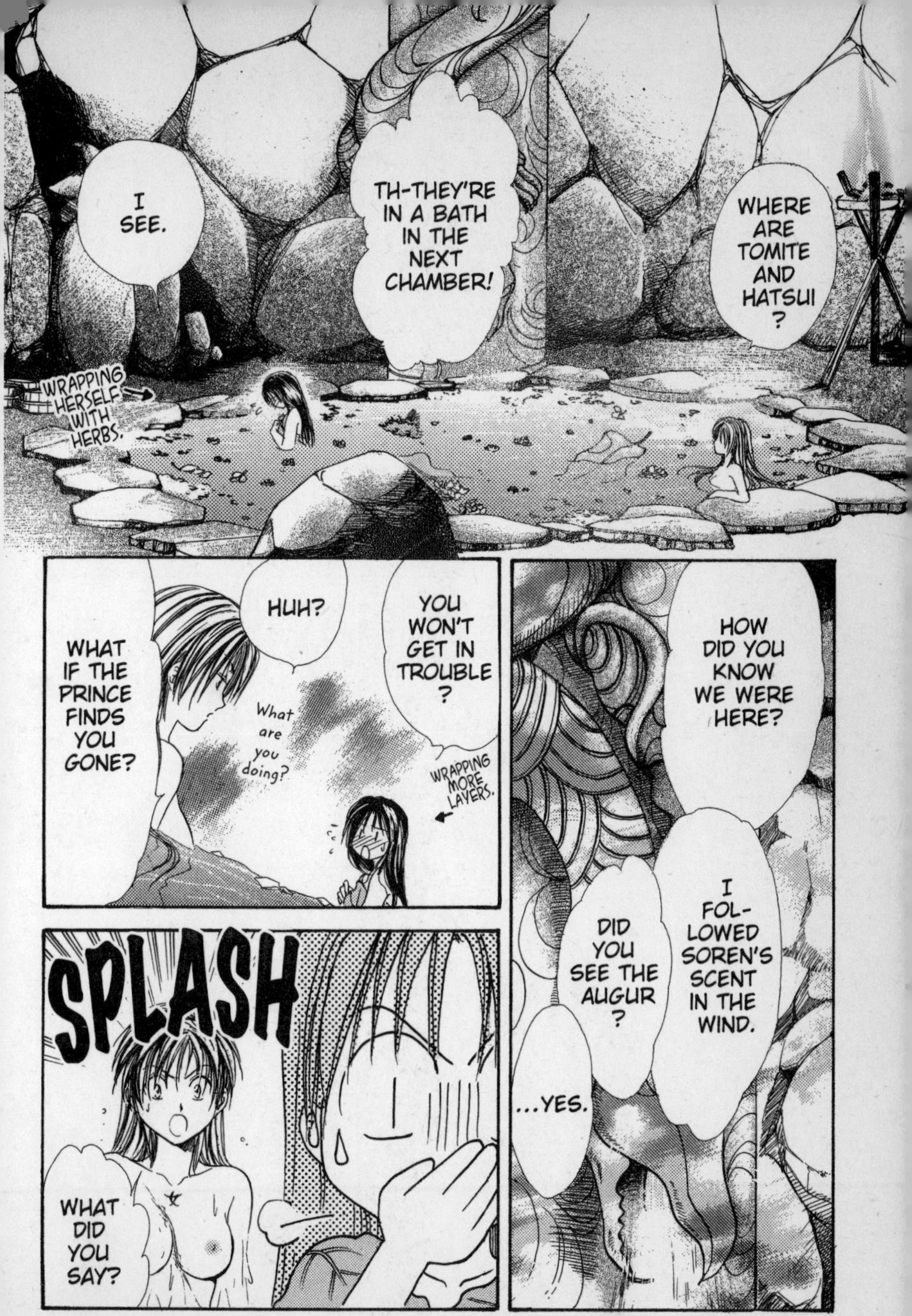
WHERE ARE TOMITE AND HATSUI?
TH-THEY'RE IN A BATH IN THE NEXT CHAMBER!
I SEE.
WRAPPING HERSELF WITH HERBS.
HOW DID YOU KNOW WE WERE HERE?
I FOL-LOWED SOREN'S SCENT IN THE WIND.
DID YOU SEE THE AUGUR?
...YES.
YOU WON'T GET IN TROUBLE?
HUH?
WHAT IF THE PRINCE FINDS YOU GONE?
What are you doing?
WRAPPING MORE LAYERS.
SPLASH
WHAT DID YOU SAY?

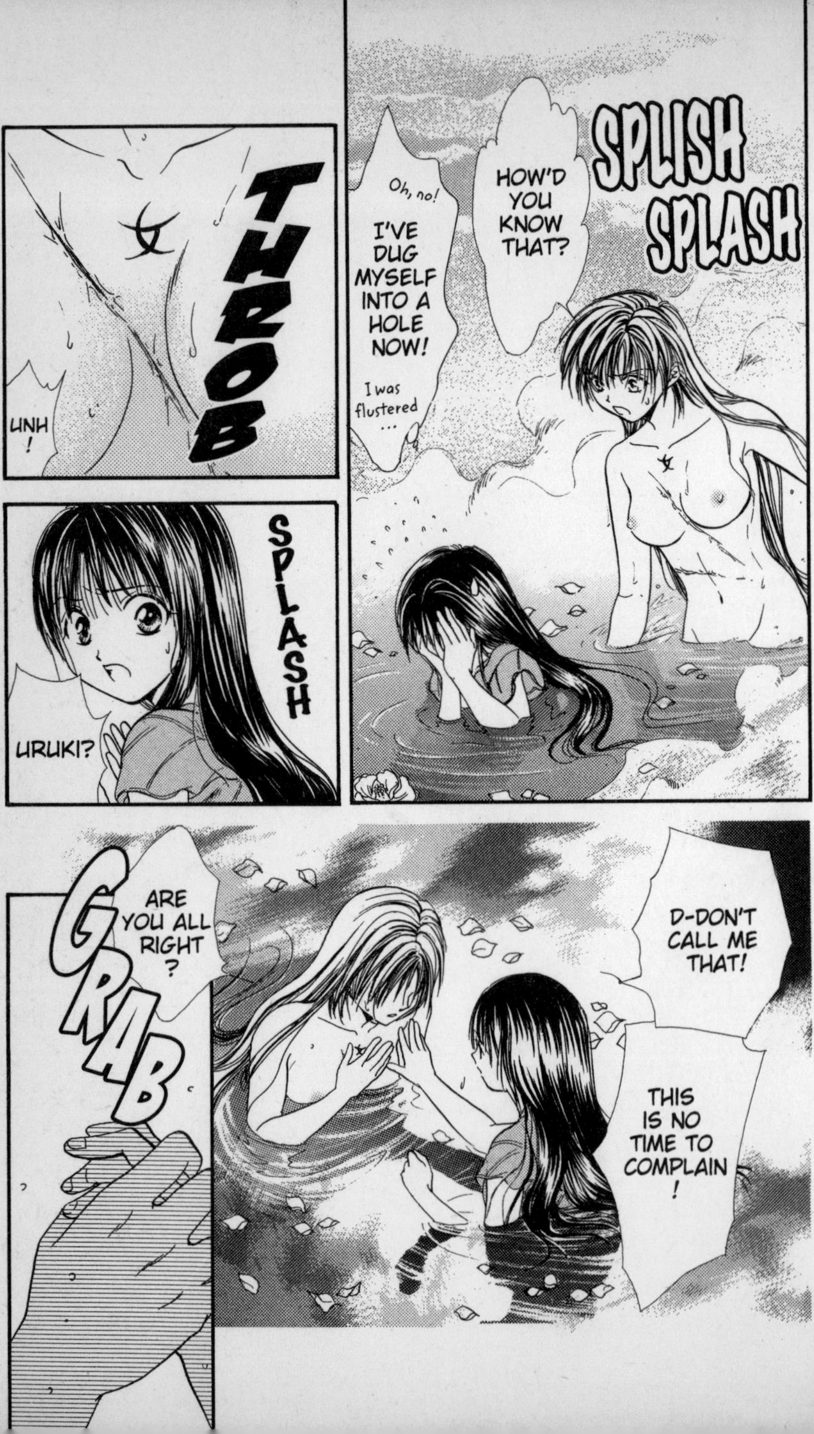
SPLISH SPLASH
HOW'D YOU KNOW THAT?
Oh, no!
I'VE DUG MYSELF INTO A HOLE NOW!
I was flustered...
THROB
UNH!
SPLASH
URUKI?
D-DON'T CALL ME THAT!
THIS IS NO TIME TO COMPLAIN!
ARE YOU ALL RIGHT?
GRAB

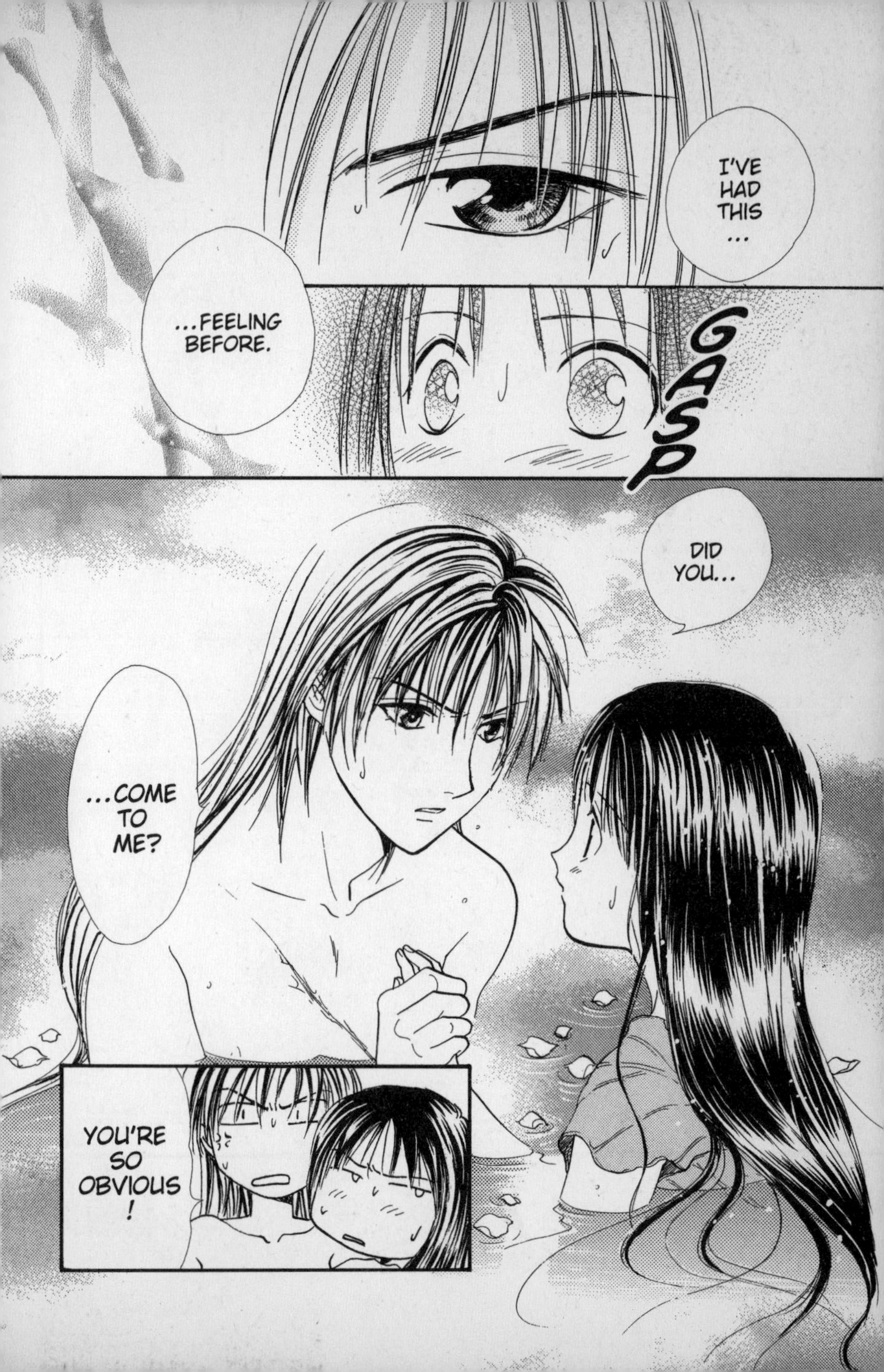
I'VE HAD THIS...
...FEELING BEFORE.
GASP
DID YOU...
...COME TO ME?
YOU'RE SO OBVIOUS!

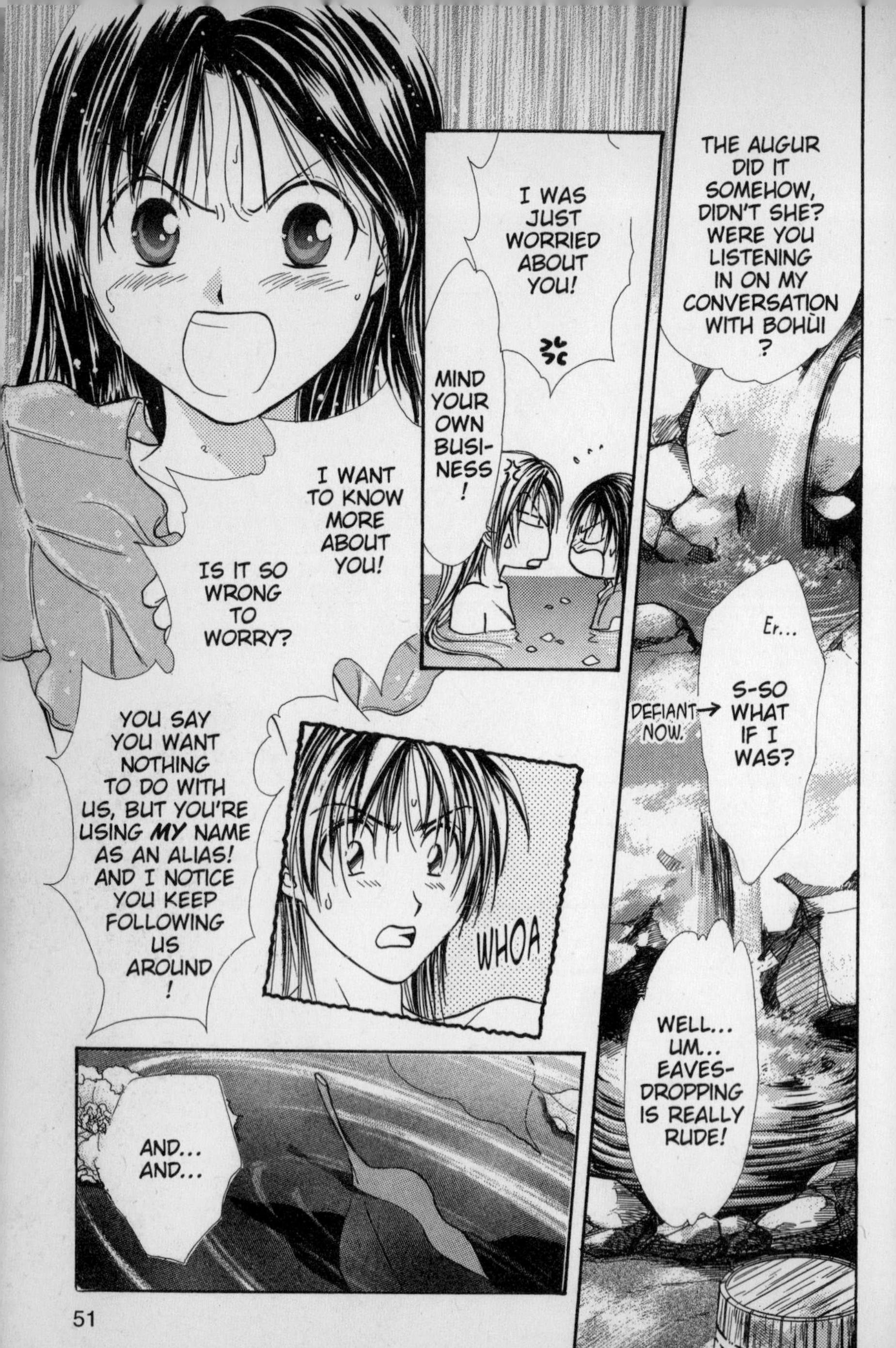
THE AUGUR DID IT SOMEHOW, DIDN'T SHE? WERE YOU LISTENING IN ON MY CONVERSATION WITH BOHÙI?
Er...
S-SO WHAT IF I WAS?
DEFIANT NOW.
WELL... UM... EAVES-DROPPING IS REALLY RUDE!
I WAS JUST WORRIED ABOUT YOU!
MIND YOUR OWN BUSI-NESS!
I WANT TO KNOW MORE ABOUT YOU!
IS IT SO WRONG TO WORRY?
YOU SAY YOU WANT NOTHING TO DO WITH US, BUT YOU'RE USING *MY* NAME AS AN ALIAS! AND I NOTICE YOU KEEP FOLLOWING US AROUND!
WHOA
AND... AND...

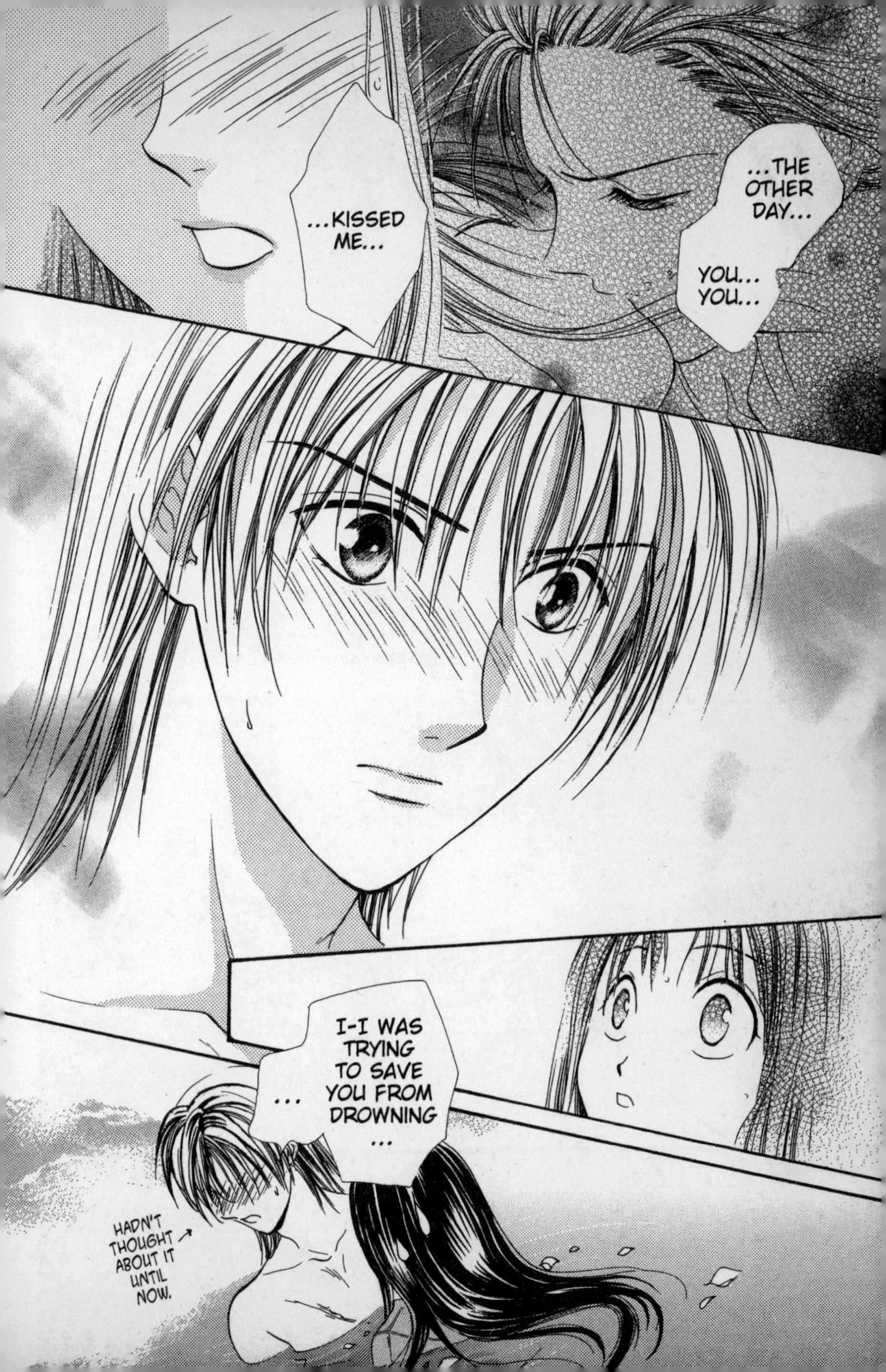
...THE OTHER DAY...
YOU... YOU...
...KISSED ME...
...
I-I WAS TRYING TO SAVE YOU FROM DROWNING ...
HADN'T THOUGHT ABOUT IT UNTIL NOW.

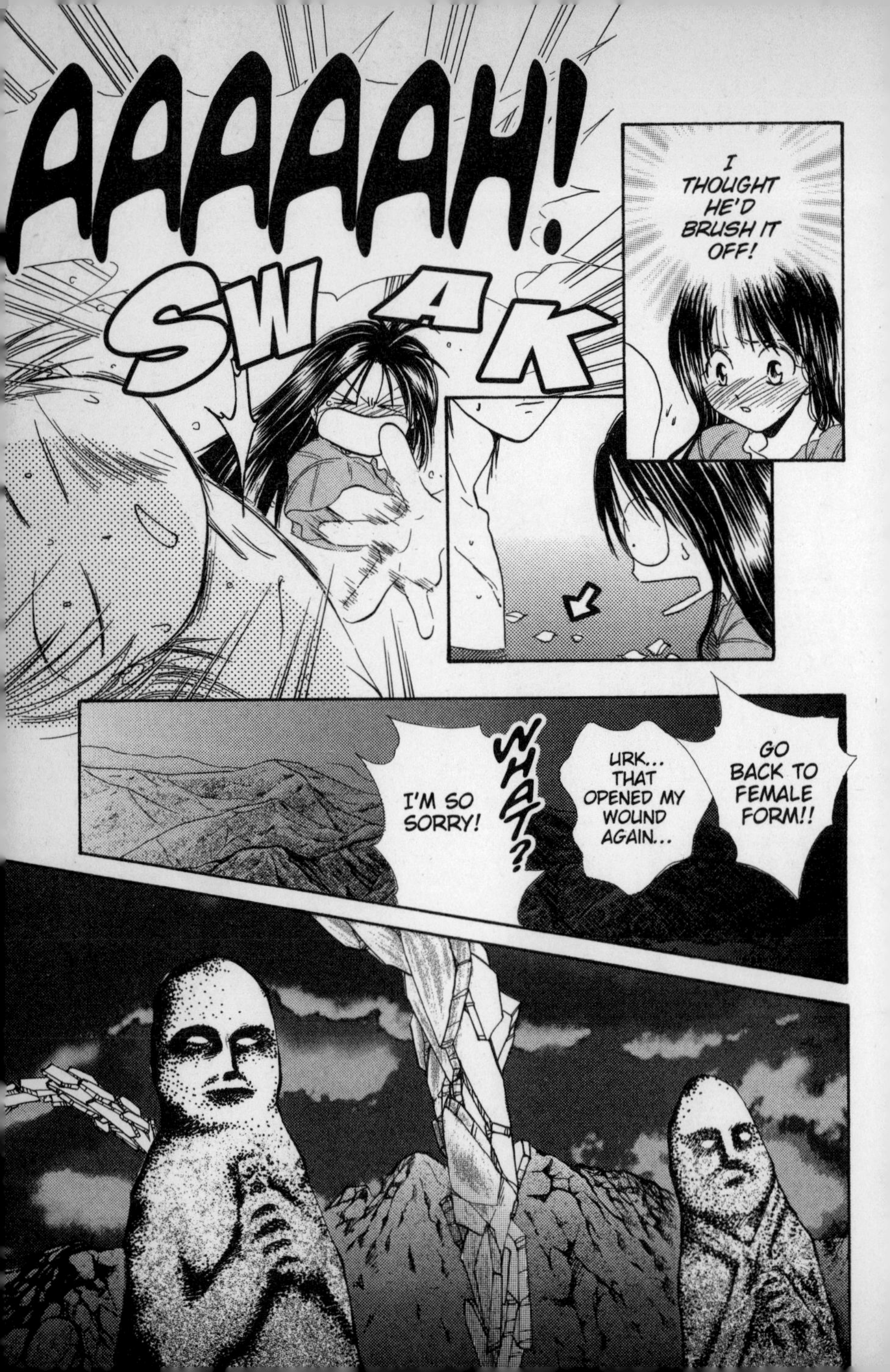
I THOUGHT HE'D BRUSH IT OFF!
AAAAAH!
SWAK
GO BACK TO FEMALE FORM!!
URK... THAT OPENED MY WOUND AGAIN...
WHAT?
I'M SO SORRY!

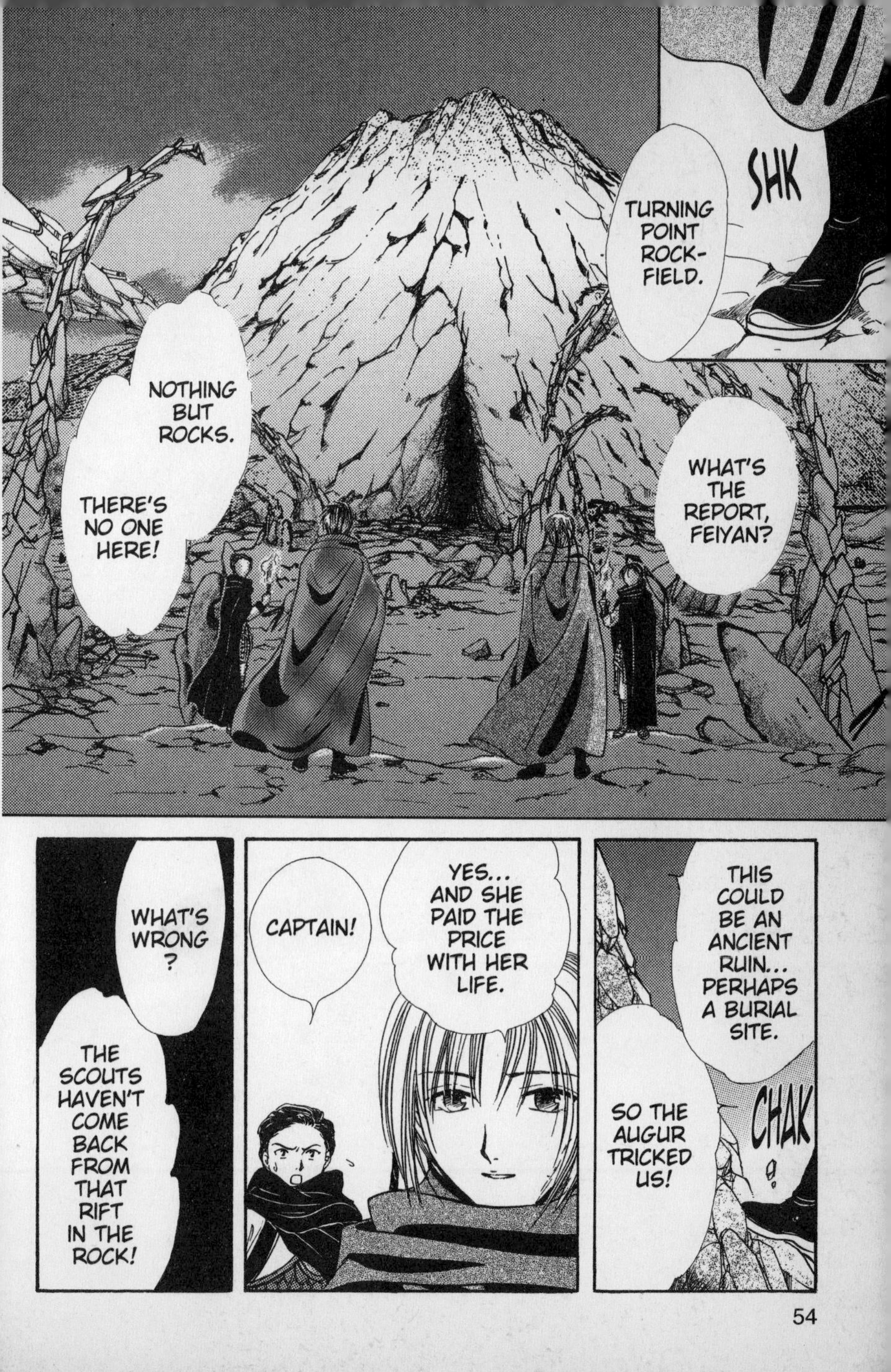
SHK
TURNING POINT ROCK-FIELD.
WHAT'S THE REPORT, FEIYAN?
NOTHING BUT ROCKS.
THERE'S NO ONE HERE!
THIS COULD BE AN ANCIENT RUIN... PERHAPS A BURIAL SITE.
CHAK
SO THE AUGUR TRICKED US!
YES... AND SHE PAID THE PRICE WITH HER LIFE.
CAPTAIN!
WHAT'S WRONG?
THE SCOUTS HAVEN'T COME BACK FROM THAT RIFT IN THE ROCK!

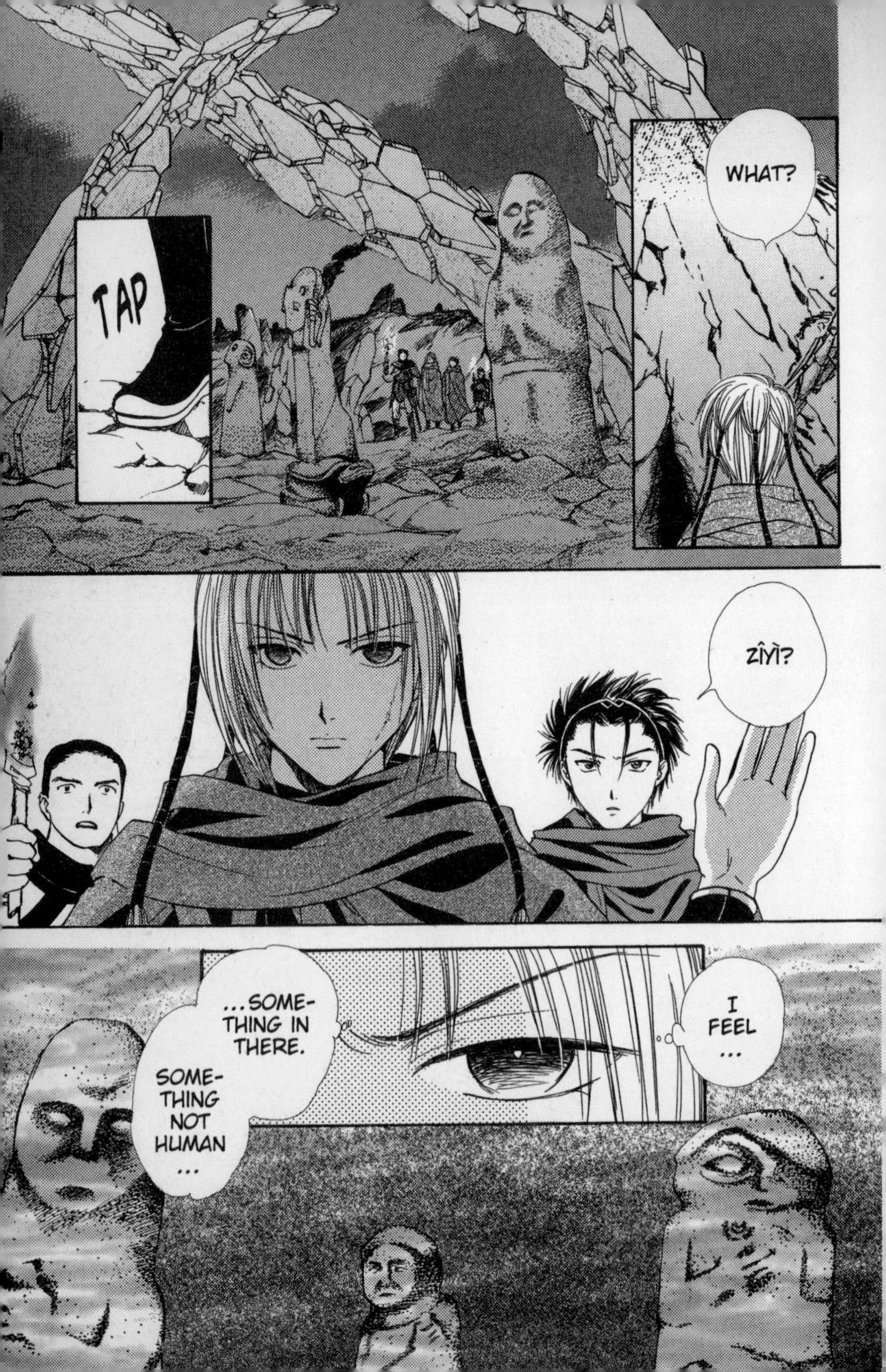
WHAT?
TAP
ZÎYÌ?
I FEEL ...
...SOME-THING IN THERE.
SOME-THING NOT HUMAN ...

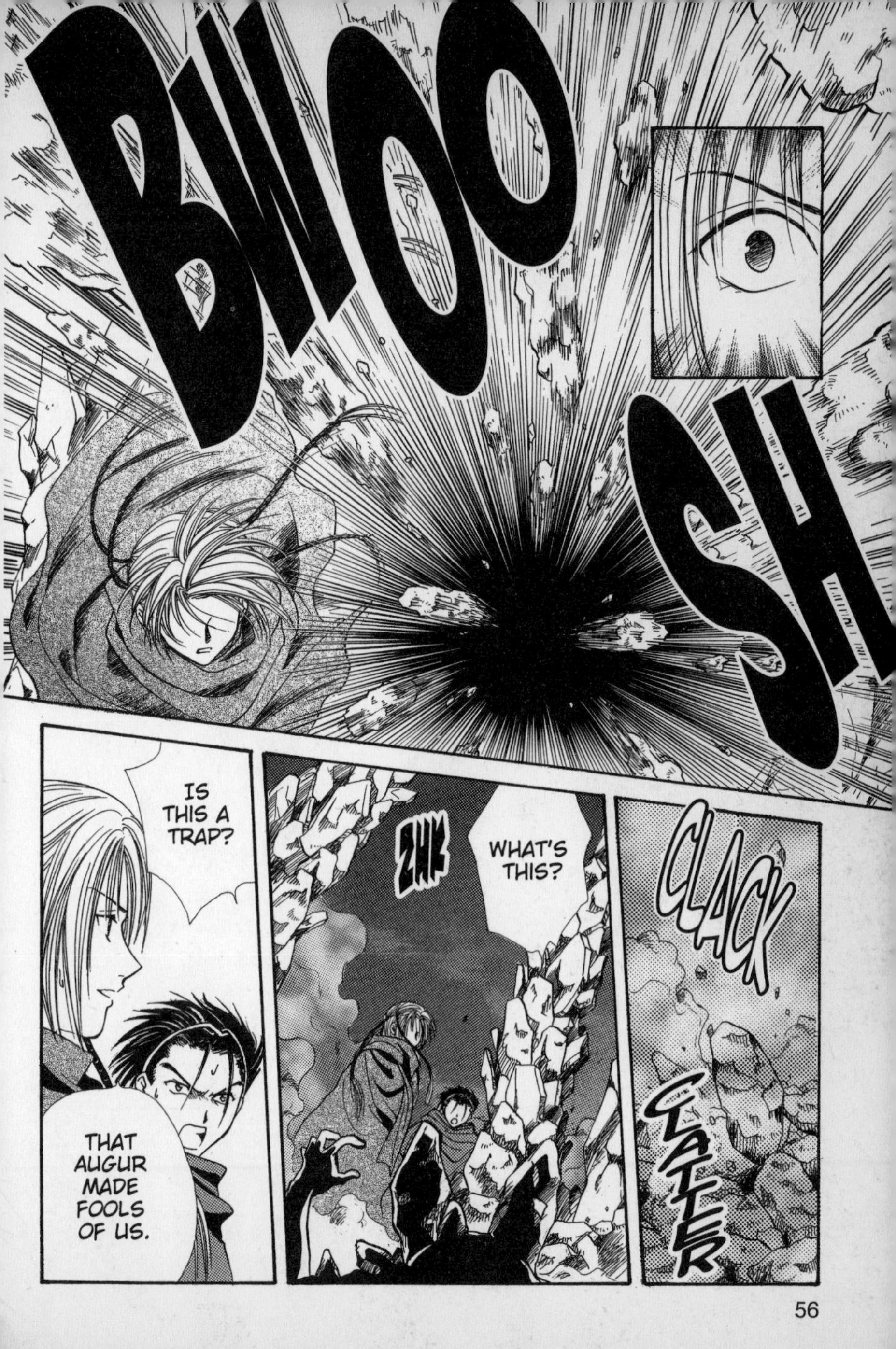
BWOOSH
CLACK
CLATTER
ZHK
WHAT'S THIS?
IS THIS A TRAP?
THAT AUGUR MADE FOOLS OF US.

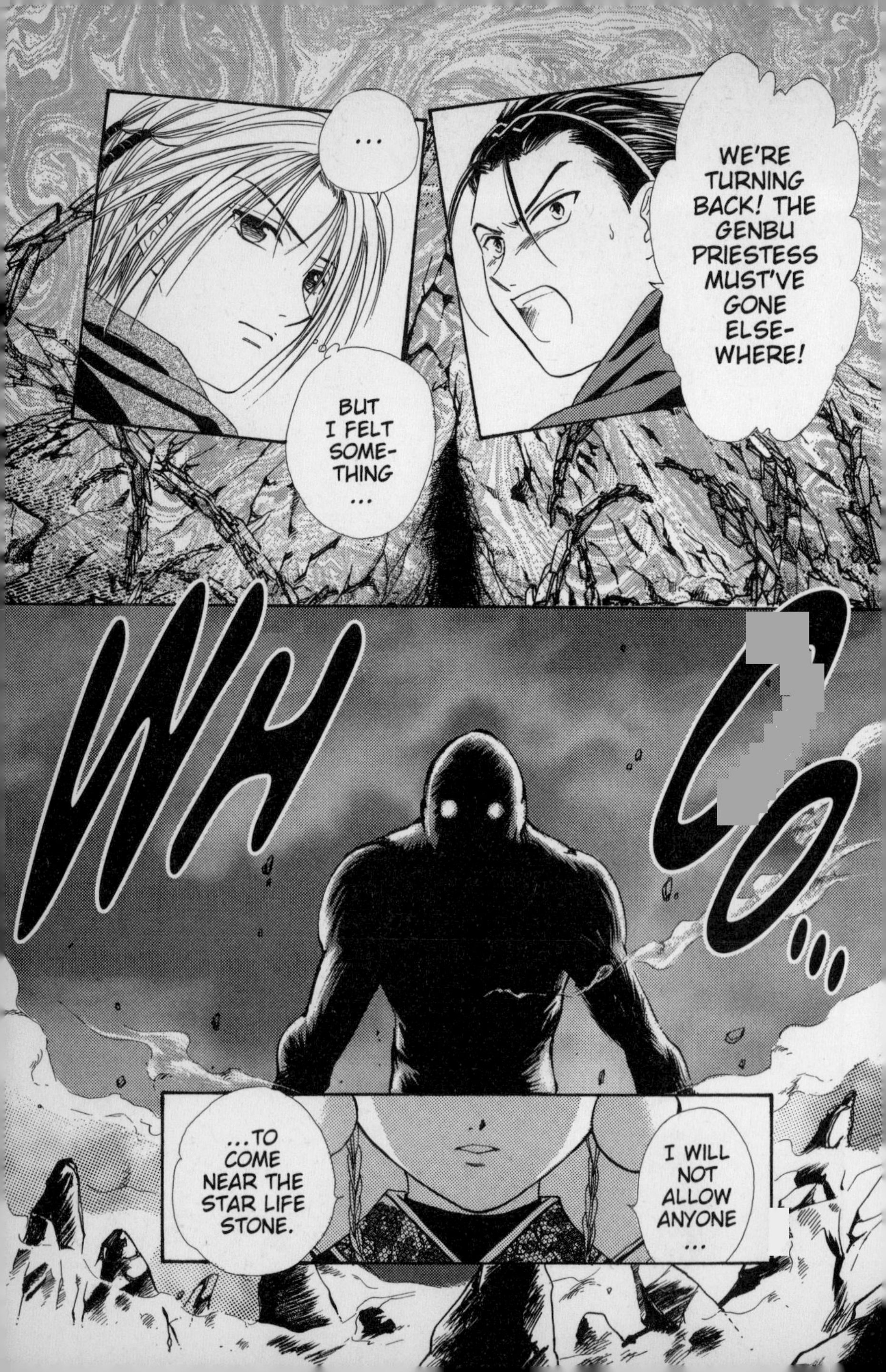
WE'RE TURNING BACK! THE GENBU PRIESTESS MUST'VE GONE ELSE-WHERE!
...
BUT I FELT SOME-THING ...
WH
OO...
I WILL NOT ALLOW ANYONE ...
...TO COME NEAR THE STAR LIFE STONE.

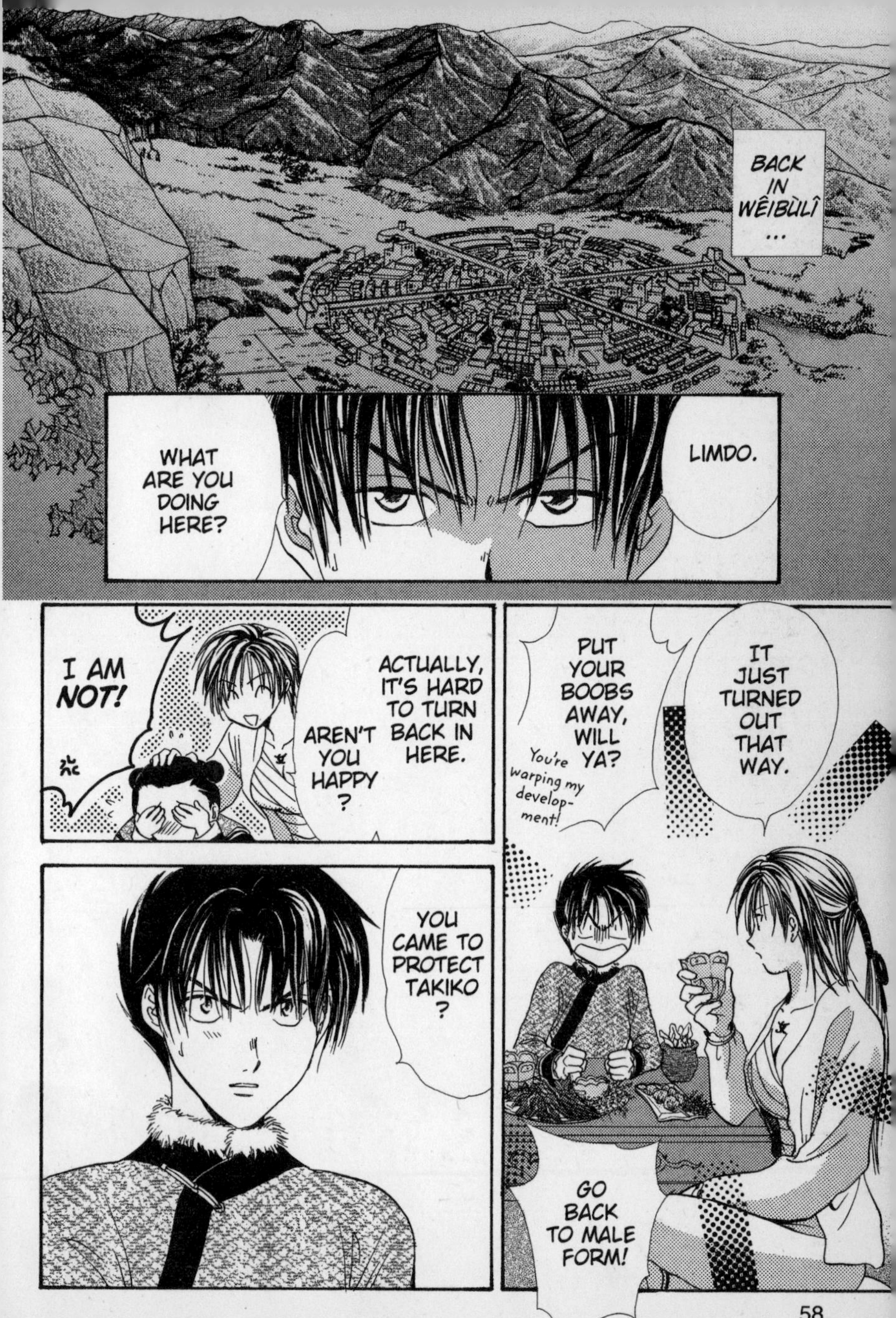
BACK IN WÊIBÙLÎ ...
LIMDO.
WHAT ARE YOU DOING HERE?
IT JUST TURNED OUT THAT WAY.
PUT YOUR BOOBS AWAY, WILL YA?
You're warping my development!
GO BACK TO MALE FORM!
ACTUALLY, IT'S HARD TO TURN BACK IN HERE.
AREN'T YOU HAPPY?
I AM NOT!
YOU CAME TO PROTECT TAKIKO?

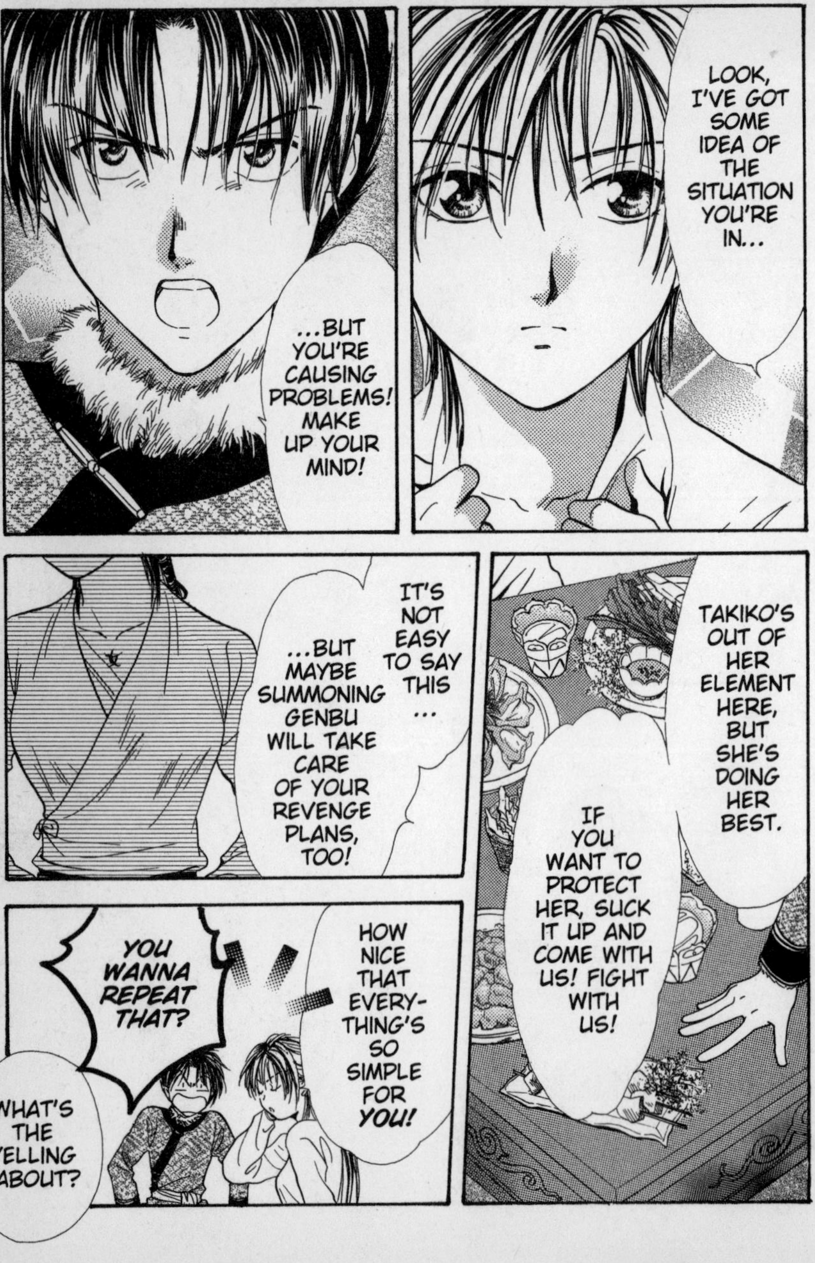
LOOK, I'VE GOT SOME IDEA OF THE SITUATION YOU'RE IN...
...BUT YOU'RE CAUSING PROBLEMS! MAKE UP YOUR MIND!
TAKIKO'S OUT OF HER ELEMENT HERE, BUT SHE'S DOING HER BEST.
IF YOU WANT TO PROTECT HER, SUCK IT UP AND COME WITH US! FIGHT WITH US!
IT'S NOT EASY TO SAY THIS...
...BUT MAYBE SUMMONING GENBU WILL TAKE CARE OF YOUR REVENGE PLANS, TOO!
HOW NICE THAT EVERY-THING'S SO SIMPLE FOR *YOU!*
YOU WANNA REPEAT THAT?
WHAT'S THE YELLING ABOUT?

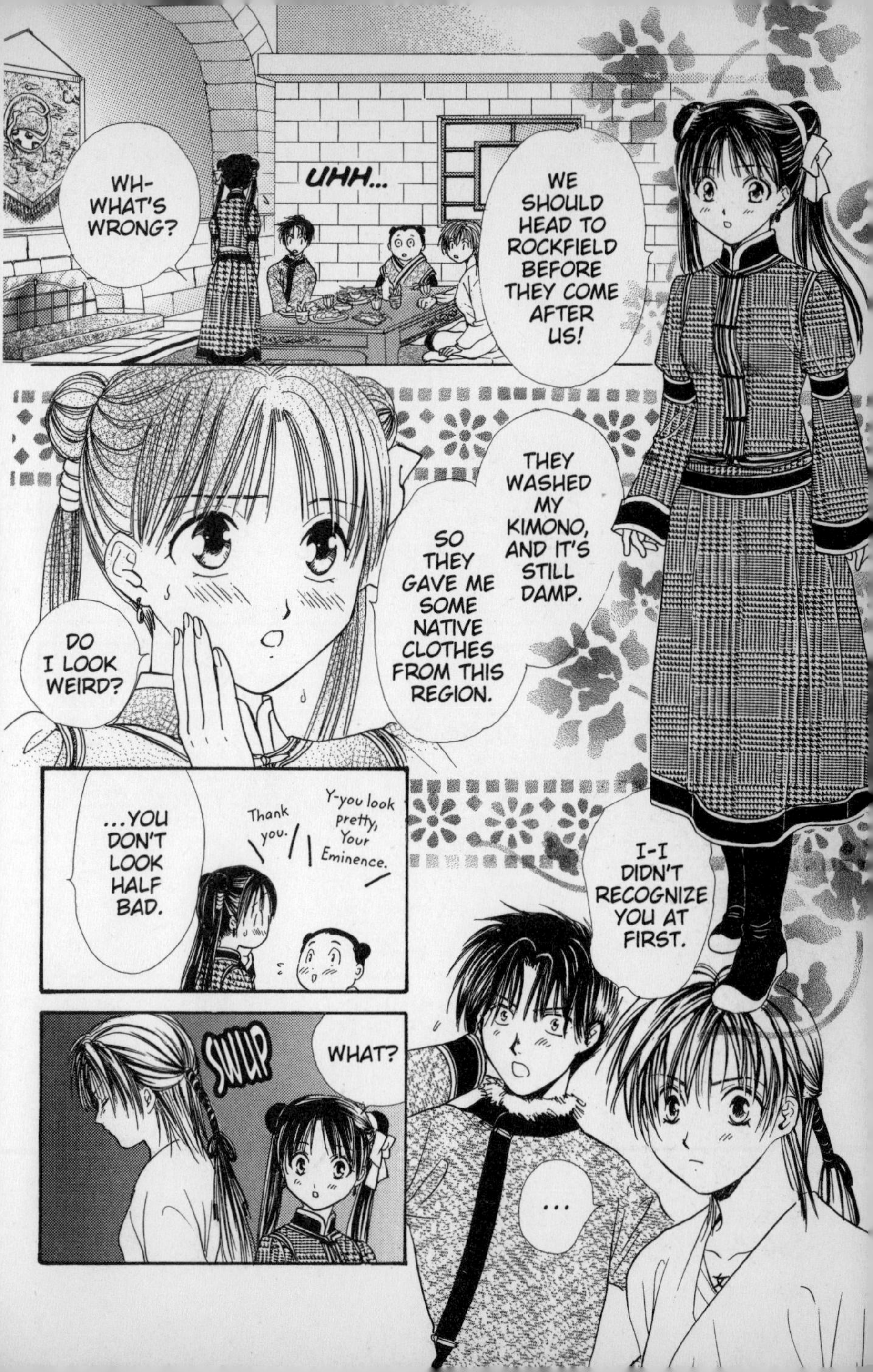
WE SHOULD HEAD TO ROCKFIELD BEFORE THEY COME AFTER US!
UHH...
WH- WHAT'S WRONG?
THEY WASHED MY KIMONO, AND IT'S STILL DAMP.
SO THEY GAVE ME SOME NATIVE CLOTHES FROM THIS REGION.
DO I LOOK WEIRD?
I-I DIDN'T RECOGNIZE YOU AT FIRST.
Y-you look pretty, Your Eminence.
Thank you.
...YOU DON'T LOOK HALF BAD.
...
WHAT?
SWUP

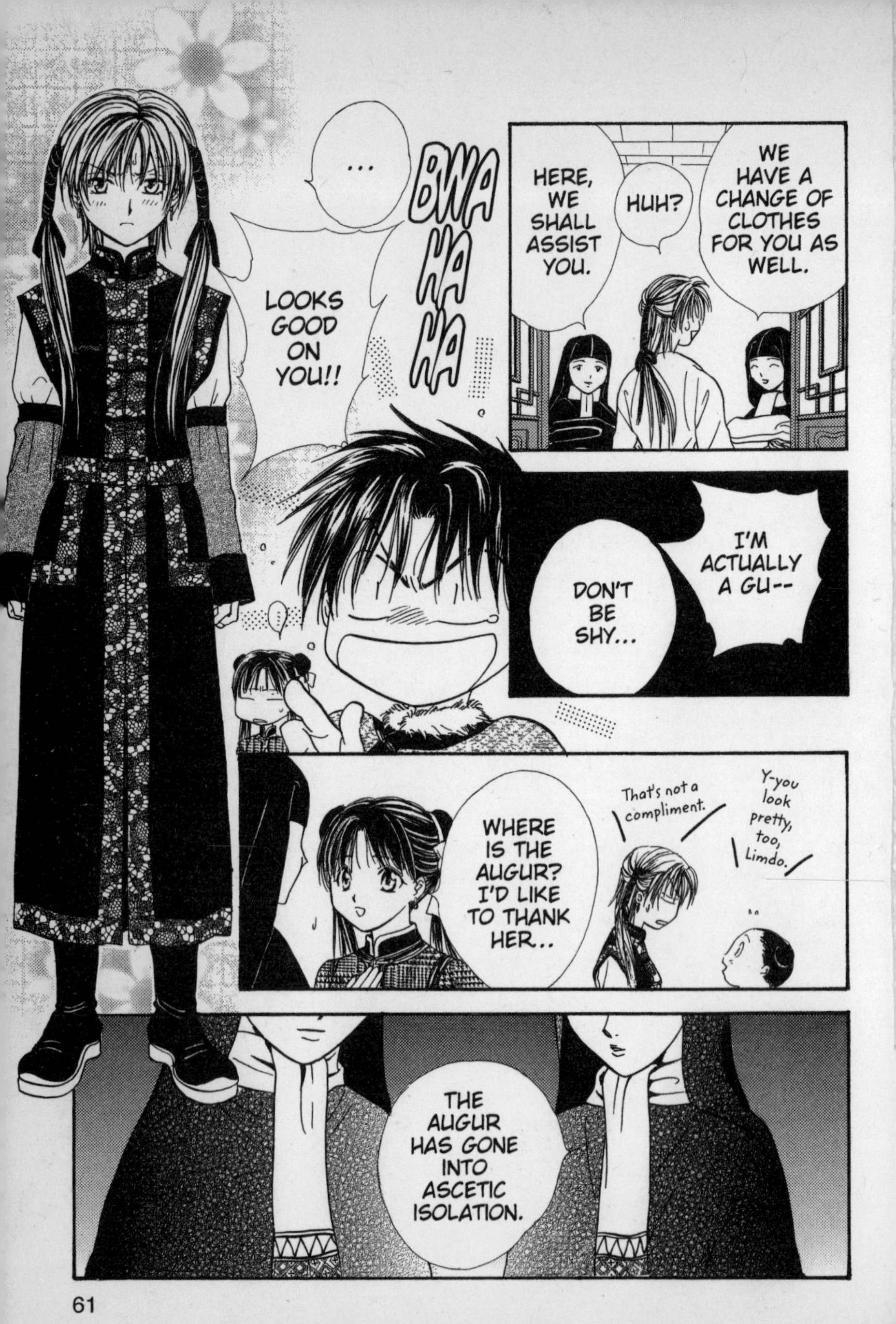

WE HAVE A CHANGE OF CLOTHES FOR YOU AS WELL.
HUH?
HERE, WE SHALL ASSIST YOU.
I'M ACTUALLY A GU--
DON'T BE SHY...
...
BWA HA HA
LOOKS GOOD ON YOU!!
Y-you look pretty, too, Limdo.
That's not a compliment.
WHERE IS THE AUGUR? I'D LIKE TO THANK HER..
THE AUGUR HAS GONE INTO ASCETIC ISOLATION.

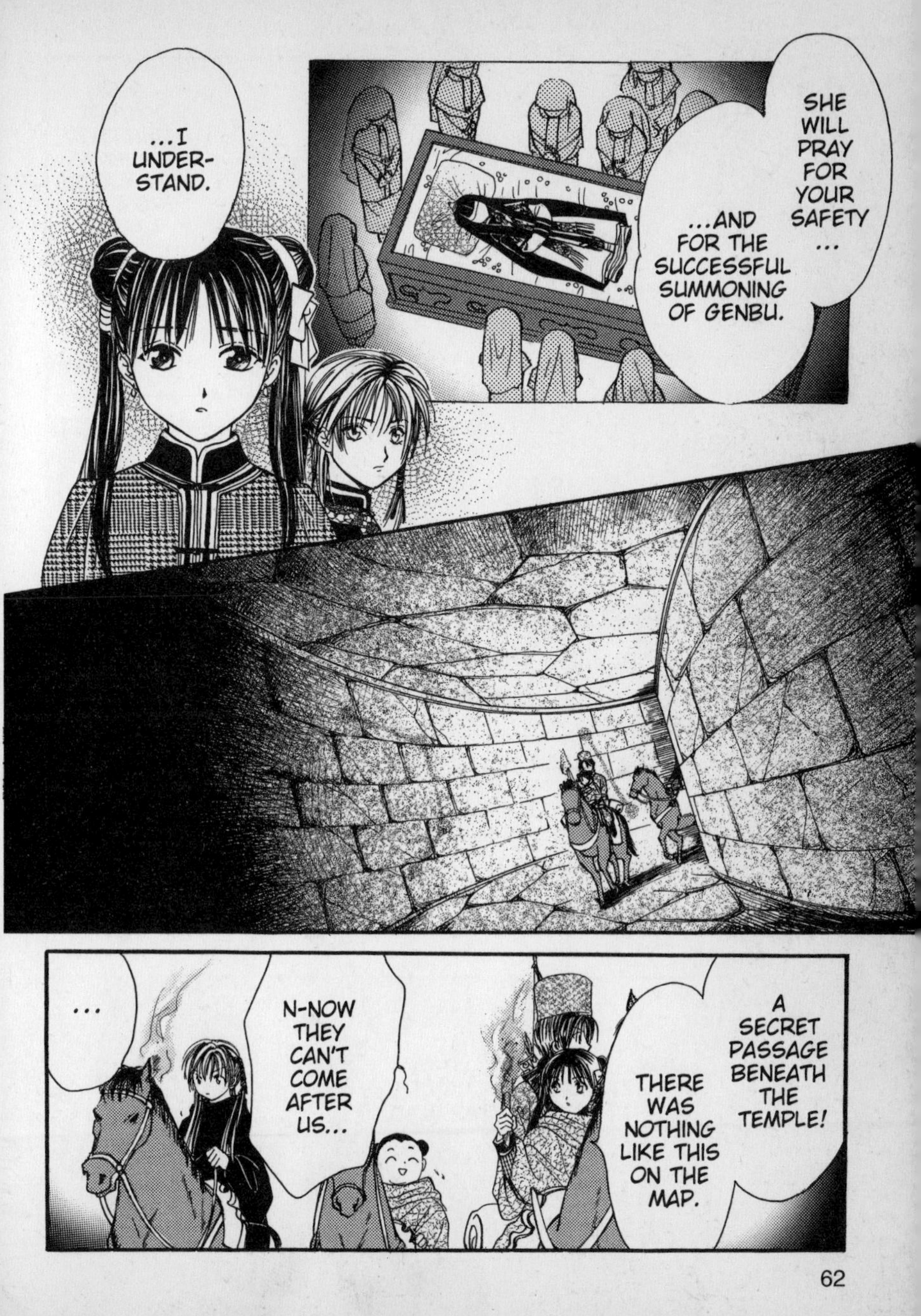
SHE WILL PRAY FOR YOUR SAFETY...
...AND FOR THE SUCCESSFUL SUMMONING OF GENBU.
...I UNDER-STAND.
A SECRET PASSAGE BENEATH THE TEMPLE!
THERE WAS NOTHING LIKE THIS ON THE MAP.
N-NOW THEY CAN'T COME AFTER US...
...

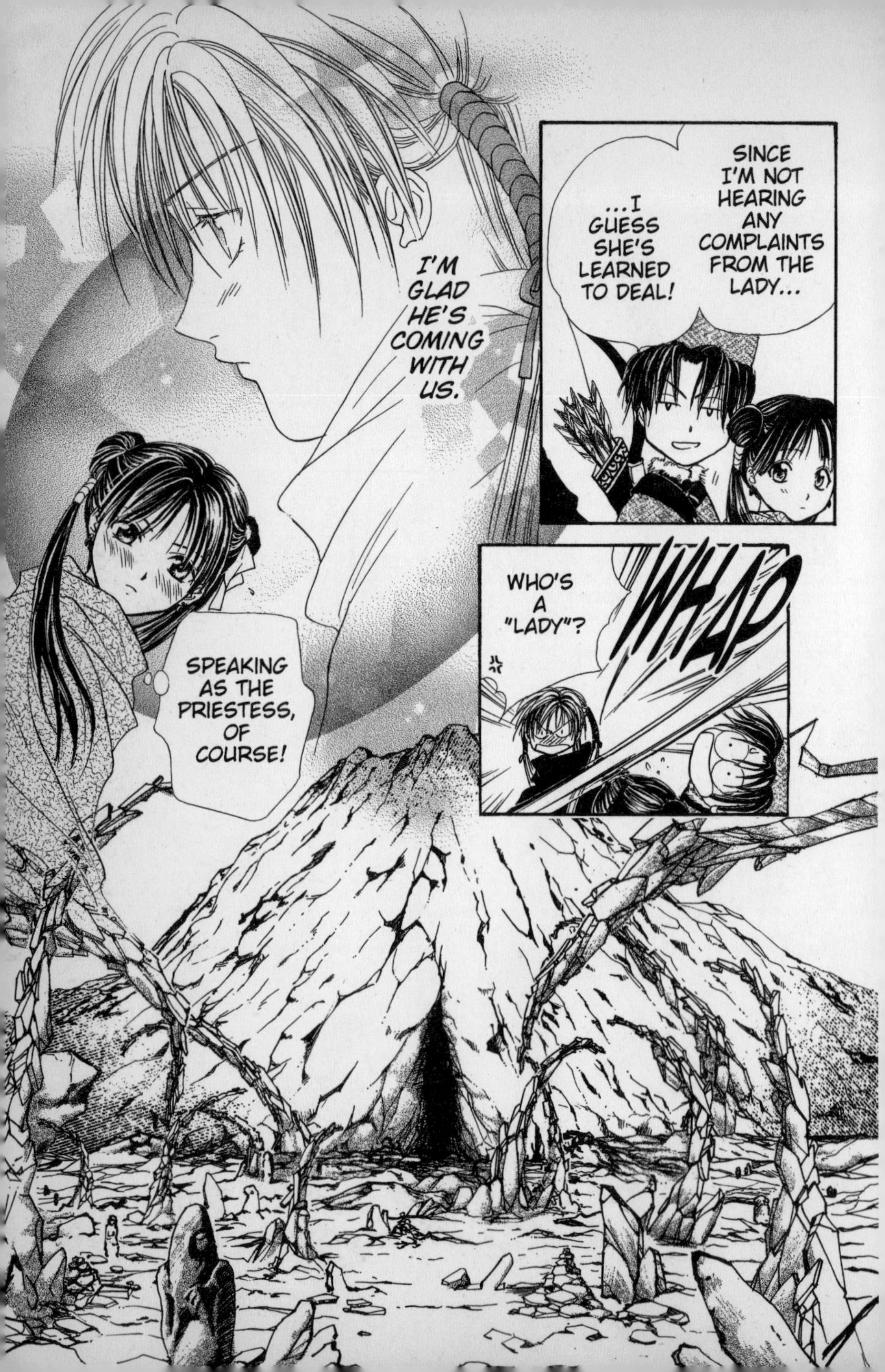
SINCE I'M NOT HEARING ANY COMPLAINTS FROM THE LADY...
...I GUESS SHE'S LEARNED TO DEAL!
WHO'S A "LADY"?
WHAP
I'M GLAD HE'S COMING WITH US.
SPEAKING AS THE PRIESTESS, OF COURSE!

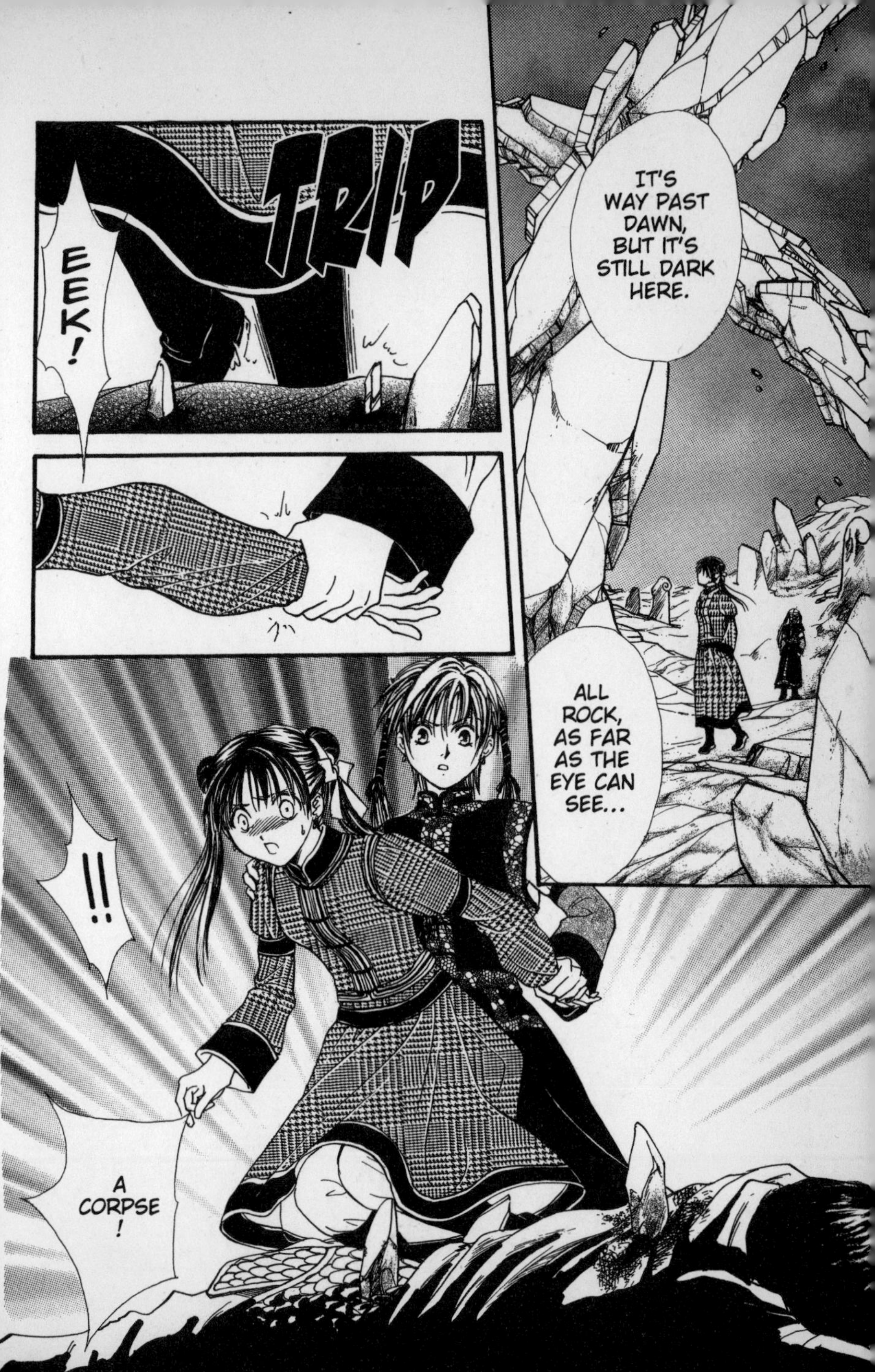
IT'S WAY PAST DAWN, BUT IT'S STILL DARK HERE.
ALL ROCK, AS FAR AS THE EYE CAN SEE...
TRIP
EEK!
!!
A CORPSE!

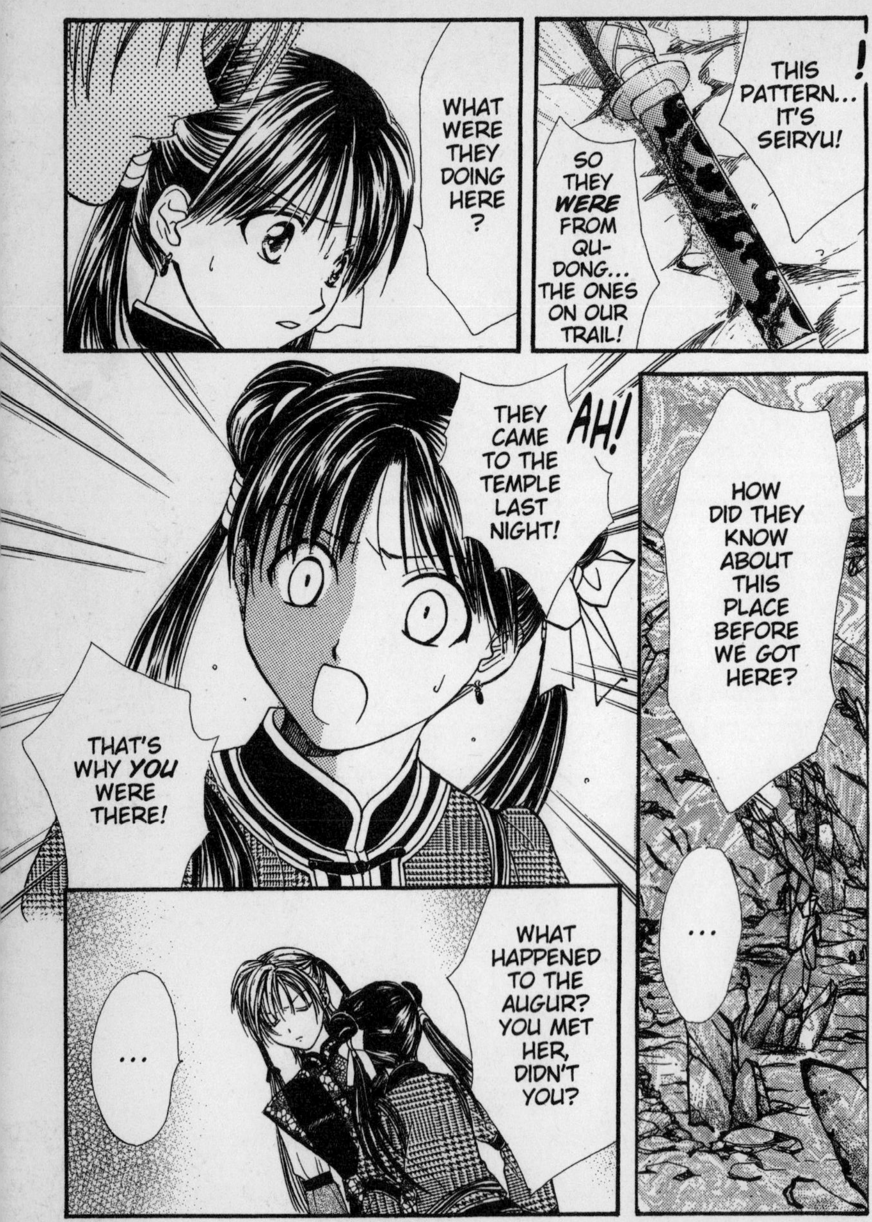
!
THIS PATTERN... IT'S SEIRYU!
SO THEY *WERE* FROM QU-DONG... THE ONES ON OUR TRAIL!
WHAT WERE THEY DOING HERE?
HOW DID THEY KNOW ABOUT THIS PLACE BEFORE WE GOT HERE?
...
AH!
THEY CAME TO THE TEMPLE LAST NIGHT!
THAT'S WHY *YOU* WERE THERE!
WHAT HAPPENED TO THE AUGUR? YOU MET HER, DIDN'T YOU?
...

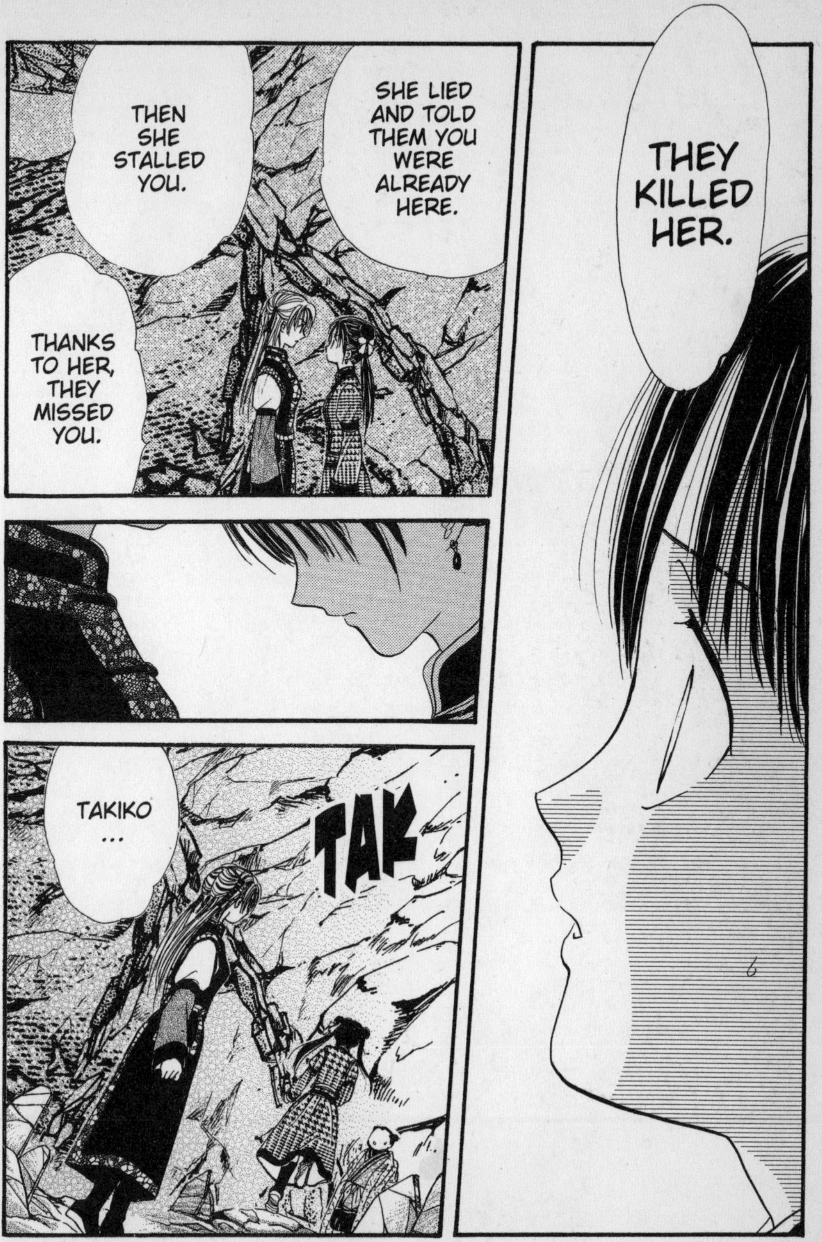
THEY KILLED HER.
SHE LIED AND TOLD THEM YOU WERE ALREADY HERE.
THEN SHE STALLED YOU.
THANKS TO HER, THEY MISSED YOU.
TAK
TAKIKO ...

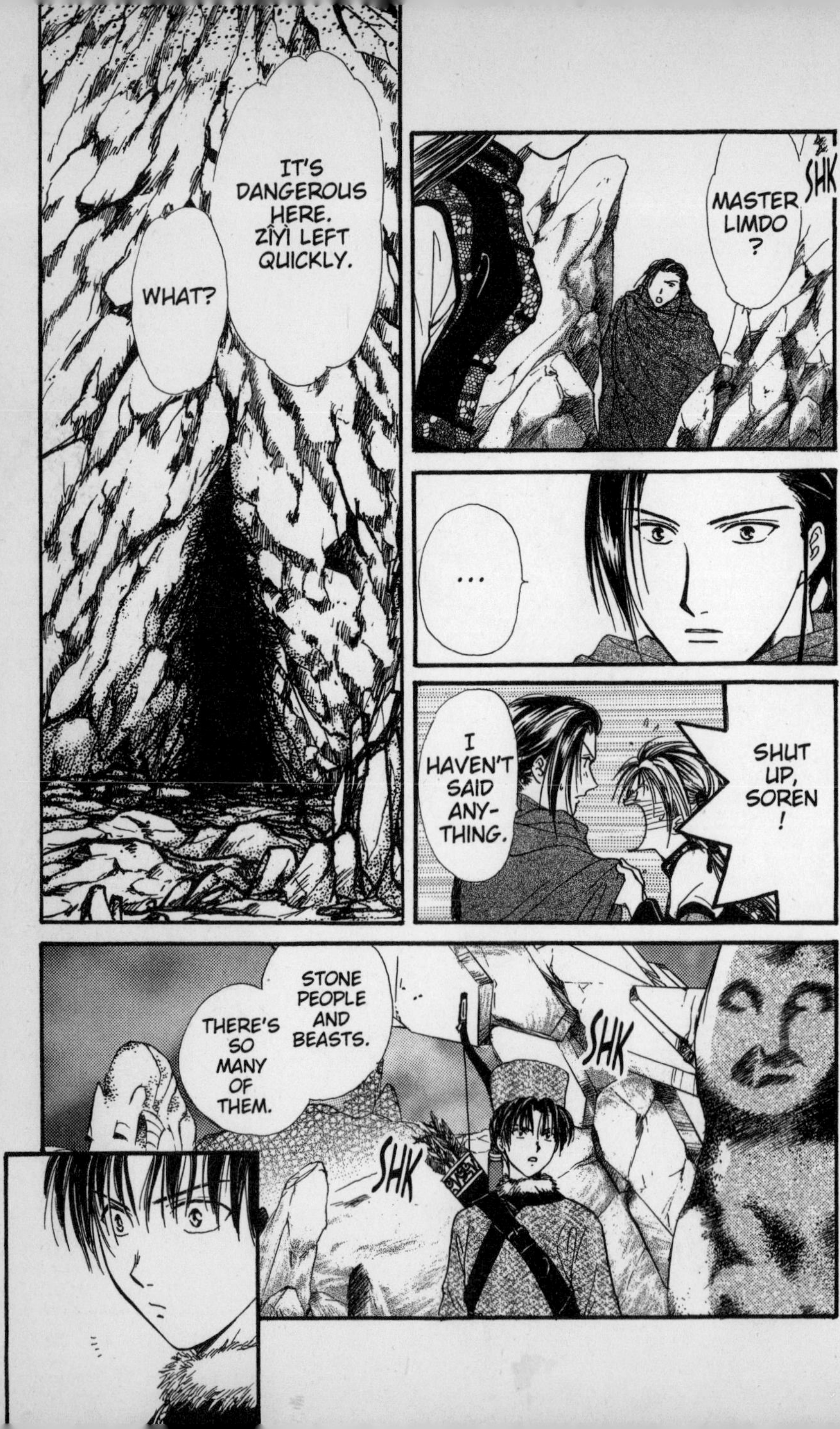
SHK
MASTER LIMDO?
...
SHUT UP, SOREN!
I HAVEN'T SAID ANY-THING.
IT'S DANGEROUS HERE. ZÎYÎ LEFT QUICKLY.
WHAT?
SHK
STONE PEOPLE AND BEASTS.
THERE'S SO MANY OF THEM.
SHK

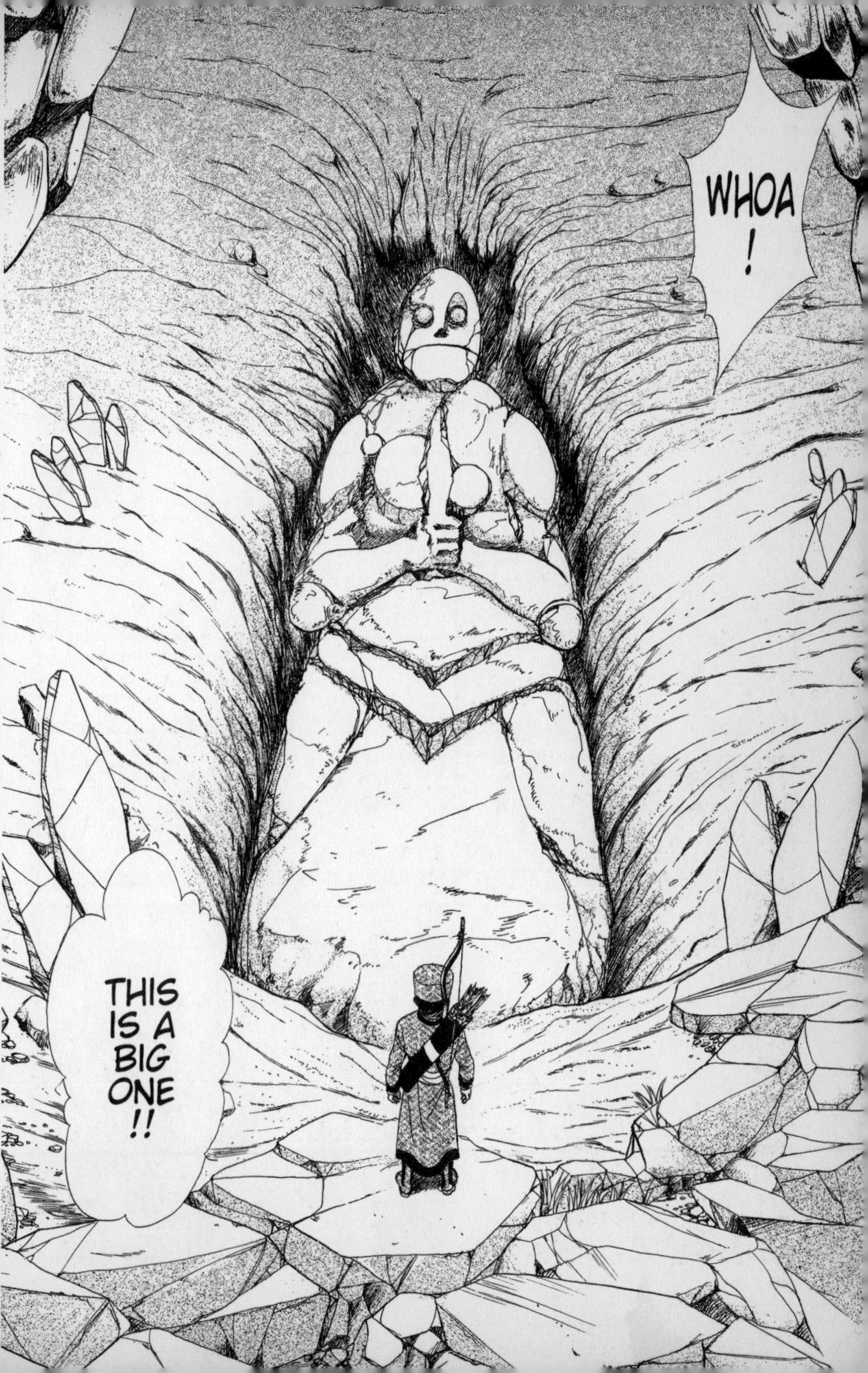
WHOA!
THIS IS A BIG ONE!!

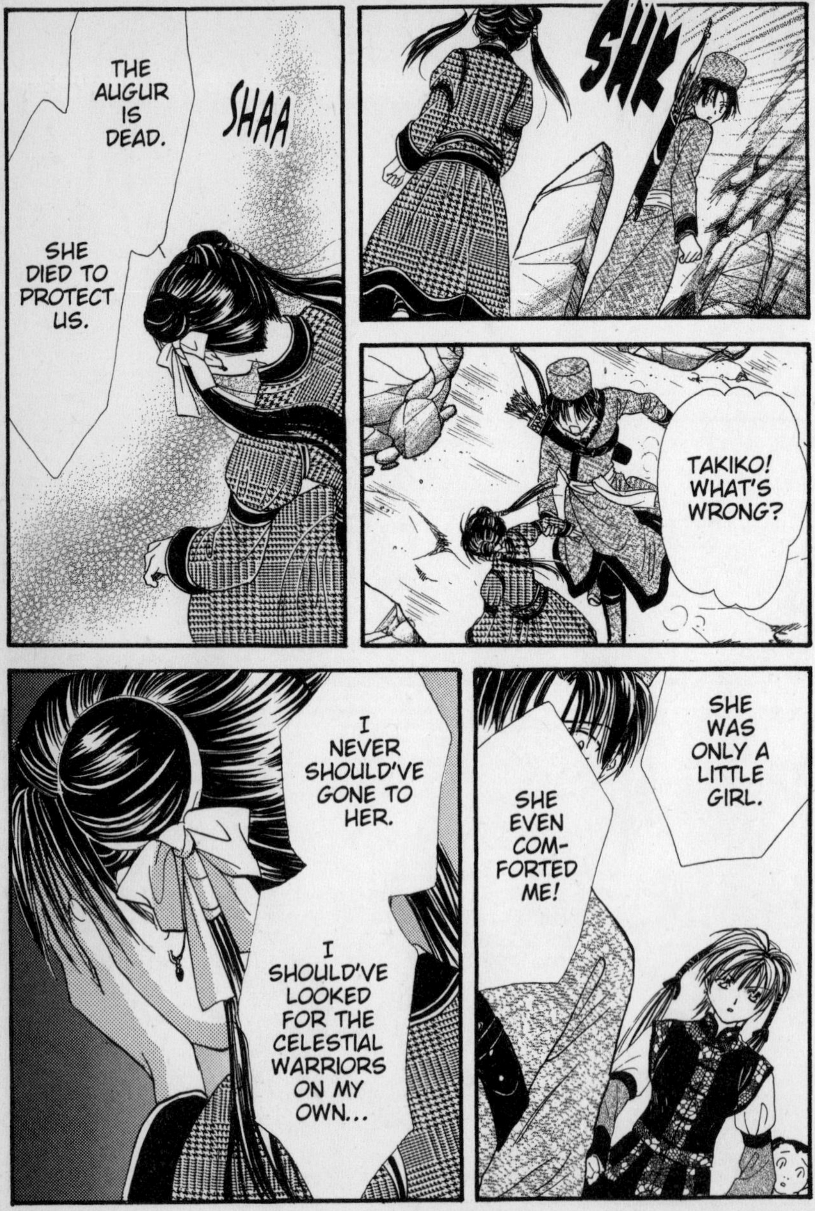
SHK
TAKIKO! WHAT'S WRONG?
THE AUGUR IS DEAD.
SHAA
SHE DIED TO PROTECT US.
SHE WAS ONLY A LITTLE GIRL.
SHE EVEN COM-FORTED ME!
I NEVER SHOULD'VE GONE TO HER.
I SHOULD'VE LOOKED FOR THE CELESTIAL WARRIORS ON MY OWN...

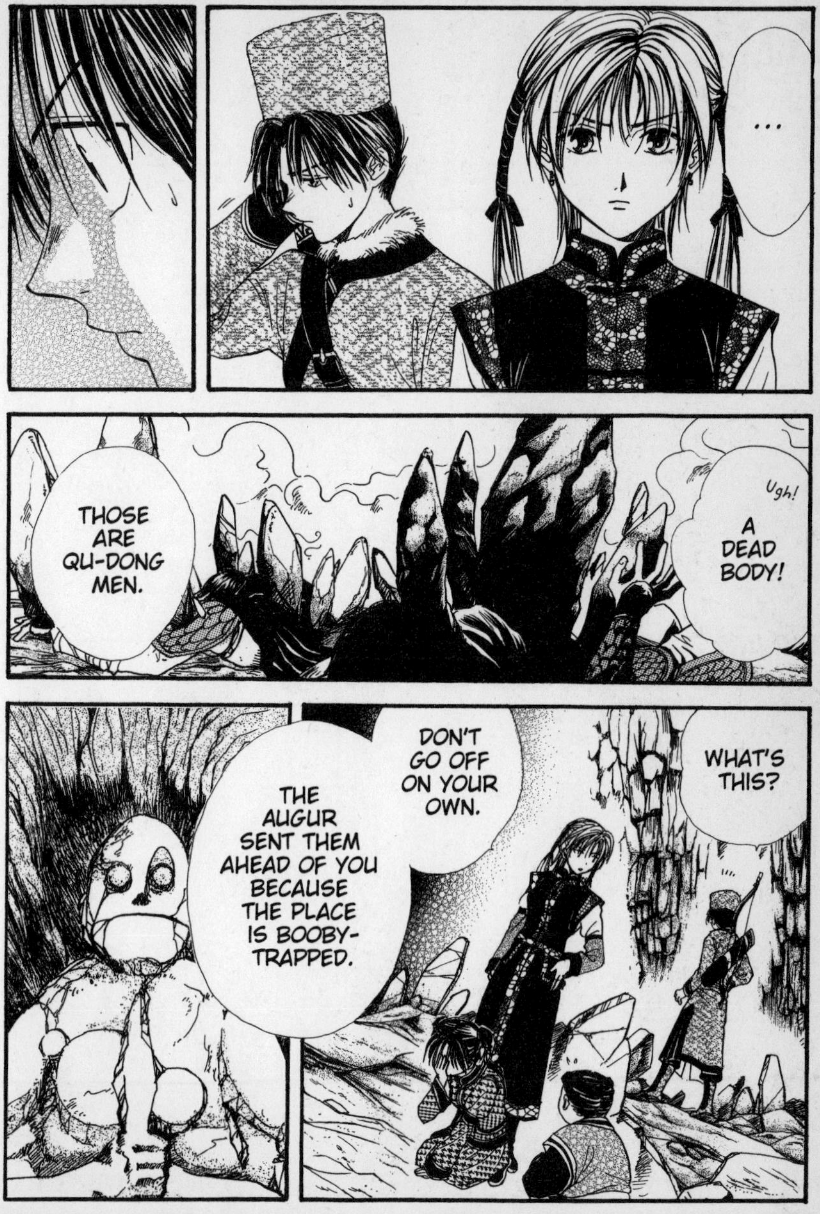
...
Ugh!
A DEAD BODY!
THOSE ARE QU-DONG MEN.
WHAT'S THIS?
DON'T GO OFF ON YOUR OWN.
THE AUGUR SENT THEM AHEAD OF YOU BECAUSE THE PLACE IS BOOBY-TRAPPED.

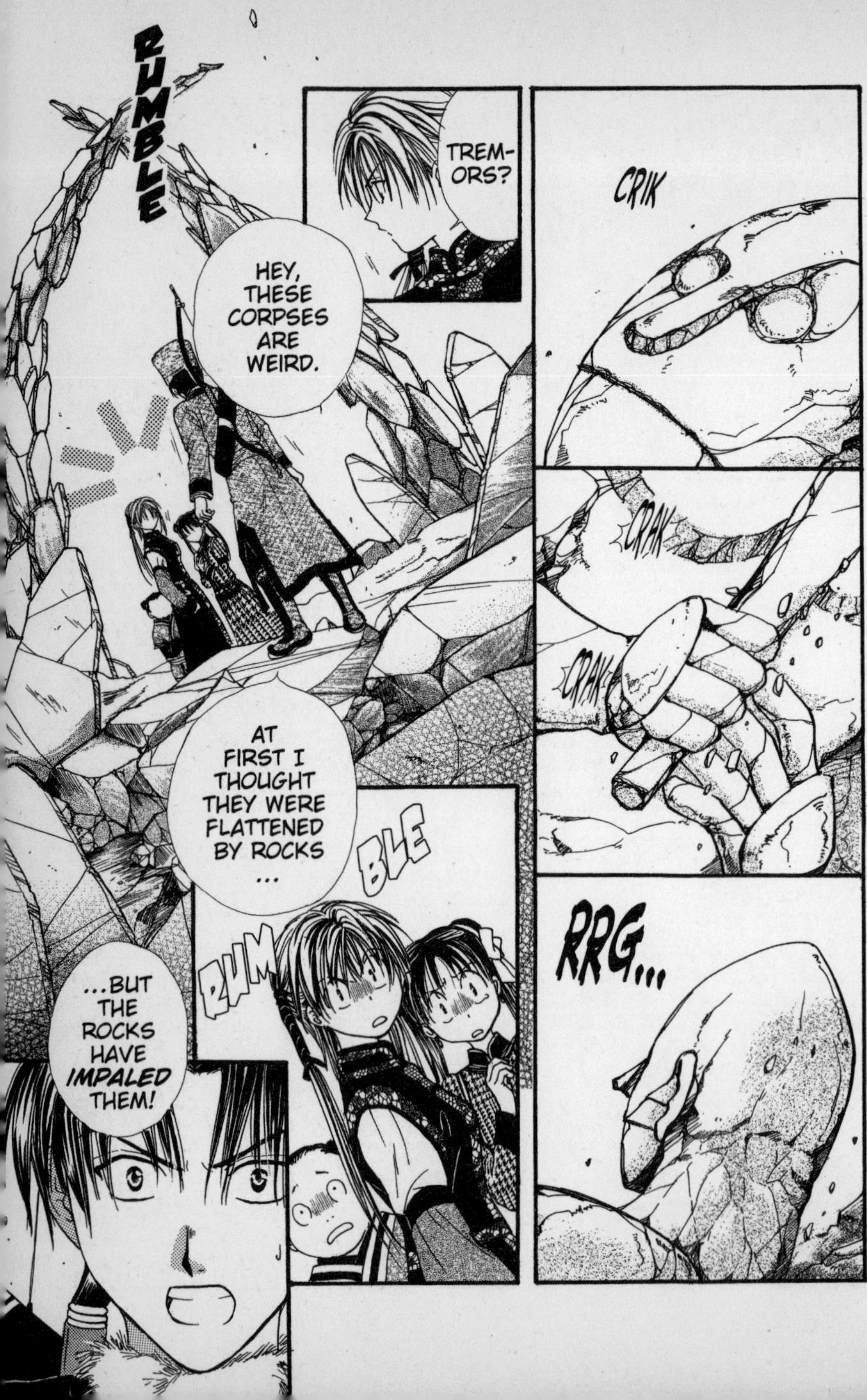
CRIK
CRAK
CRAK
RRG...
TREM-ORS?
RUMBLE
HEY, THESE CORPSES ARE WEIRD.
AT FIRST I THOUGHT THEY WERE FLATTENED BY ROCKS ...
RUMBLE
...BUT THE ROCKS HAVE *IMPALED* THEM!

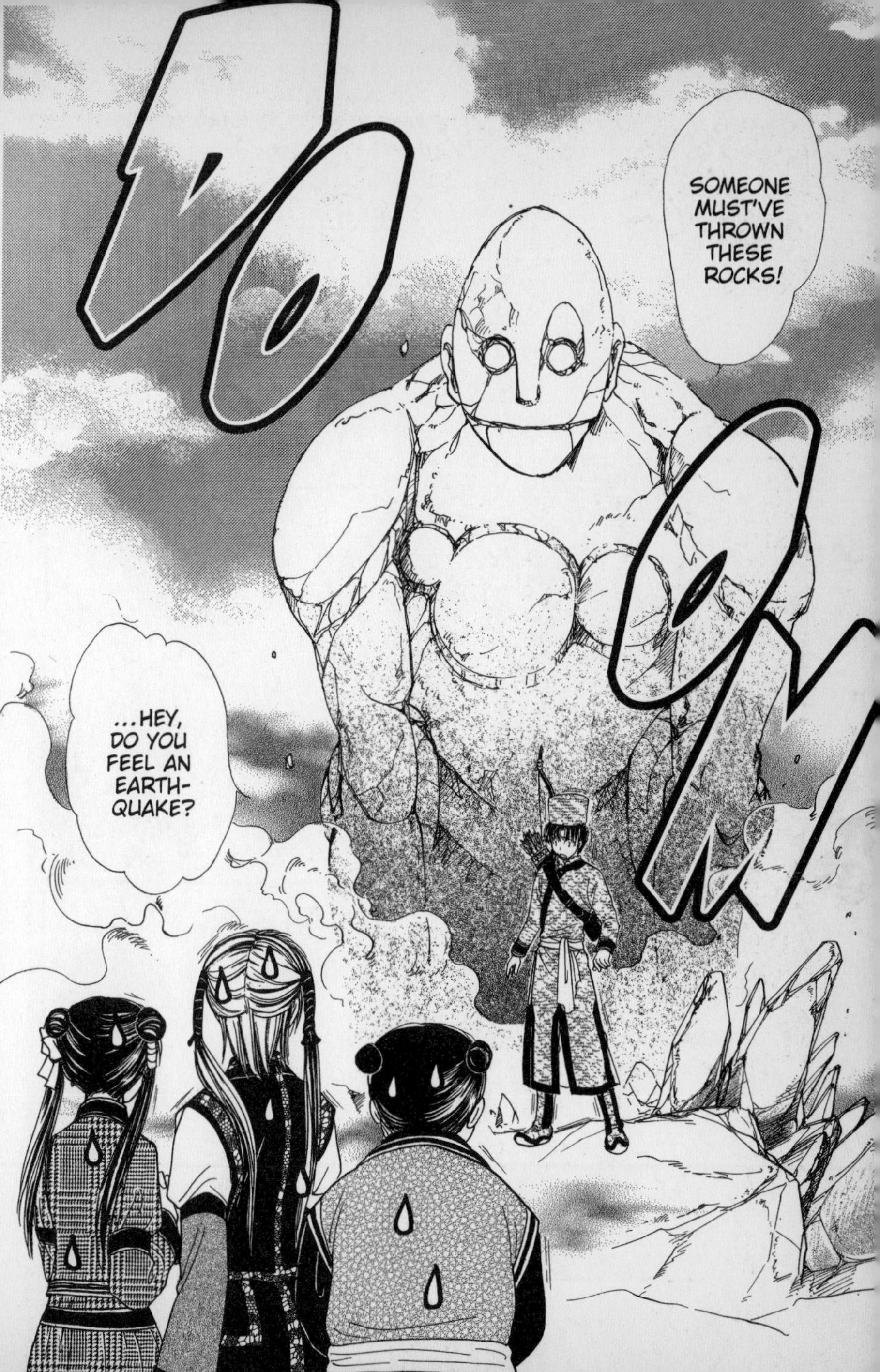
SOMEONE MUST'VE THROWN THESE ROCKS!
DOOM
...HEY, DO YOU FEEL AN EARTHQUAKE?

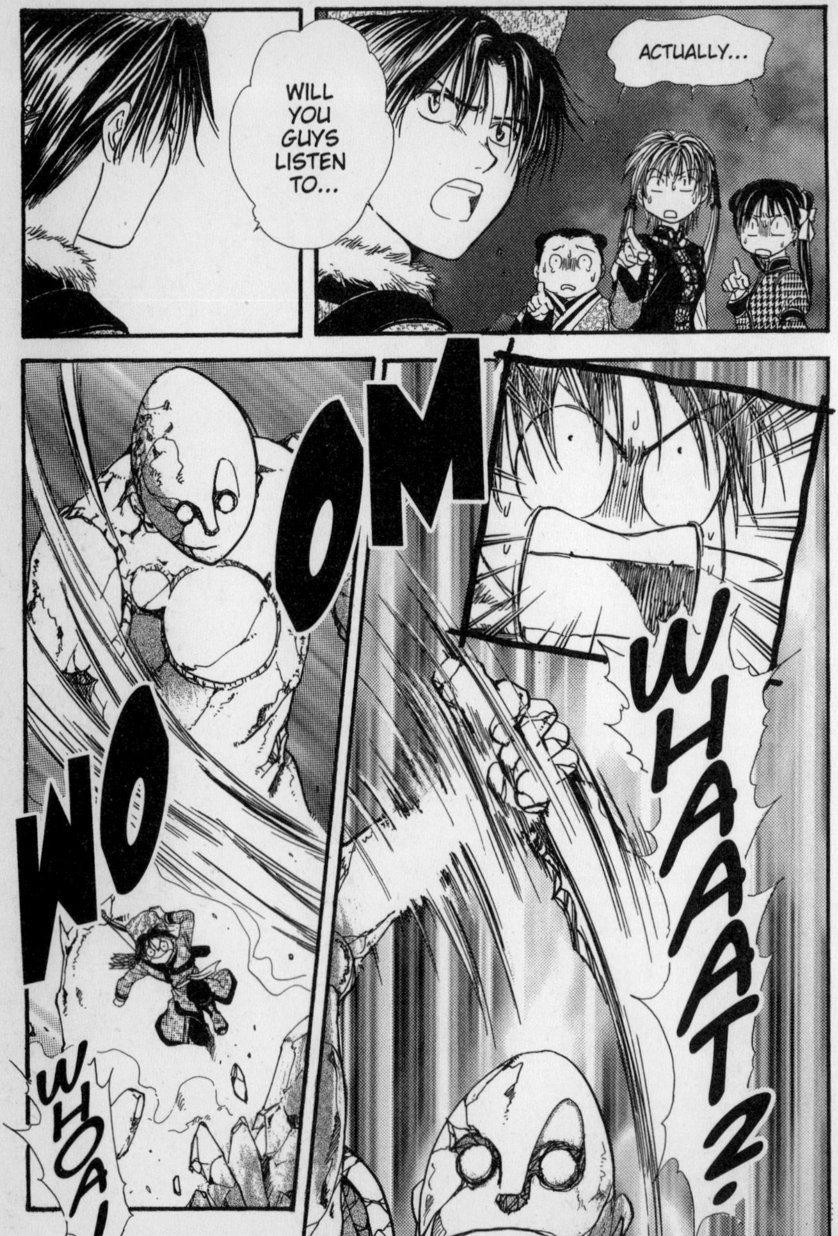
ACTUALLY...
WILL YOU GUYS LISTEN TO...
WHAAAT?!
WOOM
WHOA!

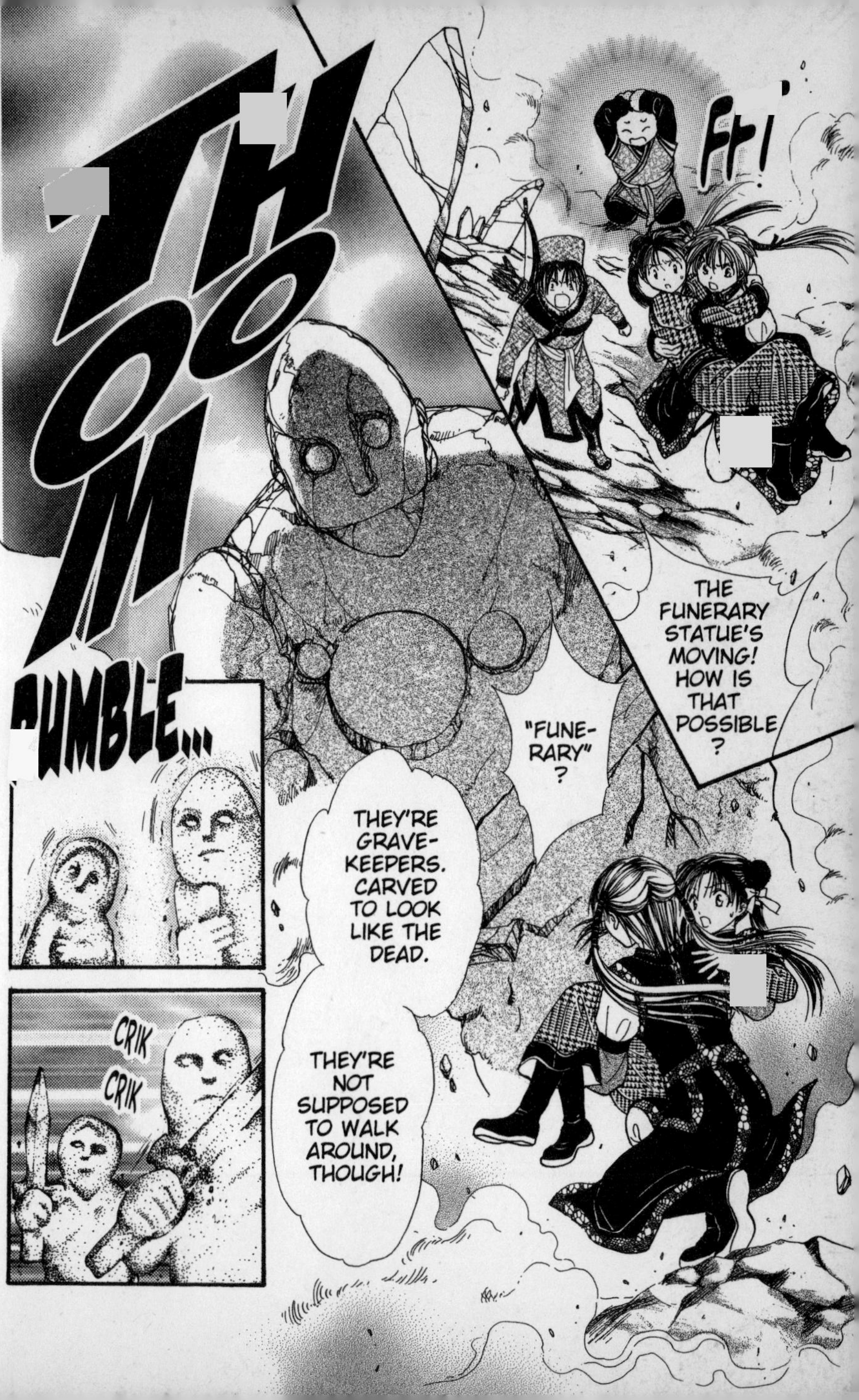
Ff!
THE FUNERARY STATUE'S MOVING! HOW IS THAT POSSIBLE?
THOOM
"FUNE-RARY"?
THEY'RE GRAVE-KEEPERS. CARVED TO LOOK LIKE THE DEAD.
THEY'RE NOT SUPPOSED TO WALK AROUND, THOUGH!
UMBLE...
CRIK CRIK

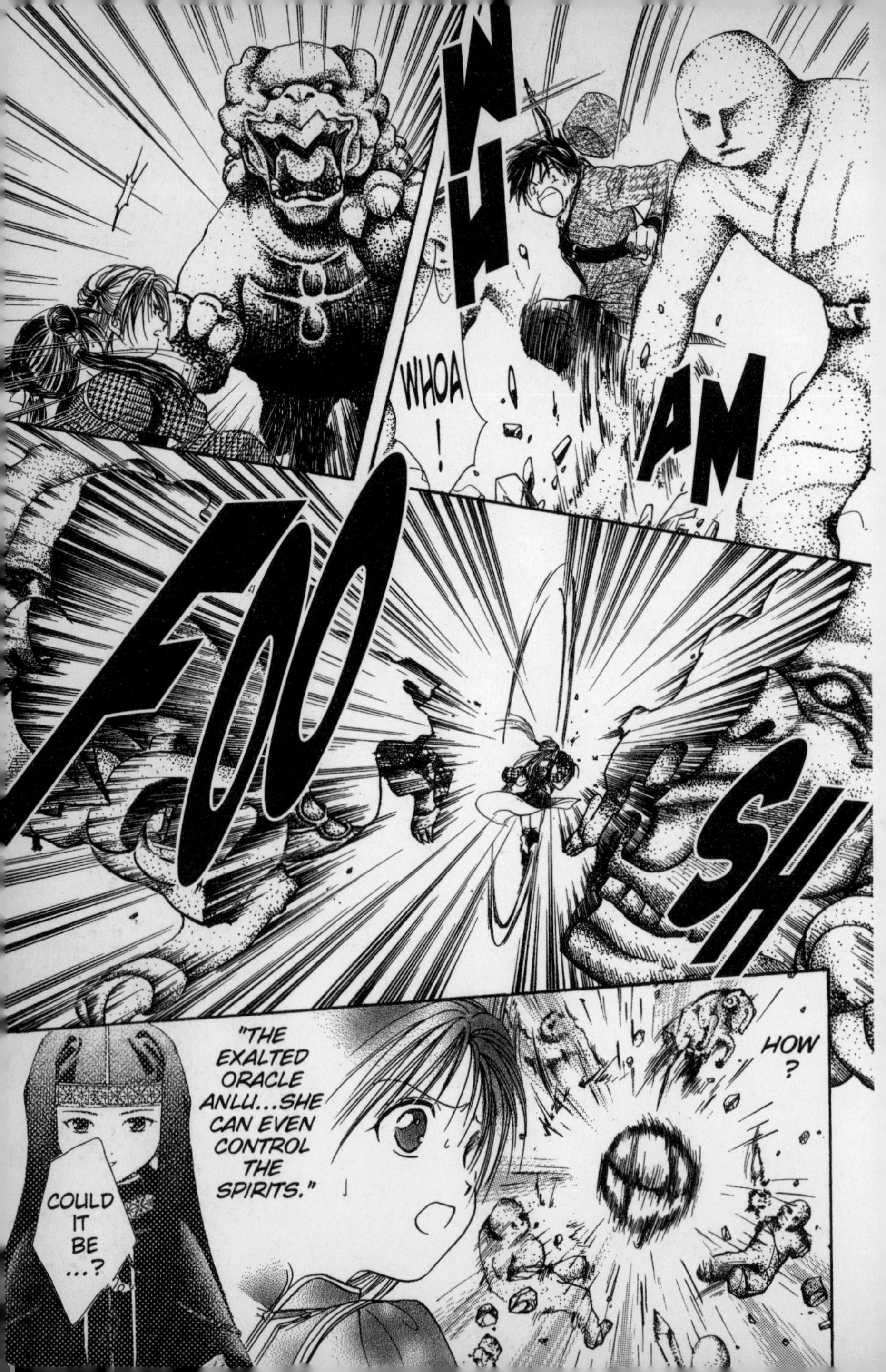
WHOA!
AM
SH
HOW?
"THE EXALTED ORACLE ANLU...SHE CAN EVEN CONTROL THE SPIRITS."
COULD IT BE ...?

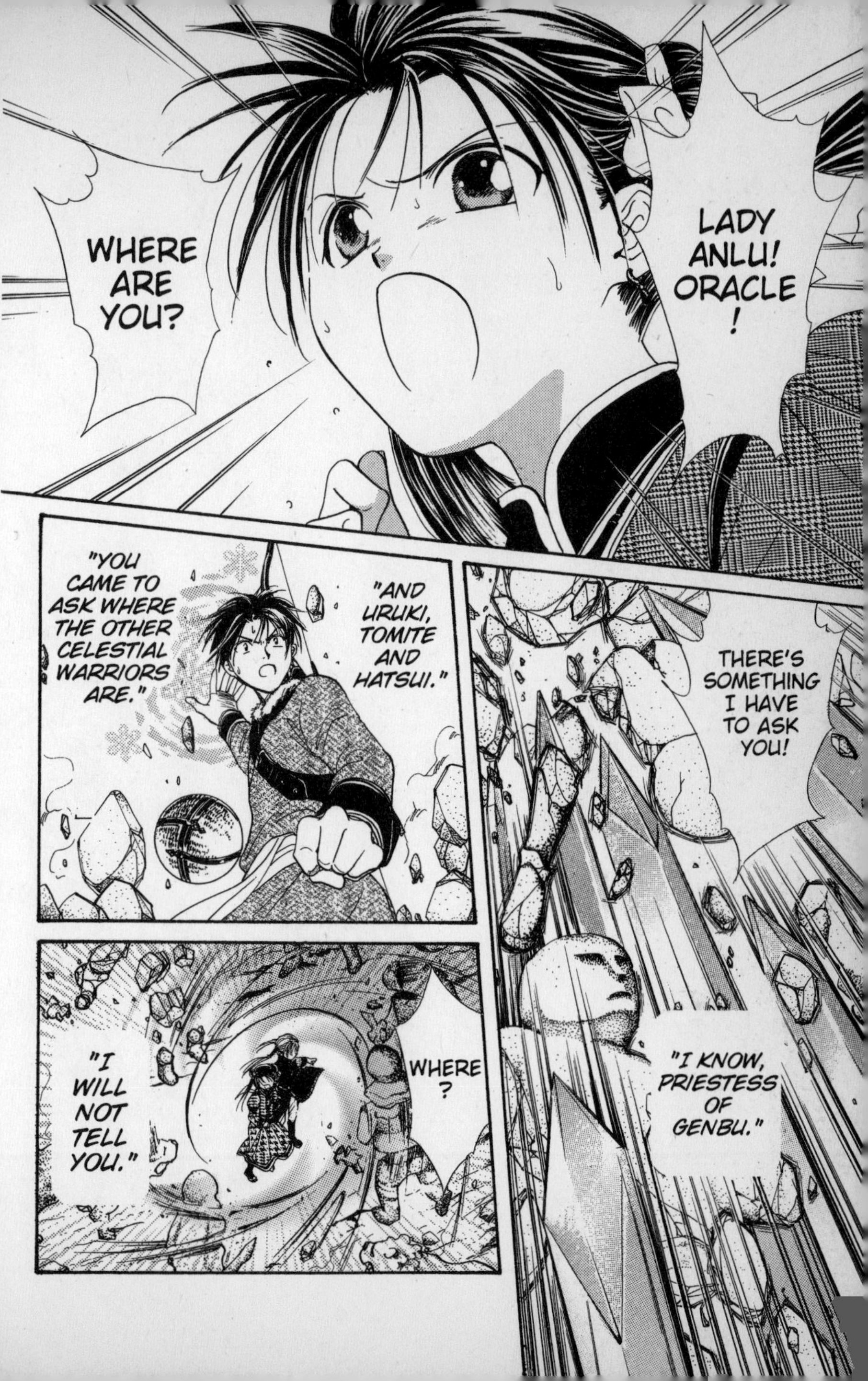
LADY ANLU! ORACLE!
WHERE ARE YOU?
THERE'S SOMETHING I HAVE TO ASK YOU!
"I KNOW, PRIESTESS OF GENBU."
"YOU CAME TO ASK WHERE THE OTHER CELESTIAL WARRIORS ARE."
"AND URUKI, TOMITE AND HATSUI."
WHERE?
"I WILL NOT TELL YOU."

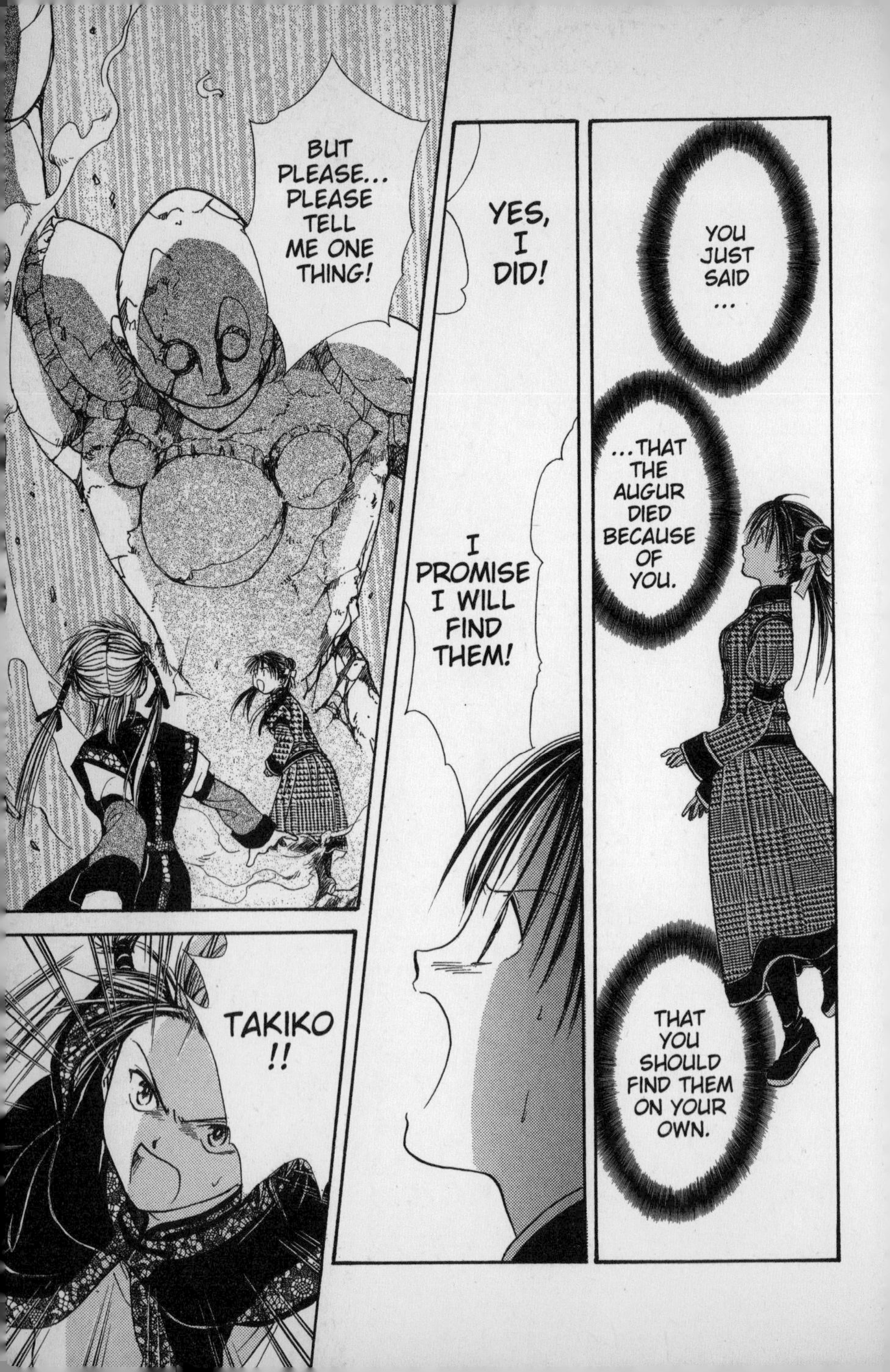
YOU JUST SAID ...
...THAT THE AUGUR DIED BECAUSE OF YOU.
THAT YOU SHOULD FIND THEM ON YOUR OWN.
YES, I DID!
I PROMISE I WILL FIND THEM!
BUT PLEASE... PLEASE TELL ME ONE THING!
TAKIKO !!

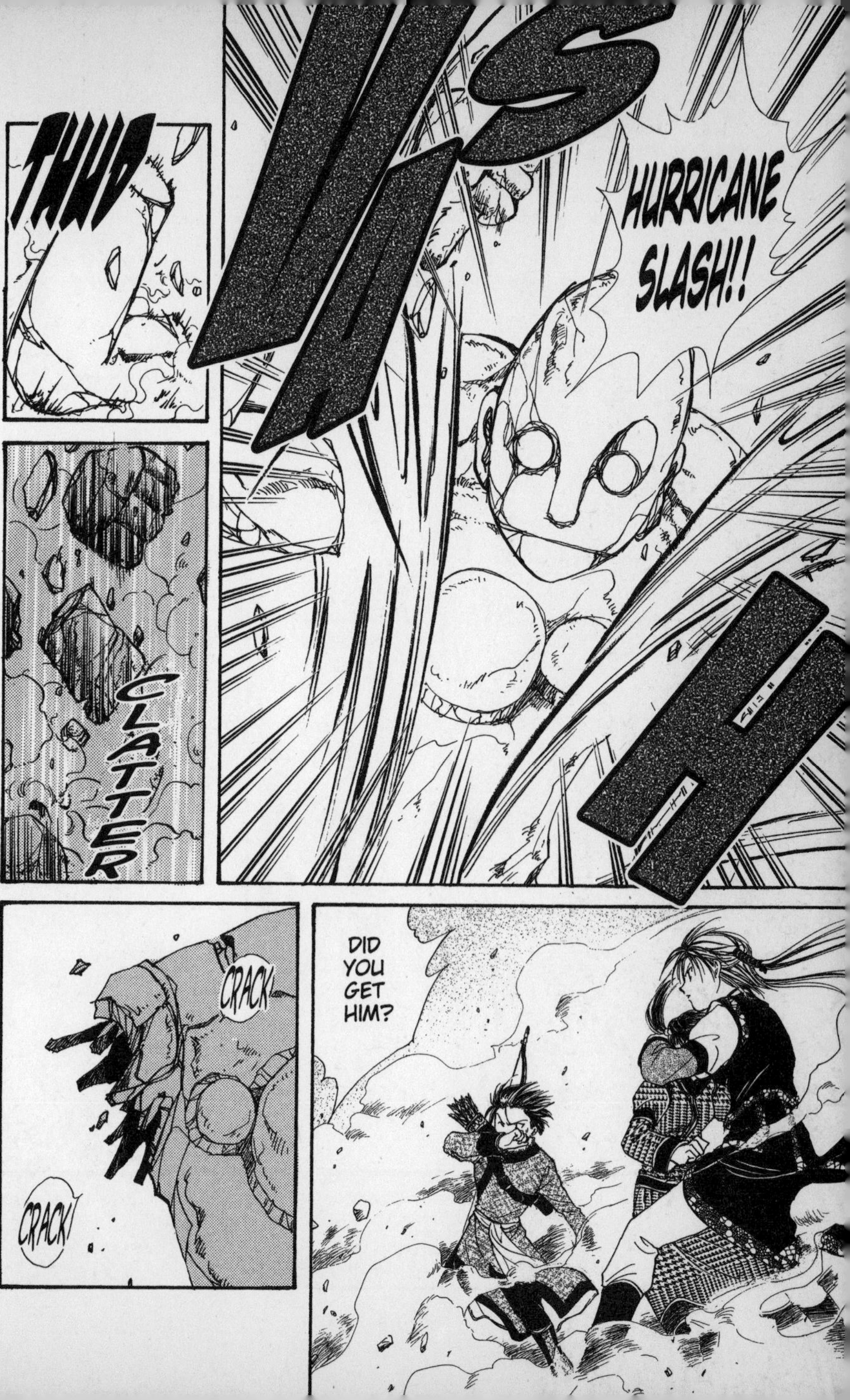
HURRICANE SLASH!!
THUD
CLATTER
DID YOU GET HIM?
CRACK
CRACK

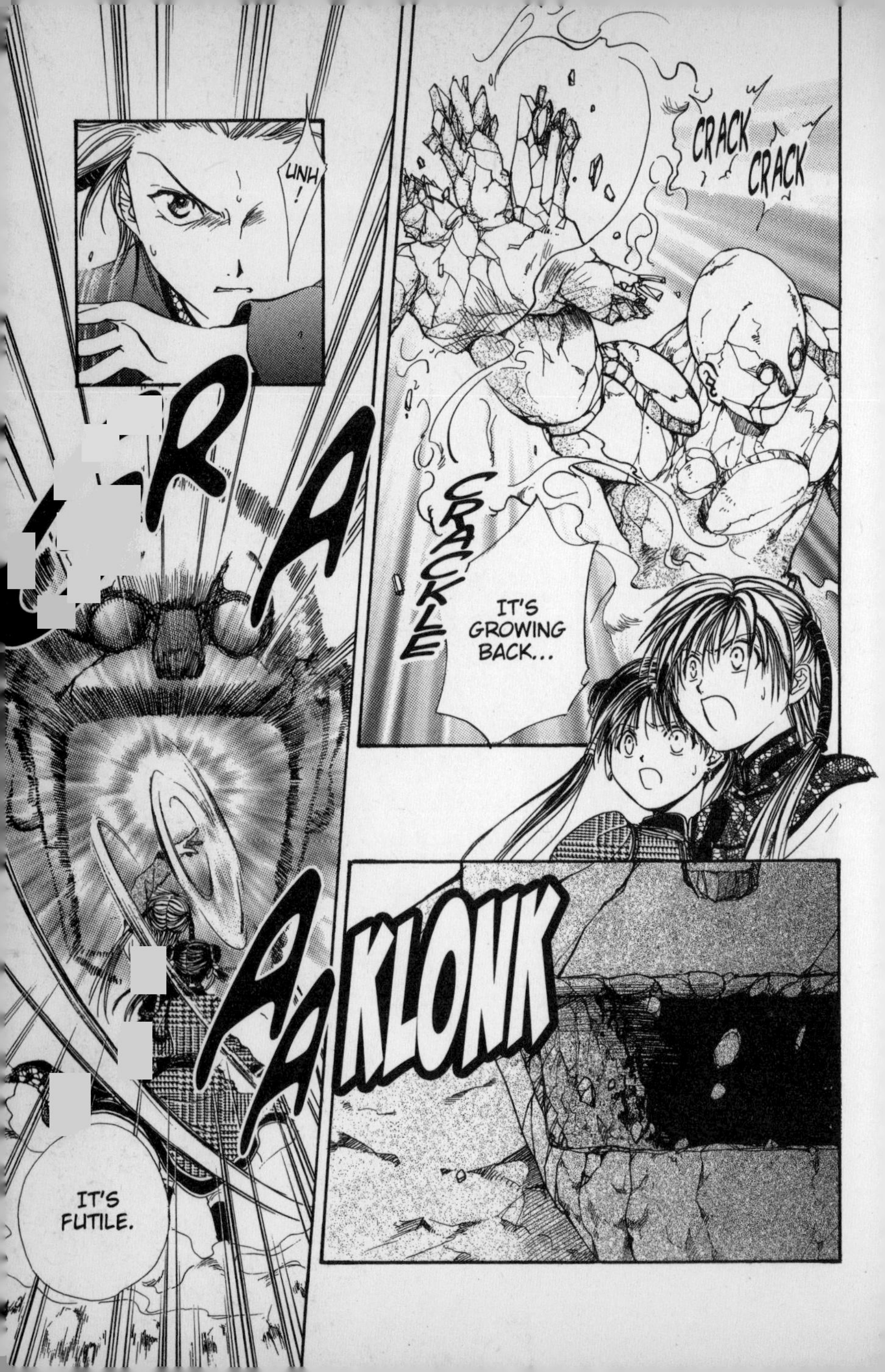
CRACK
CRACK
CRACKLE
IT'S GROWING BACK...
KLONK
UNH!
IT'S FUTILE.

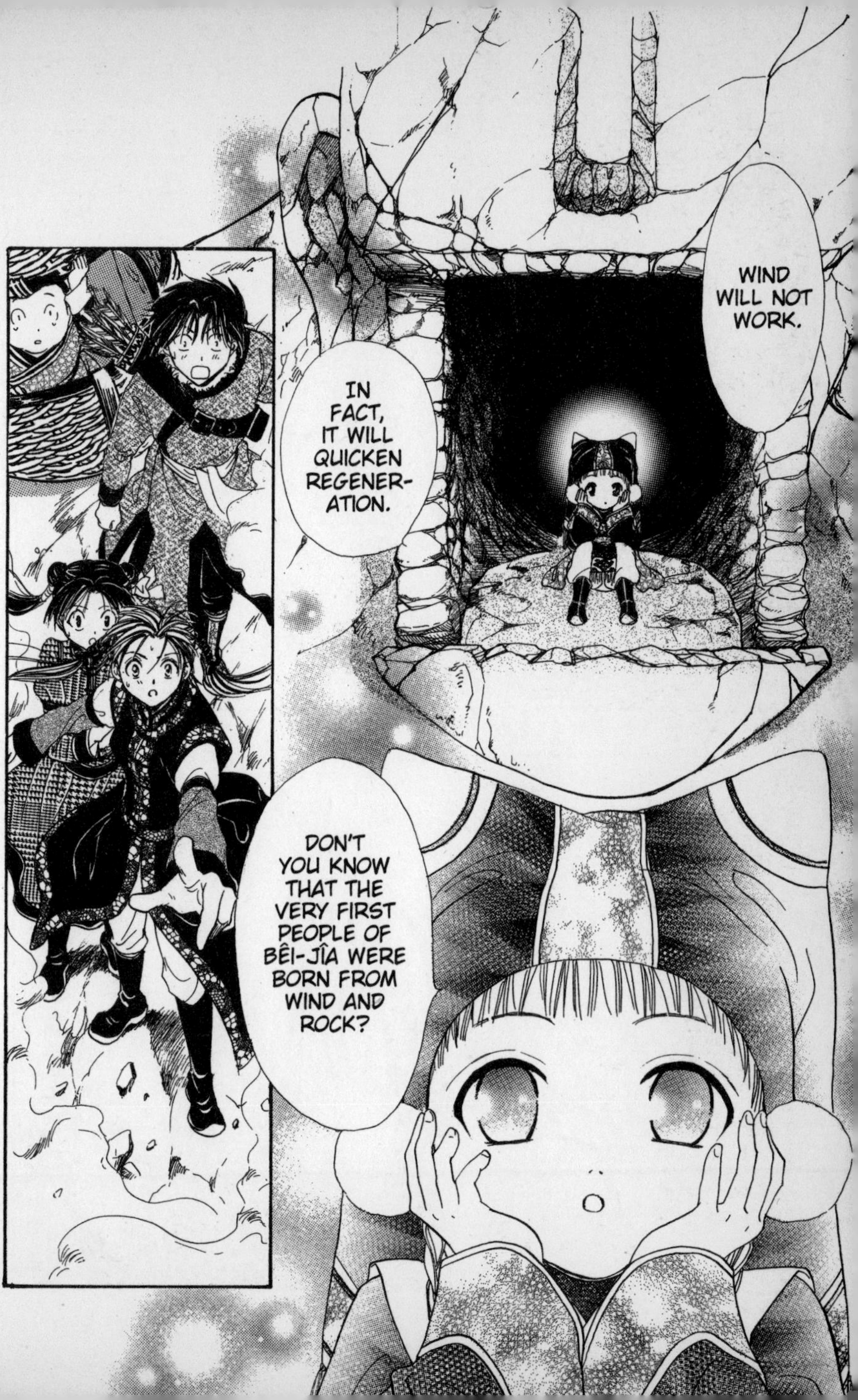
WIND WILL NOT WORK.
IN FACT, IT WILL QUICKEN REGENER-ATION.
DON'T YOU KNOW THAT THE VERY FIRST PEOPLE OF BÊI-JÎA WERE BORN FROM WIND AND ROCK?

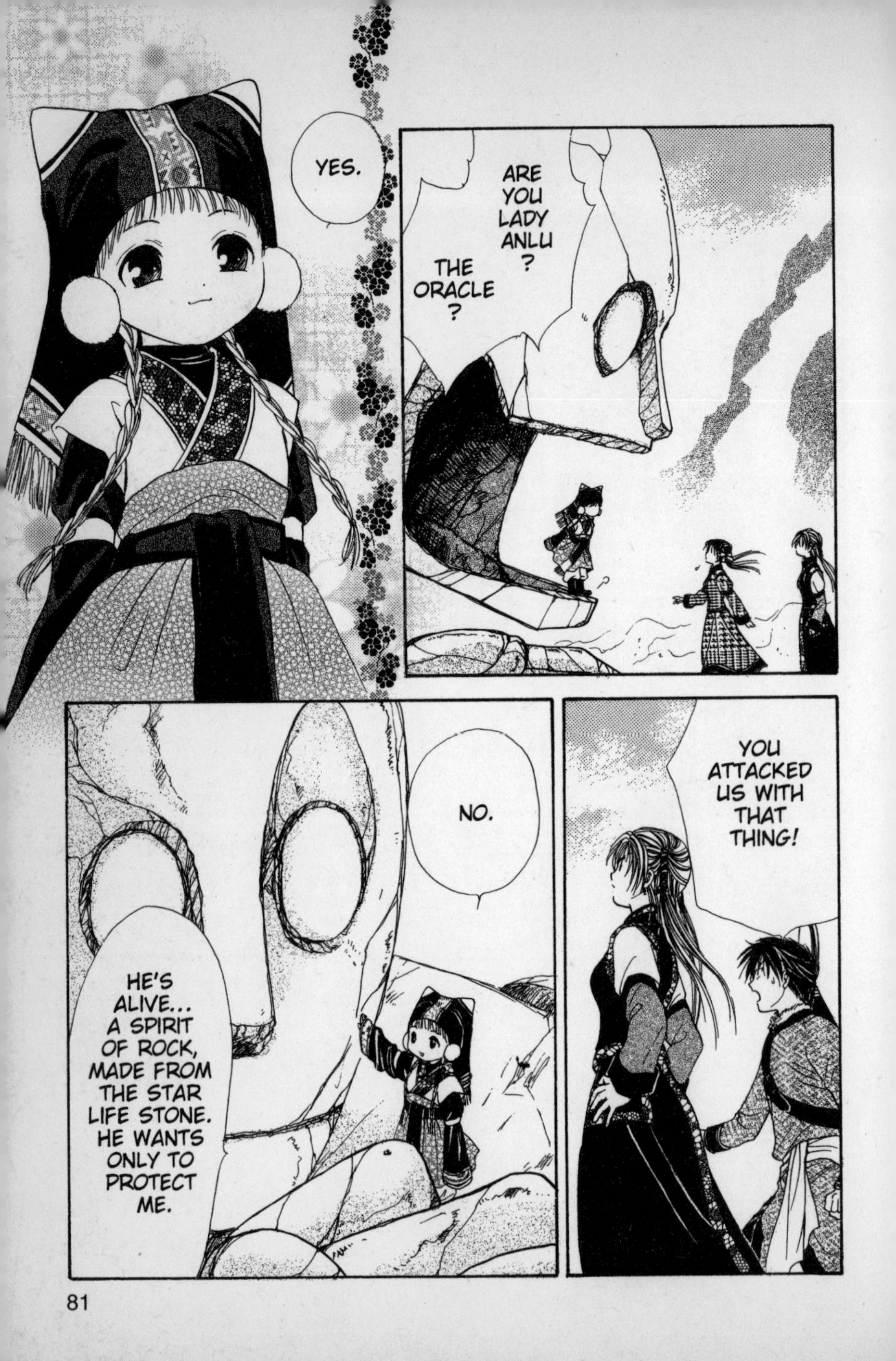
ARE YOU LADY ANLU?
THE ORACLE?
YES.
YOU ATTACKED US WITH THAT THING!
NO.
HE'S ALIVE... A SPIRIT OF ROCK, MADE FROM THE STAR LIFE STONE. HE WANTS ONLY TO PROTECT ME.

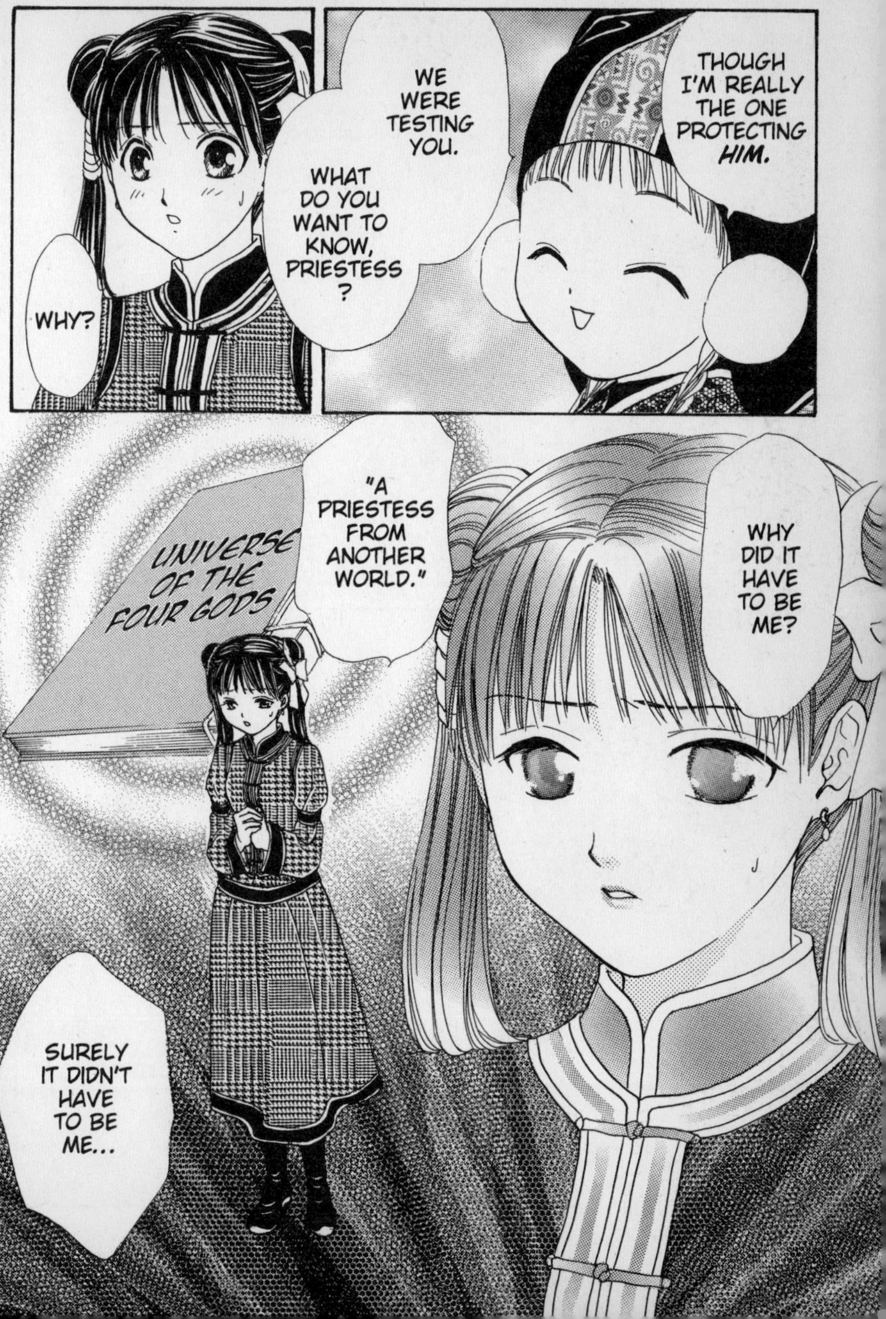
THOUGH I'M REALLY THE ONE PROTECTING *HIM.*
WE WERE TESTING YOU.
WHAT DO YOU WANT TO KNOW, PRIESTESS?
WHY?
WHY DID IT HAVE TO BE ME?
"A PRIESTESS FROM ANOTHER WORLD."
UNIVERSE OF THE FOUR GODS
SURELY IT DIDN'T HAVE TO BE ME...

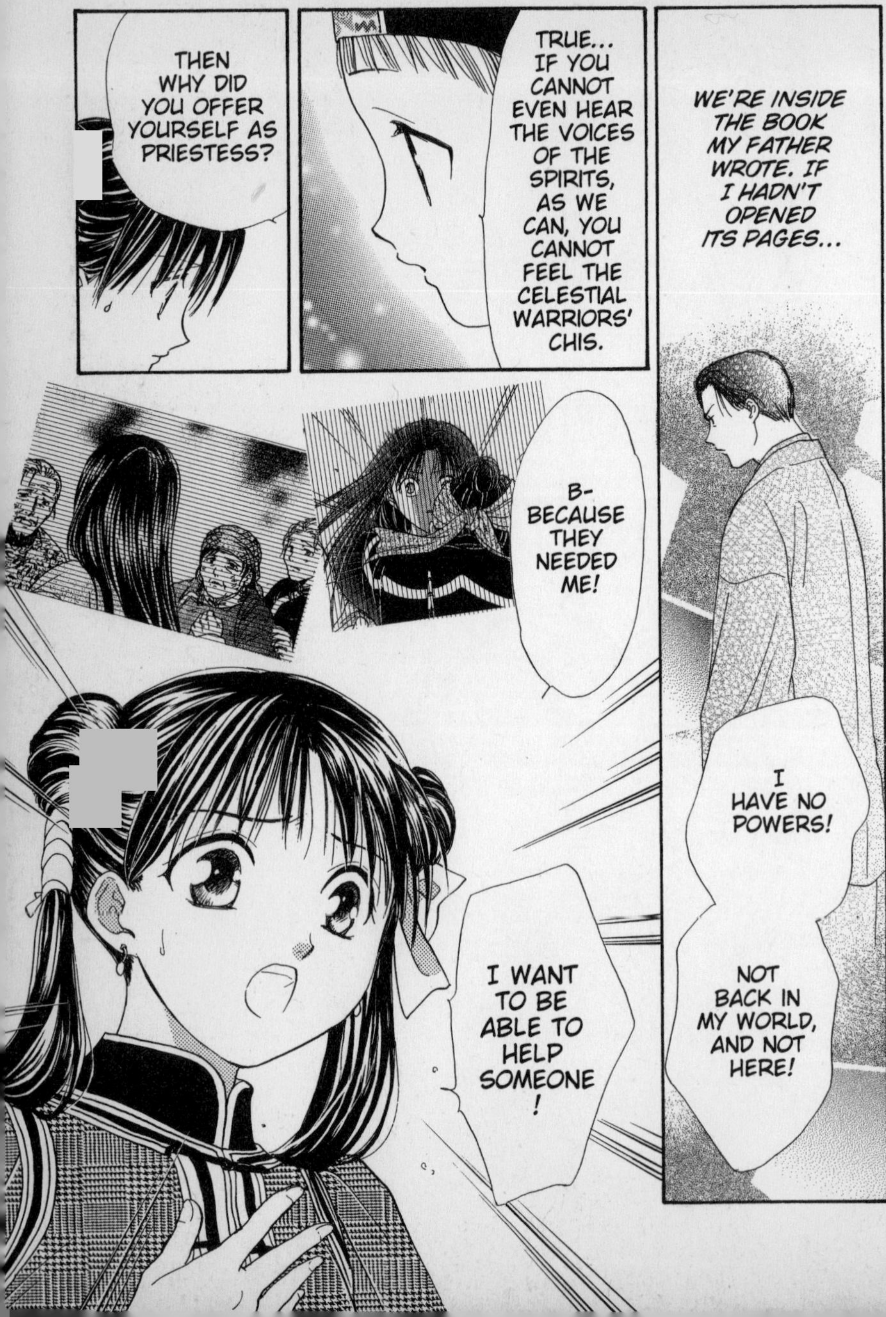
WE'RE INSIDE THE BOOK MY FATHER WROTE. IF I HADN'T OPENED ITS PAGES...
I HAVE NO POWERS!
NOT BACK IN MY WORLD, AND NOT HERE!
TRUE... IF YOU CANNOT EVEN HEAR THE VOICES OF THE SPIRITS, AS WE CAN, YOU CANNOT FEEL THE CELESTIAL WARRIORS' CHIS.
THEN WHY DID YOU OFFER YOURSELF AS PRIESTESS?
B-BECAUSE THEY NEEDED ME!
I WANT TO BE ABLE TO HELP SOMEONE!

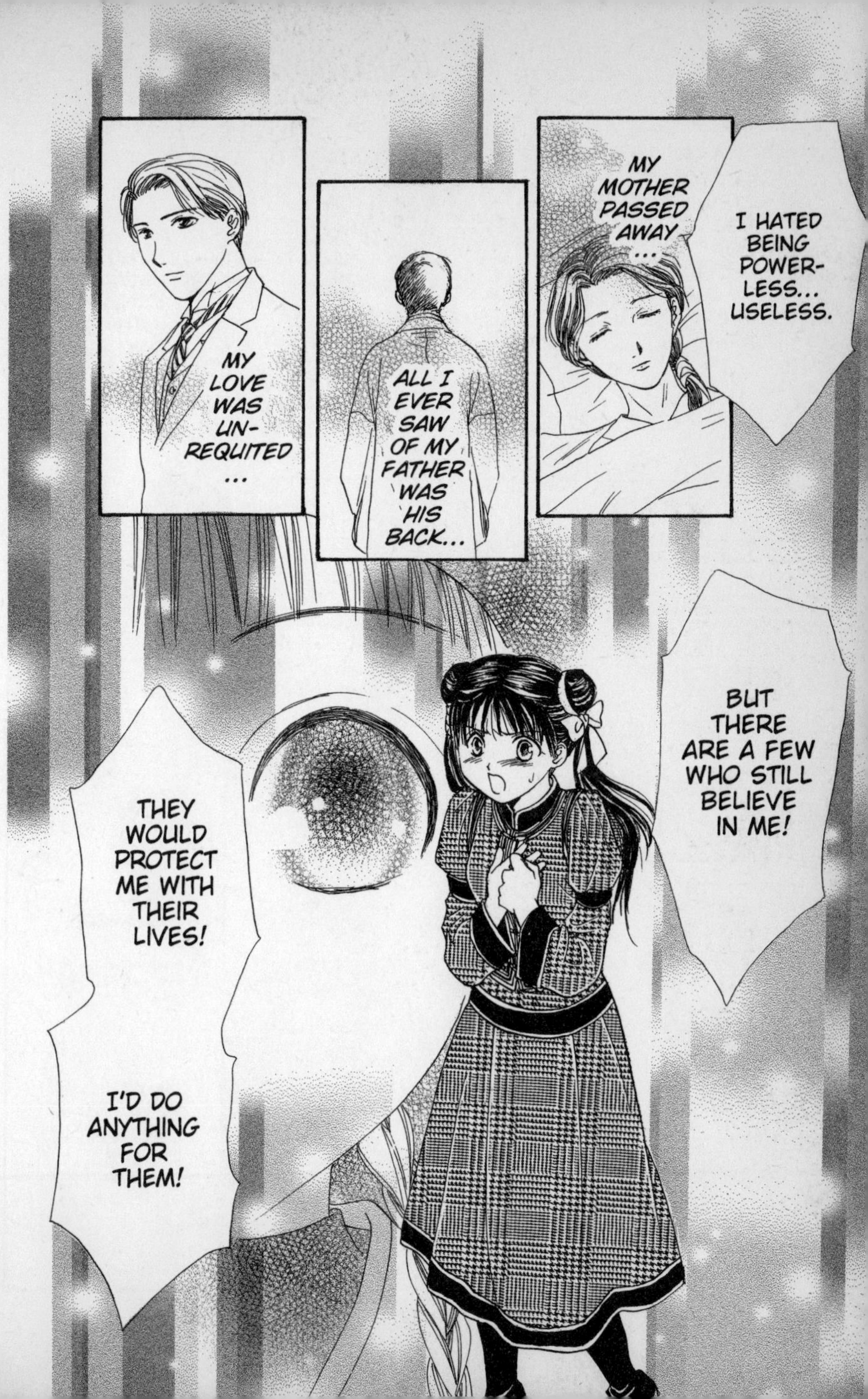
I HATED BEING POWERLESS... USELESS.
MY MOTHER PASSED AWAY...
ALL I EVER SAW OF MY FATHER WAS HIS BACK...
MY LOVE WAS UNREQUITED...
BUT THERE ARE A FEW WHO STILL BELIEVE IN ME!
THEY WOULD PROTECT ME WITH THEIR LIVES!
I'D DO ANYTHING FOR THEM!

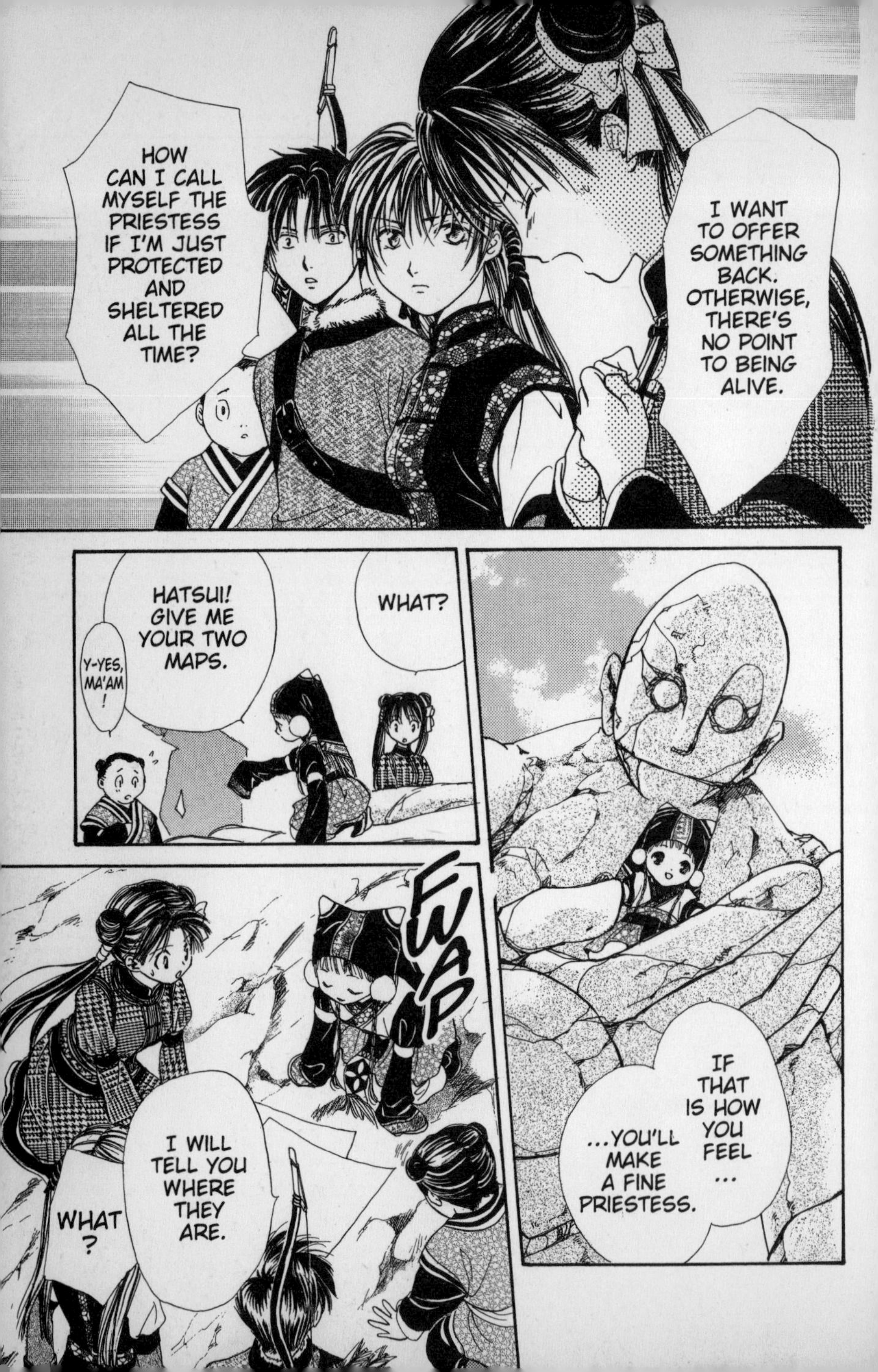
I WANT TO OFFER SOMETHING BACK. OTHERWISE, THERE'S NO POINT TO BEING ALIVE.
HOW CAN I CALL MYSELF THE PRIESTESS IF I'M JUST PROTECTED AND SHELTERED ALL THE TIME?
IF THAT IS HOW YOU FEEL...
...YOU'LL MAKE A FINE PRIESTESS.
WHAT?
HATSUI! GIVE ME YOUR TWO MAPS.
Y-YES, MA'AM!
FWAP
I WILL TELL YOU WHERE THEY ARE.
WHAT?

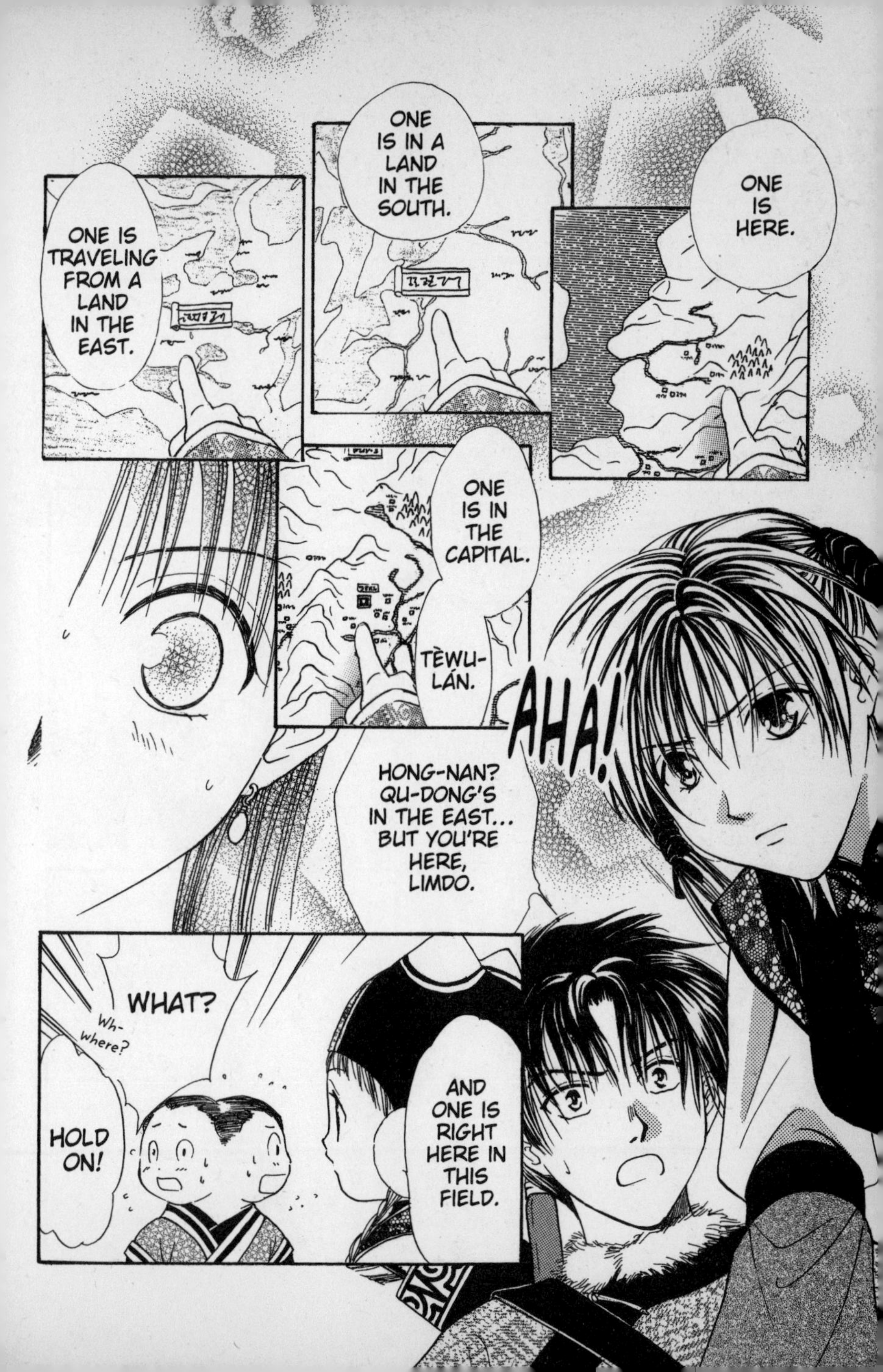
ONE IS HERE.
ONE IS IN A LAND IN THE SOUTH.
ONE IS TRAVELING FROM A LAND IN THE EAST.
ONE IS IN THE CAPITAL.
TÈWULÁN.
AHA!
HONG-NAN? QU-DONG'S IN THE EAST... BUT YOU'RE HERE, LIMDO.
AND ONE IS RIGHT HERE IN THIS FIELD.
WHAT?
Wh-where?
HOLD ON!

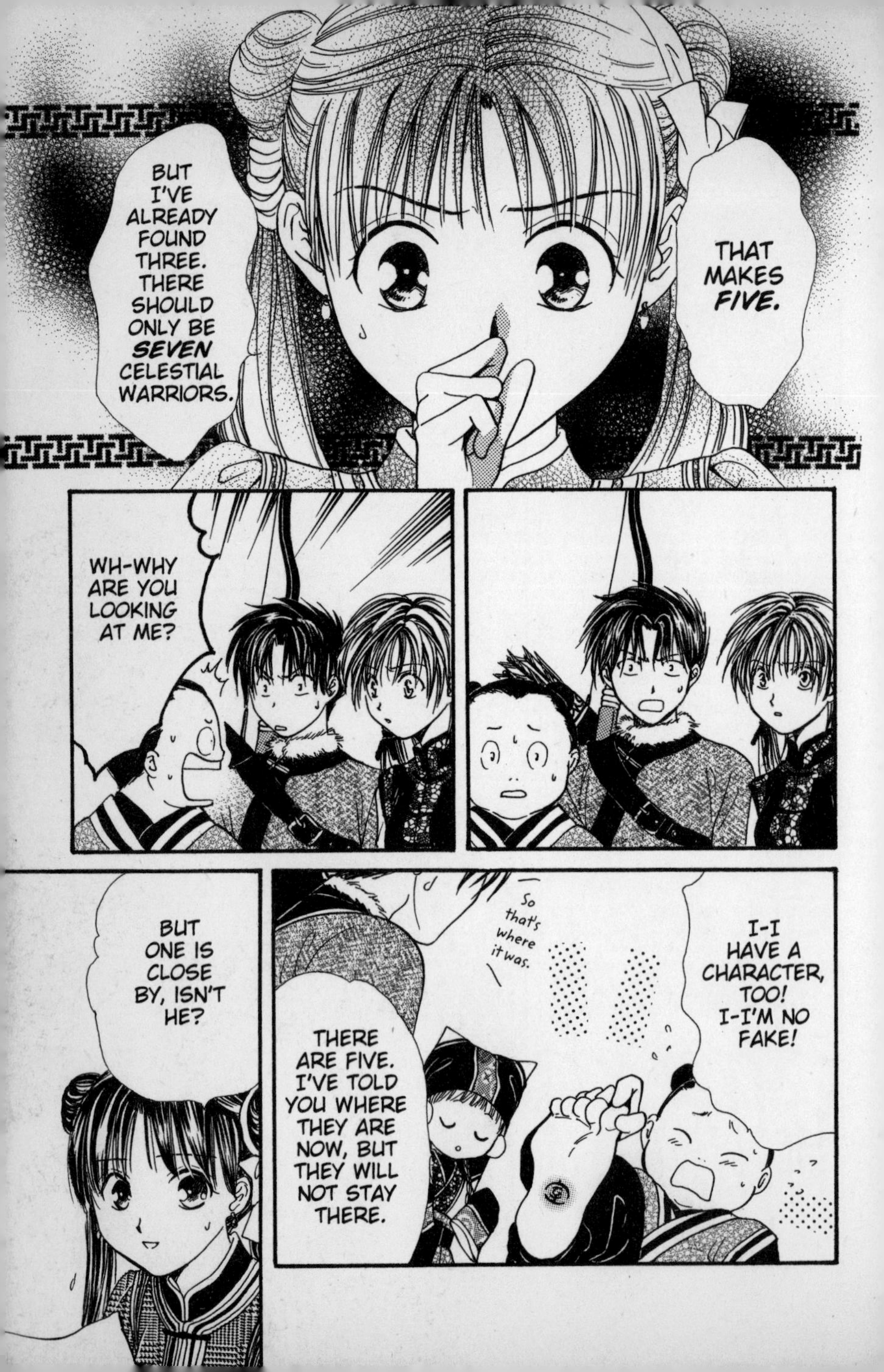
THAT MAKES *FIVE.*
BUT I'VE ALREADY FOUND THREE. THERE SHOULD ONLY BE ***SEVEN*** CELESTIAL WARRIORS.
WH-WHY ARE YOU LOOKING AT ME?
I-I HAVE A CHARACTER, TOO! I-I'M NO FAKE!
So that's where it was.
THERE ARE FIVE. I'VE TOLD YOU WHERE THEY ARE NOW, BUT THEY WILL NOT STAY THERE.
BUT ONE IS CLOSE BY, ISN'T HE?

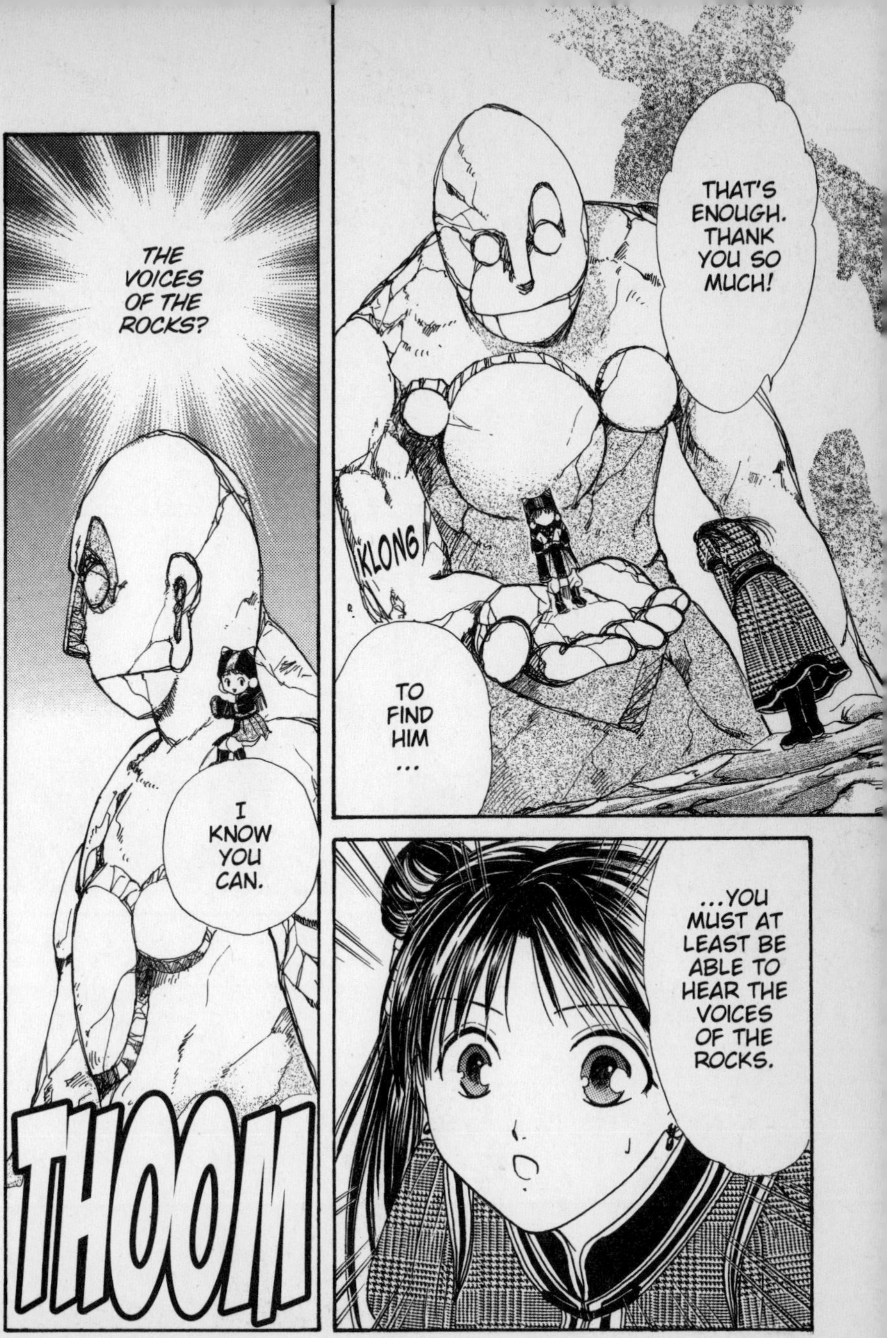
THAT'S ENOUGH. THANK YOU SO MUCH!
KLONG
TO FIND HIM ...
...YOU MUST AT LEAST BE ABLE TO HEAR THE VOICES OF THE ROCKS.
THE VOICES OF THE ROCKS?
I KNOW YOU CAN.
THOOM

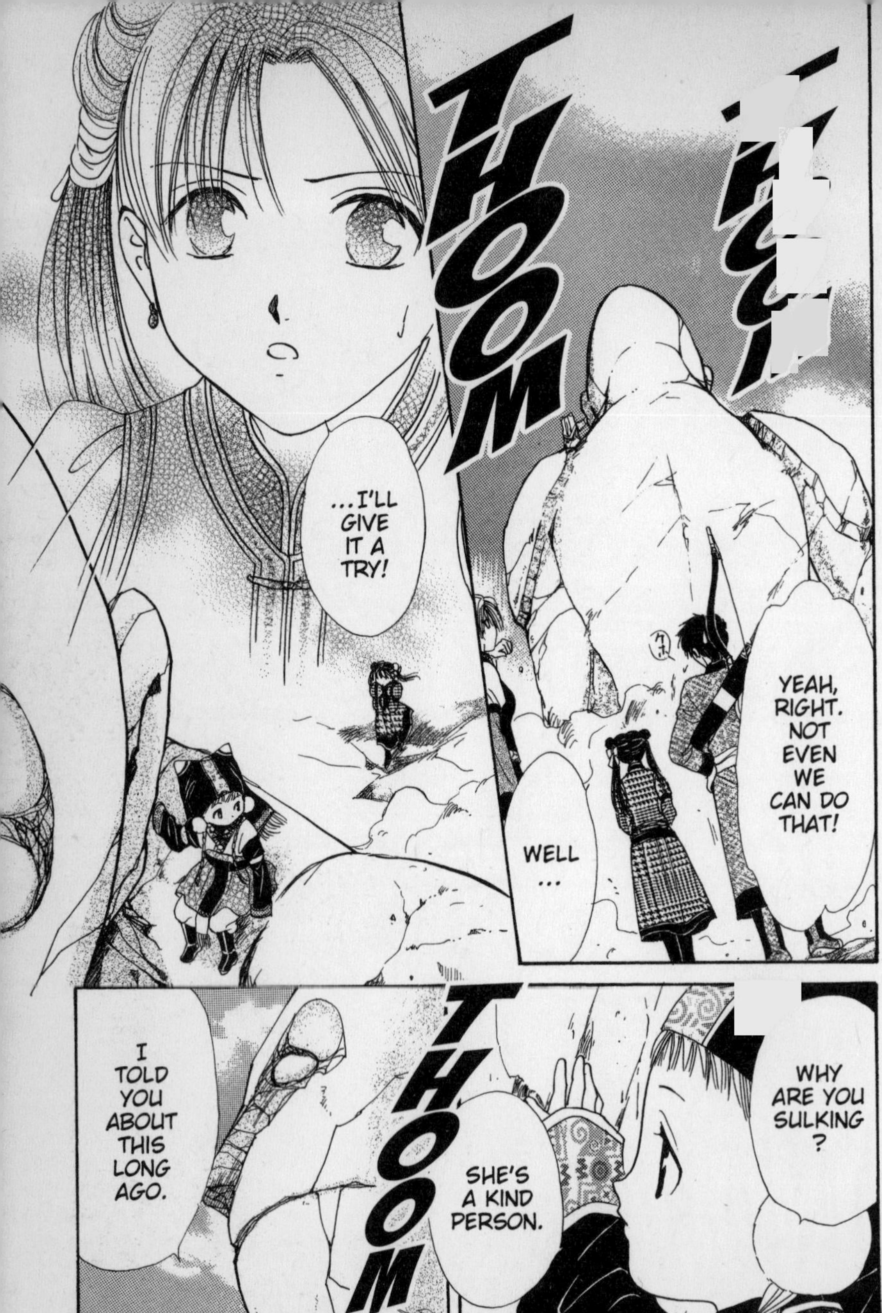
THOOM
YEAH, RIGHT. NOT EVEN WE CAN DO THAT!
WELL ...
...I'LL GIVE IT A TRY!
WHY ARE YOU SULKING ?
SHE'S A KIND PERSON.
THOOM
I TOLD YOU ABOUT THIS LONG AGO.

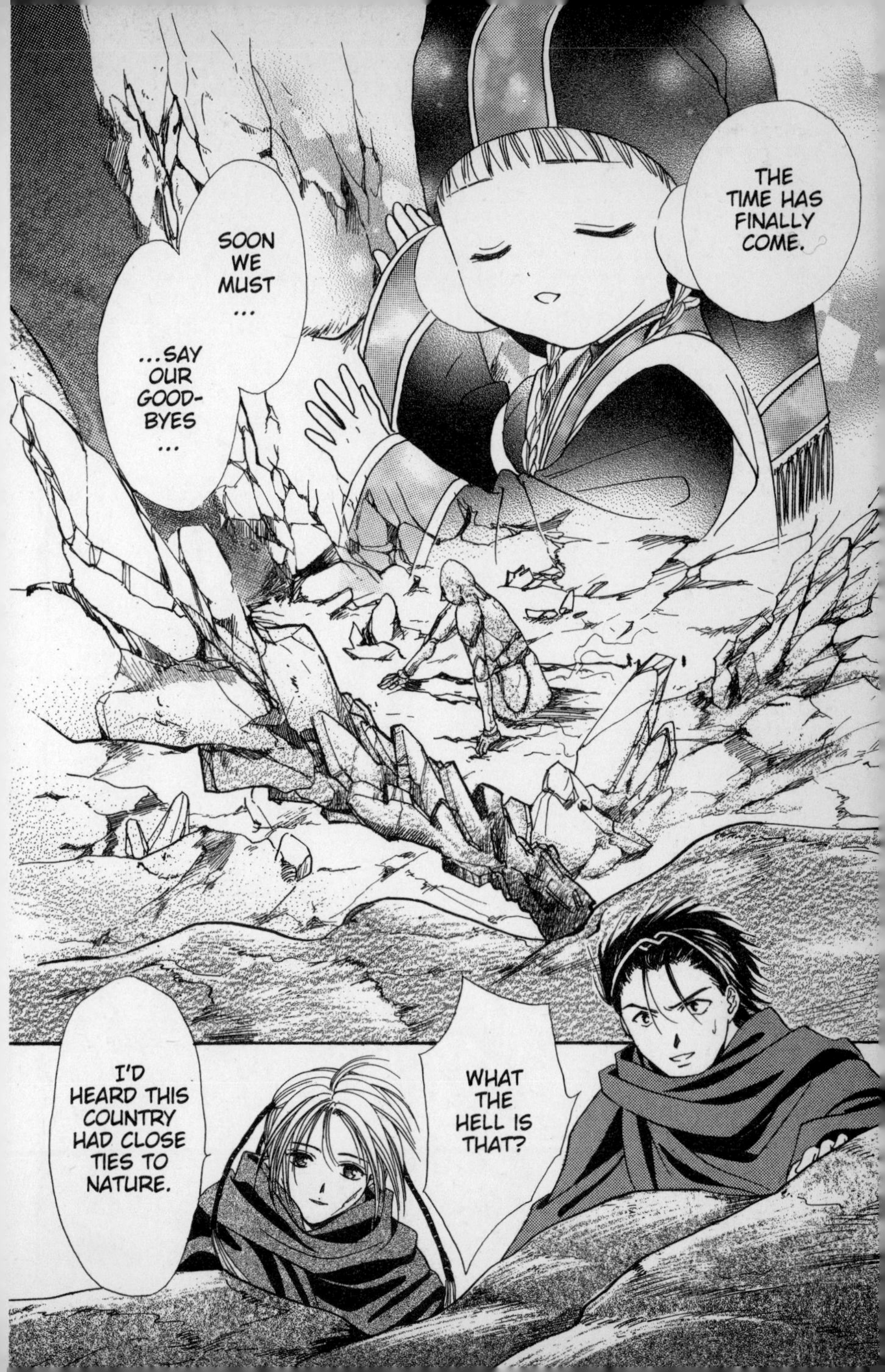
THE TIME HAS FINALLY COME.
SOON WE MUST ...
...SAY OUR GOOD-BYES ...
WHAT THE HELL IS THAT?
I'D HEARD THIS COUNTRY HAD CLOSE TIES TO NATURE.

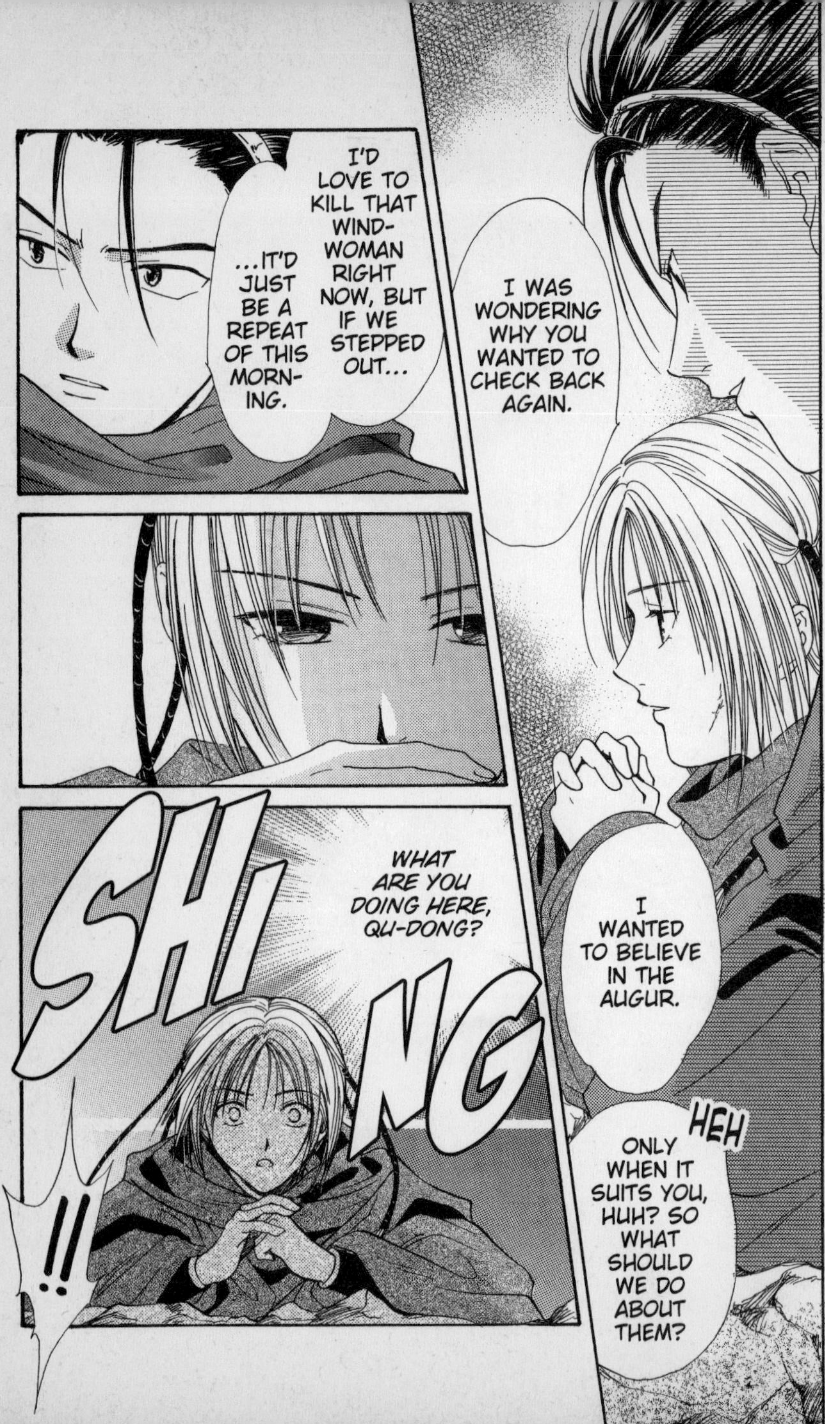
I WAS WONDERING WHY YOU WANTED TO CHECK BACK AGAIN.
I WANTED TO BELIEVE IN THE AUGUR.
HEH
ONLY WHEN IT SUITS YOU, HUH? SO WHAT SHOULD WE DO ABOUT THEM?
I'D LOVE TO KILL THAT WIND-WOMAN RIGHT NOW, BUT IF WE STEPPED OUT...
...IT'D JUST BE A REPEAT OF THIS MORNING.
SHING
WHAT ARE YOU DOING HERE, QU-DONG?
!!

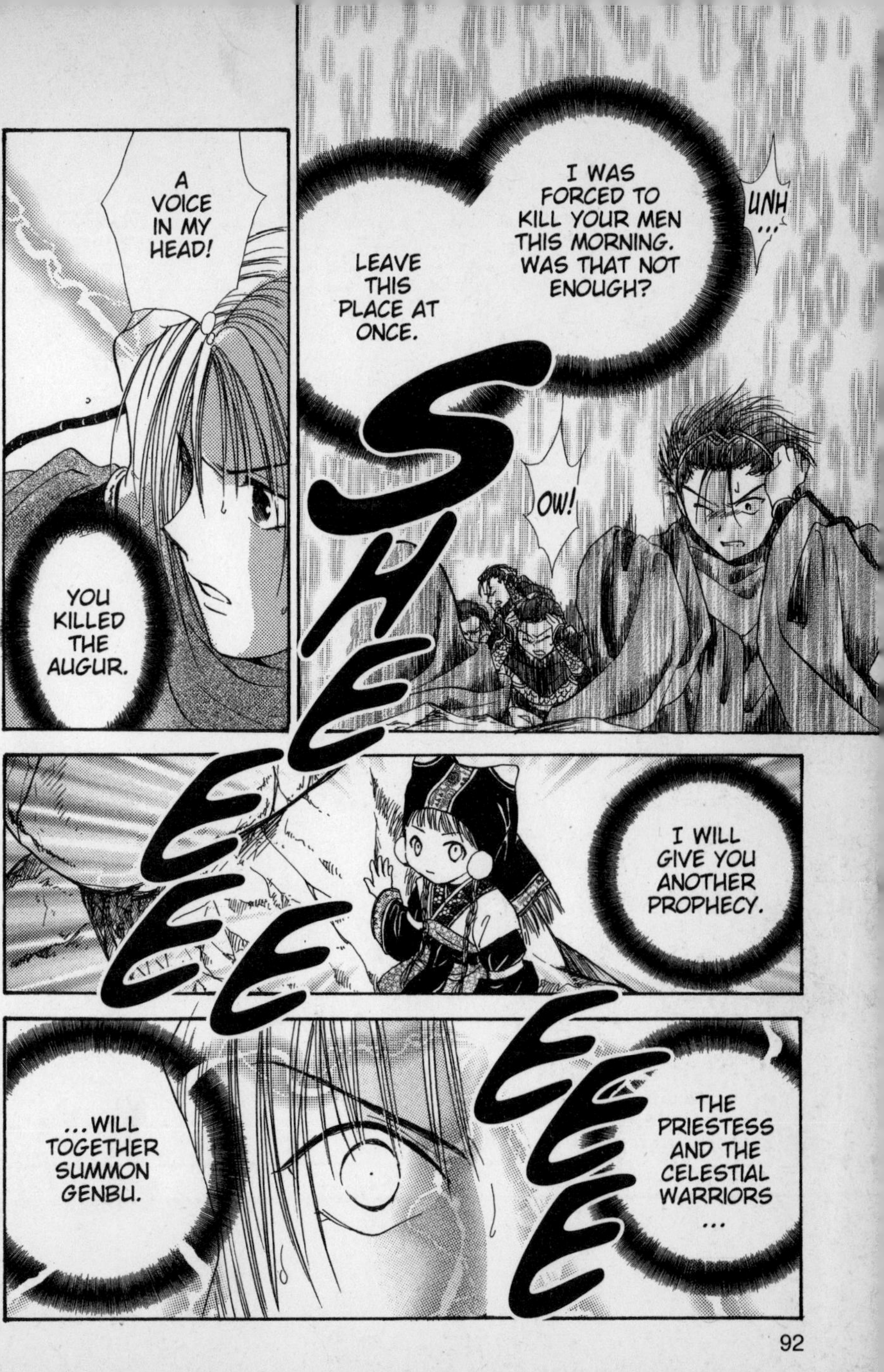
UNH ...
I WAS FORCED TO KILL YOUR MEN THIS MORNING. WAS THAT NOT ENOUGH?
LEAVE THIS PLACE AT ONCE.
OW!
A VOICE IN MY HEAD!
YOU KILLED THE AUGUR.
SHEEEEEEEEE
I WILL GIVE YOU ANOTHER PROPHECY.
THE PRIESTESS AND THE CELESTIAL WARRIORS ...
...WILL TOGETHER SUMMON GENBU.

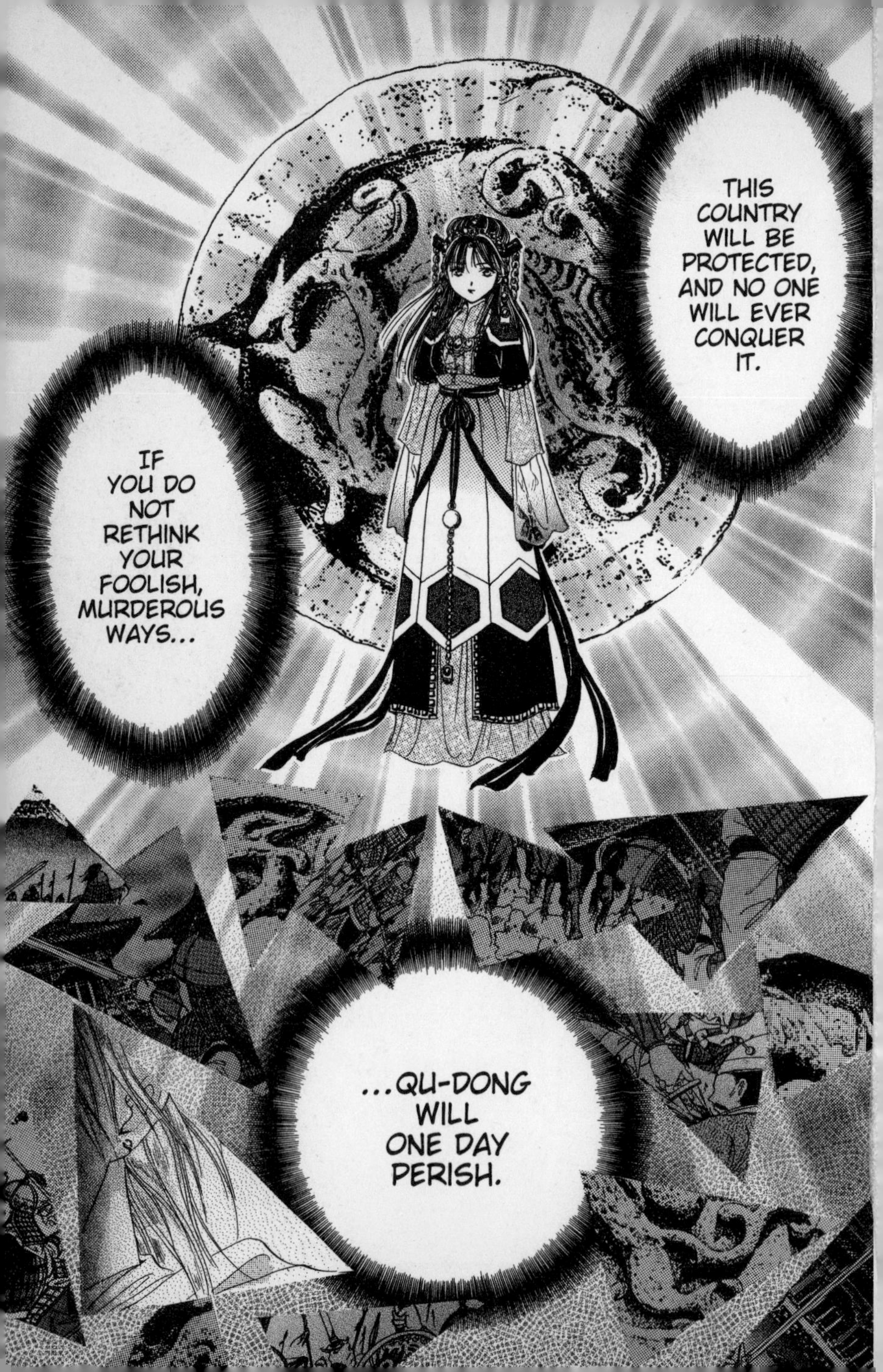
THIS COUNTRY WILL BE PROTECTED, AND NO ONE WILL EVER CONQUER IT.
IF YOU DO NOT RETHINK YOUR FOOLISH, MURDEROUS WAYS...
...QU-DONG WILL ONE DAY PERISH.

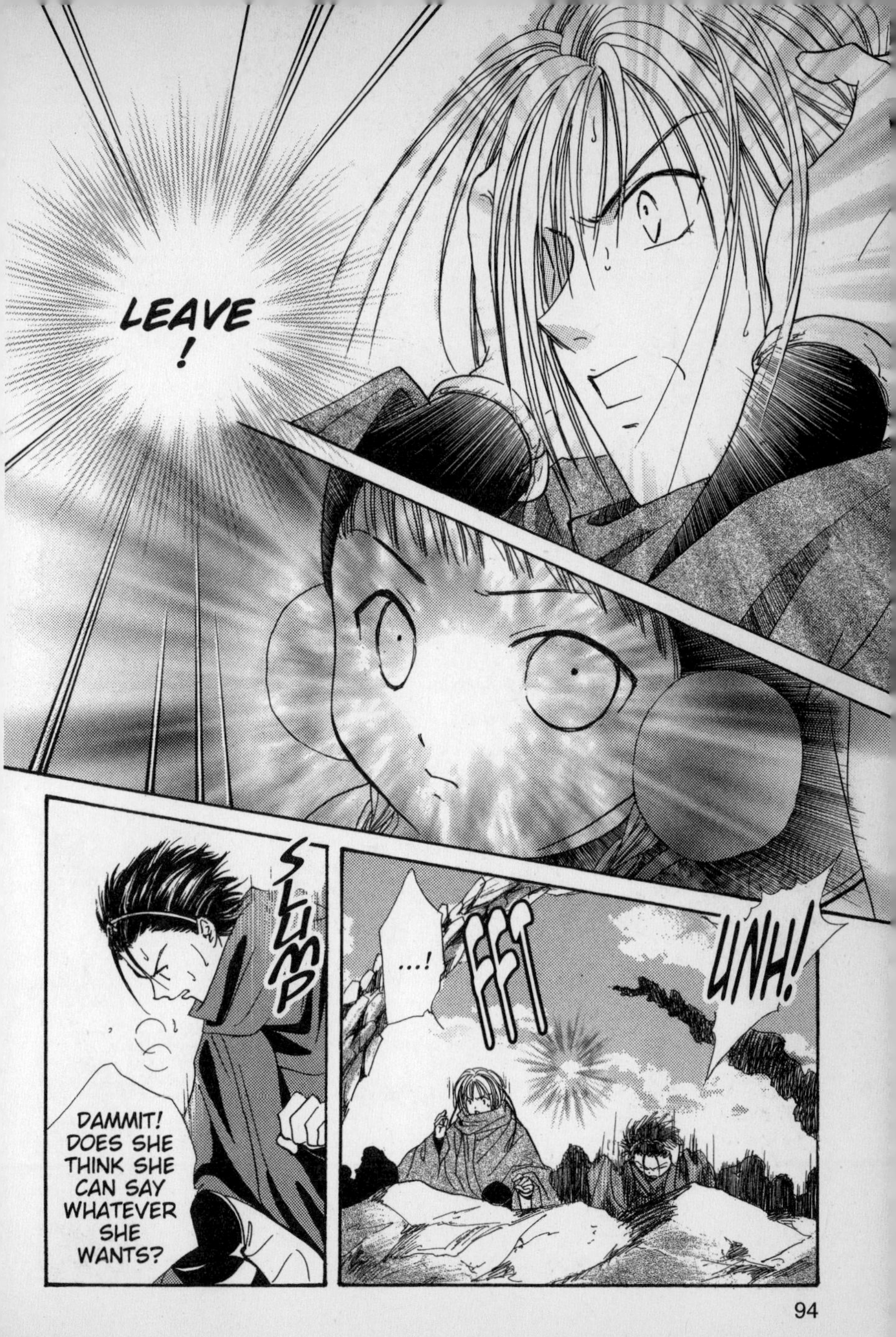
LEAVE
!
UNH!
FFT
...!
SLUMP
DAMMIT! DOES SHE THINK SHE CAN SAY WHATEVER SHE WANTS?

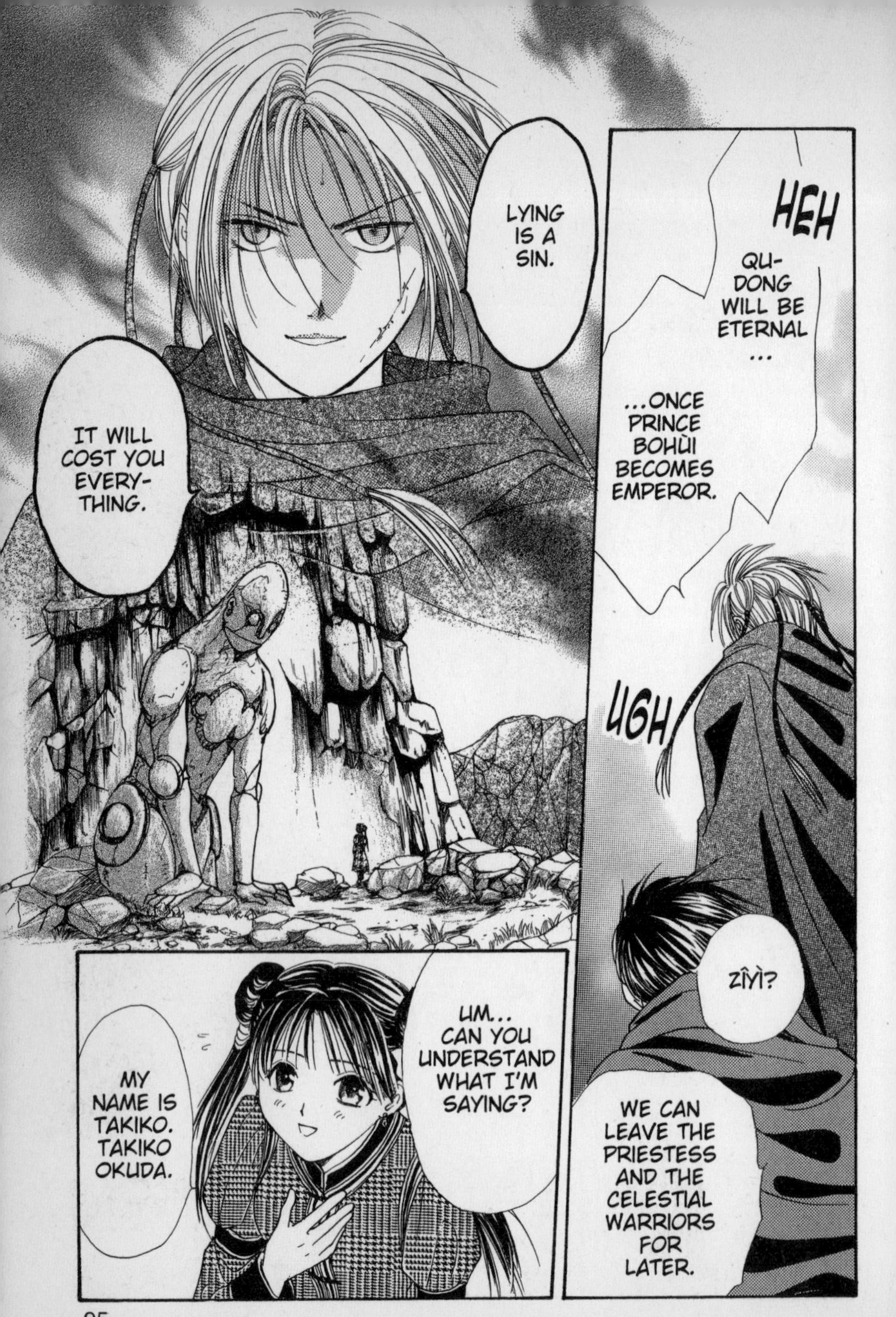
LYING IS A SIN.
IT WILL COST YOU EVERY-THING.
HEH
QU-DONG WILL BE ETERNAL ...
...ONCE PRINCE BOHÙI BECOMES EMPEROR.
UGH
ZÎYÌ?
WE CAN LEAVE THE PRIESTESS AND THE CELESTIAL WARRIORS FOR LATER.
UM... CAN YOU UNDERSTAND WHAT I'M SAYING?
MY NAME IS TAKIKO. TAKIKO OKUDA.

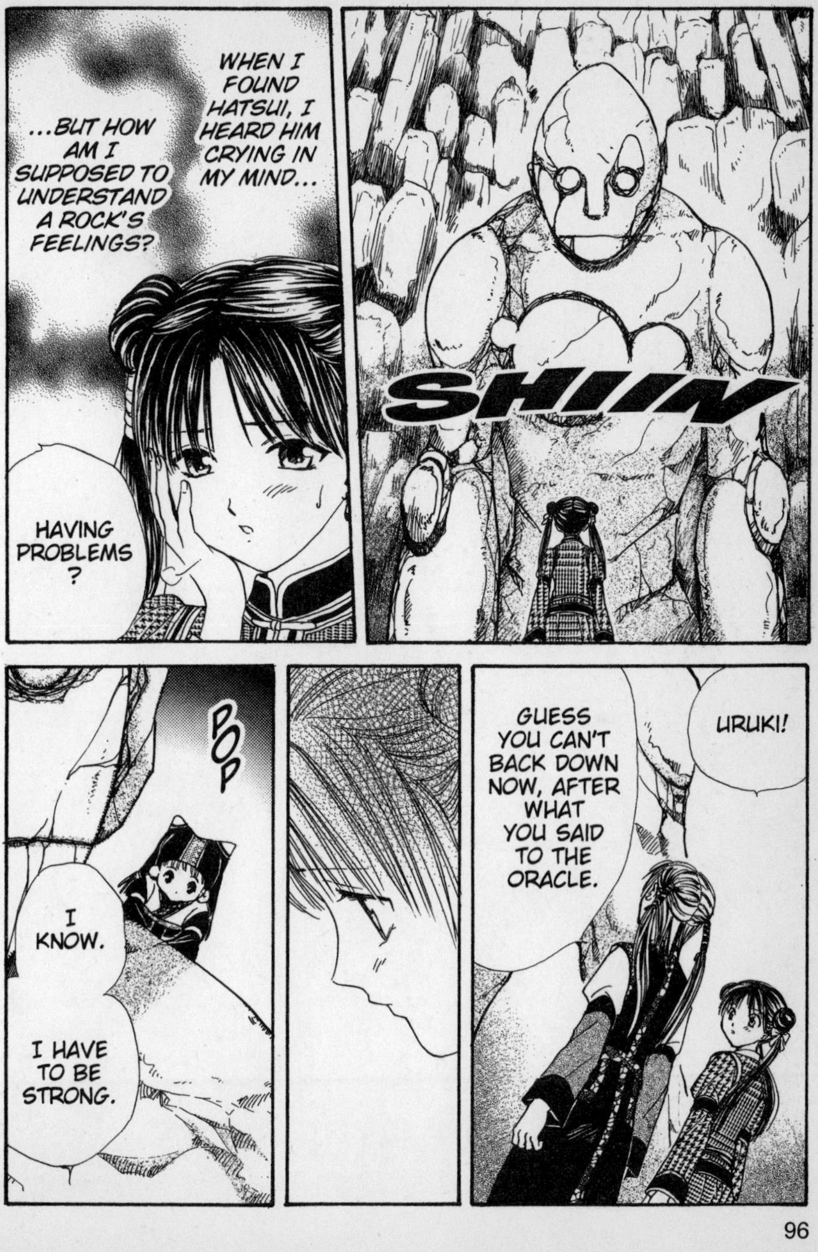
SHIN
WHEN I FOUND HATSUI, I HEARD HIM CRYING IN MY MIND...
...BUT HOW AM I SUPPOSED TO UNDERSTAND A ROCK'S FEELINGS?
HAVING PROBLEMS?
URUKI!
GUESS YOU CAN'T BACK DOWN NOW, AFTER WHAT YOU SAID TO THE ORACLE.
POP
I KNOW.
I HAVE TO BE STRONG.

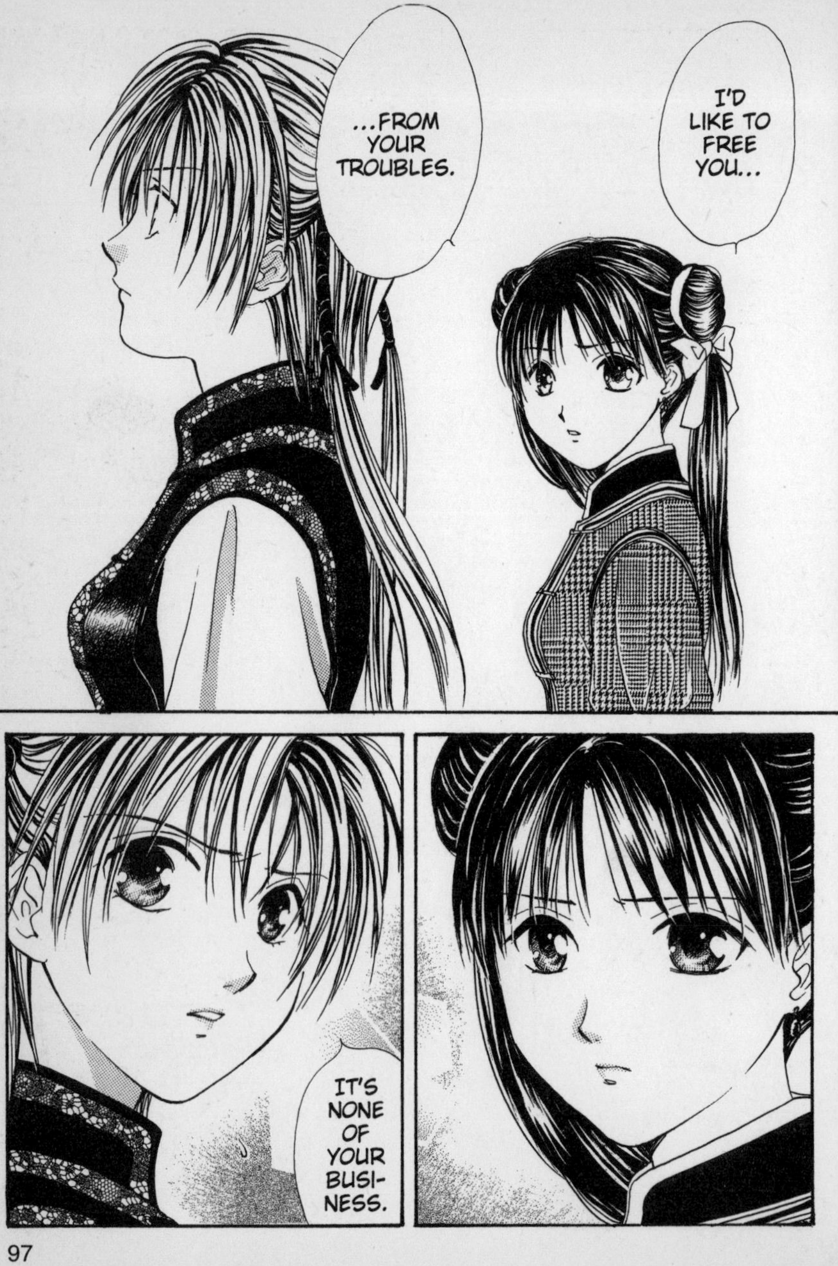
I'D LIKE TO FREE YOU...
...FROM YOUR TROUBLES.
IT'S NONE OF YOUR BUSI- NESS.

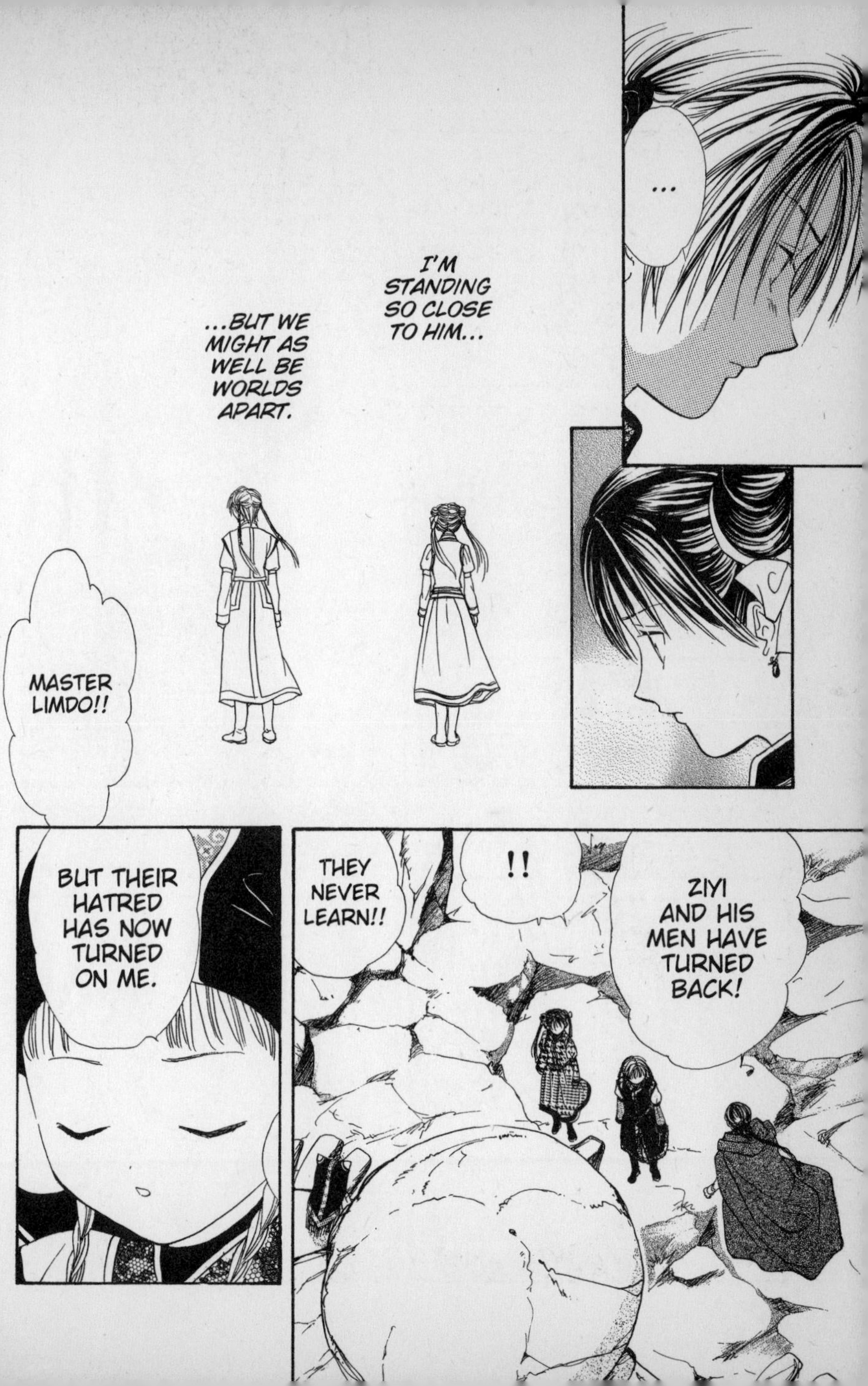
...
I'M STANDING SO CLOSE TO HIM...
...BUT WE MIGHT AS WELL BE WORLDS APART.
MASTER LIMDO!!
ZIYI AND HIS MEN HAVE TURNED BACK!
!!
THEY NEVER LEARN!!
BUT THEIR HATRED HAS NOW TURNED ON ME.

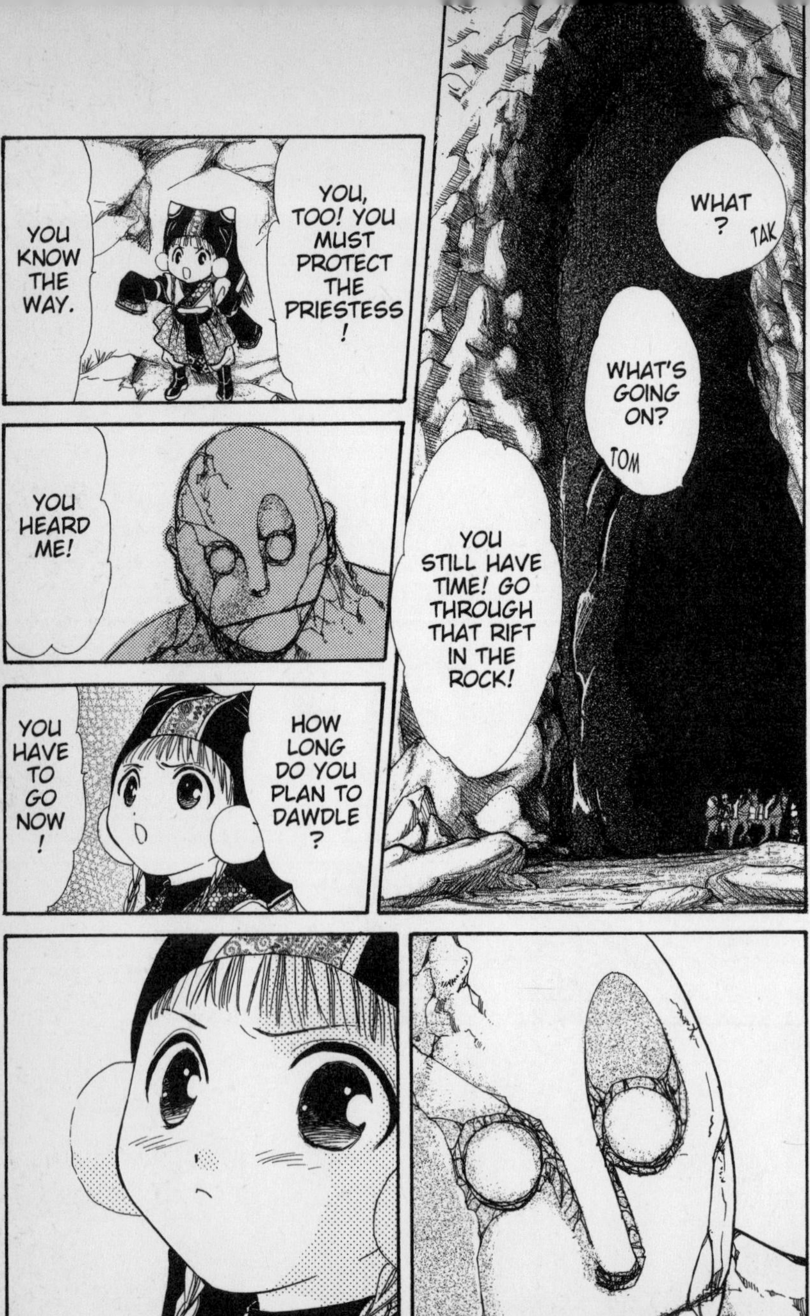
WHAT?
TAK
WHAT'S GOING ON?
TOM
YOU STILL HAVE TIME! GO THROUGH THAT RIFT IN THE ROCK!
YOU, TOO! YOU MUST PROTECT THE PRIESTESS!
YOU KNOW THE WAY.
YOU HEARD ME!
HOW LONG DO YOU PLAN TO DAWDLE?
YOU HAVE TO GO NOW!

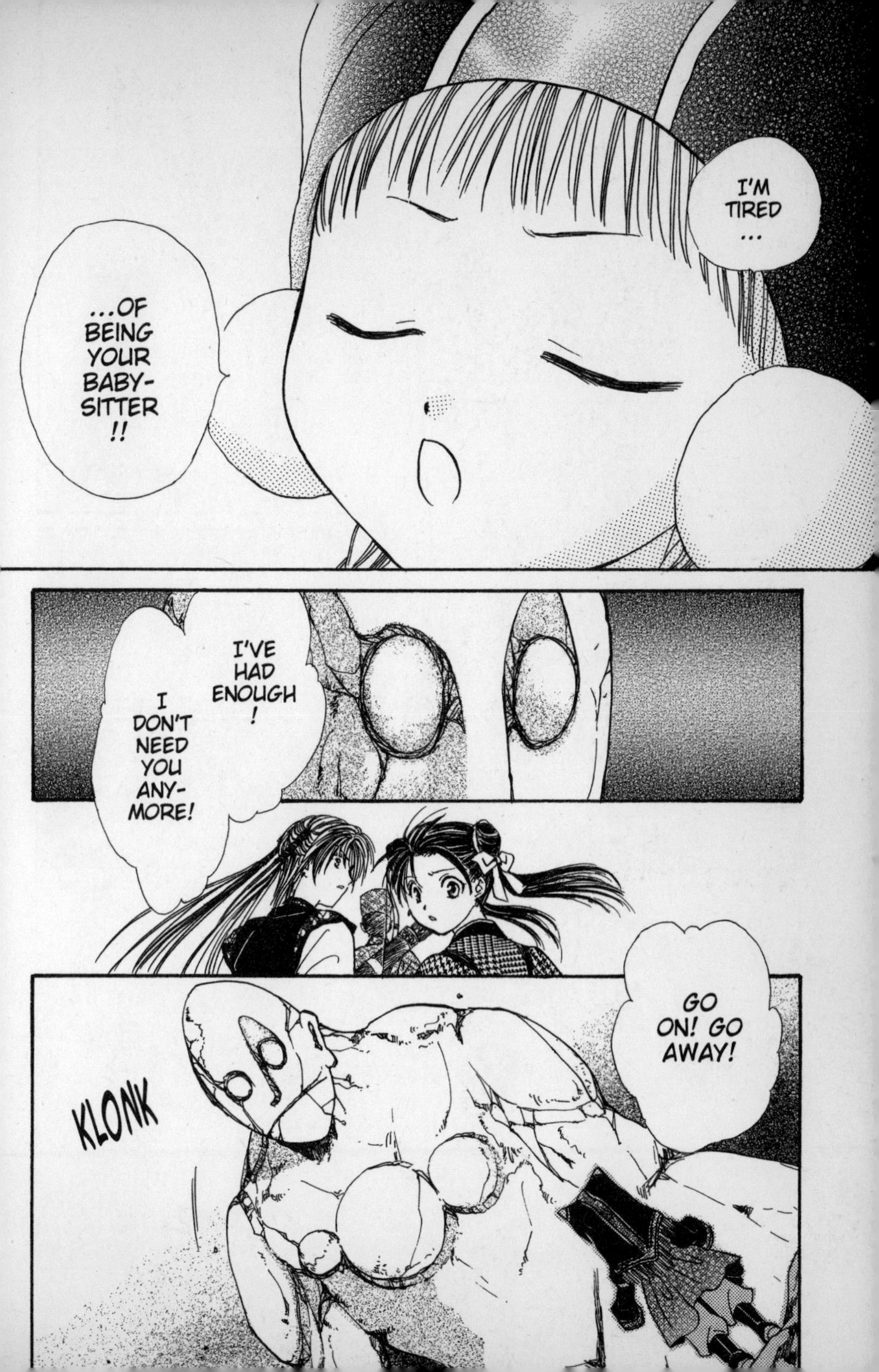
I'M TIRED ...
...OF BEING YOUR BABY-SITTER !!
I'VE HAD ENOUGH !
I DON'T NEED YOU ANY-MORE!
GO ON! GO AWAY!
KLONK

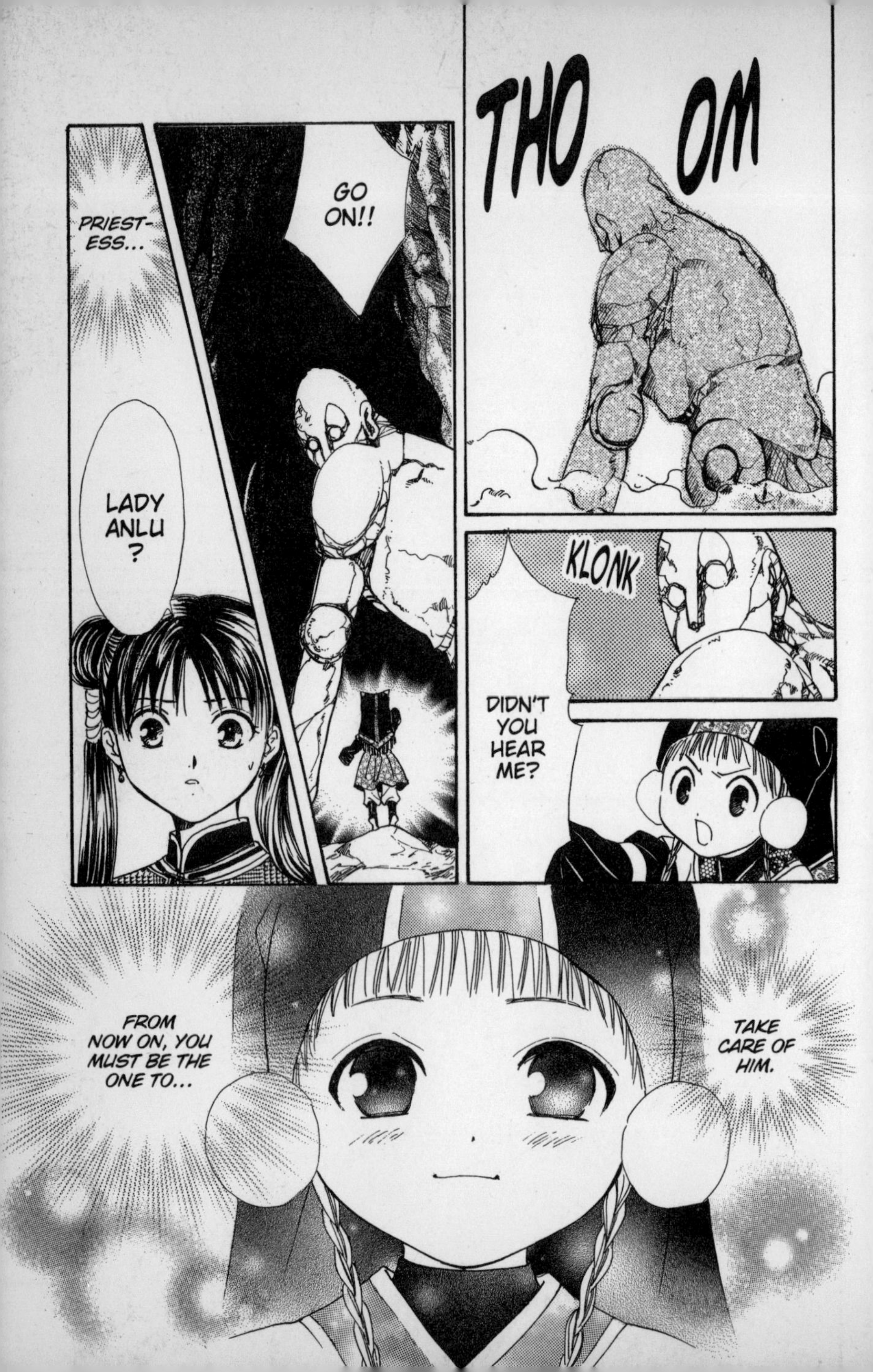
THO OM
KLONK
DIDN'T YOU HEAR ME?
GO ON!!
PRIEST-ESS...
LADY ANLU ?
TAKE CARE OF HIM.
FROM NOW ON, YOU MUST BE THE ONE TO...

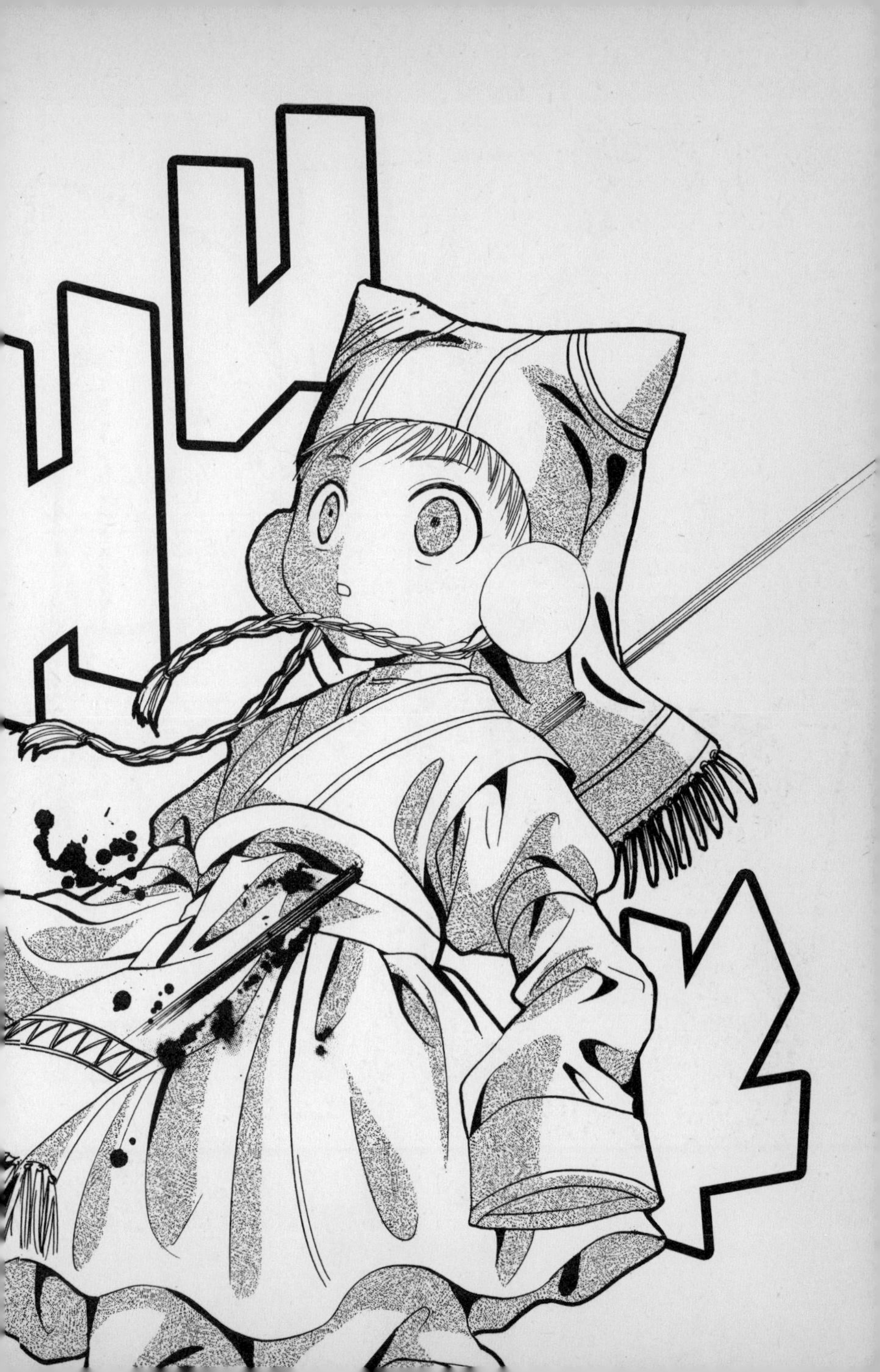

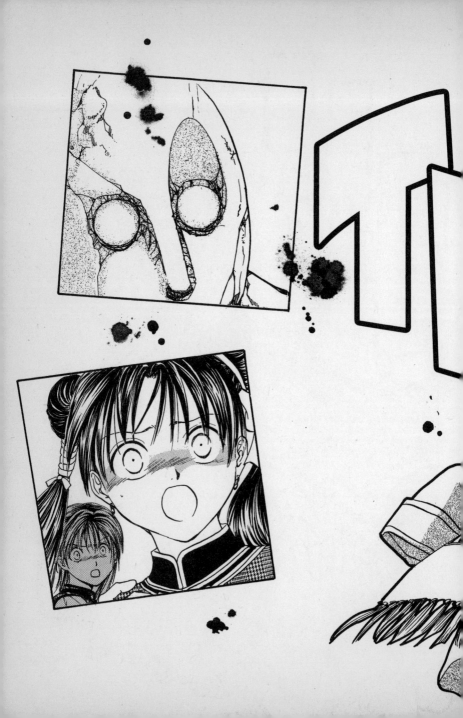

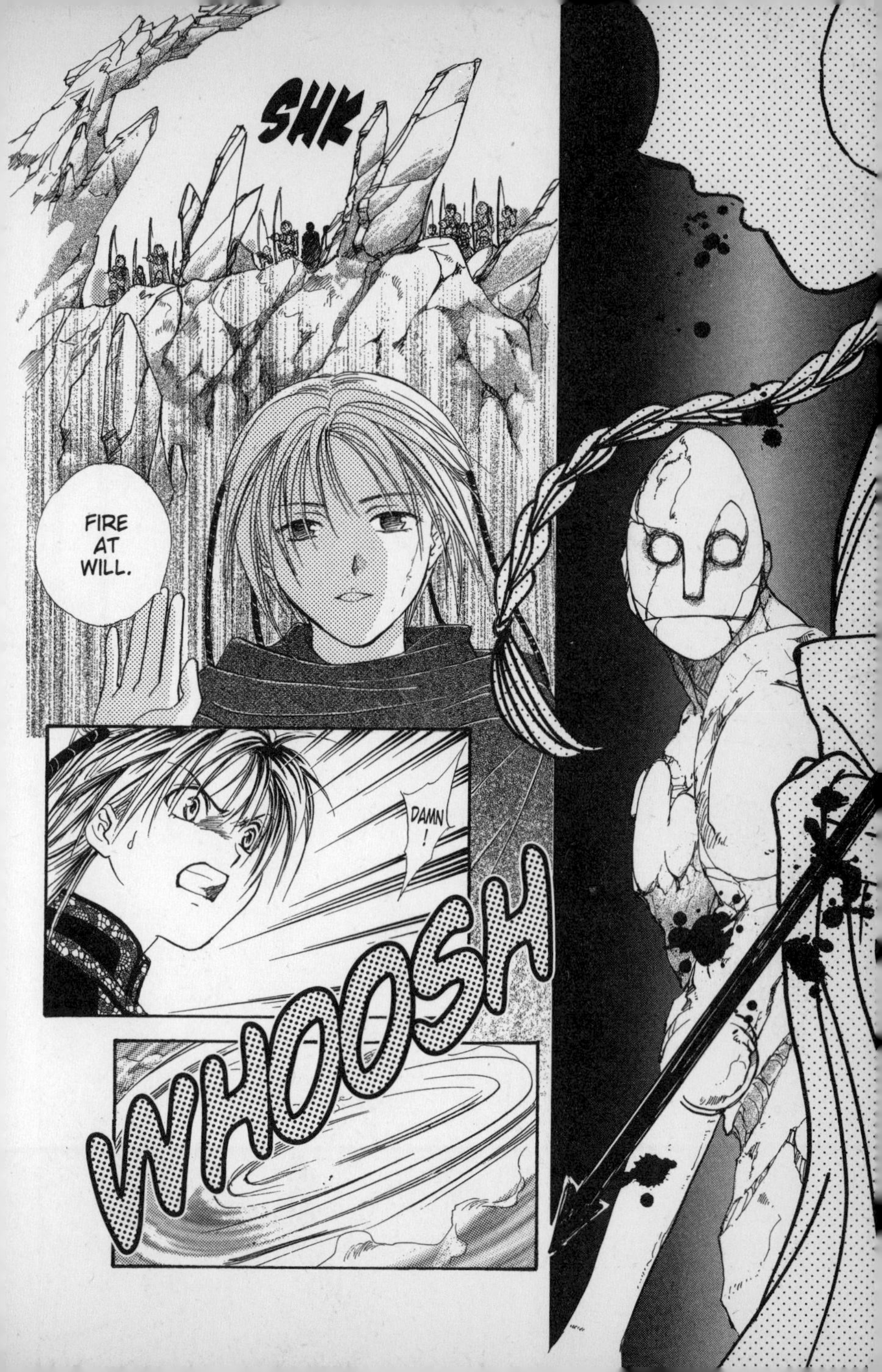
SHK
FIRE AT WILL.
DAMN!
WHOOSH

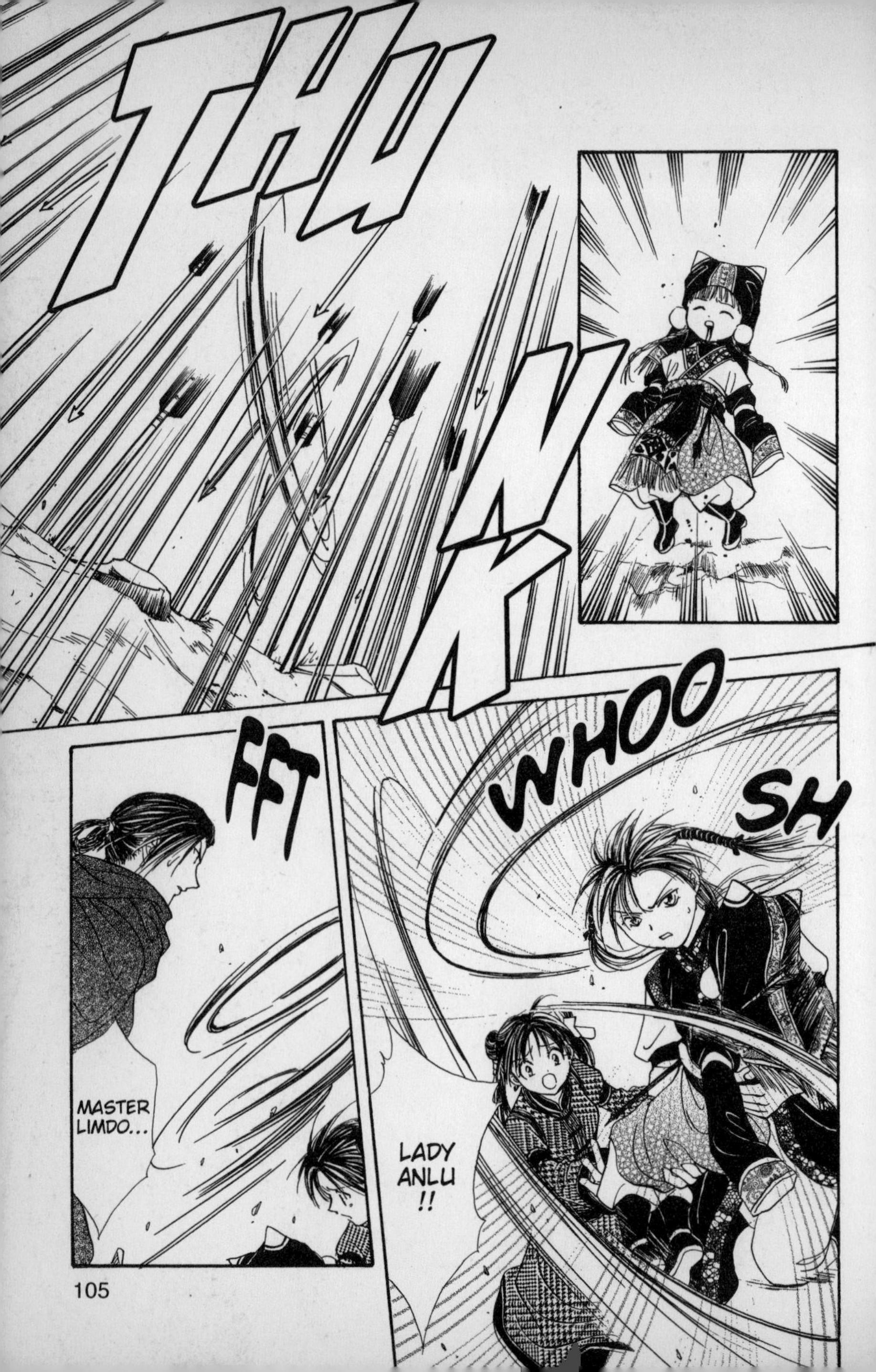
THUNK
WHOOOSH
LADY ANLU !!
FFT
MASTER LIMDO...

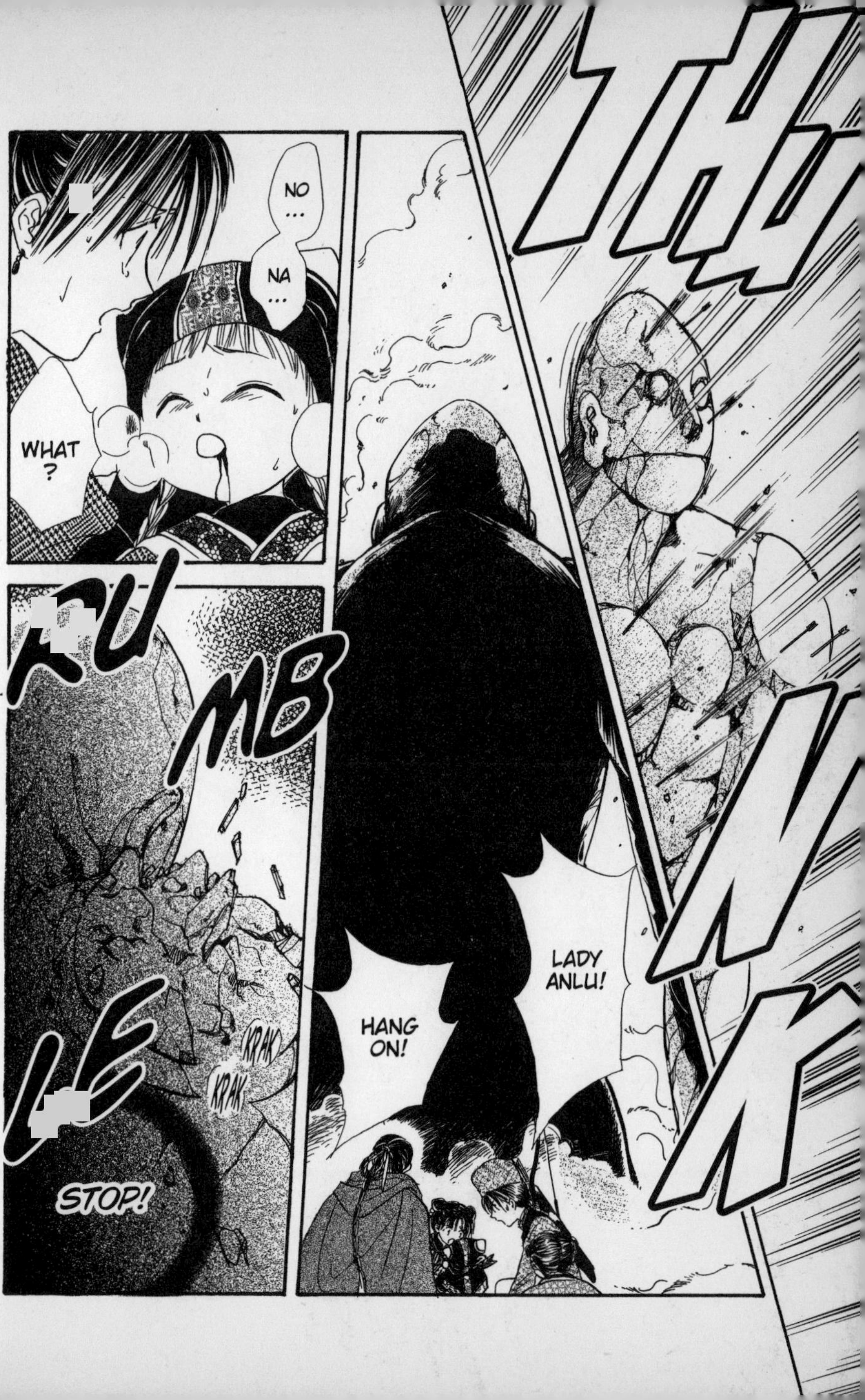
LADY ANLU!
HANG ON!
NO ...
NA ...
WHAT ?
KRAK
KRAK
STOP!

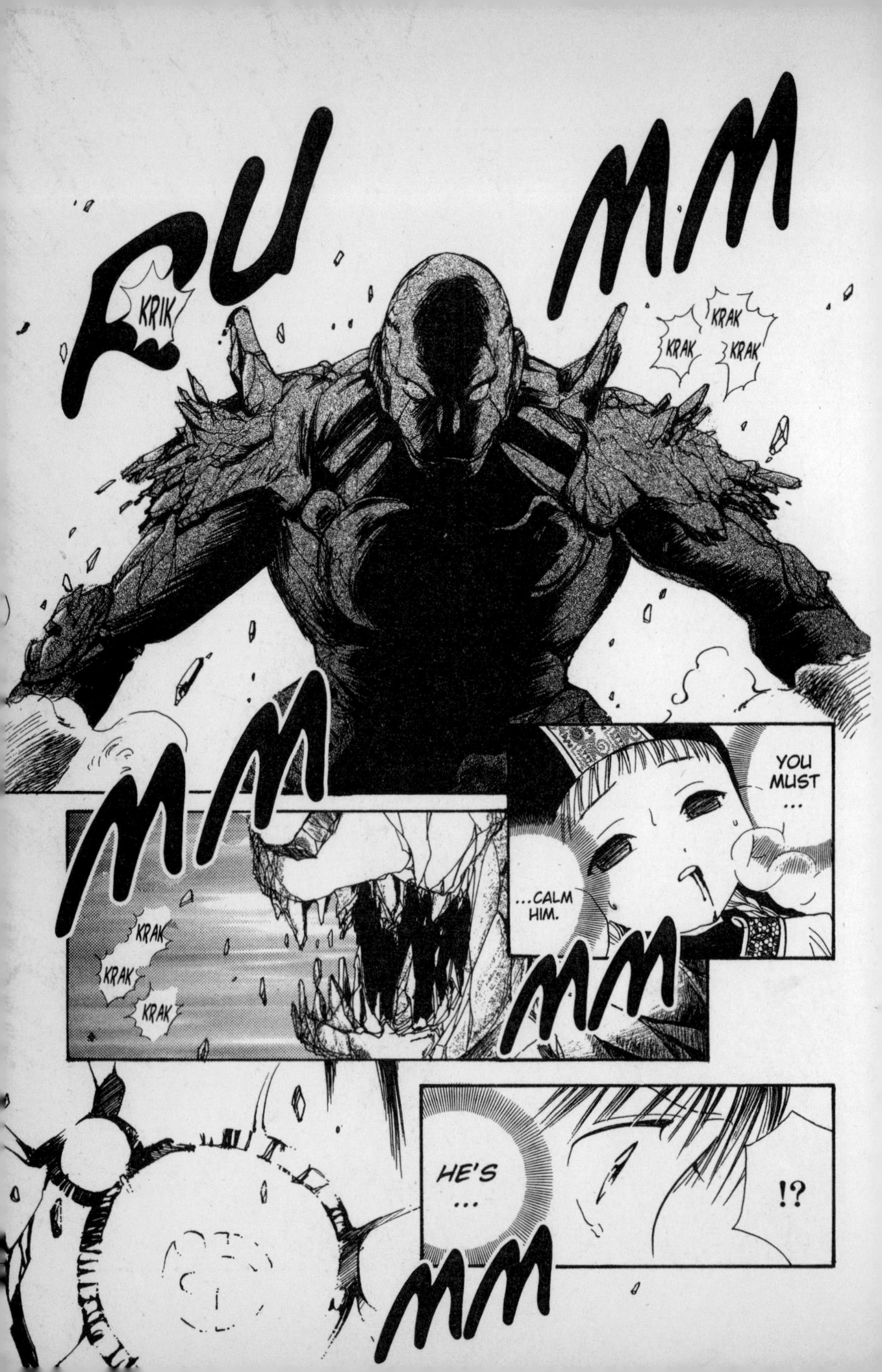
RUMMMMMMMM
KRAK KRAK KRAK
KRIK
YOU MUST ...
...CALM HIM.
KRAK KRAK KRAK
!?
HE'S ...

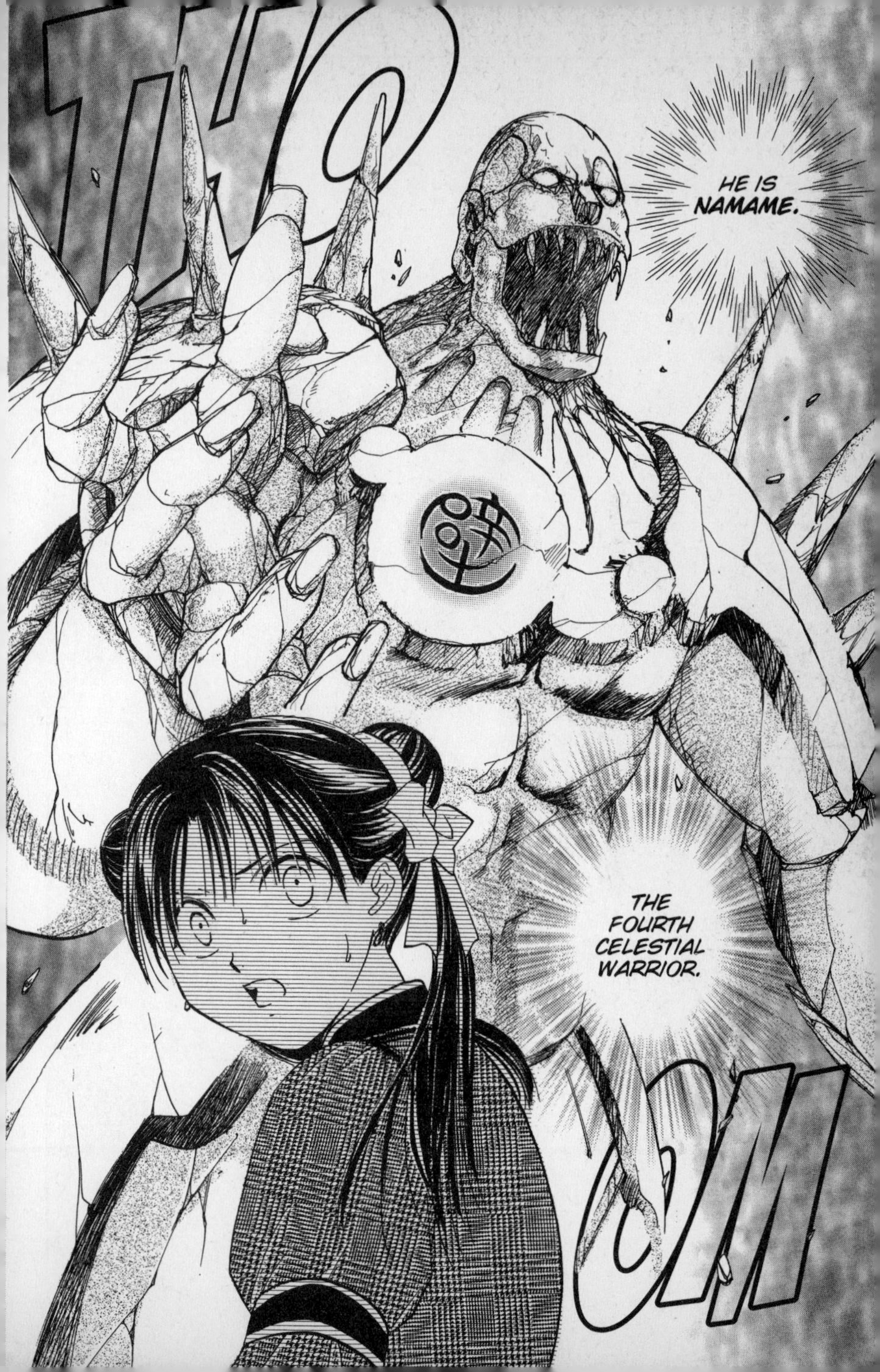
HE IS NAMAME.
THOOM
THE FOURTH CELESTIAL WARRIOR.

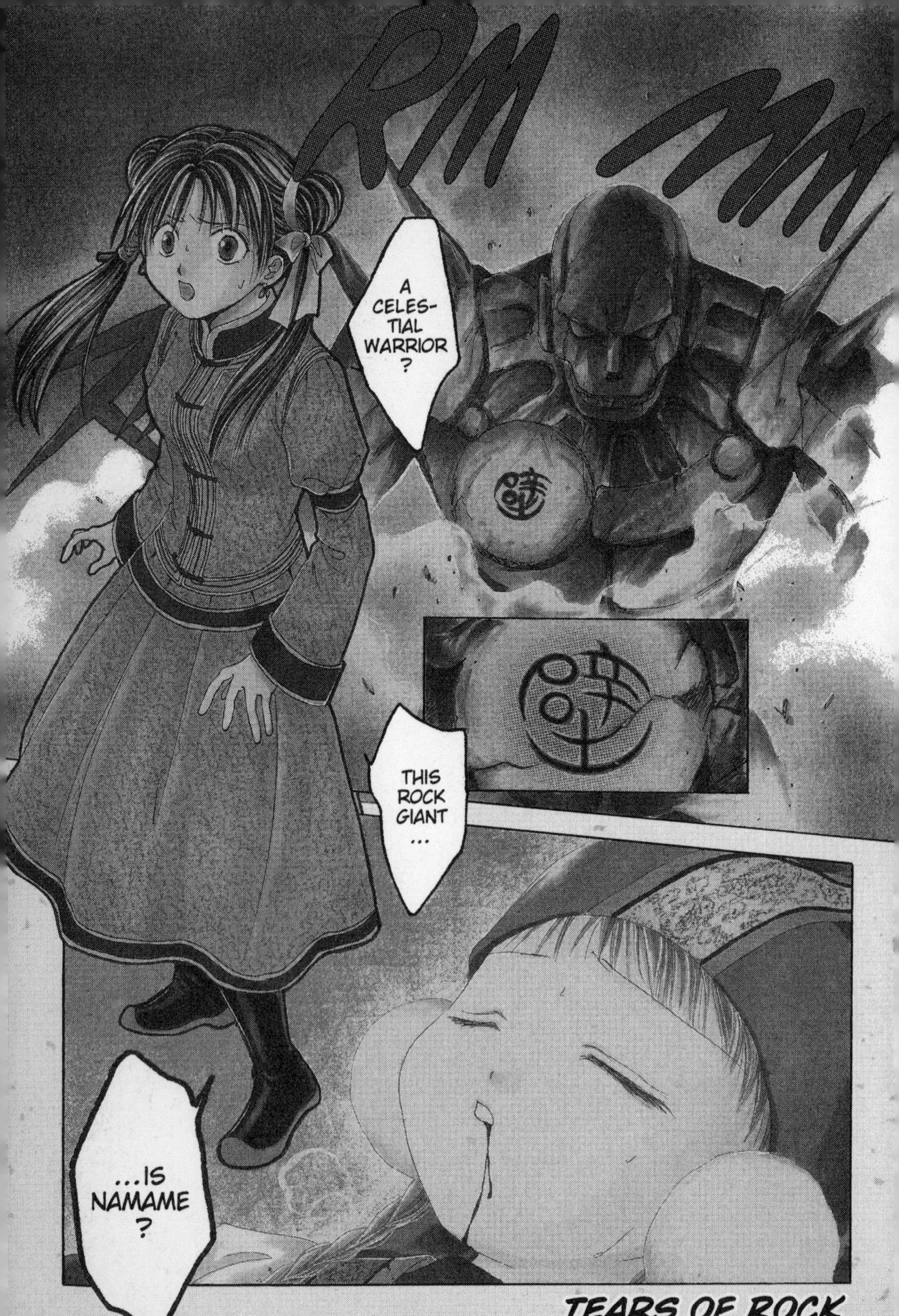
A CELES-TIAL WARRIOR?
THIS ROCK GIANT...
...IS NAMAME?

TEARS OF ROCK

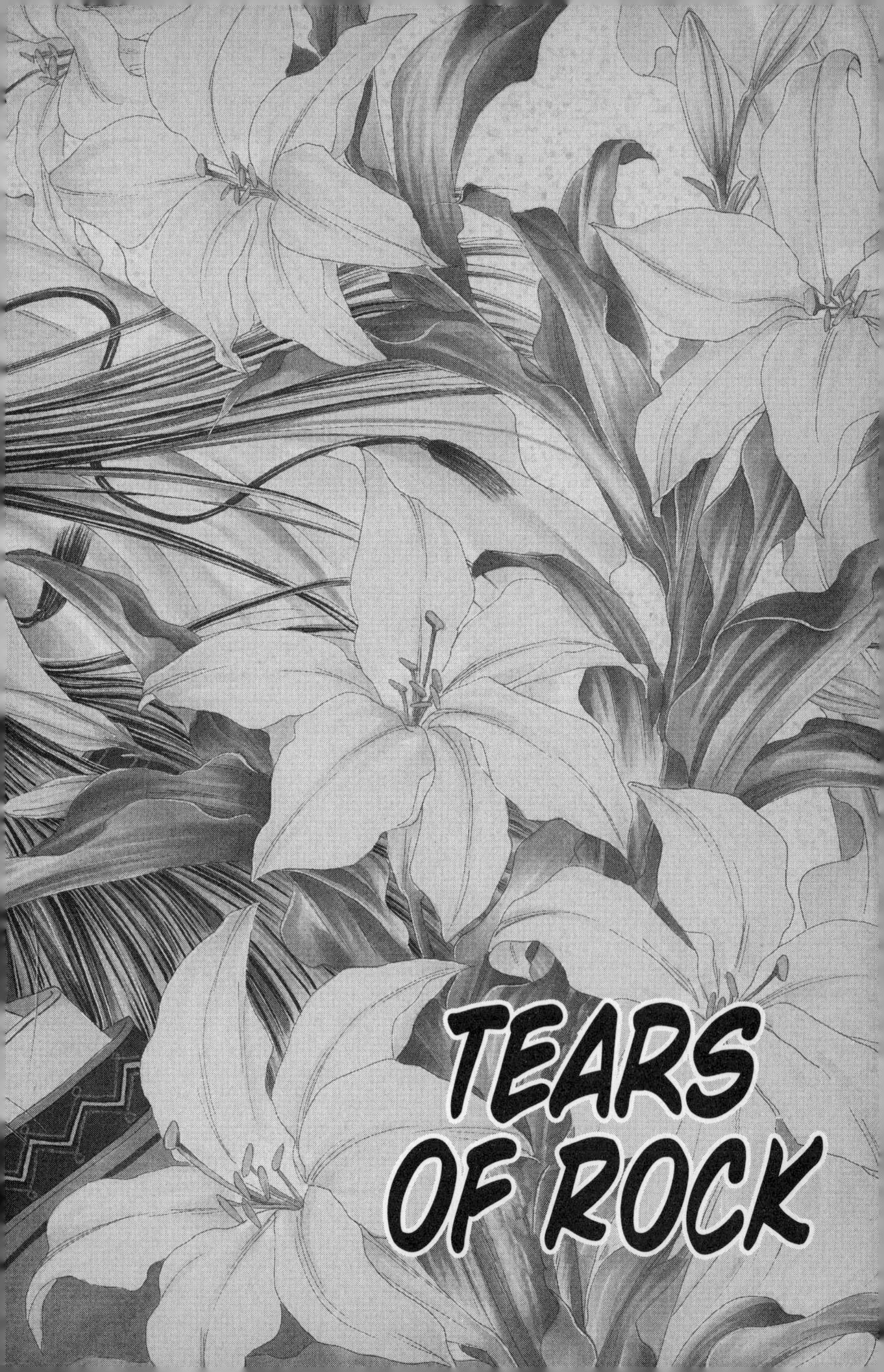
TEARS
OF ROCK

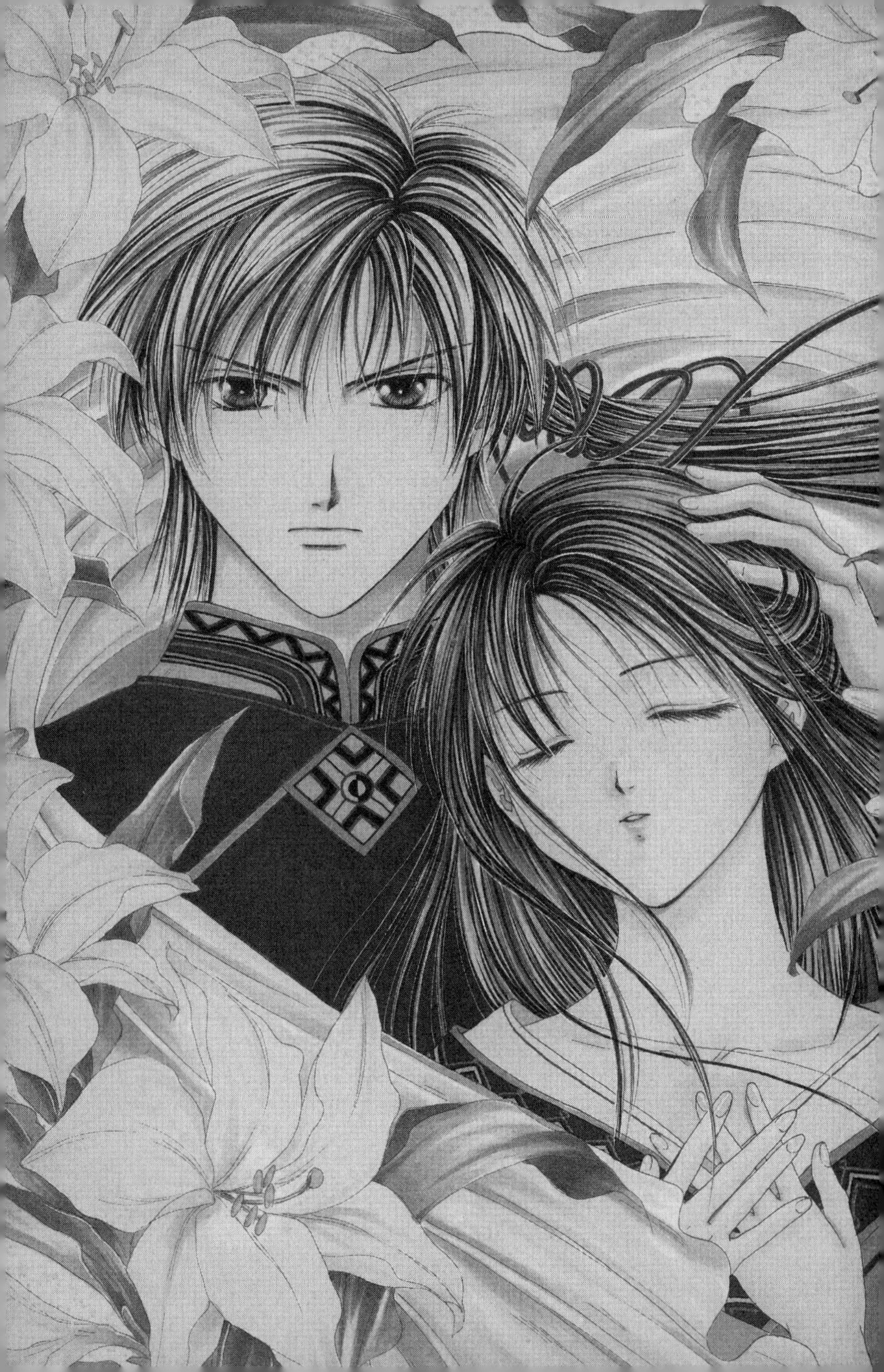

Here we are at Volume 3!! FY:GK gets published slowly, at a pace of two volumes a year. I'm sorry, but I can't go any faster. *Yuu Watase Perfect World: FY*, the magazine that publishes it, comes out every three months, and there's 90 pages of FY:GK in each issue. So, basically, I draw 30 pages a month. People have cruelly demanded that it run monthly, but then there would only be 30 pages per issue. It would be a pretty thin magazine. You want me to increase the page count? Ha ha ha... Do you want to kill me? 🗯 Sure, I'd do it if I had the time and the energy (which means I don't). I think it would kill the editors, too. Anyway, please show your support for the magazine. Issue 3 is coming out on the same day as this graphic novel, along with a drama CD. The voice actor lineup is awesome. Plus, it's comedy. A drama CD that follows the main story will come out next year. But this bonus CD will be a comedic side story. Limdo (voiced by Mr. Takahiro Sakurai) assumed this bonus CD would come out after the main CD. But the comedy will make its appearance first. I wonder what people will think of Tomite. His wild acting job will blow your mind. I drew new art for the CD, too. I'm so overworked. (But I'm always like that.) Oh, the main story CD will be sold normally in music stores.

Now then. (I'm so sleepy.) Since the story has progressed a bit, I think I'll talk a little about the characters. There isn't much space, though.

First, Takiko. She's more popular with my female readers than the previous heroine, Miaka. 😆 Drawing her kimono and hakama is tough work. Picking the colors is especially tricky. What colors did they wear in the Taisho era? I looked up books like *How Kimono Were Worn Long Ago* and photographs and paintings of kimono from that era. The way they wore the hakama was slightly different, too, so I've been studying photographs from that time period (which are black and white and blurry, of course ♪). Oh, well...so what if I end up being wrong?

The famous arrow-pattern kimono was worn only from the Meiji to the early Taisho eras, so I won't use it for Takiko.

I'm also looking at catalogues of traditional dress, and the models strike these unbelievably exaggerated poses. It's good in a way—I get ideas for action shots.

The fact that Takiko can fight with a naginata has been well received. Girls sure like strong, fighting women. She's always so tense, so I hope she'll get to relax soon... 💢

Readers are already nervous about what happens to her at the end. Please be patient. I like Takiko, too. Or maybe girls from that era in general appeal to me. They were hard-working and modest, and they really were "genteel young ladies." Oh, the scene with the "Song of the Gondola" in chapter 6 was also well received. I wanted to do that scene so much—I wanted to have Takiko sing that song. I have two renditions on CD and I like both. It's a pretty famous song. When I read the lyrics, I knew I had to get Takiko to sing it! I really love it.

Please sing it, Miss Satsuki Yukino!*

Next, Limdo/Uruki. He's 16 years old. He first appeared as a girl, so everyone naturally figured "she" was Uruki, the warrior with the character for "woman"! Nobody thought he might be a guy, but he's extremely popular, so that's good. I figured having him turn female would be a good play on his name. Ten years ago, when I mapped out all the Celestial Warriors, I thought of him as a regular Celestial Warrior, not a love interest.

My idea back then was that he'd also be a hermaphrodite. That didn't make for a good plot, so I merely split him into two sexes. I also thought it would be interesting to give him a handicap—that he has to turn into a woman to use his powers. But I never expected him to be so well received!

I'll see you next time in Volume 4!

Two volumes a year is really tough! ♪ Don't forget, everyone!!! ☺

*Voice actress who plays Takiko in the FY:GK drama CDs.

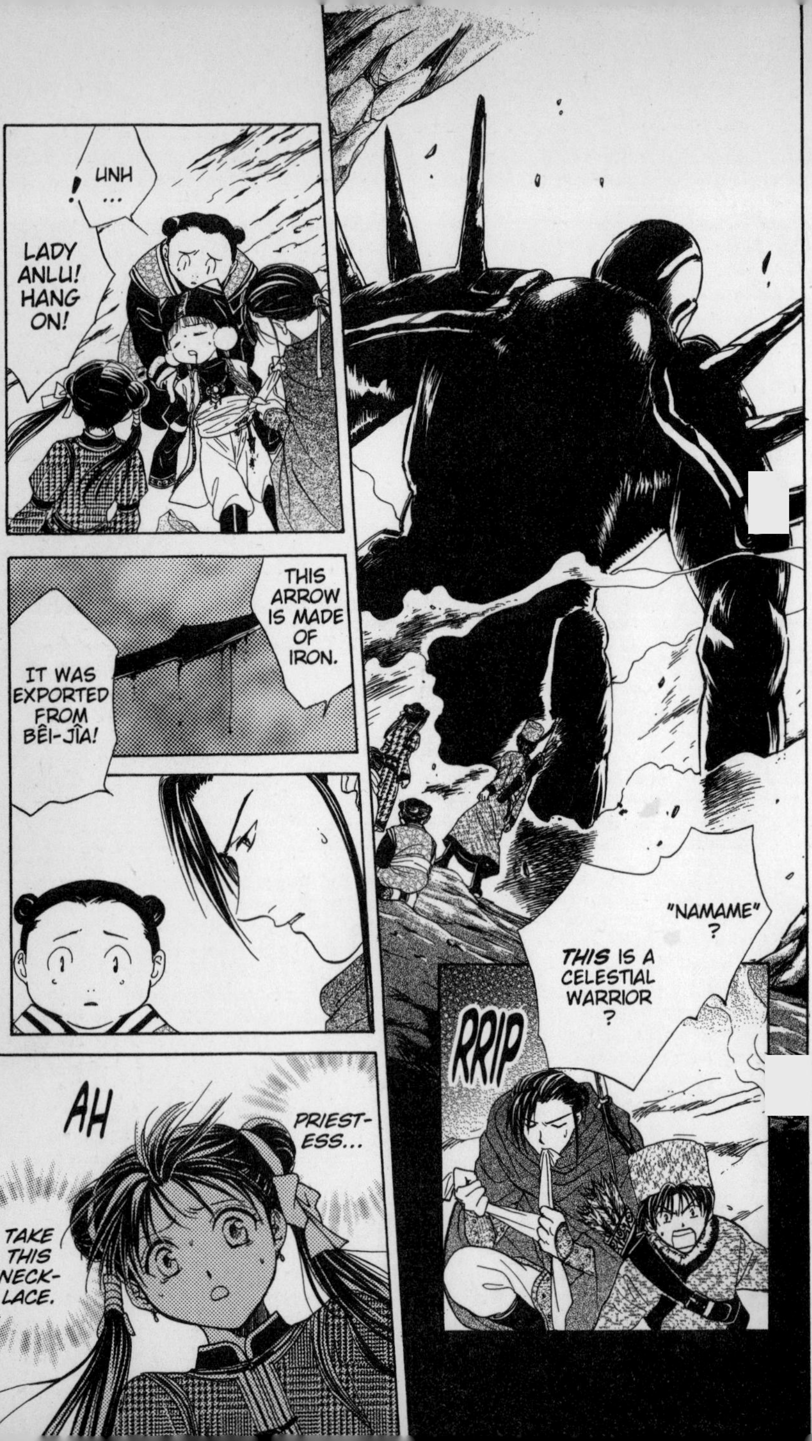
"NAMAME"?
THIS IS A CELESTIAL WARRIOR?
RRIP
UNH...
LADY ANLU! HANG ON!
THIS ARROW IS MADE OF IRON.
IT WAS EXPORTED FROM BÊI-JÌA!
PRIEST-ESS...
AH
TAKE THIS NECK-LACE.

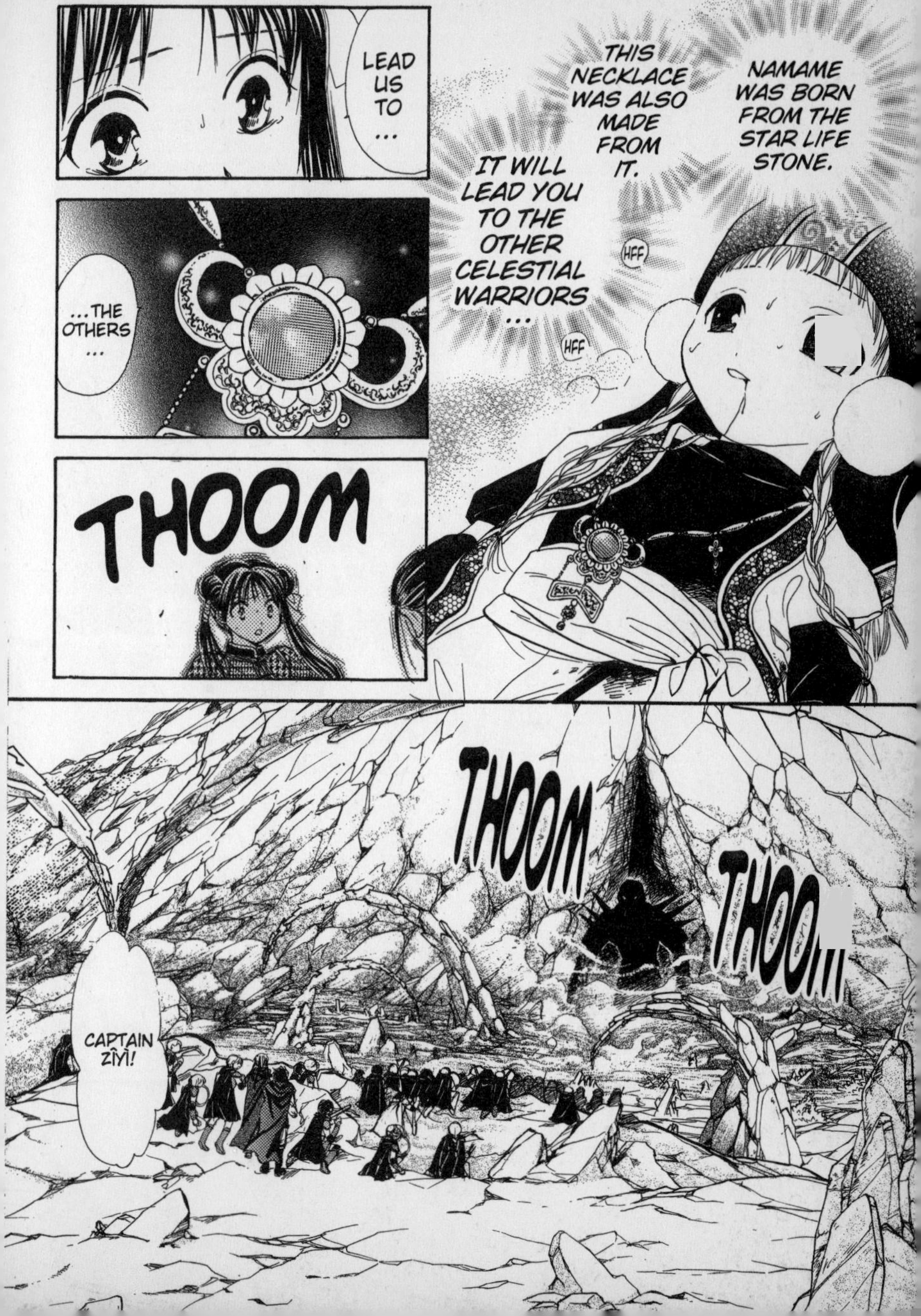
NAMAME WAS BORN FROM THE STAR LIFE STONE.
THIS NECKLACE WAS ALSO MADE FROM IT.
IT WILL LEAD YOU TO THE OTHER CELESTIAL WARRIORS ...
HFF
HFF
LEAD US TO ...
...THE OTHERS ...
THOOM
THOOM
THOO
CAPTAIN ZÎYÎ!

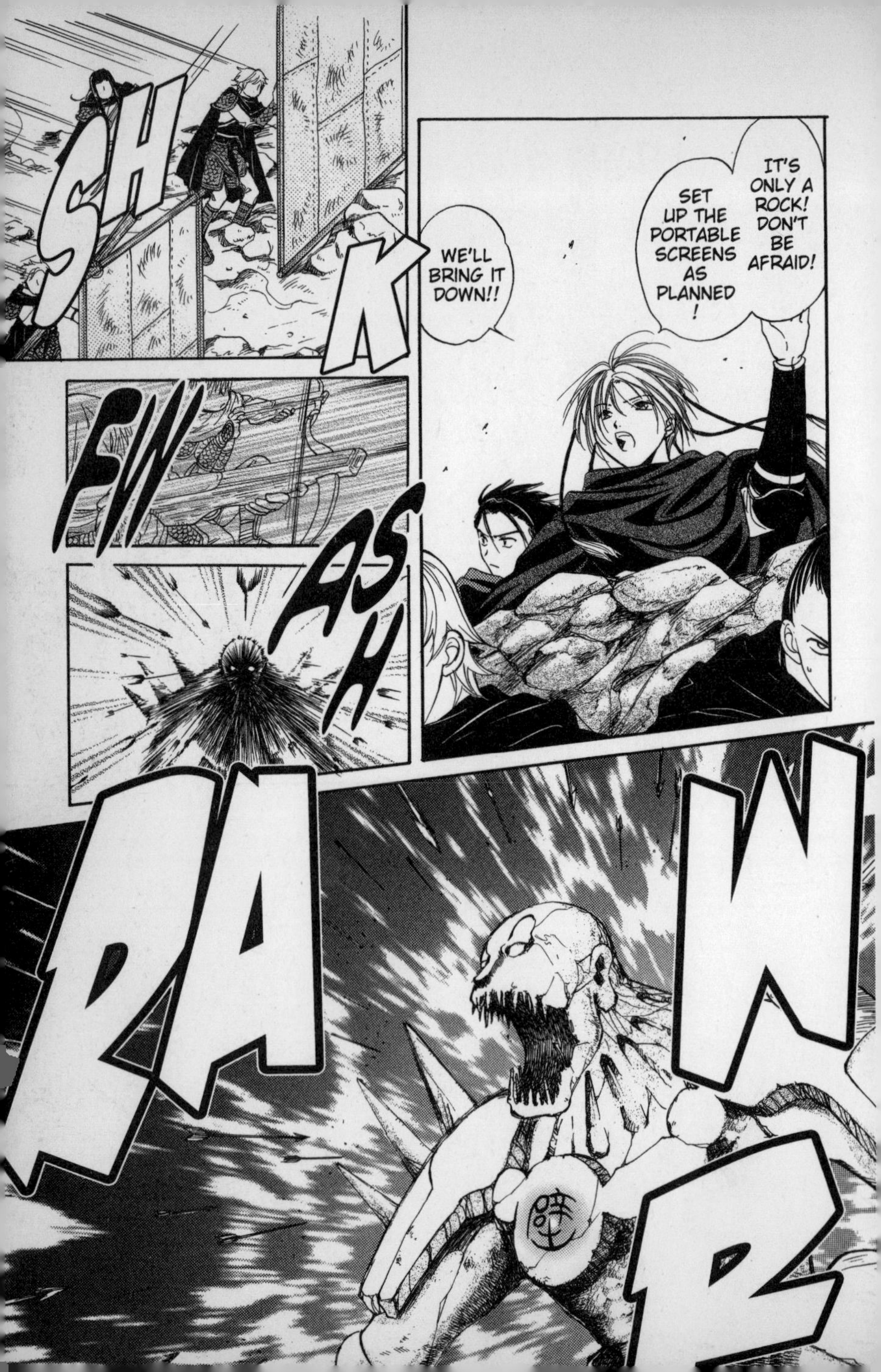
IT'S ONLY A ROCK! DON'T BE AFRAID!
SET UP THE PORTABLE SCREENS AS PLANNED!
WE'LL BRING IT DOWN!!
SHK
FWASH

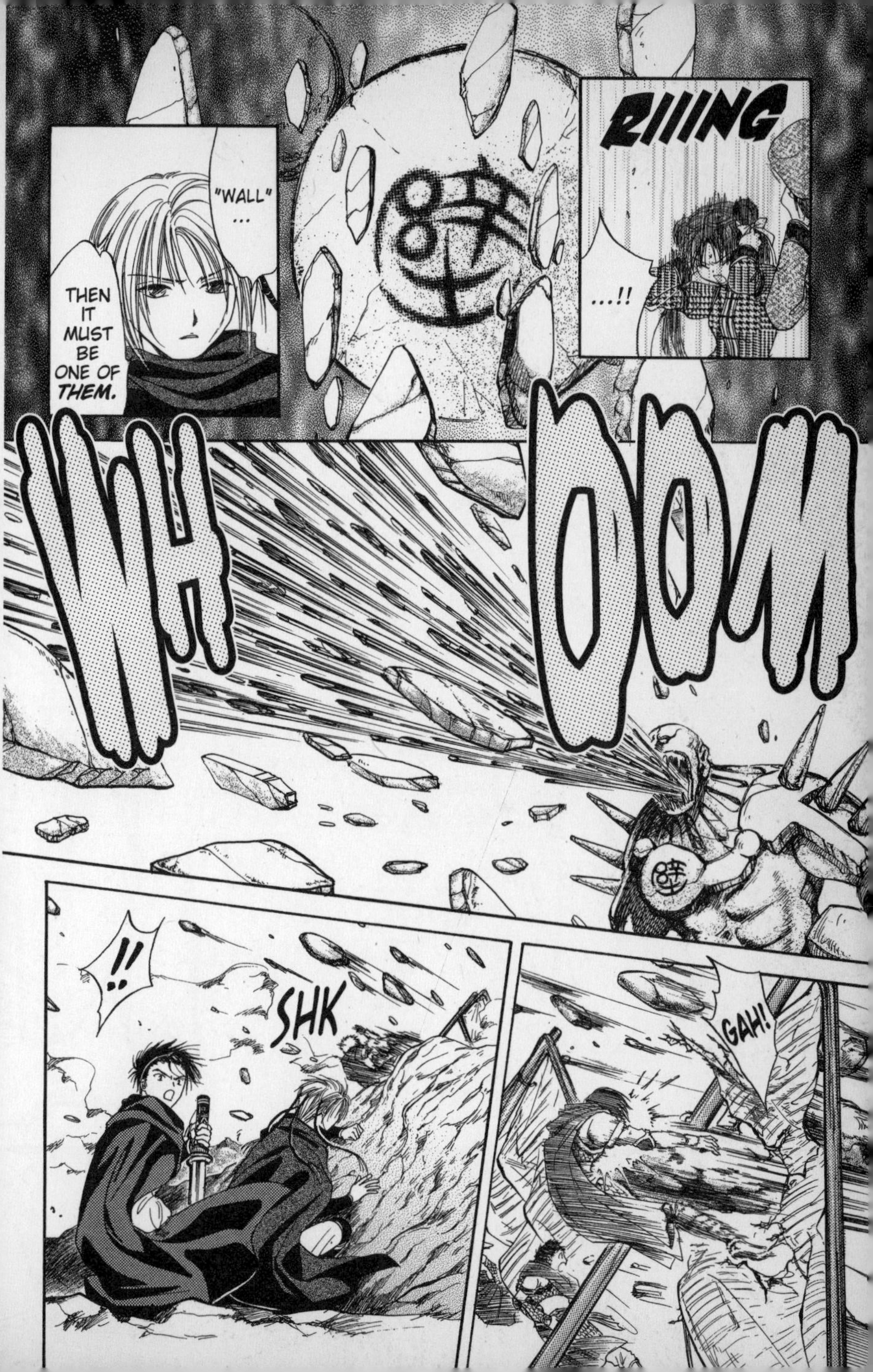
RIIING
...!!
"WALL" ...
THEN IT MUST BE ONE OF THEM.
WHOOM
GAH!
!!
SHK

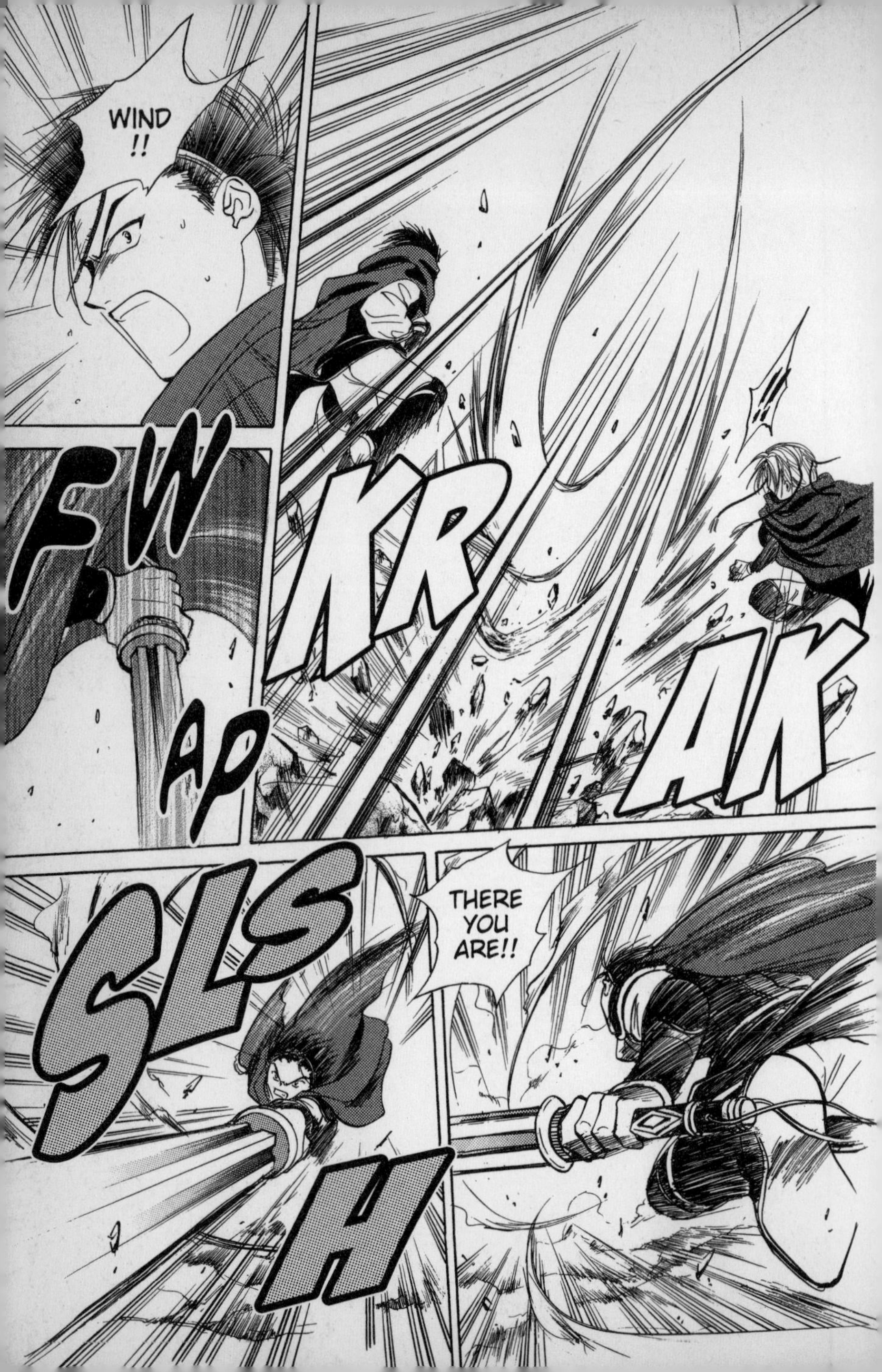
KRAK
!!
WIND !!
FWAP
THERE YOU ARE!!
SLSH

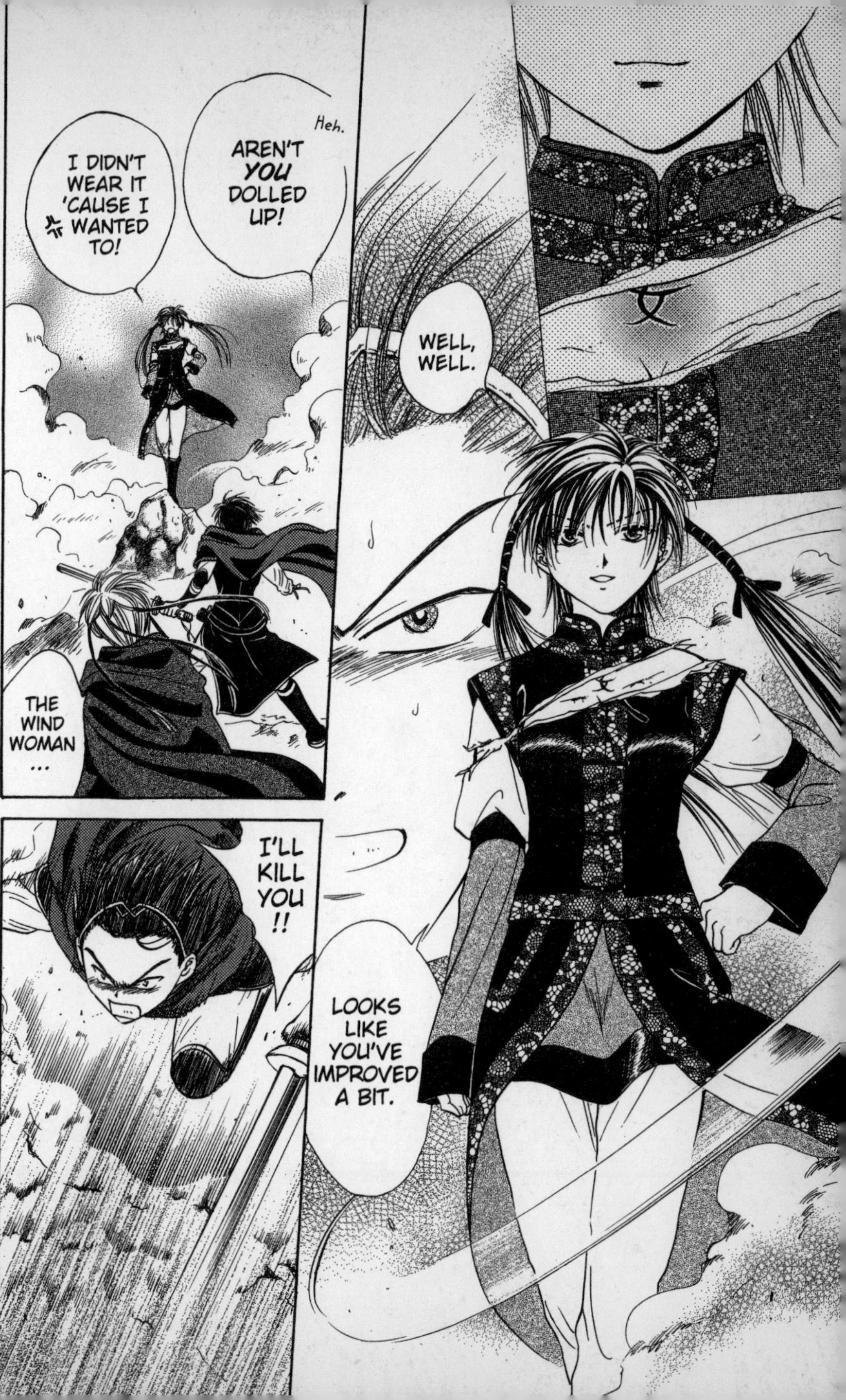

WELL, WELL.
...
LOOKS LIKE YOU'VE IMPROVED A BIT.
Heh.
AREN'T *YOU* DOLLED UP!
I DIDN'T WEAR IT 'CAUSE I WANTED TO!
THE WIND WOMAN ...
I'LL KILL YOU !!

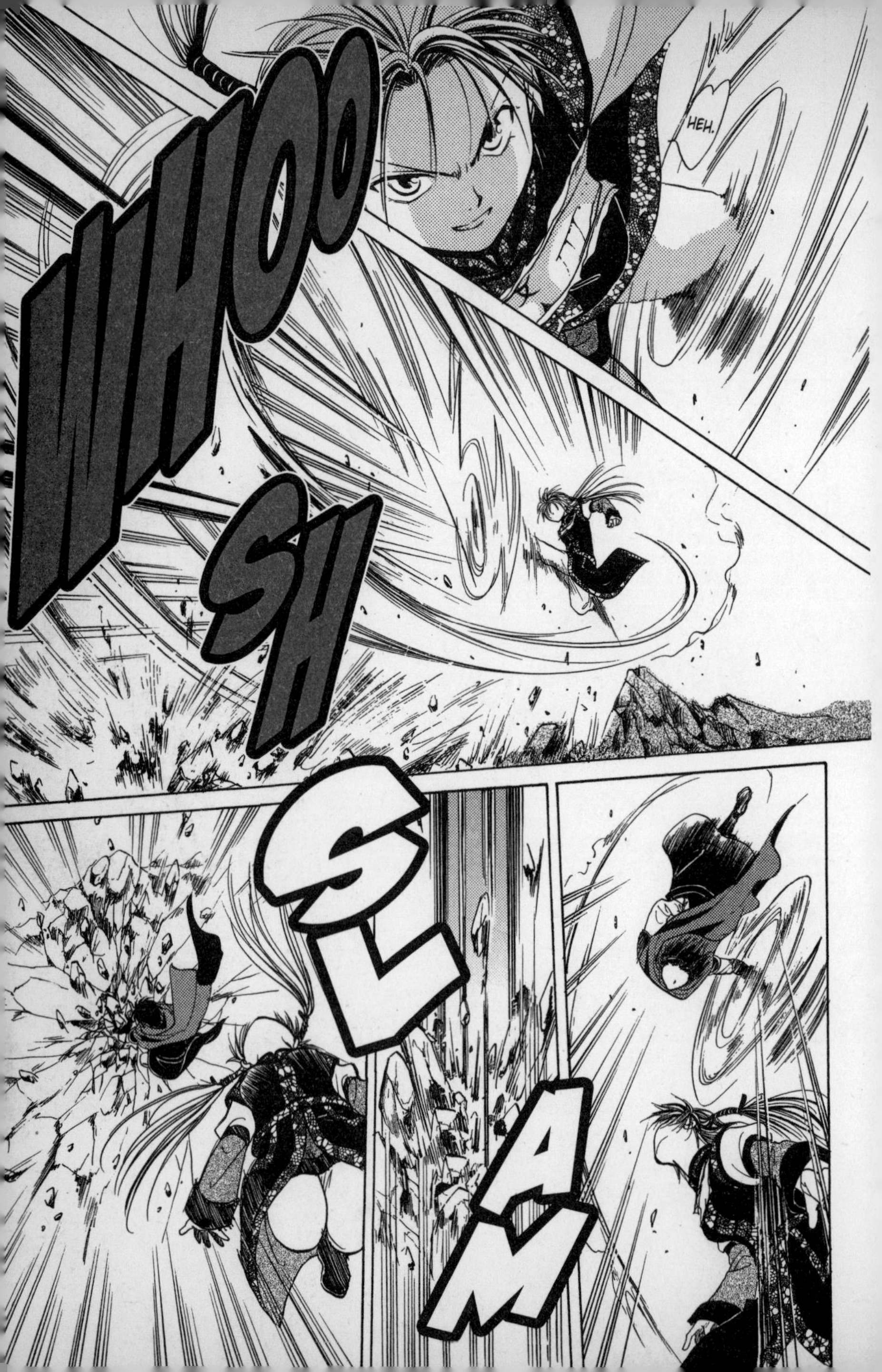
HEH.
WHOOSH
SLAM

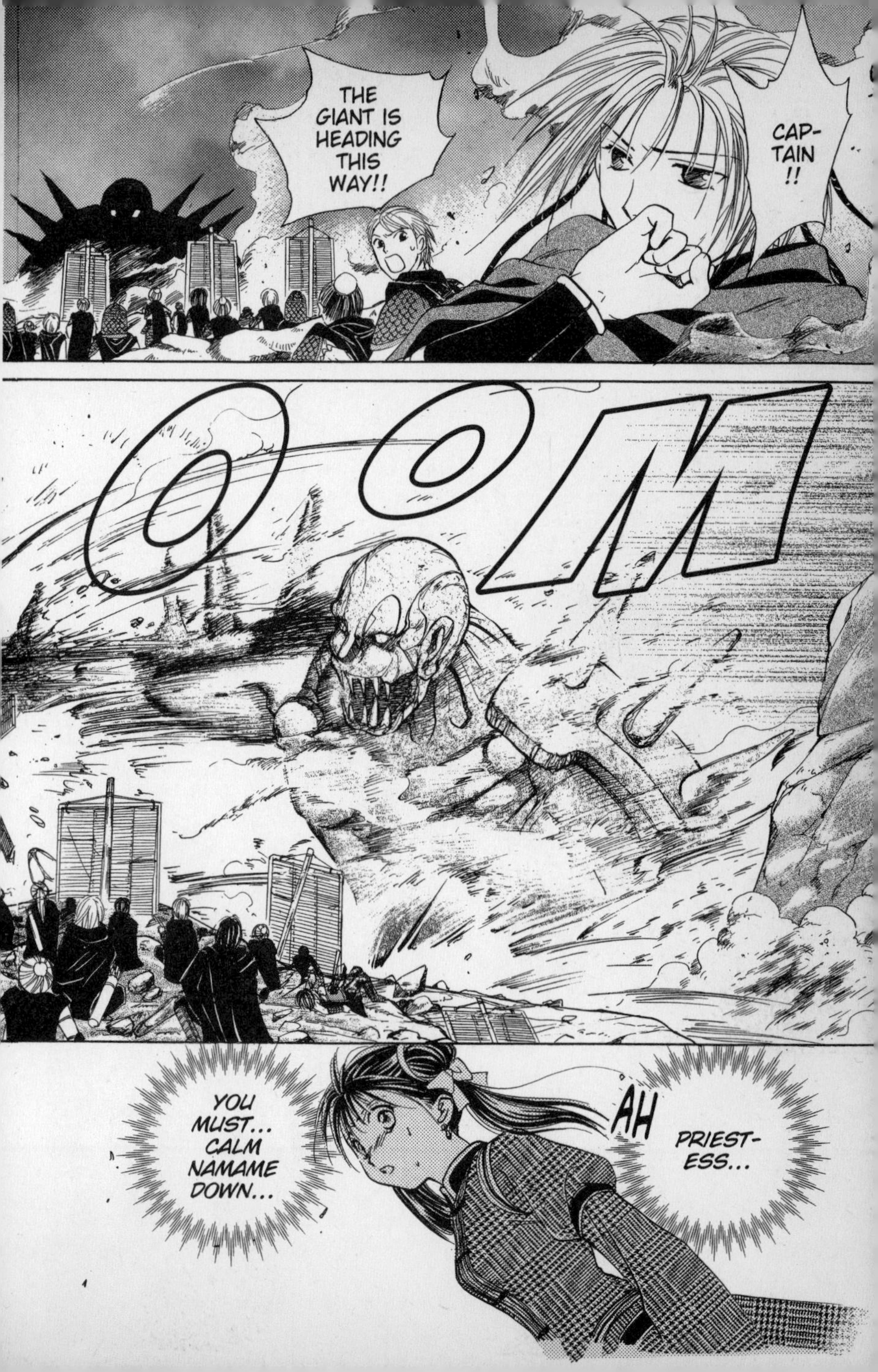
CAP-TAIN!!
THE GIANT IS HEADING THIS WAY!!
OOM
AH
PRIEST-ESS...
YOU MUST... CALM NAMAME DOWN...

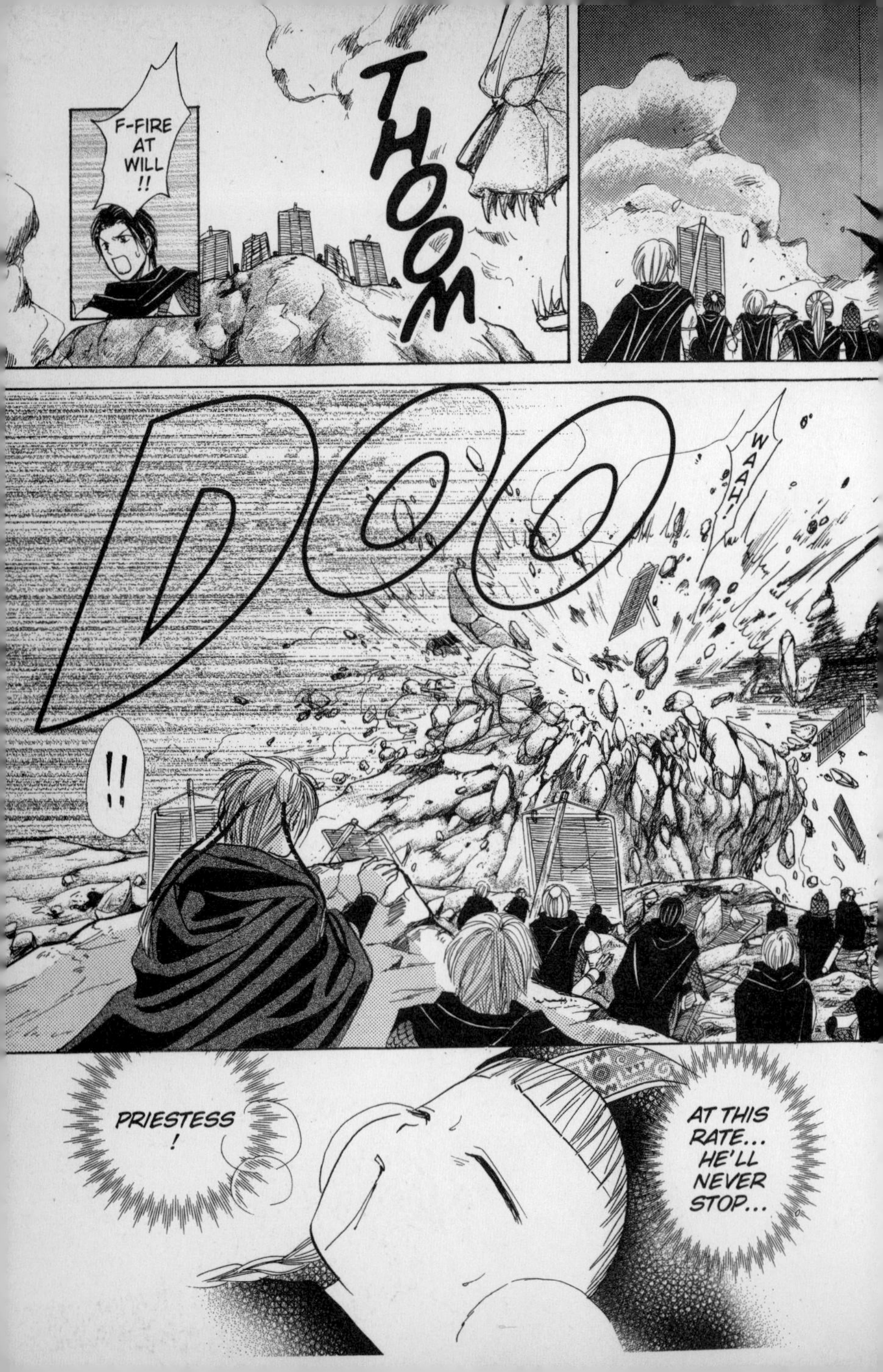
THOOM
F-FIRE AT WILL!!
WAAH!
DOOO
!!
AT THIS RATE... HE'LL NEVER STOP...
PRIESTESS!

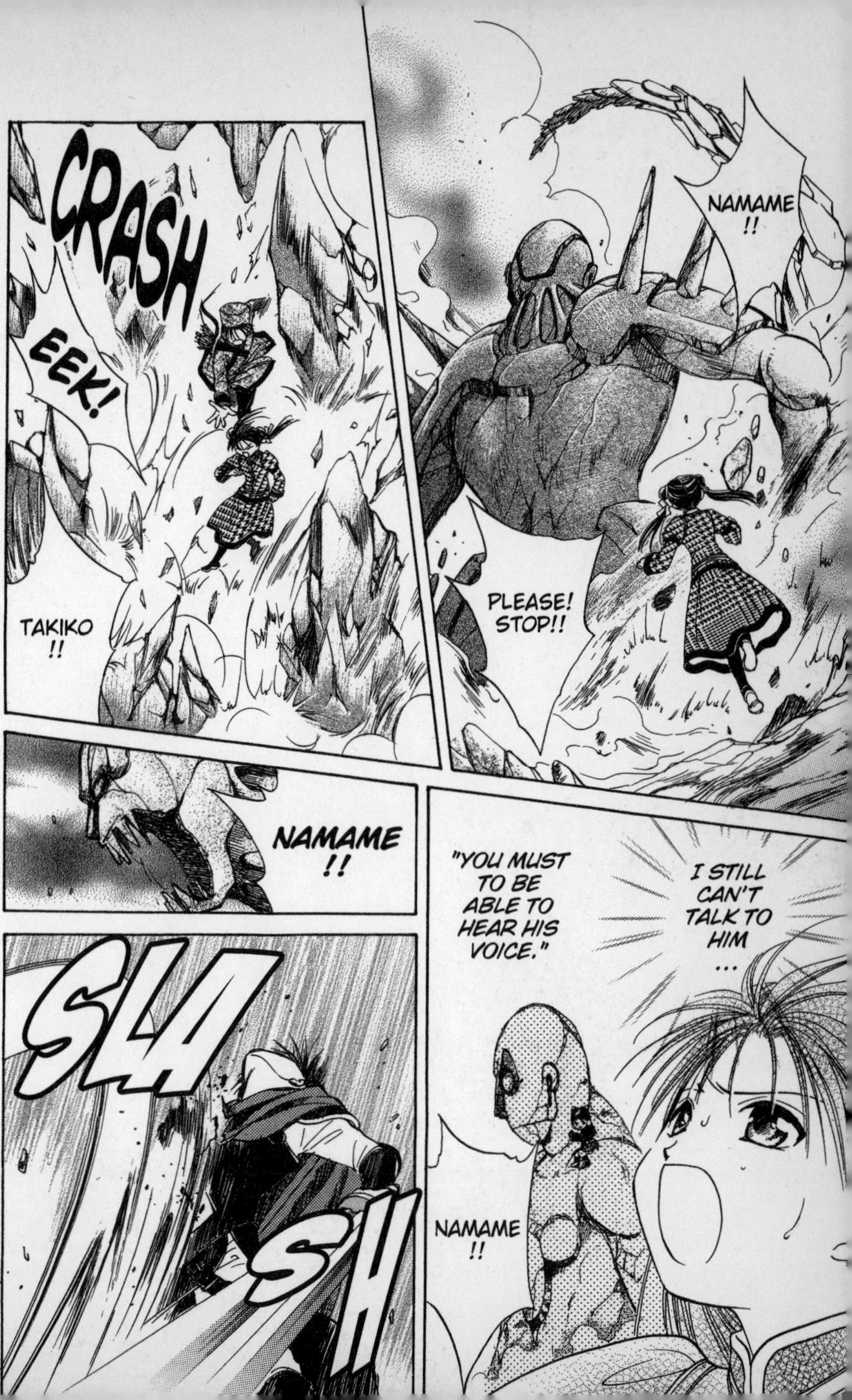
NAMAME !!
PLEASE! STOP!!
CRASH
EEK!
TAKIKO !!
I STILL CAN'T TALK TO HIM ...
"YOU MUST TO BE ABLE TO HEAR HIS VOICE."
NAMAME !!
NAMAME !!
SHA
SH

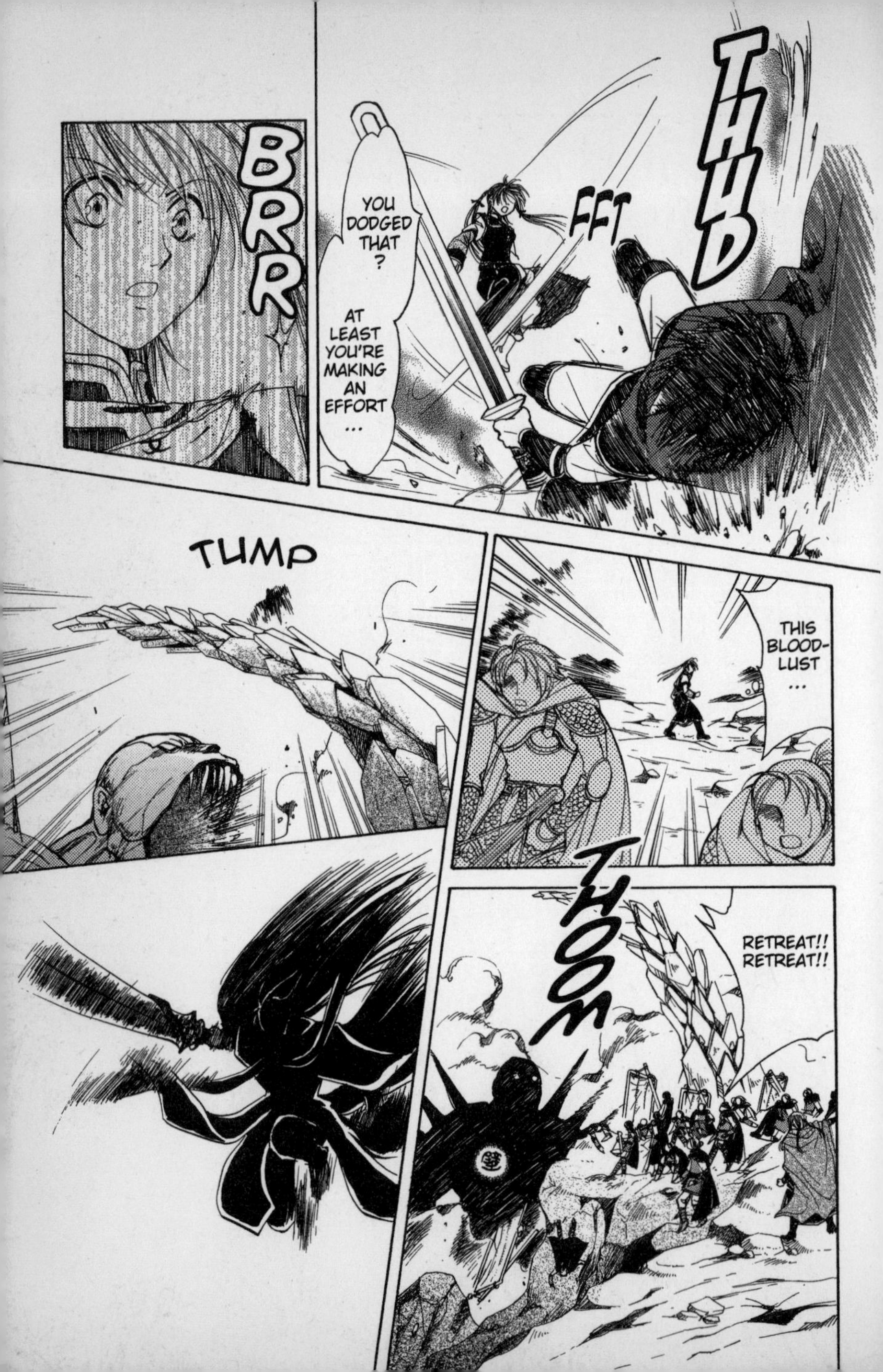
THUD
FFT
YOU DODGED THAT?
AT LEAST YOU'RE MAKING AN EFFORT...
BRR
THIS BLOOD-LUST...
TUMP
THOOM
RETREAT!! RETREAT!!

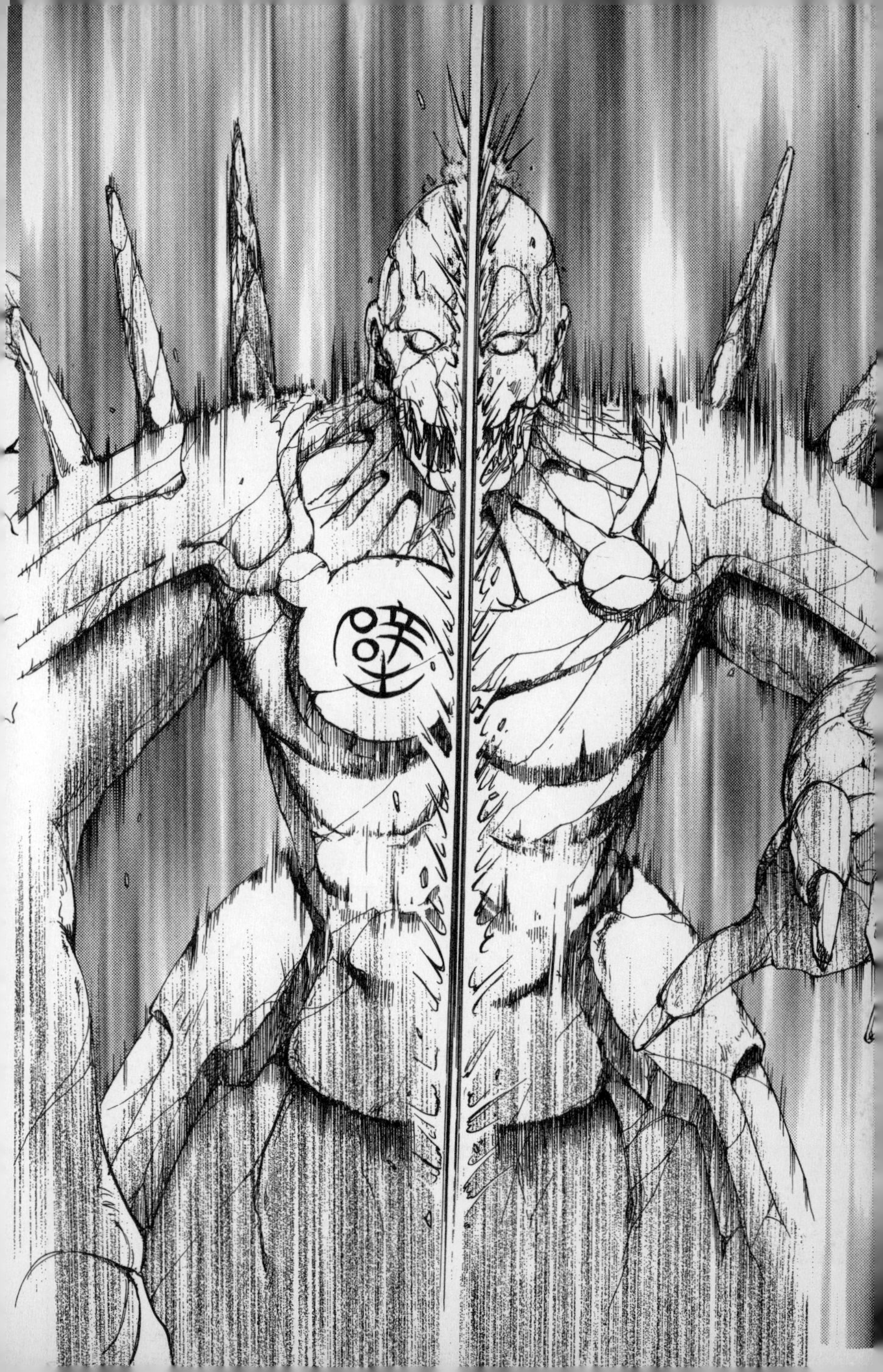

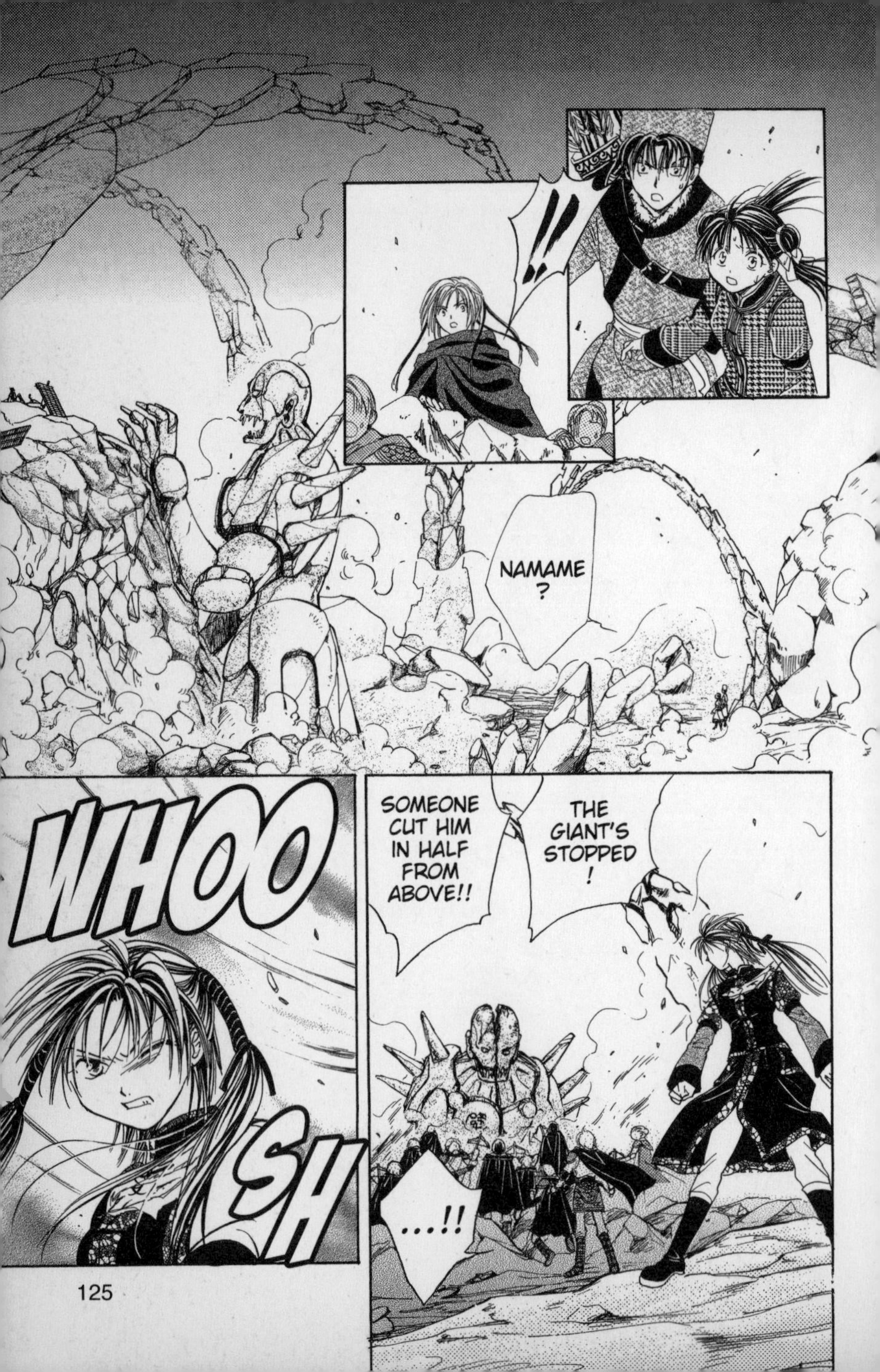
!!
NAMAME ?
THE GIANT'S STOPPED !
SOMEONE CUT HIM IN HALF FROM ABOVE!!
...!!
WHOOSH

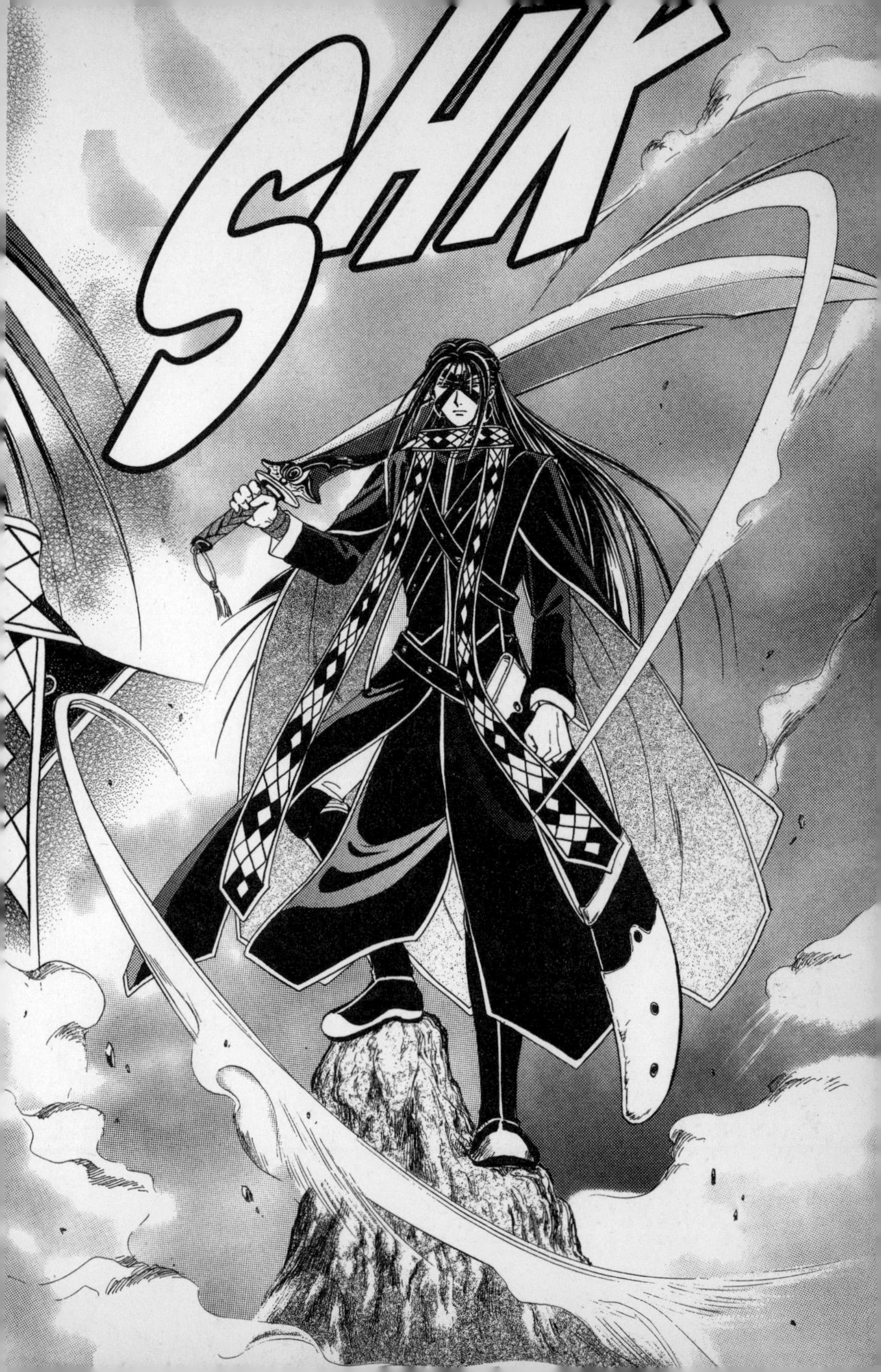
SHK

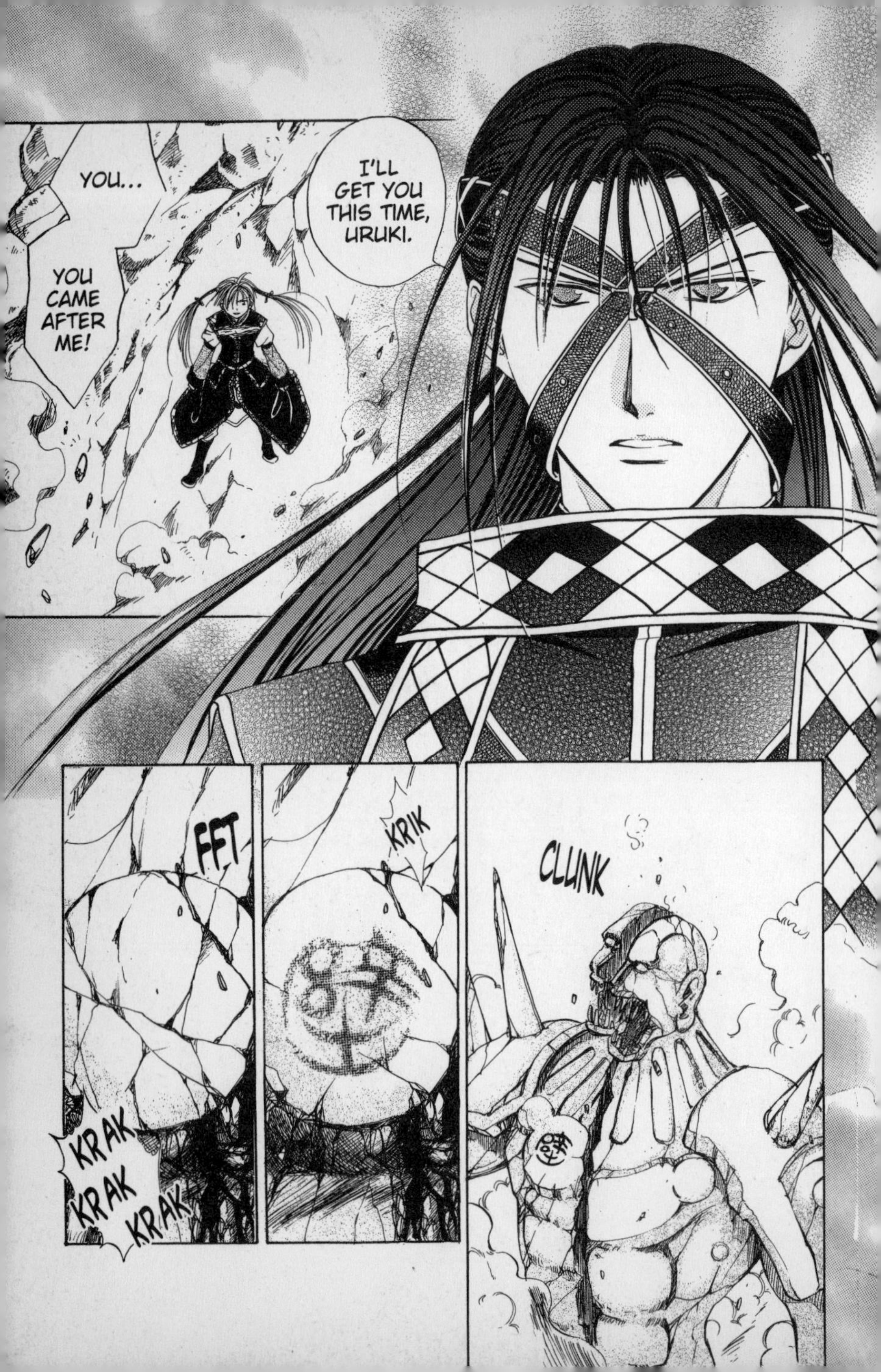
I'LL GET YOU THIS TIME, URUKI.
YOU...
YOU CAME AFTER ME!
CLUNK
KRIK
FFT
KRAK KRAK KRAK

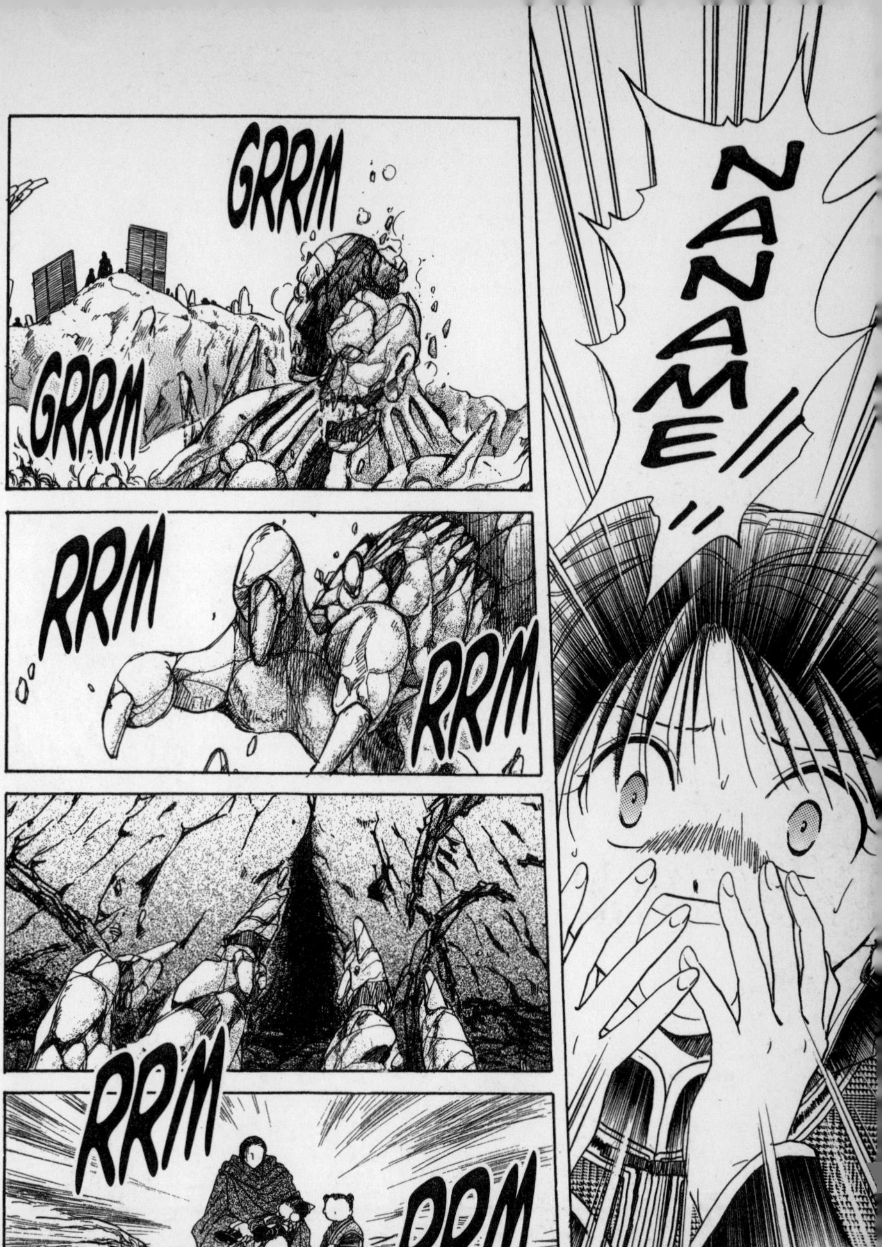
NANAME!!
GRRM
GRRM
RRM
RRM
RRM
RRM
RRM

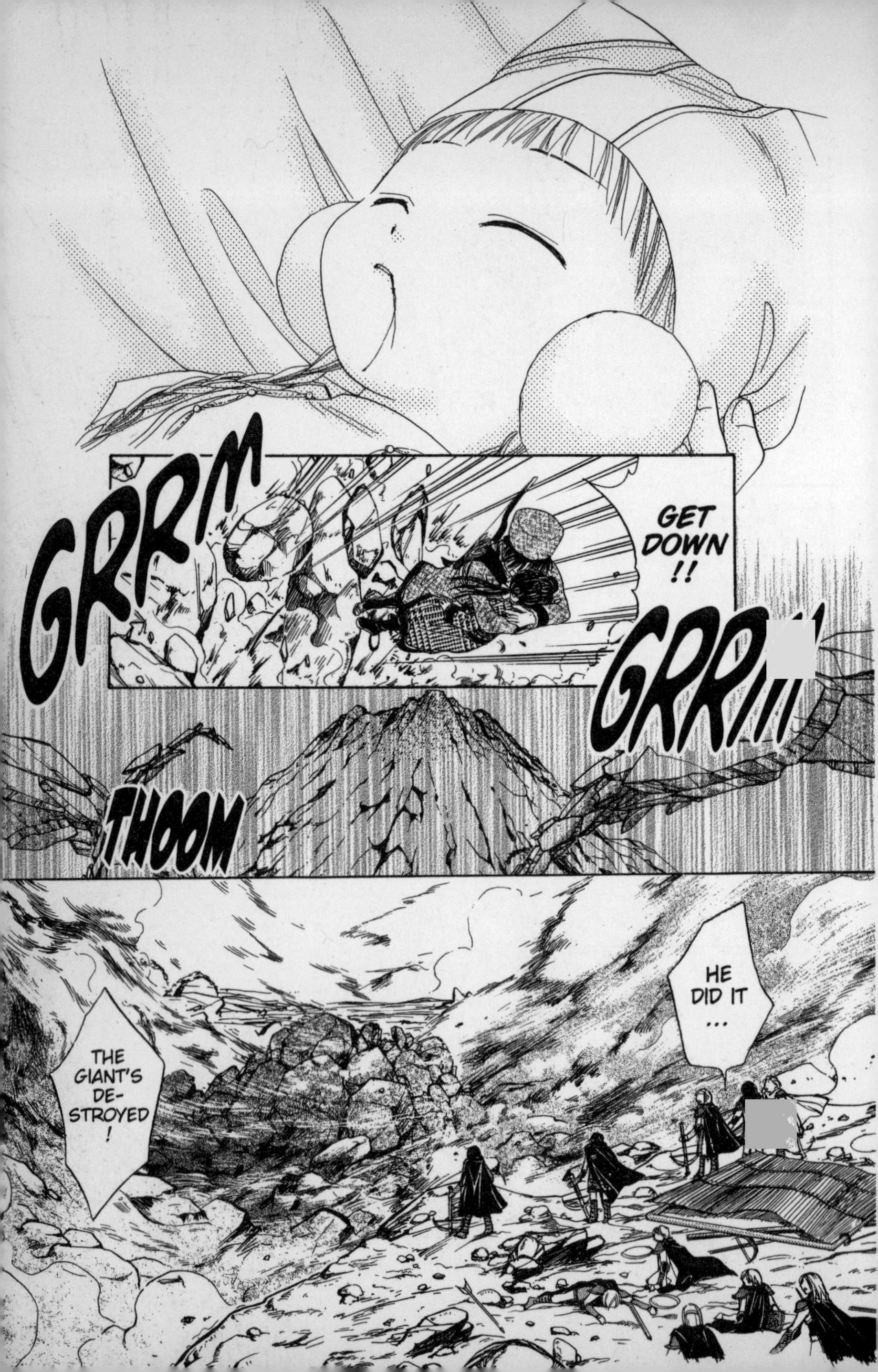
GET DOWN !!
GRR
GRRM
THOOM
HE DID IT ...
THE GIANT'S DE- STROYED !

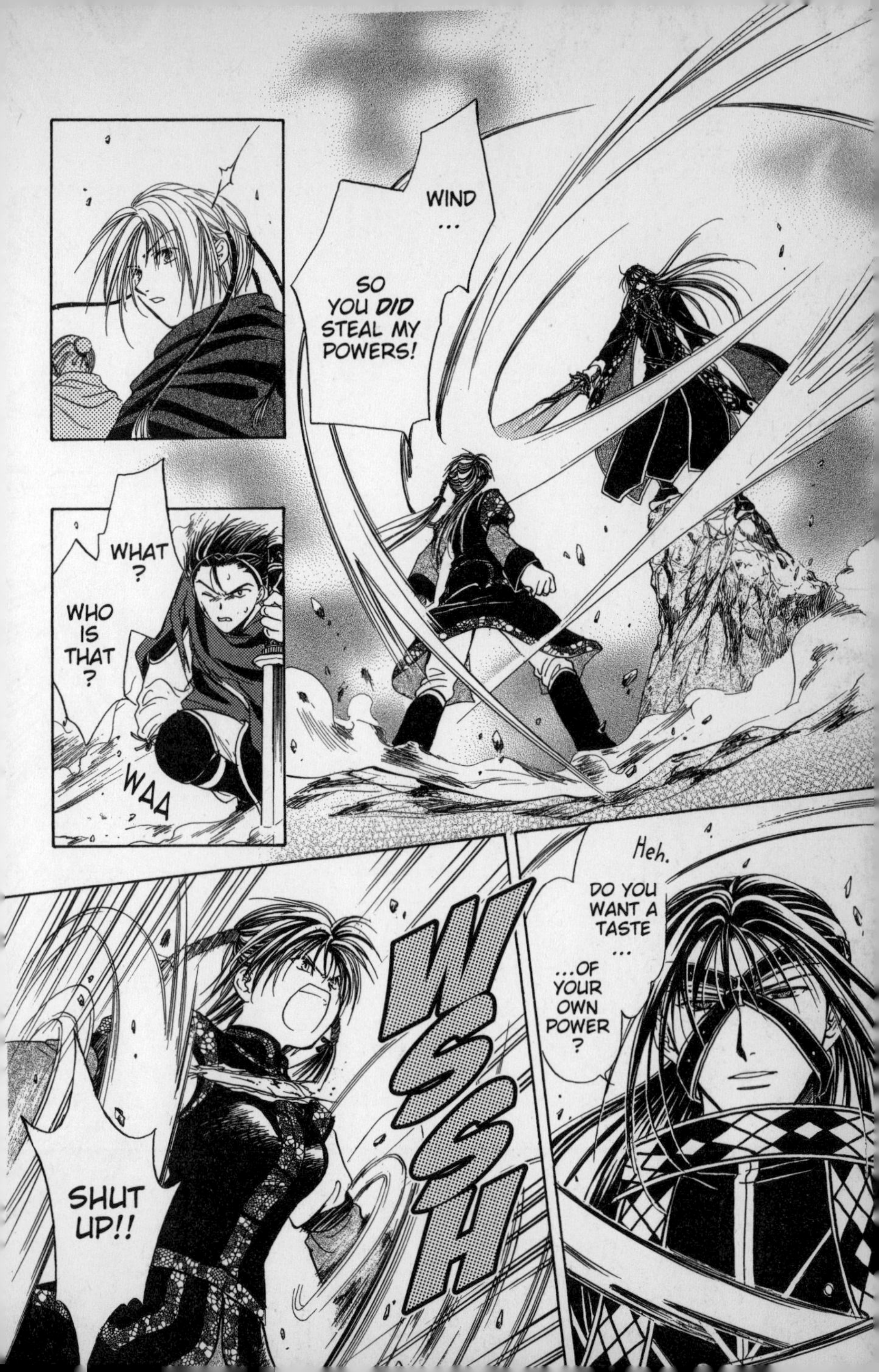
WIND ...
SO YOU *DID* STEAL MY POWERS!
WHAT?
WHO IS THAT?
WAA
Heh.
DO YOU WANT A TASTE ...
...OF YOUR OWN POWER?
WSSH
SHUT UP!!

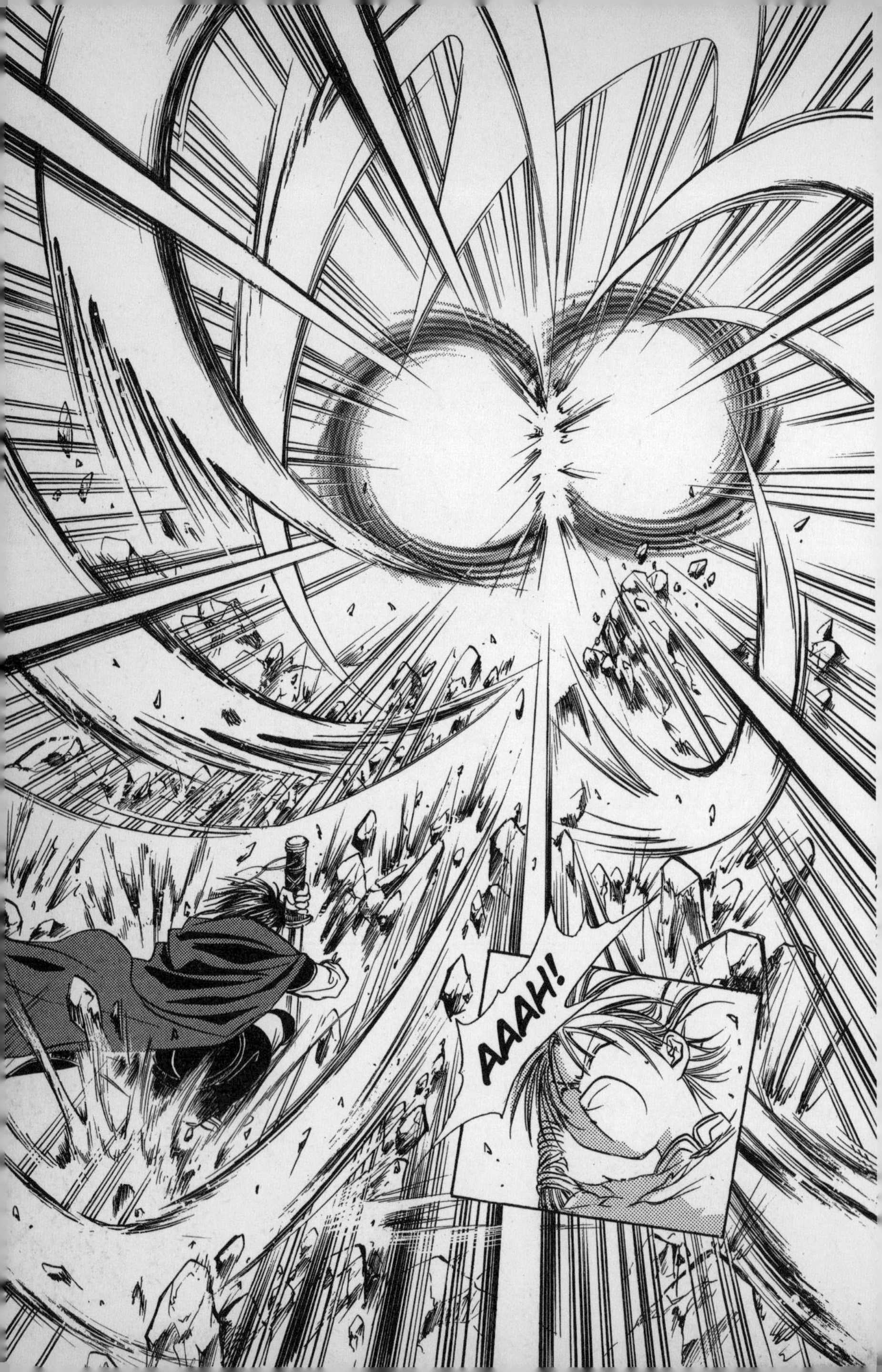
AAAH!

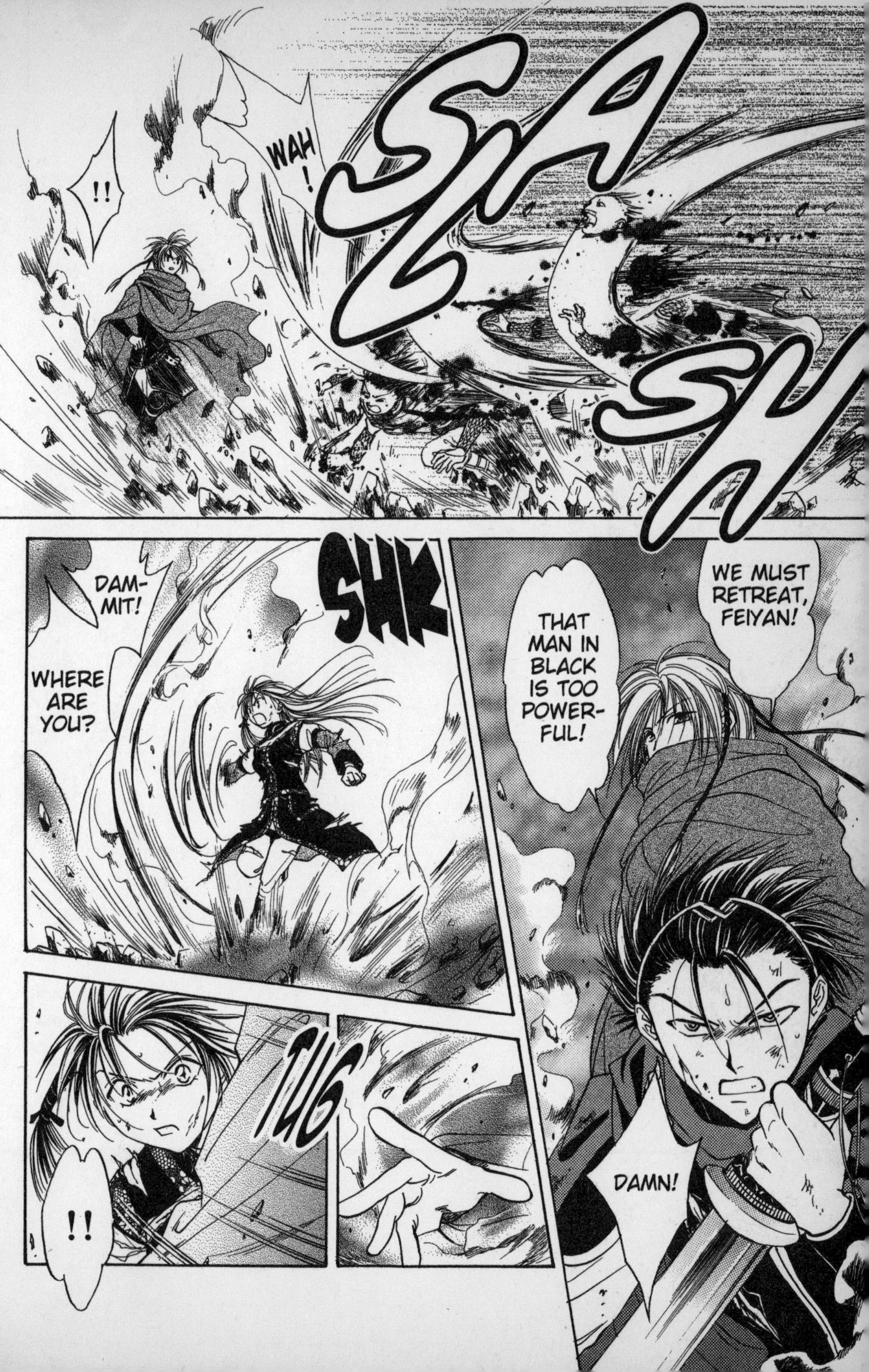
SASH
WAH!
!!
WE MUST RETREAT, FEIYAN!
THAT MAN IN BLACK IS TOO POWERFUL!
DAMN!
SHK
DAM-MIT!
WHERE ARE YOU?
TUG
!!

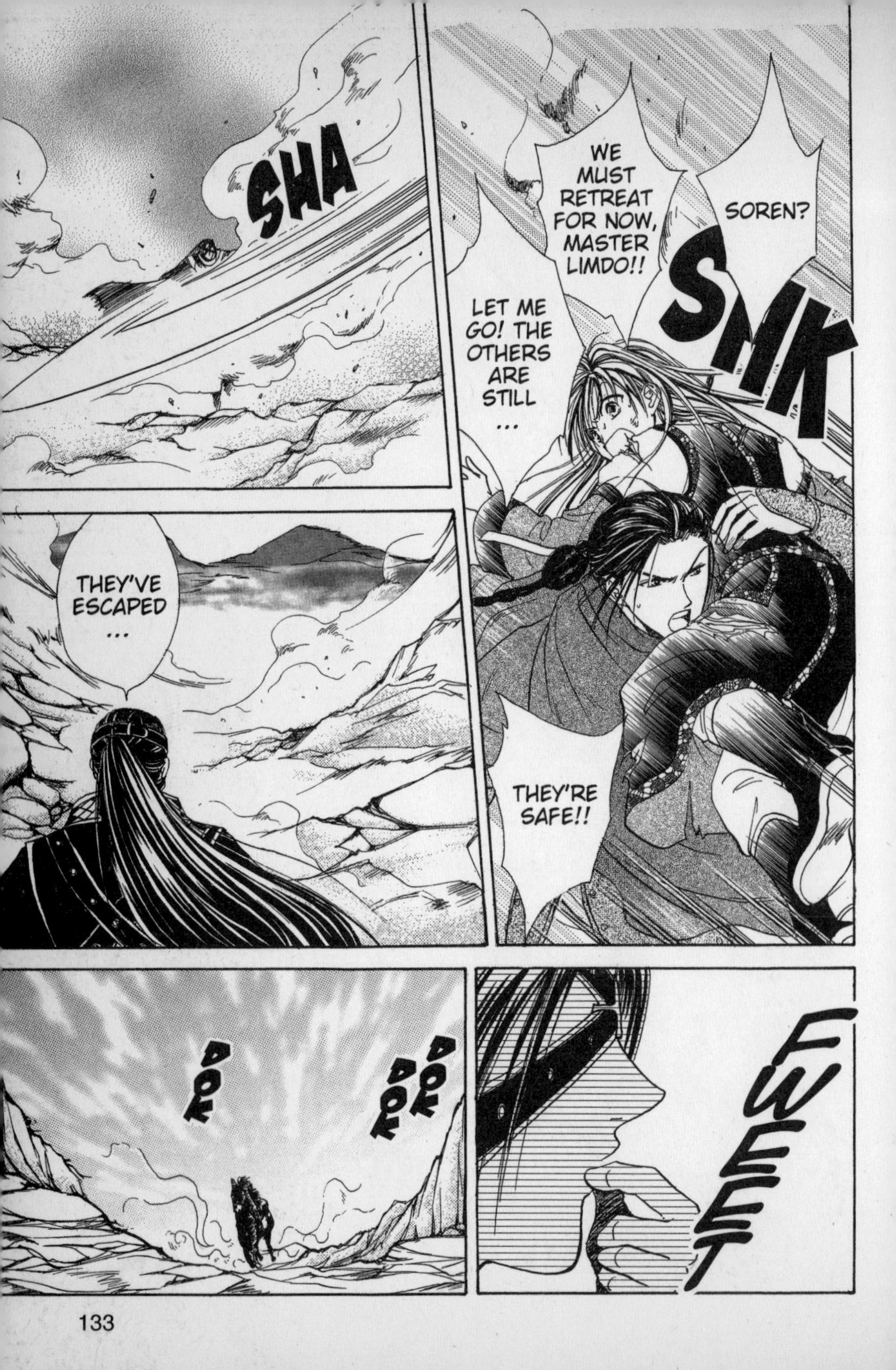
SOREN?
SMK
WE MUST RETREAT FOR NOW, MASTER LIMDO!!
LET ME GO! THE OTHERS ARE STILL ...
THEY'RE SAFE!!
SHA
THEY'VE ESCAPED ...
FWEET
DOK DOK
DOK DOK

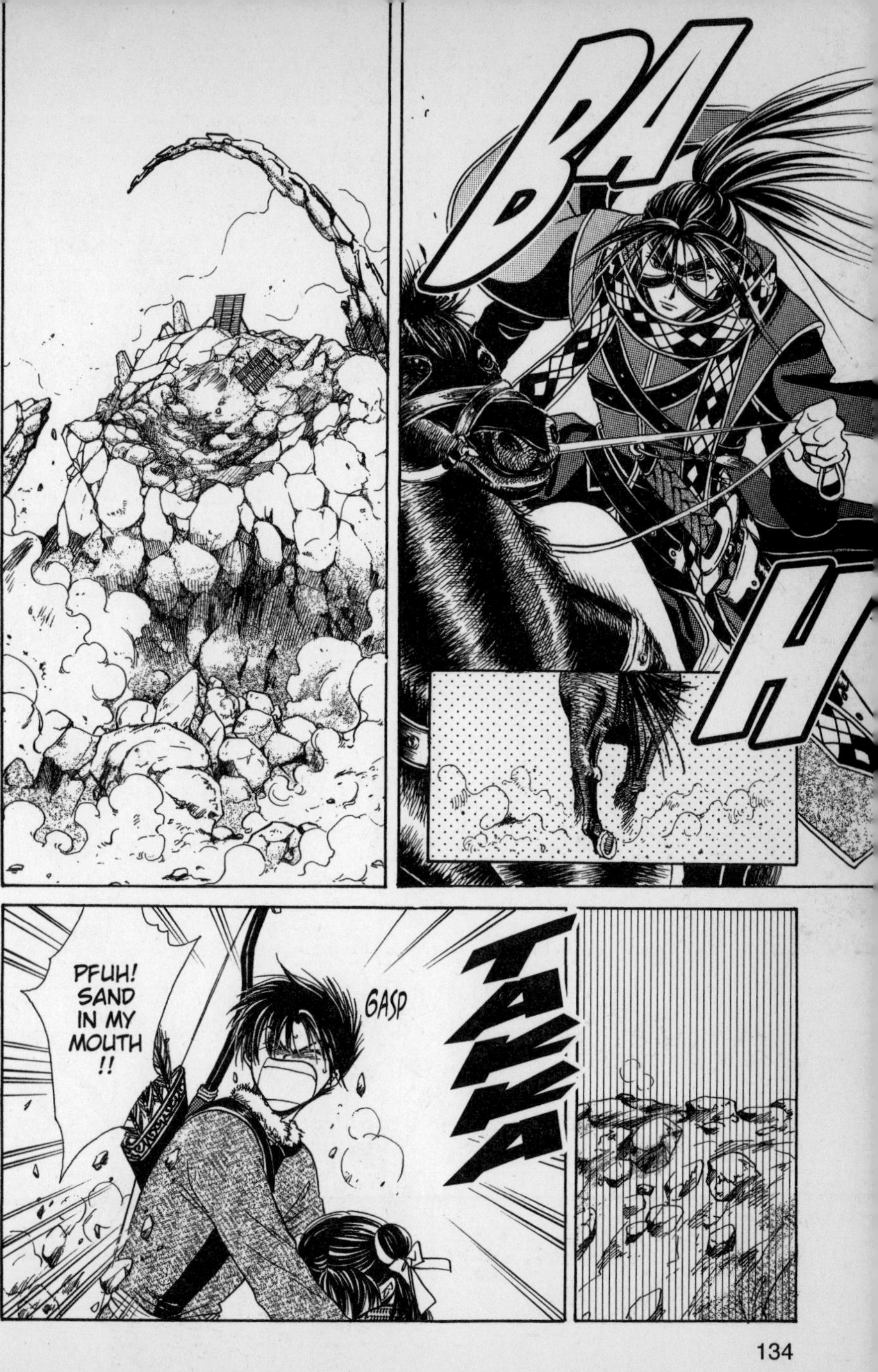
BA-H
GASP
PFUH! SAND IN MY MOUTH !!

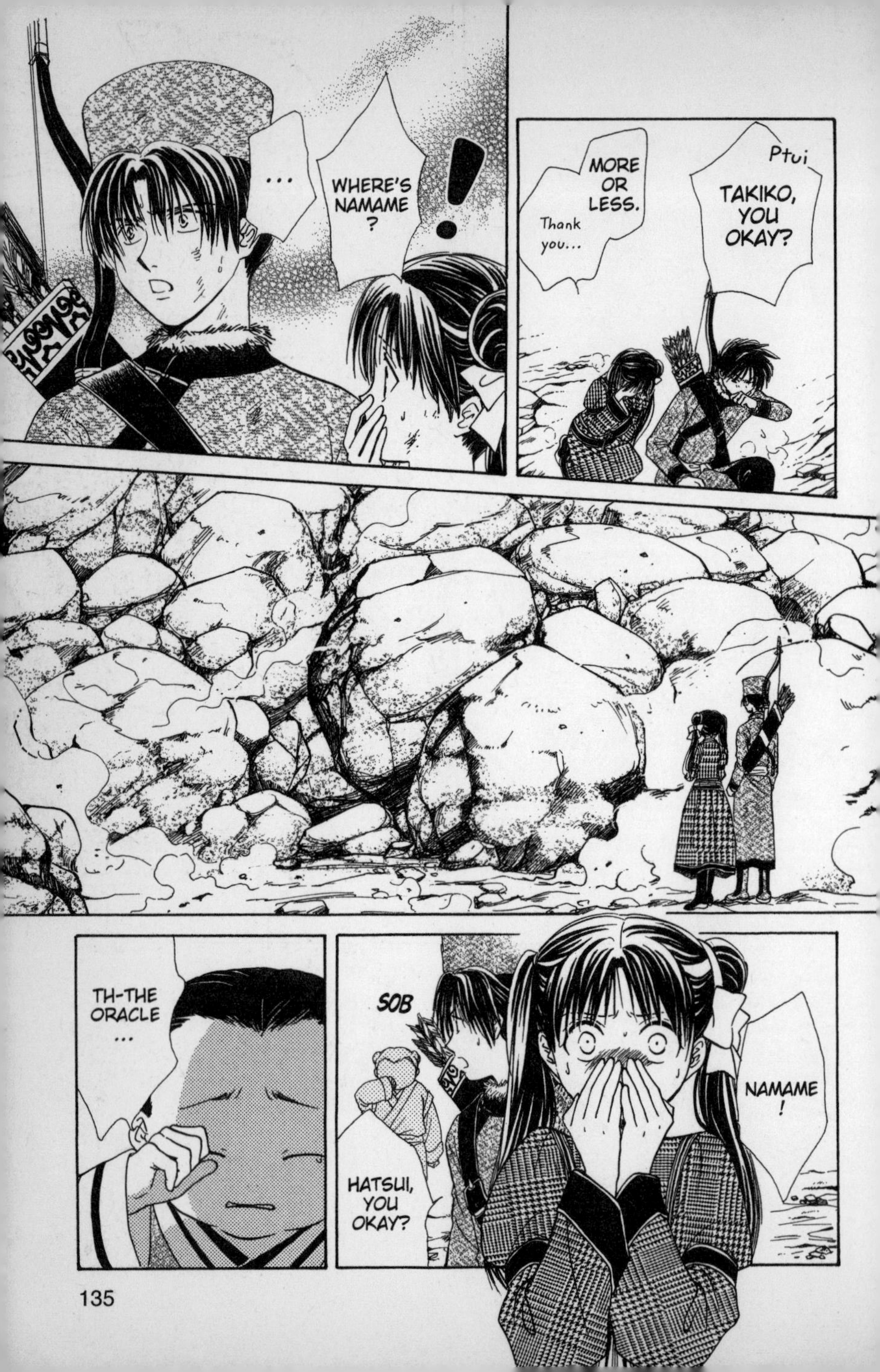
Ptui
TAKIKO, YOU OKAY?
MORE OR LESS.
Thank you...
!
WHERE'S NAMAME?
...
NAMAME!
SOB
HATSUI, YOU OKAY?
TH-THE ORACLE...

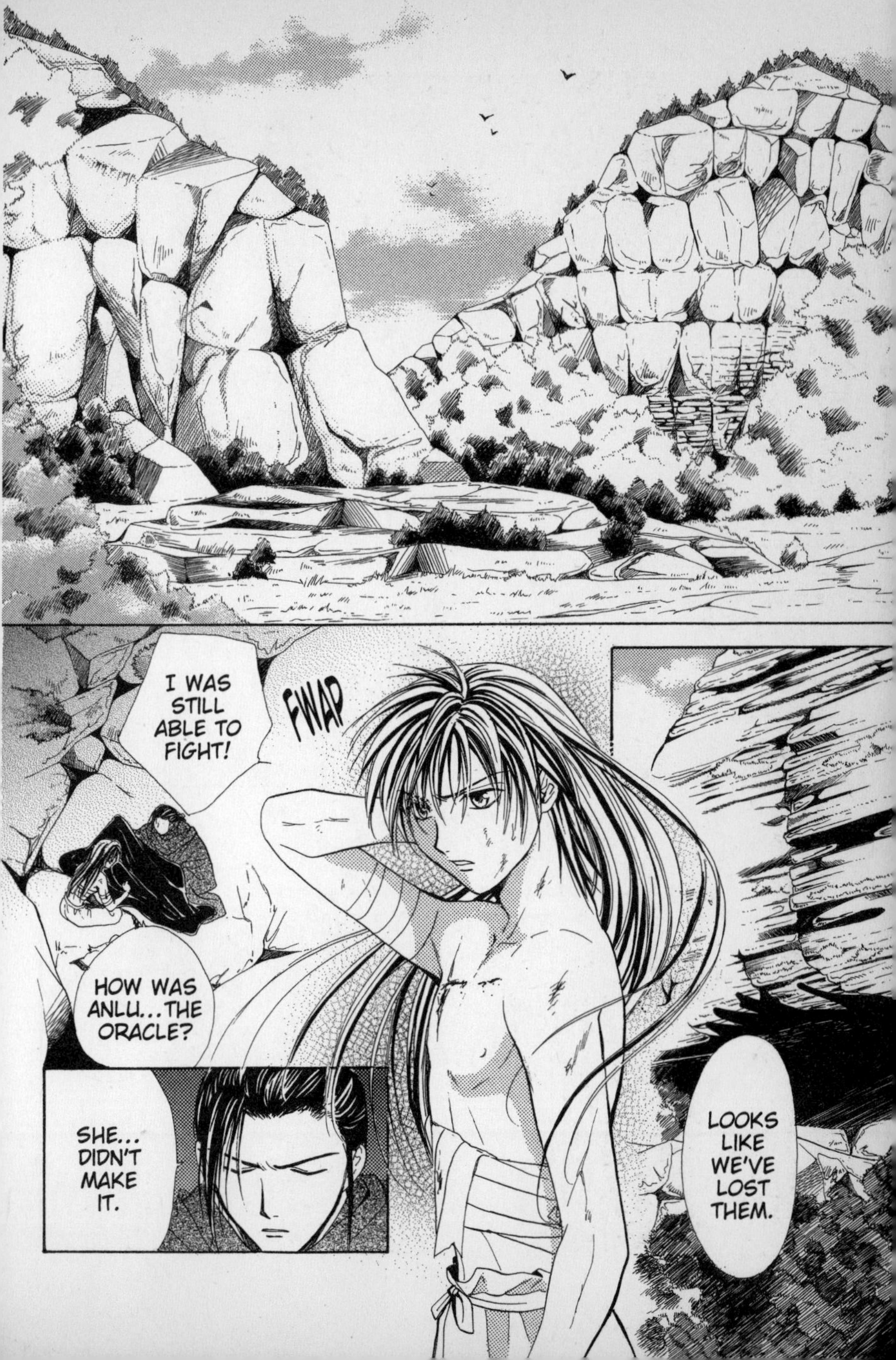
LOOKS LIKE WE'VE LOST THEM.
FWAP
I WAS STILL ABLE TO FIGHT!
HOW WAS ANLU...THE ORACLE?
SHE... DIDN'T MAKE IT.

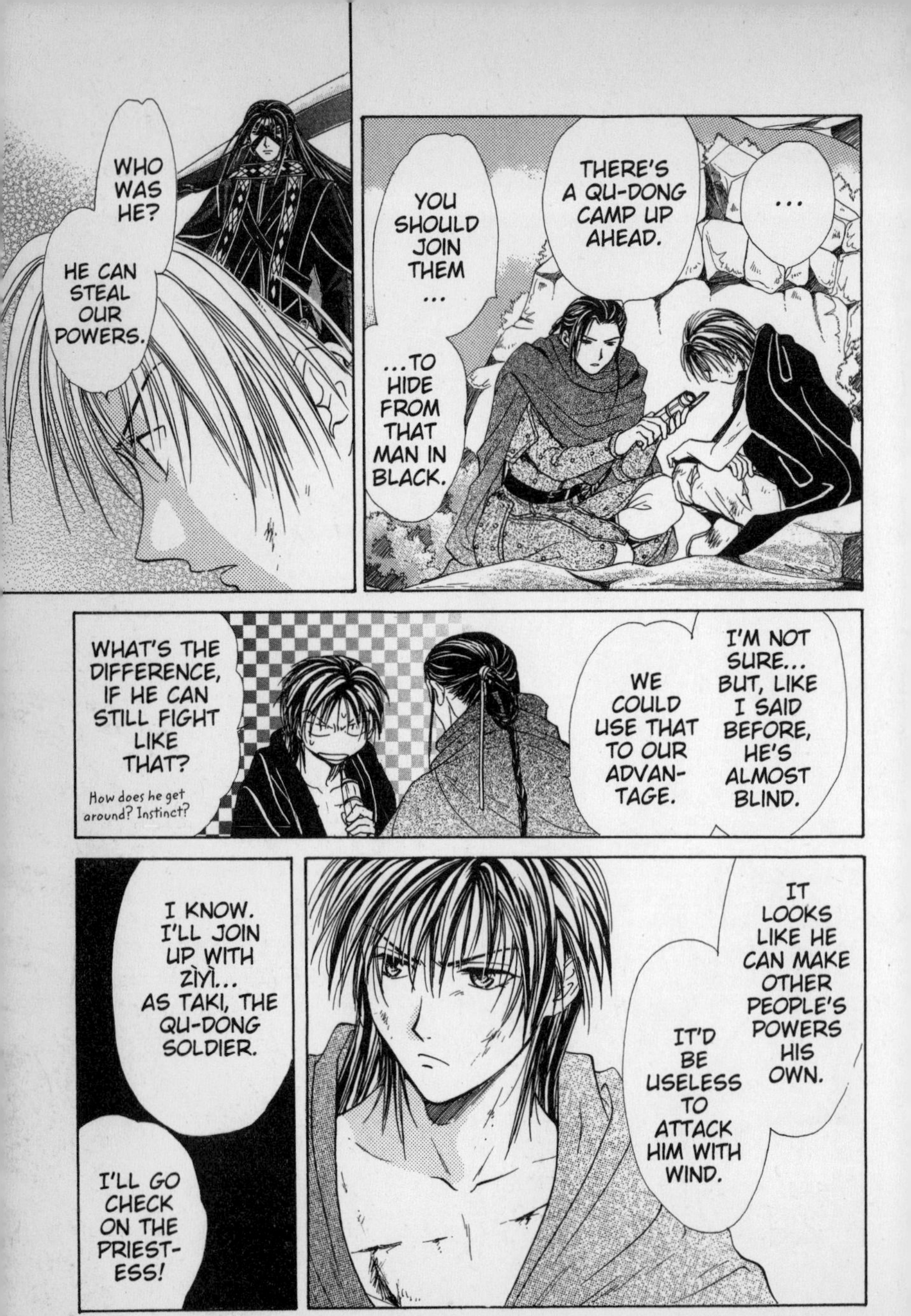
...
THERE'S A QU-DONG CAMP UP AHEAD.
YOU SHOULD JOIN THEM ...
...TO HIDE FROM THAT MAN IN BLACK.
WHO WAS HE?
HE CAN STEAL OUR POWERS.
I'M NOT SURE... BUT, LIKE I SAID BEFORE, HE'S ALMOST BLIND.
WE COULD USE THAT TO OUR ADVANTAGE.
WHAT'S THE DIFFERENCE, IF HE CAN STILL FIGHT LIKE THAT?
How does he get around? Instinct?
IT LOOKS LIKE HE CAN MAKE OTHER PEOPLE'S POWERS HIS OWN.
IT'D BE USELESS TO ATTACK HIM WITH WIND.
I KNOW. I'LL JOIN UP WITH ZÌYÌ... AS TAKI, THE QU-DONG SOLDIER.
I'LL GO CHECK ON THE PRIEST-ESS!

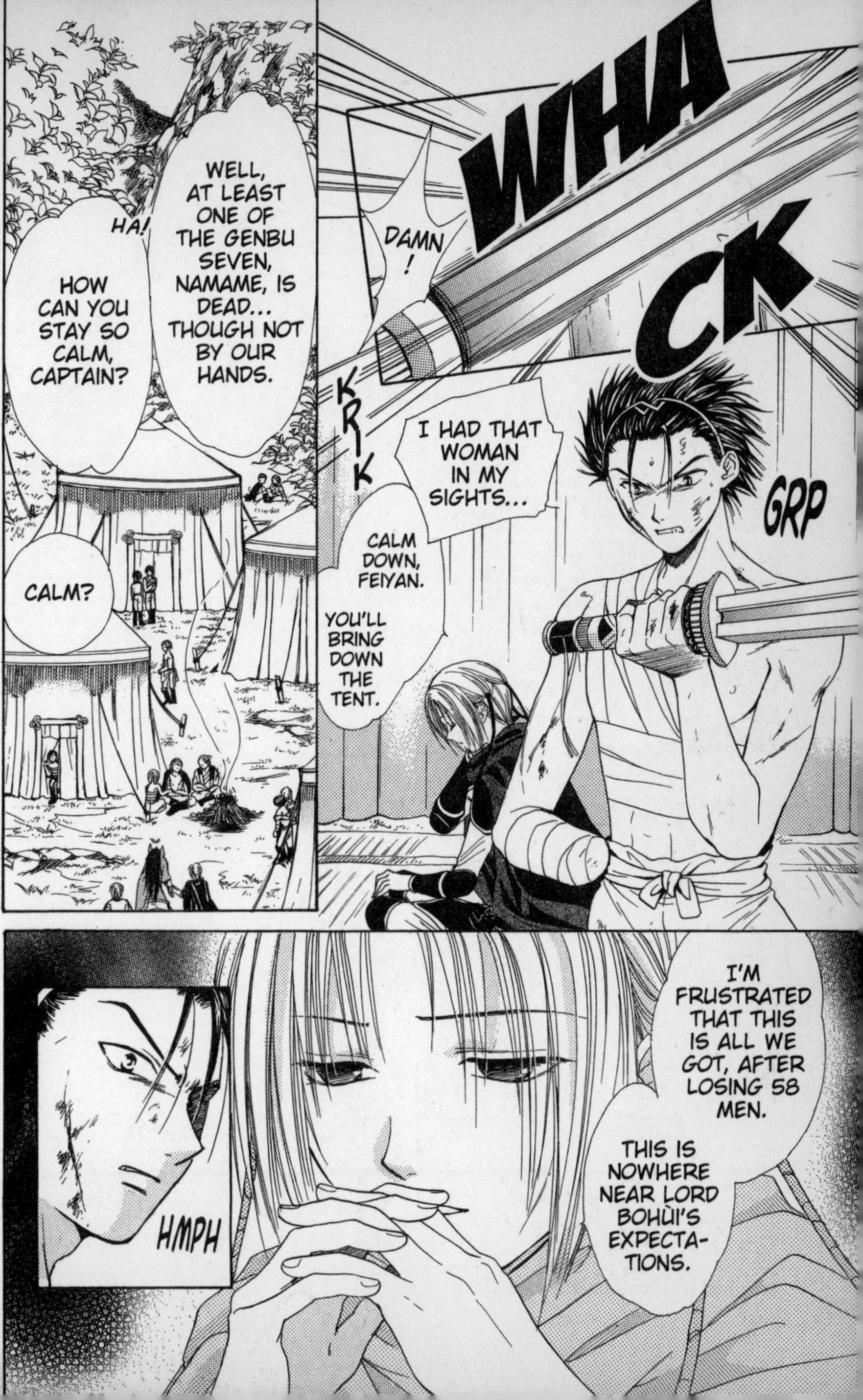
WHACK
DAMN!
KRIK
I HAD THAT WOMAN IN MY SIGHTS...
GRP
CALM DOWN, FEIYAN.
YOU'LL BRING DOWN THE TENT.
WELL, AT LEAST ONE OF THE GENBU SEVEN, NAMAME, IS DEAD... THOUGH NOT BY OUR HANDS.
HA!
HOW CAN YOU STAY SO CALM, CAPTAIN?
CALM?
I'M FRUSTRATED THAT THIS IS ALL WE GOT, AFTER LOSING 58 MEN.
THIS IS NOWHERE NEAR LORD BOHÙI'S EXPECTATIONS.
HMPH

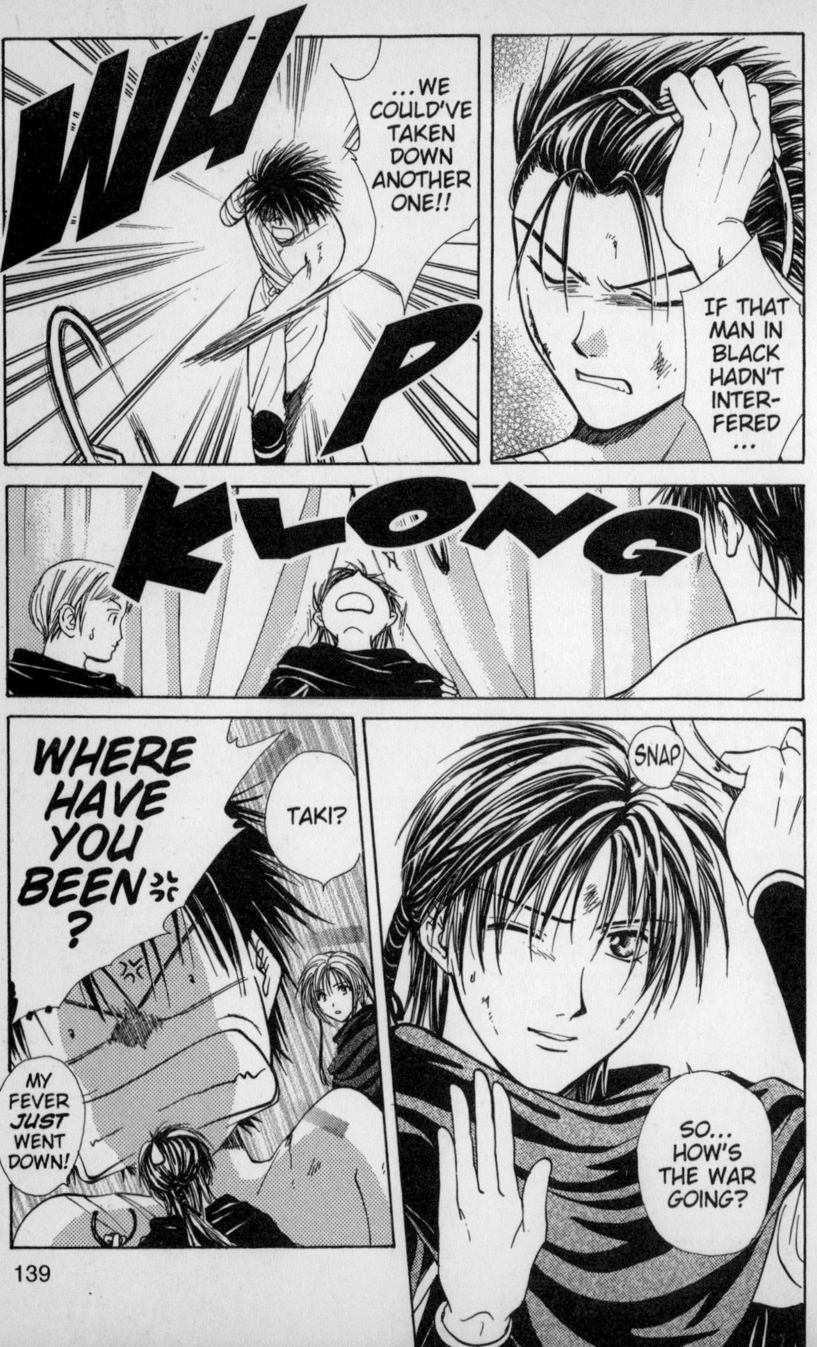
IF THAT MAN IN BLACK HADN'T INTERFERED...
...WE COULD'VE TAKEN DOWN ANOTHER ONE!!
WH
P
KLONG
SNAP
SO... HOW'S THE WAR GOING?
TAKI?
WHERE HAVE YOU BEEN?
MY FEVER JUST WENT DOWN!

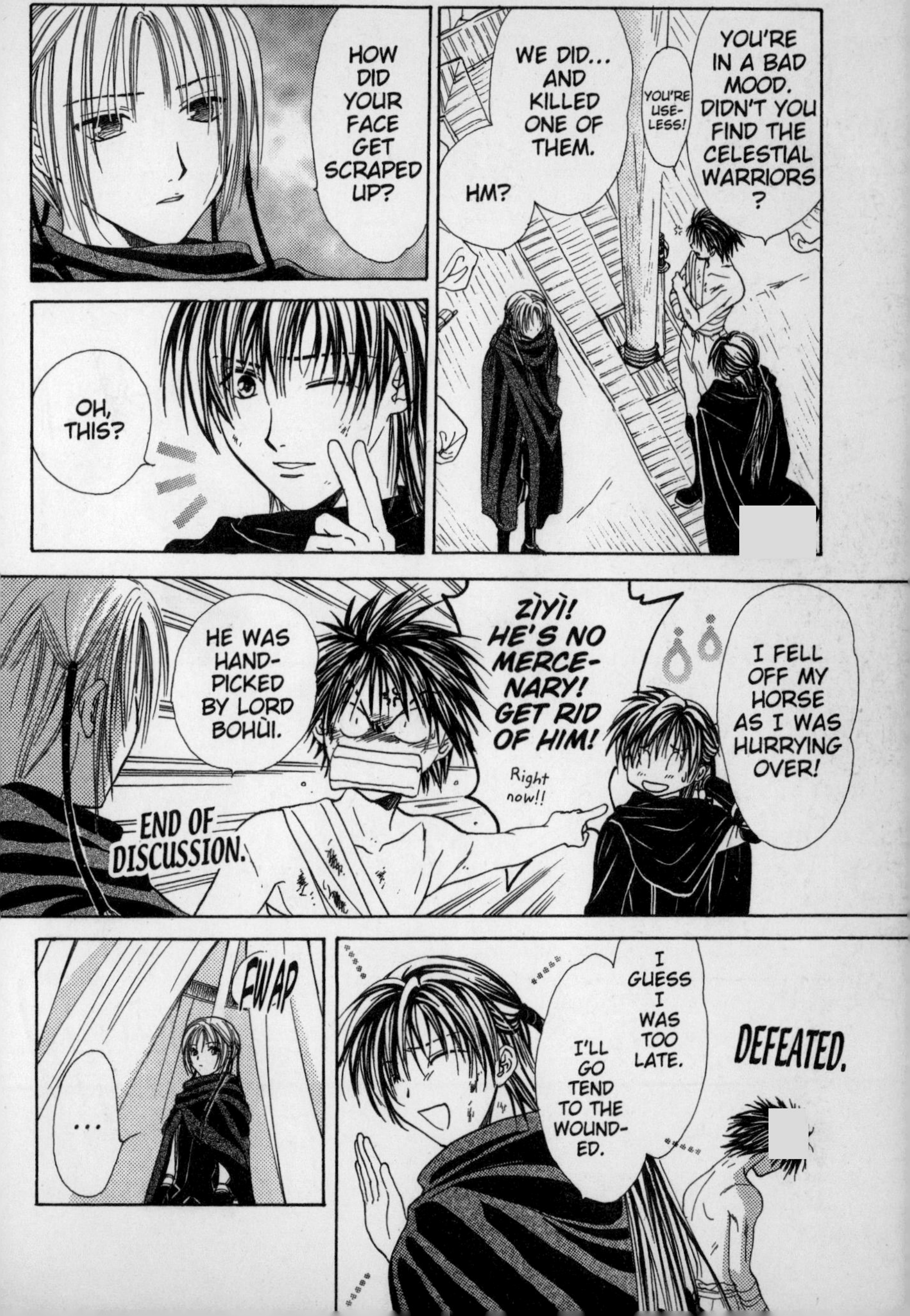
YOU'RE IN A BAD MOOD. DIDN'T YOU FIND THE CELESTIAL WARRIORS?
YOU'RE USE-LESS!
WE DID... AND KILLED ONE OF THEM.
HM?
HOW DID YOUR FACE GET SCRAPED UP?
OH, THIS?
I FELL OFF MY HORSE AS I WAS HURRYING OVER!
ZÌYÌ! HE'S NO MERCE-NARY! GET RID OF HIM!
Right now!!
HE WAS HAND-PICKED BY LORD BOHÙI.
END OF DISCUSSION.
DEFEATED.
I GUESS I WAS TOO LATE.
I'LL GO TEND TO THE WOUND-ED.
FWAP
...

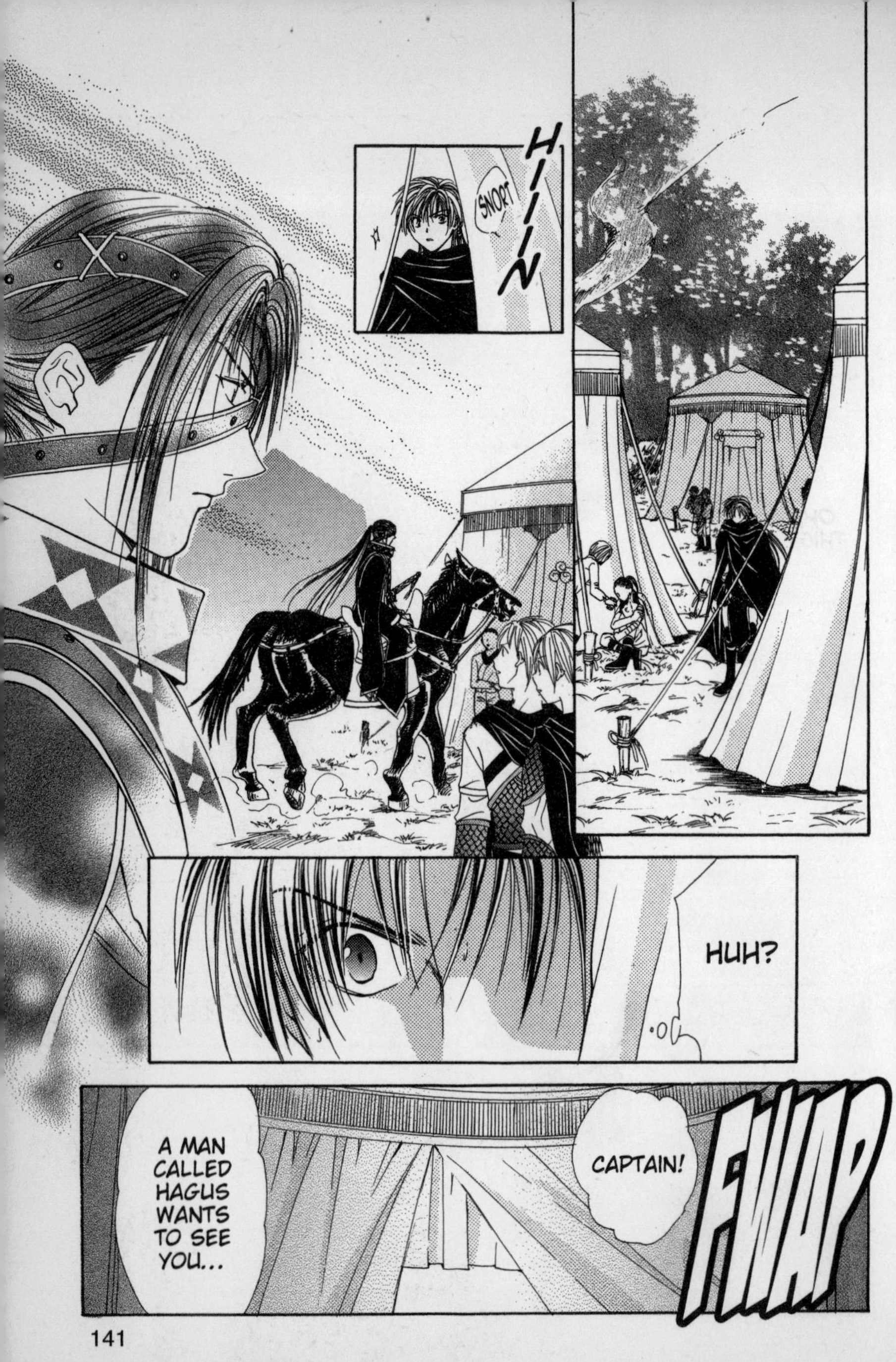
HIIIN
SNORT
HUH?
FWAP
CAPTAIN!
A MAN CALLED HAGUS WANTS TO SEE YOU...

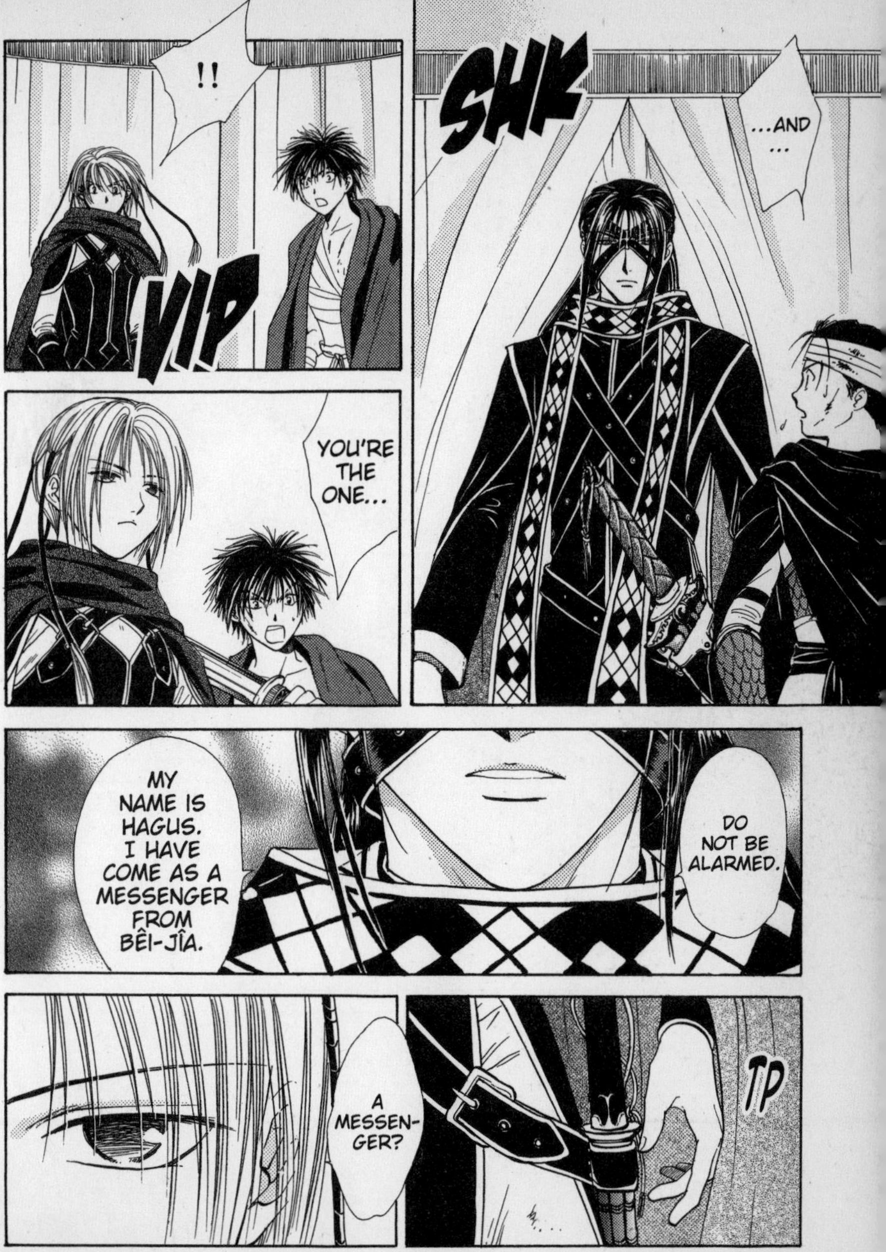
SHK
...AND ...
!!
VIP
YOU'RE THE ONE...
DO NOT BE ALARMED.
MY NAME IS HAGUS. I HAVE COME AS A MESSENGER FROM BÊI-JÎA.
TP
A MESSEN-GER?

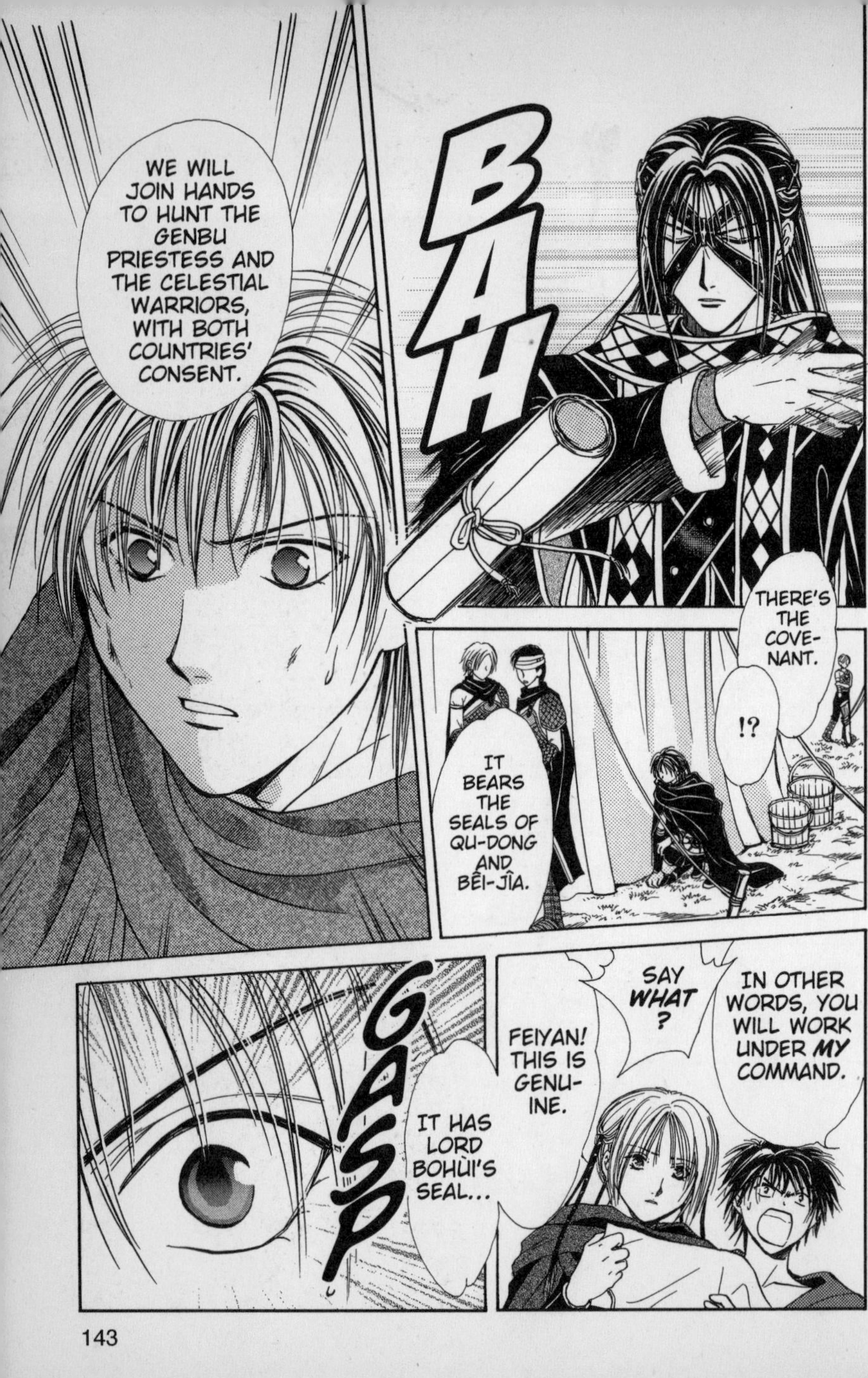
BAH
THERE'S THE COVENANT.
!?
IT BEARS THE SEALS OF QU-DONG AND BÊI-JÎA.
WE WILL JOIN HANDS TO HUNT THE GENBU PRIESTESS AND THE CELESTIAL WARRIORS, WITH BOTH COUNTRIES' CONSENT.
IN OTHER WORDS, YOU WILL WORK UNDER *MY* COMMAND.
SAY *WHAT*?
FEIYAN! THIS IS GENUINE.
IT HAS LORD BOHÙI'S SEAL...
GASP

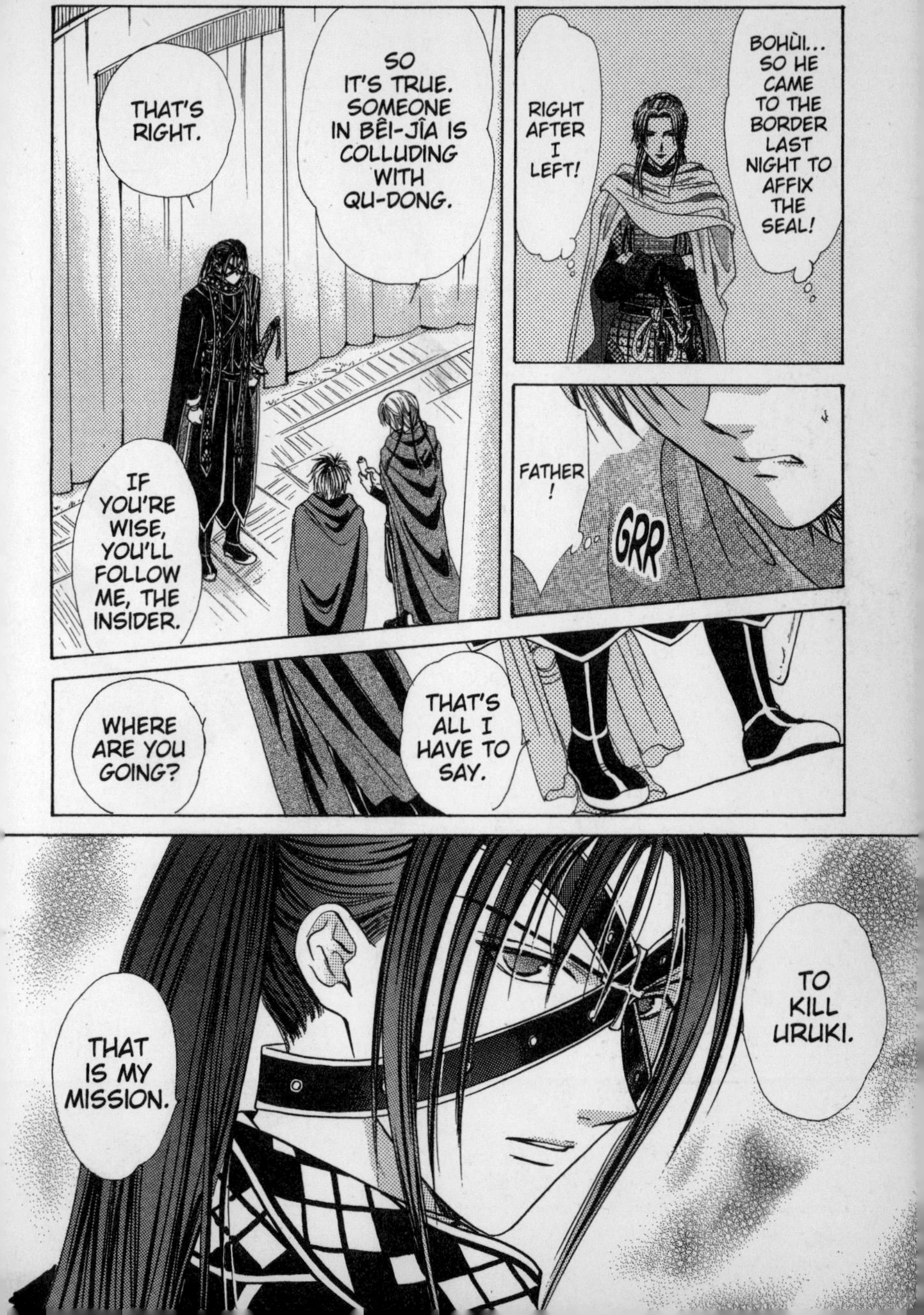
BOHÙI... SO HE CAME TO THE BORDER LAST NIGHT TO AFFIX THE SEAL!
RIGHT AFTER I LEFT!
FATHER!
GRR
SO IT'S TRUE. SOMEONE IN BÊI-JÏA IS COLLUDING WITH QU-DONG.
THAT'S RIGHT.
IF YOU'RE WISE, YOU'LL FOLLOW ME, THE INSIDER.
THAT'S ALL I HAVE TO SAY.
WHERE ARE YOU GOING?
TO KILL URUKI.
THAT IS MY MISSION.

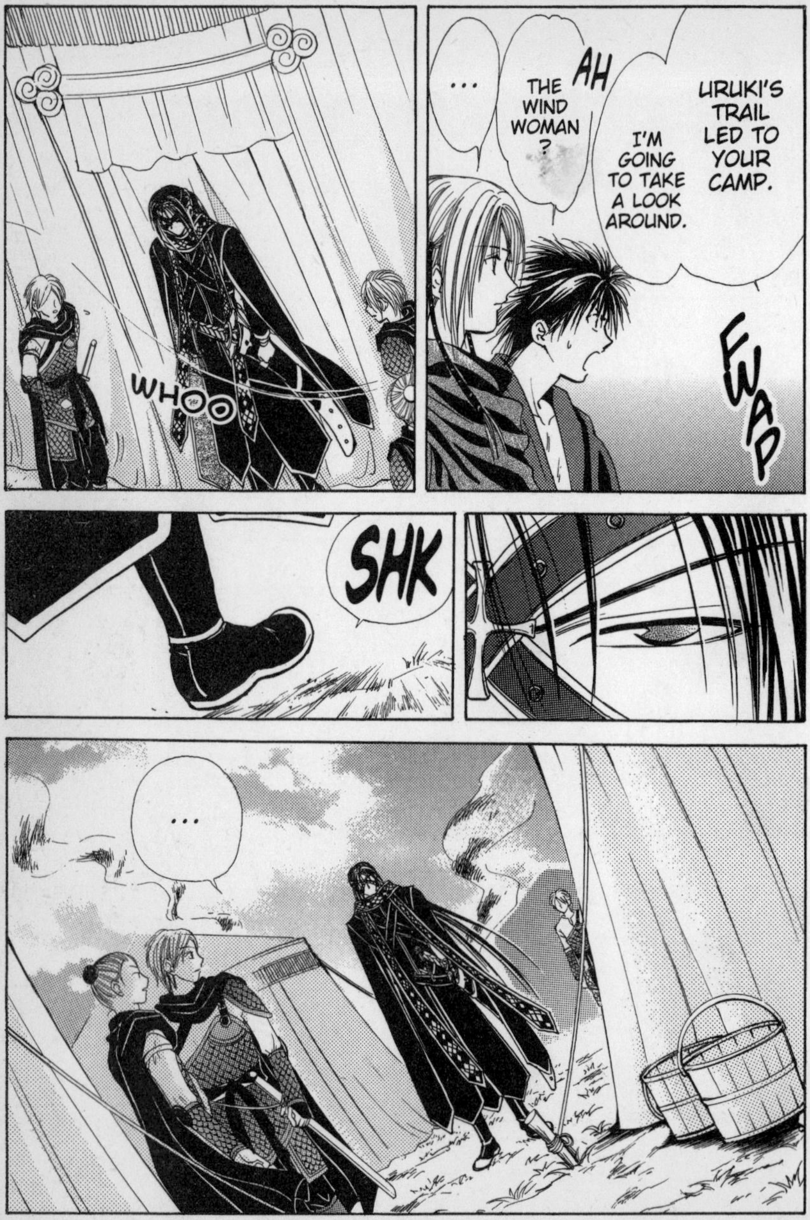
URUKI'S TRAIL LED TO YOUR CAMP.
I'M GOING TO TAKE A LOOK AROUND.
AH
THE WIND WOMAN ?
...
FWAP
WHOO
SHK
...

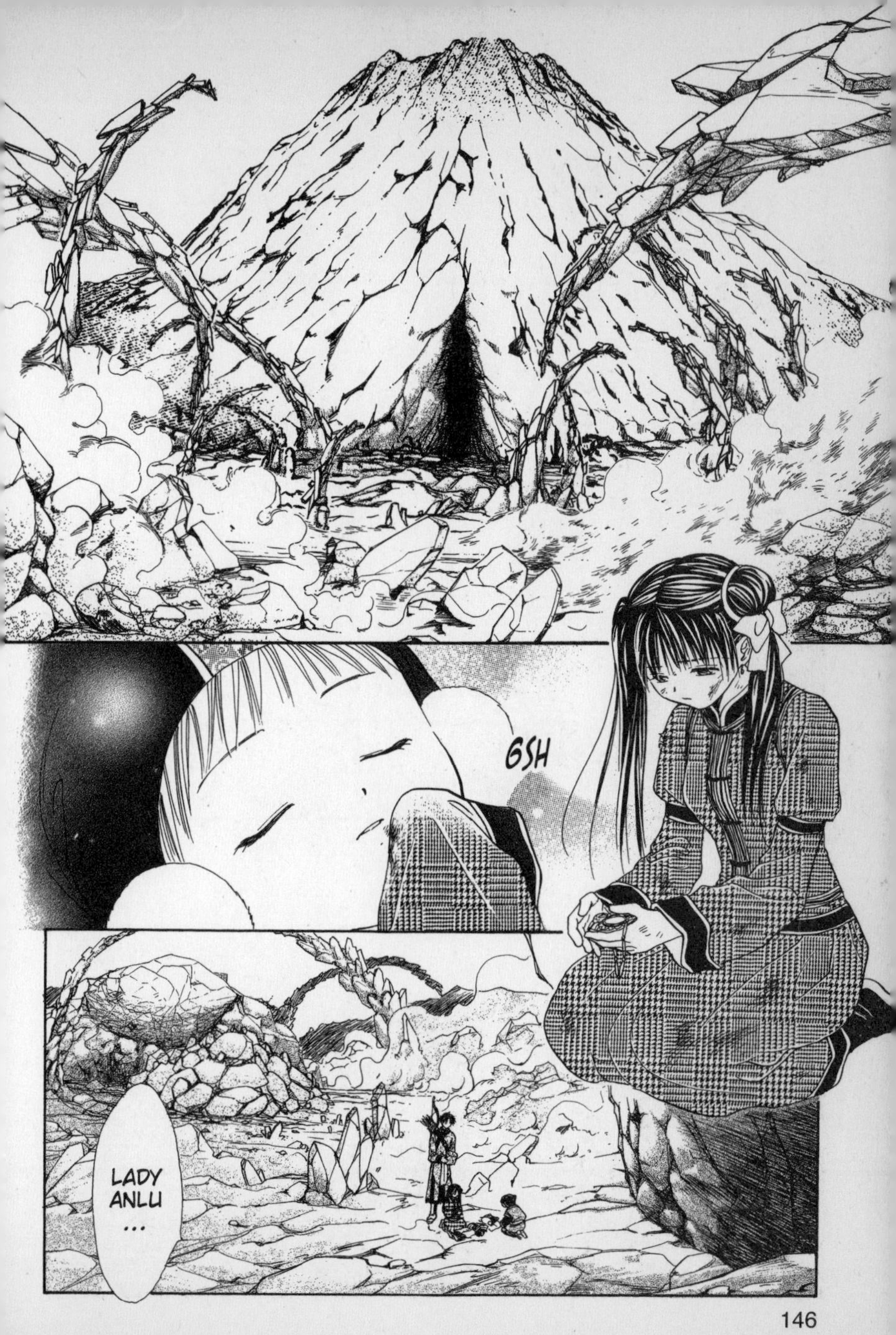
GSH
LADY ANLU ...

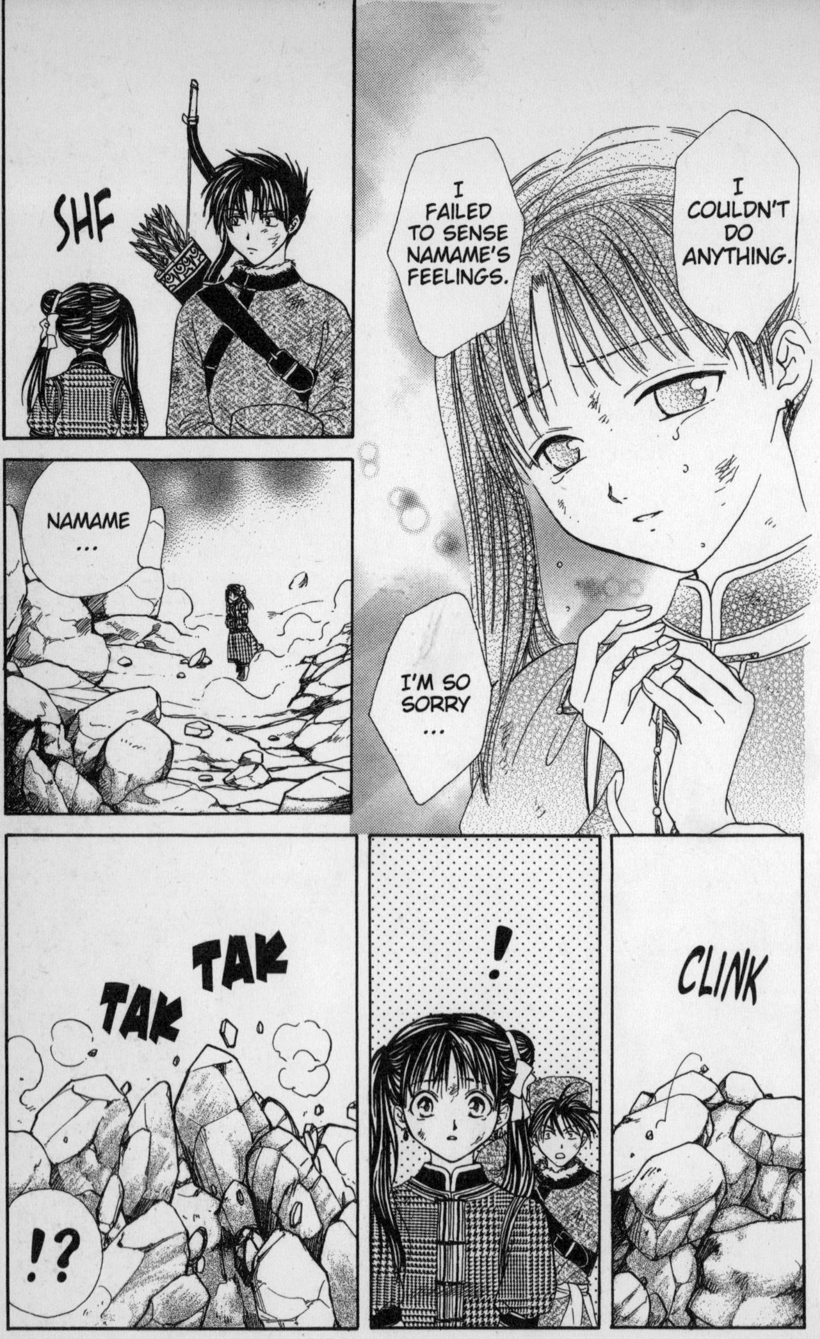
I COULDN'T DO ANYTHING.
I FAILED TO SENSE NAMAME'S FEELINGS.
I'M SO SORRY ...
SHF
NAMAME ...
CLINK
!
TAK
TAK
!?

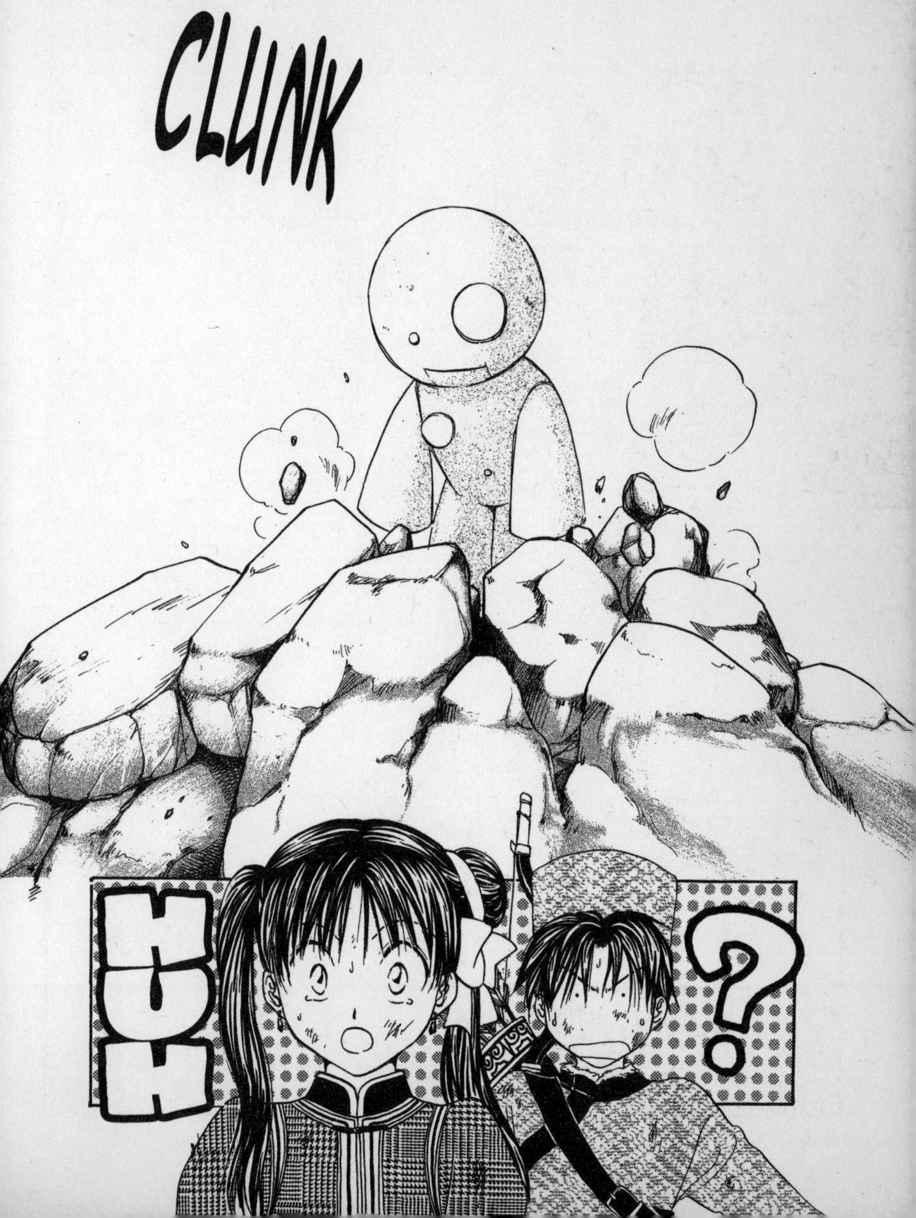
CLUNK
HUH
?

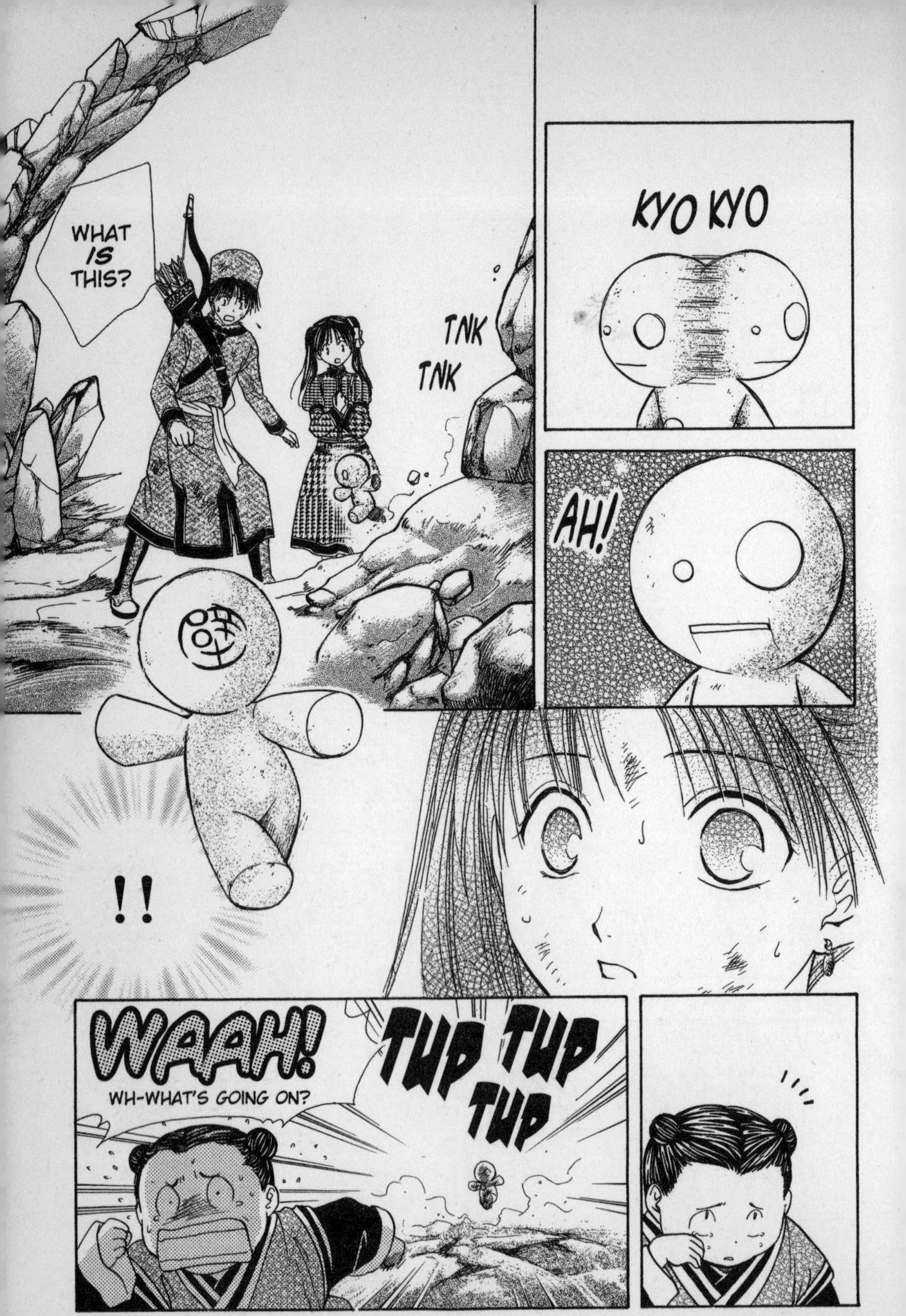
KYO KYO
AH!
TNK
TNK
WHAT IS THIS?
!!
TUP TUP TUP
WAAH!
WH-WHAT'S GOING ON?

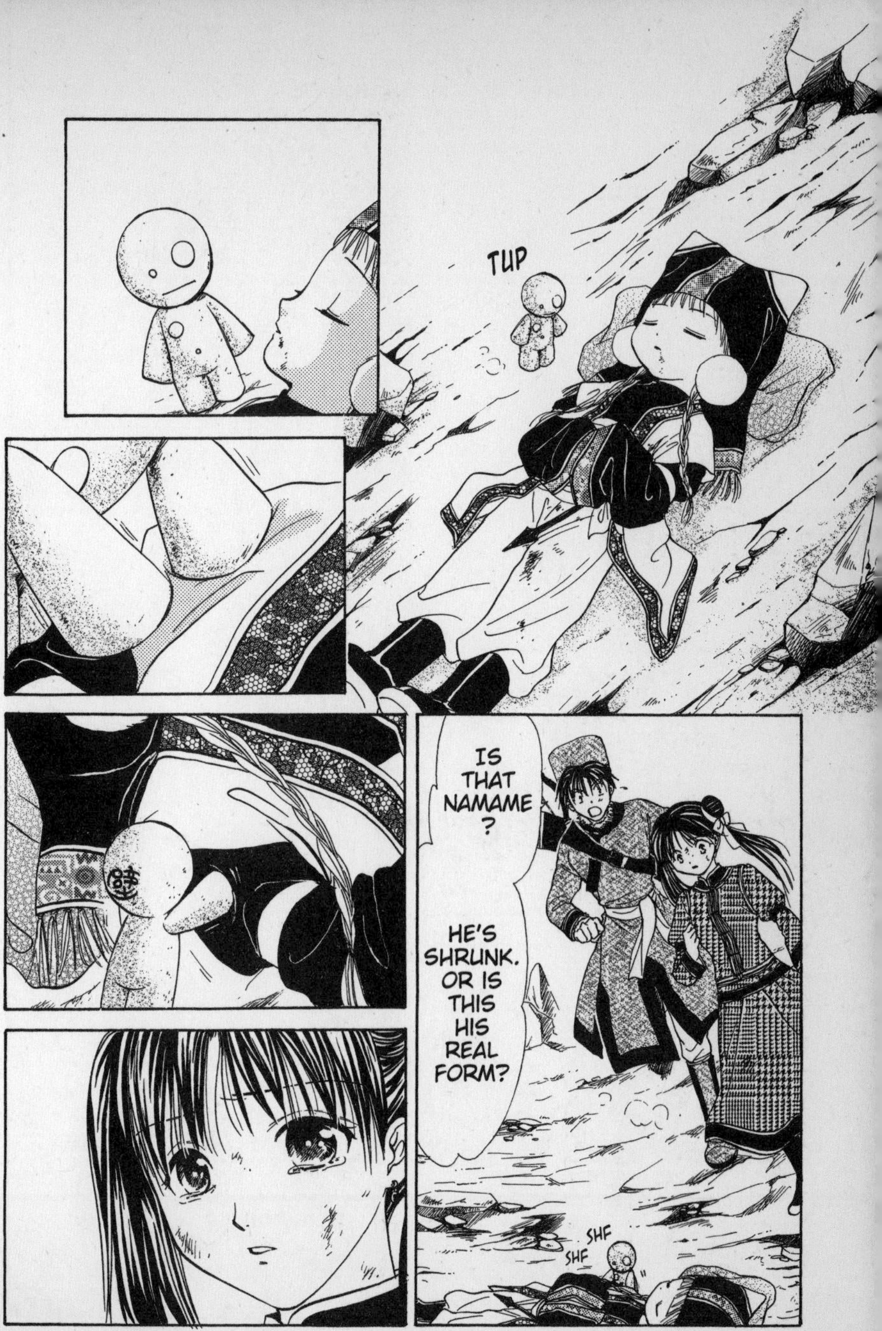
TUP
IS THAT NAMAME?
HE'S SHRUNK. OR IS THIS HIS REAL FORM?
SHF
SHF

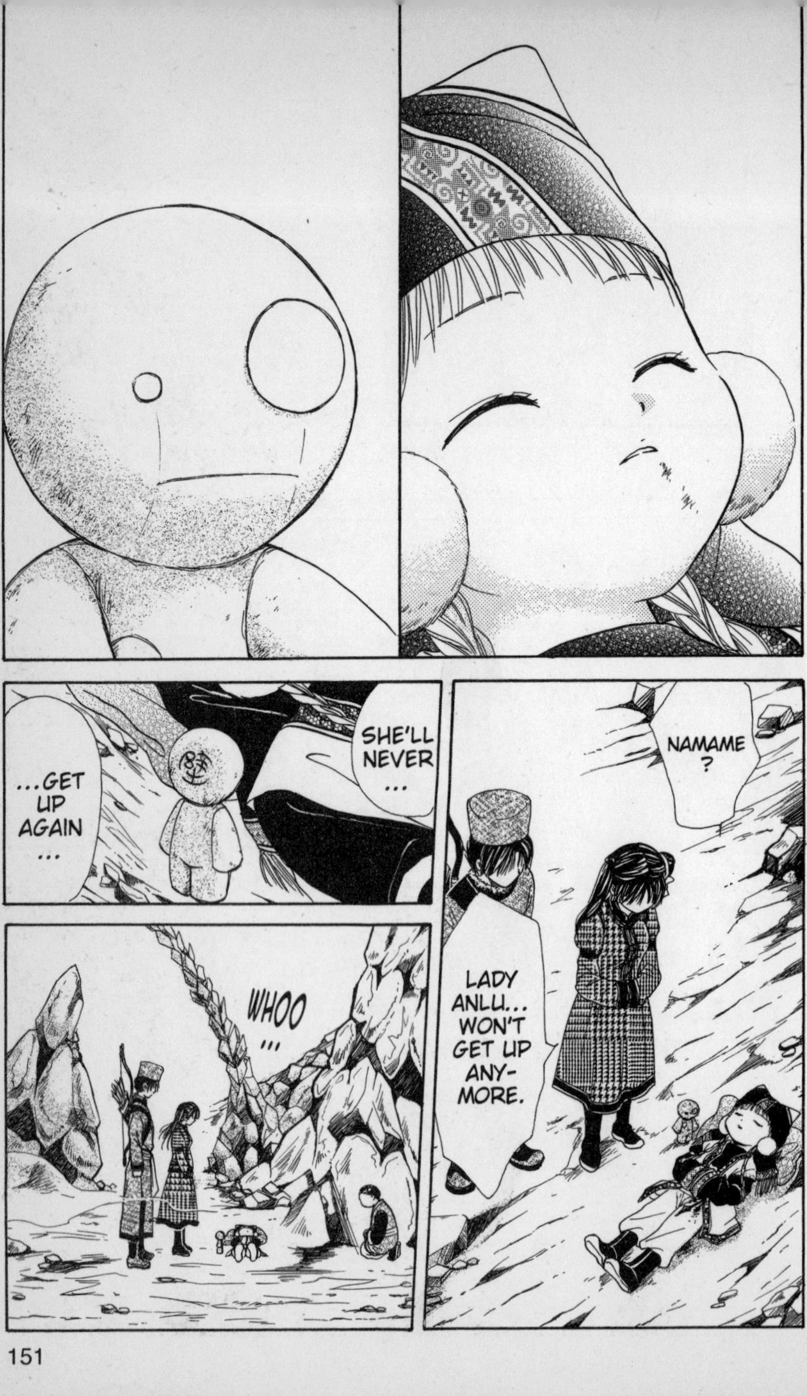
NAMAME ?
LADY ANLU... WON'T GET UP ANYMORE.
SHE'LL NEVER ...
...GET UP AGAIN ...
WHOO ...

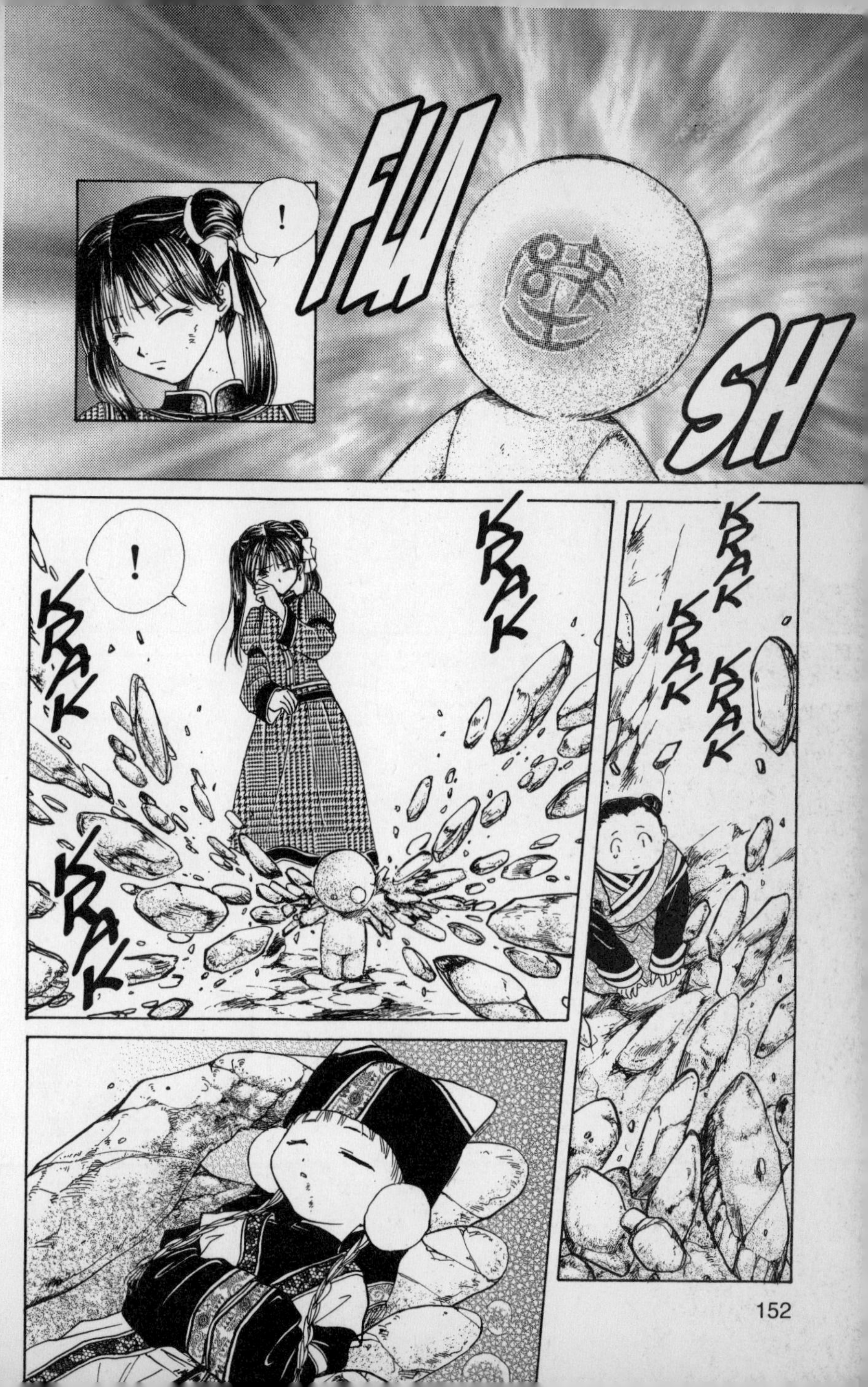
FWA
SH
!
KRAK
KRAK
KRAK
KRAK
!
KRAK
KRAK
KRAK

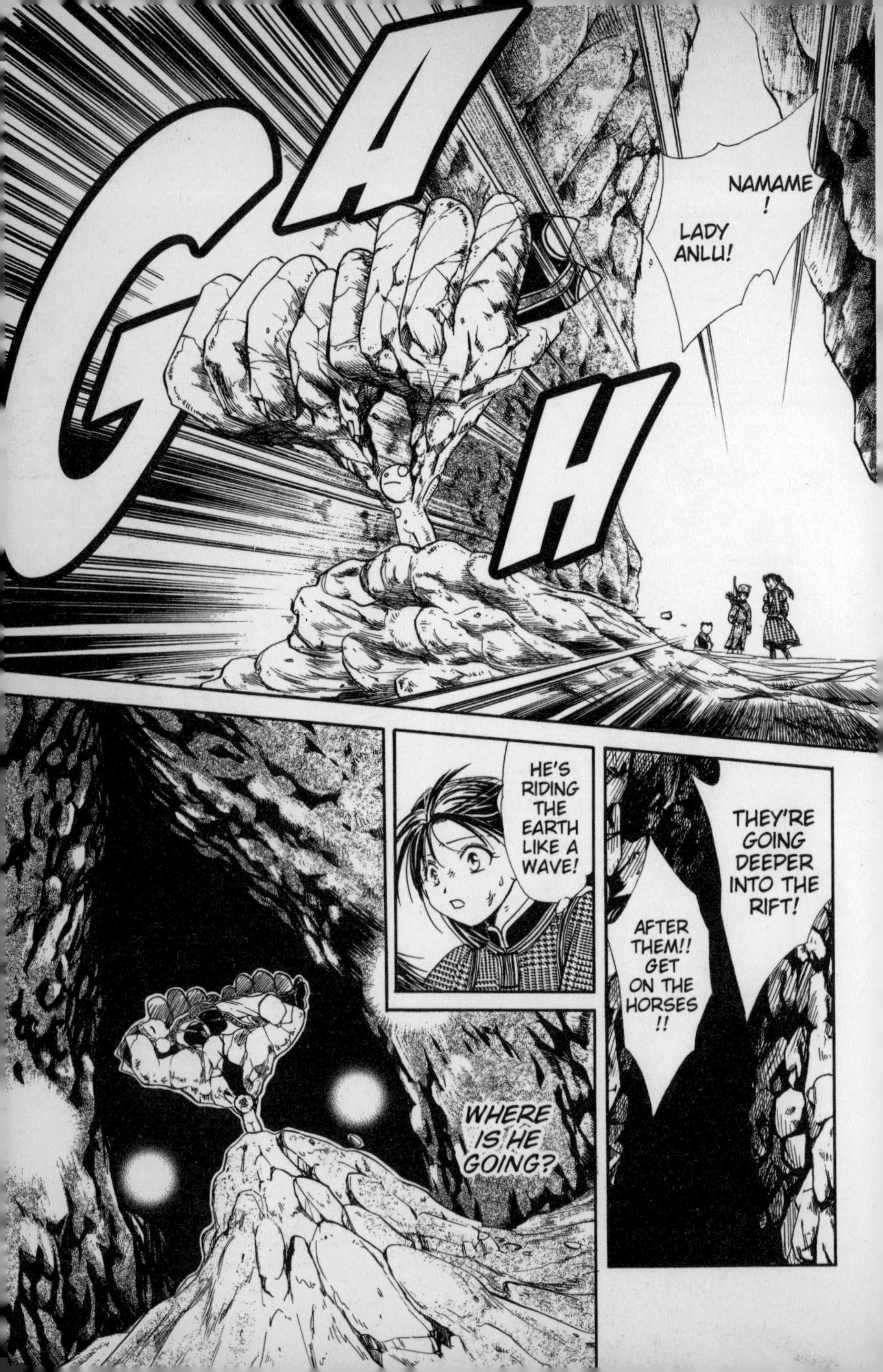
NAMAME!
LADY ANLU!
THEY'RE GOING DEEPER INTO THE RIFT!
AFTER THEM!! GET ON THE HORSES!!
HE'S RIDING THE EARTH LIKE A WAVE!
WHERE IS HE GOING?

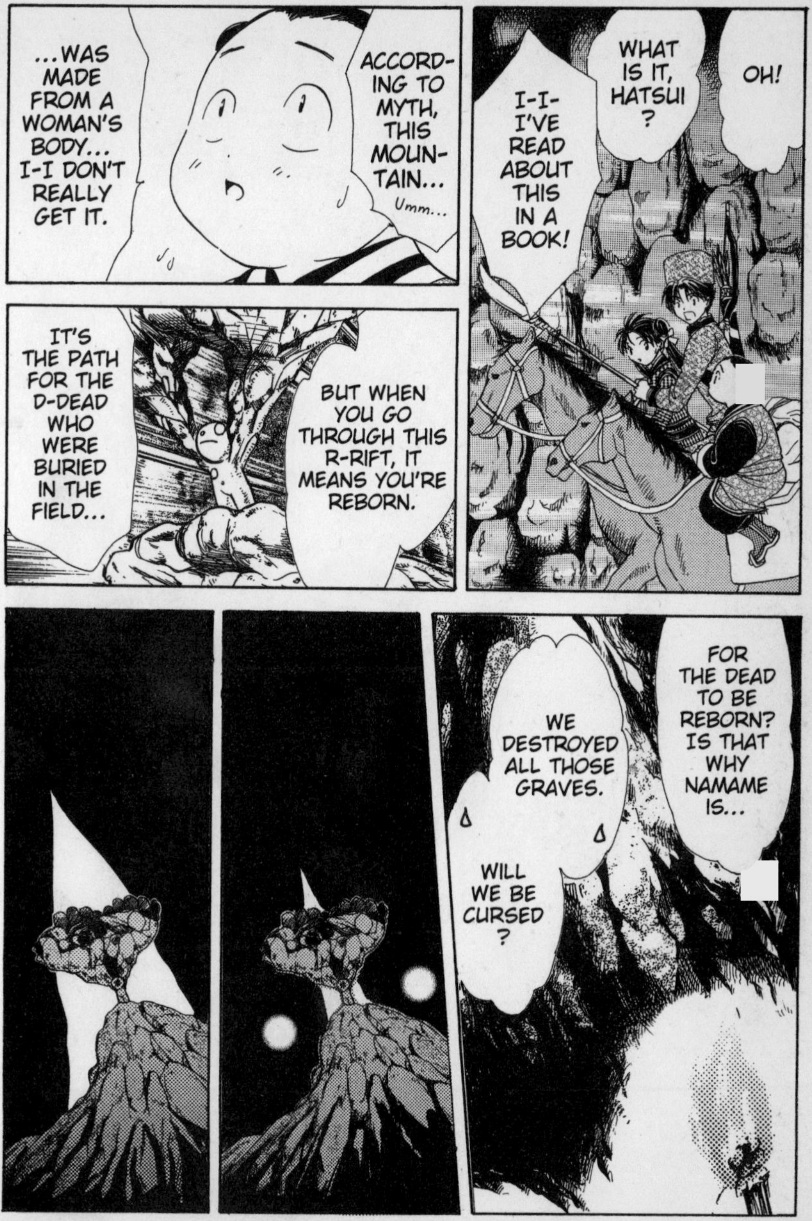
OH!
WHAT IS IT, HATSUI?
I-I-I'VE READ ABOUT THIS IN A BOOK!
ACCORDING TO MYTH, THIS MOUNTAIN...
Umm...
...WAS MADE FROM A WOMAN'S BODY... I-I DON'T REALLY GET IT.
BUT WHEN YOU GO THROUGH THIS R-RIFT, IT MEANS YOU'RE REBORN.
IT'S THE PATH FOR THE D-DEAD WHO WERE BURIED IN THE FIELD...
FOR THE DEAD TO BE REBORN? IS THAT WHY NAMAME IS...
WE DESTROYED ALL THOSE GRAVES.
WILL WE BE CURSED?

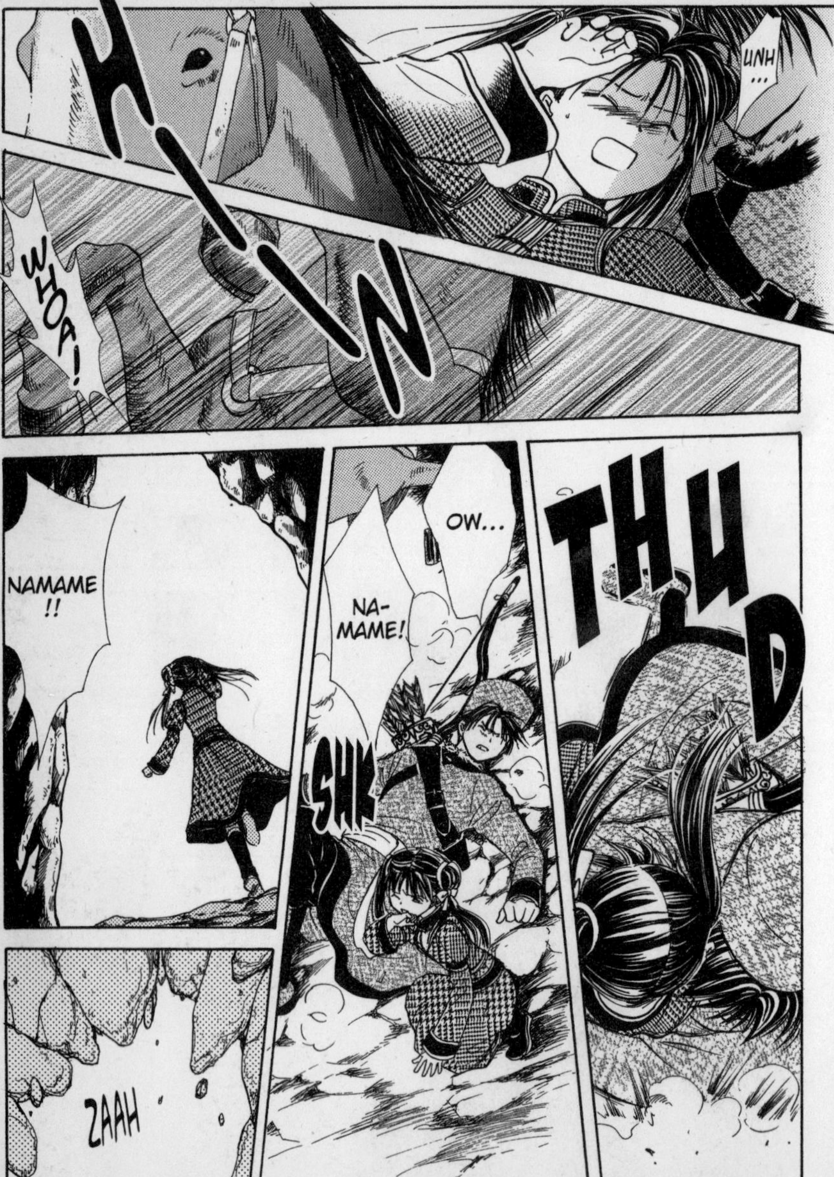
UNH ...
HI-IN
WHOA!
THUD
OW...
NA-MAME!
SHK
NAMAME !!
ZAAH

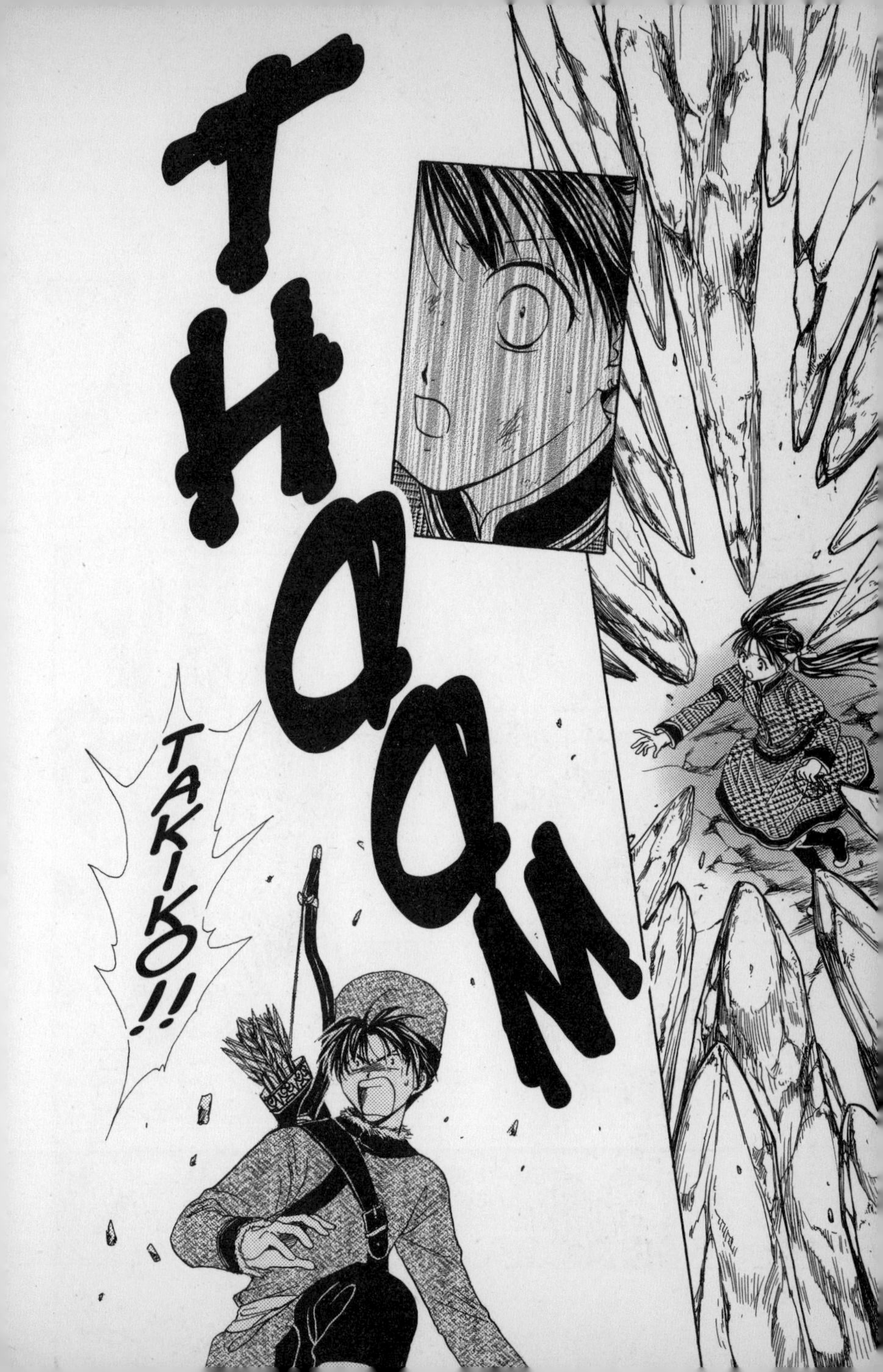
THOOOM
TAKIKO!!

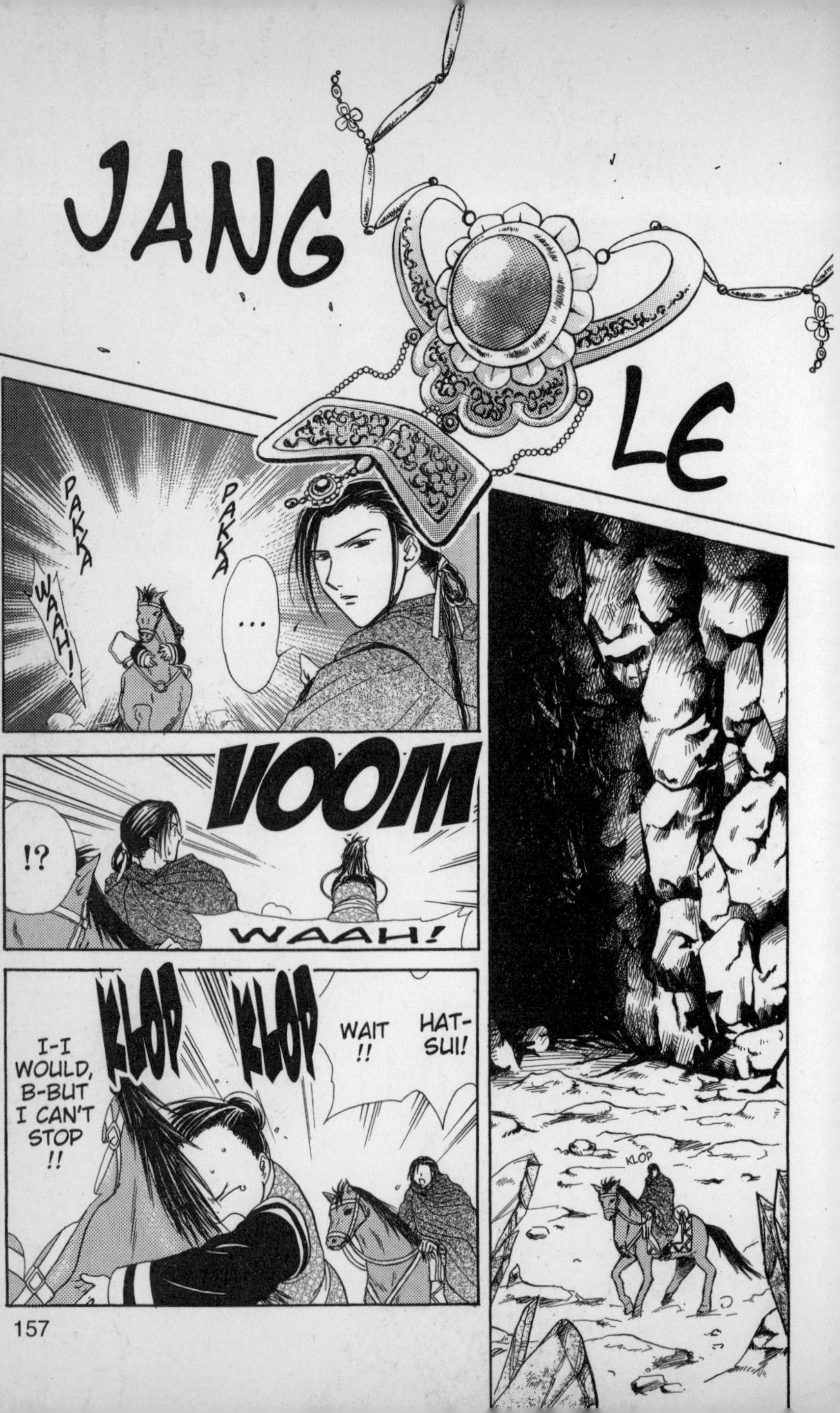
JANG
LE
KLOP
PAKKA
...
PAKKA
WAAH!
VOOM
!?
WAAH!
HAT-SUI!
WAIT!!
KLOP
KLOP
I-I WOULD, B-BUT I CAN'T STOP!!

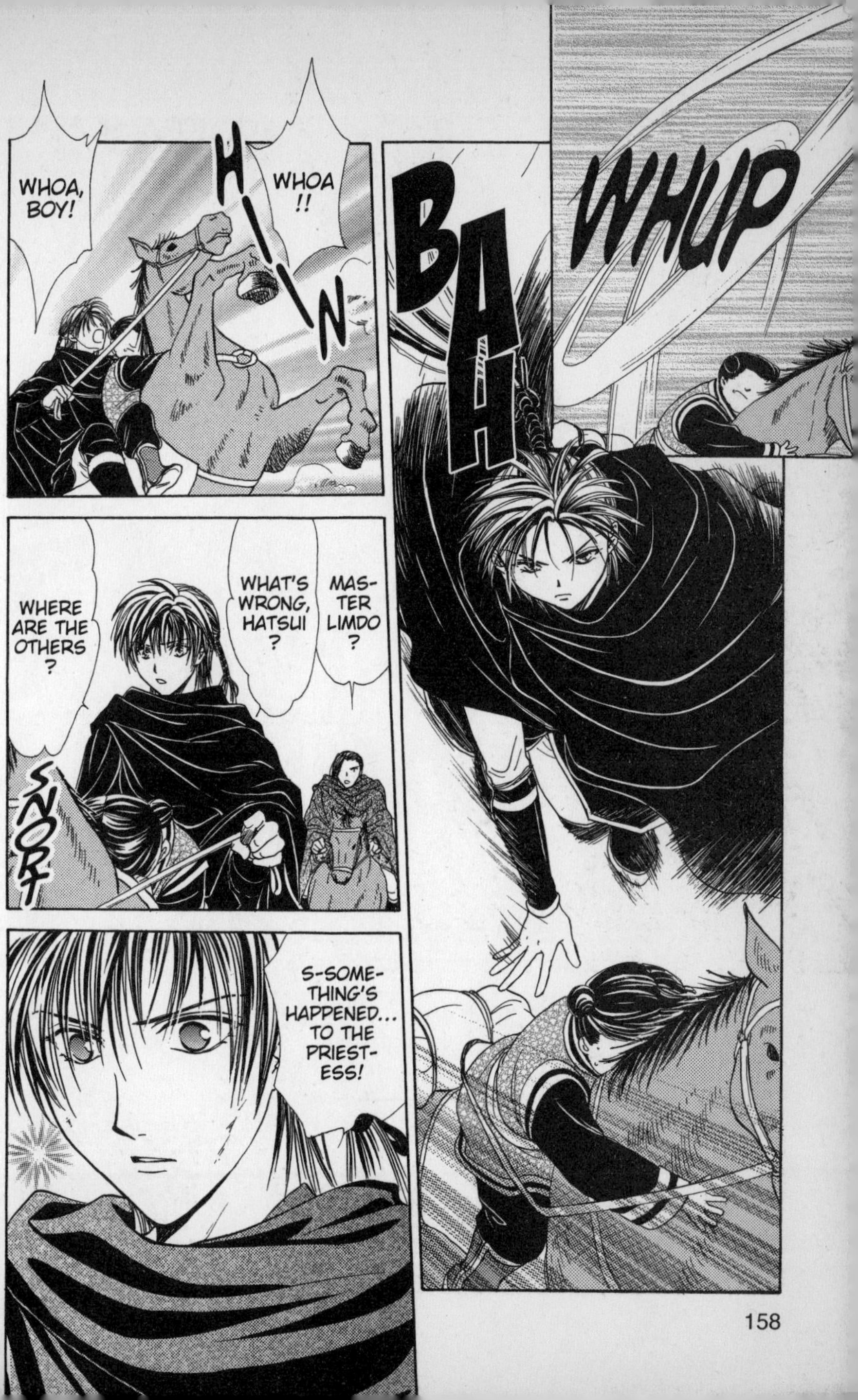
WHUP
BAAH
WHOA !!
WHOA, BOY!
HIN
MAS-TER LIMDO ?
WHAT'S WRONG, HATSUI ?
WHERE ARE THE OTHERS ?
SNORT
S-SOME-THING'S HAPPENED... TO THE PRIEST-ESS!

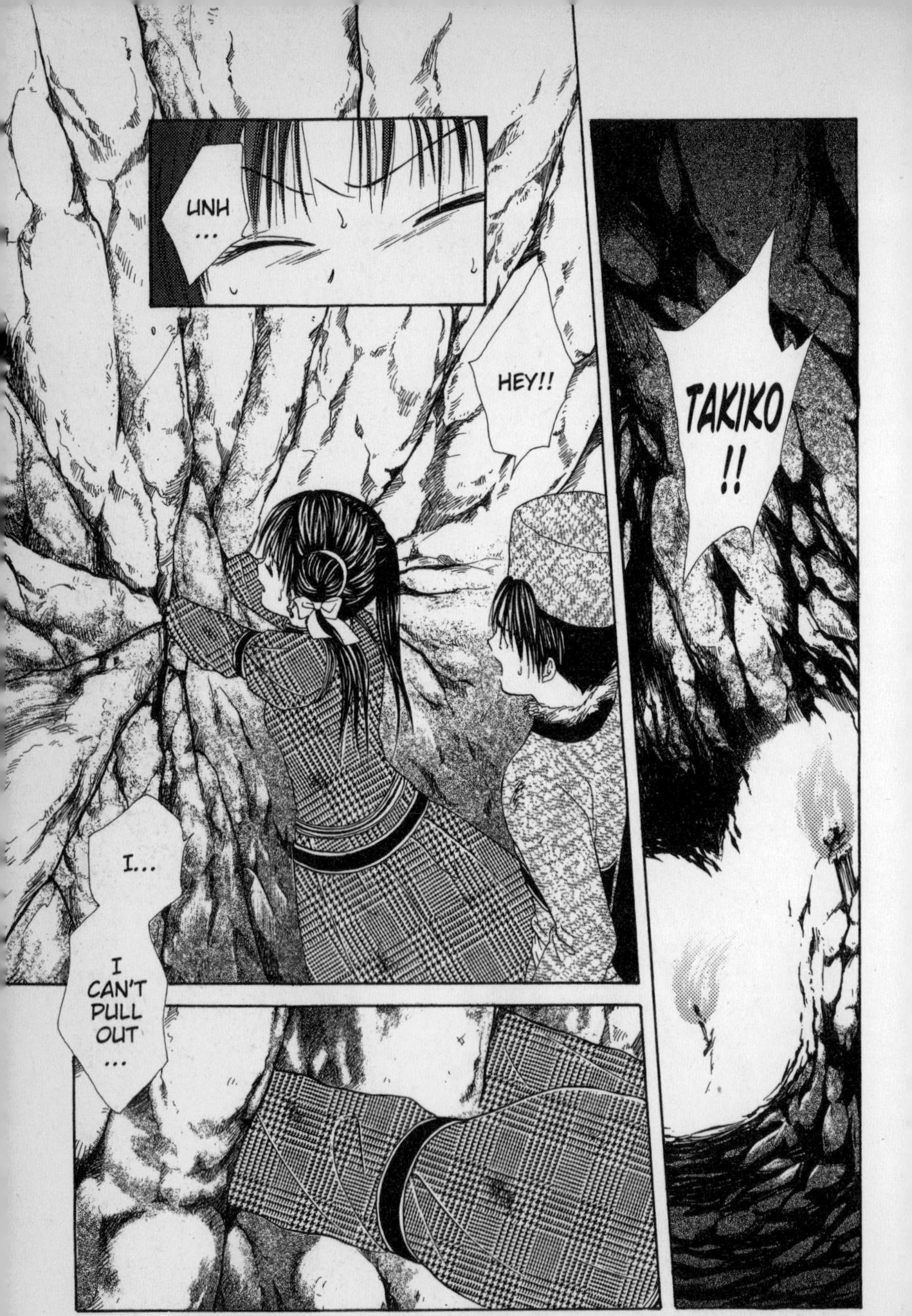
TAKIKO!!
UNH...
HEY!!
I...
I CAN'T PULL OUT...

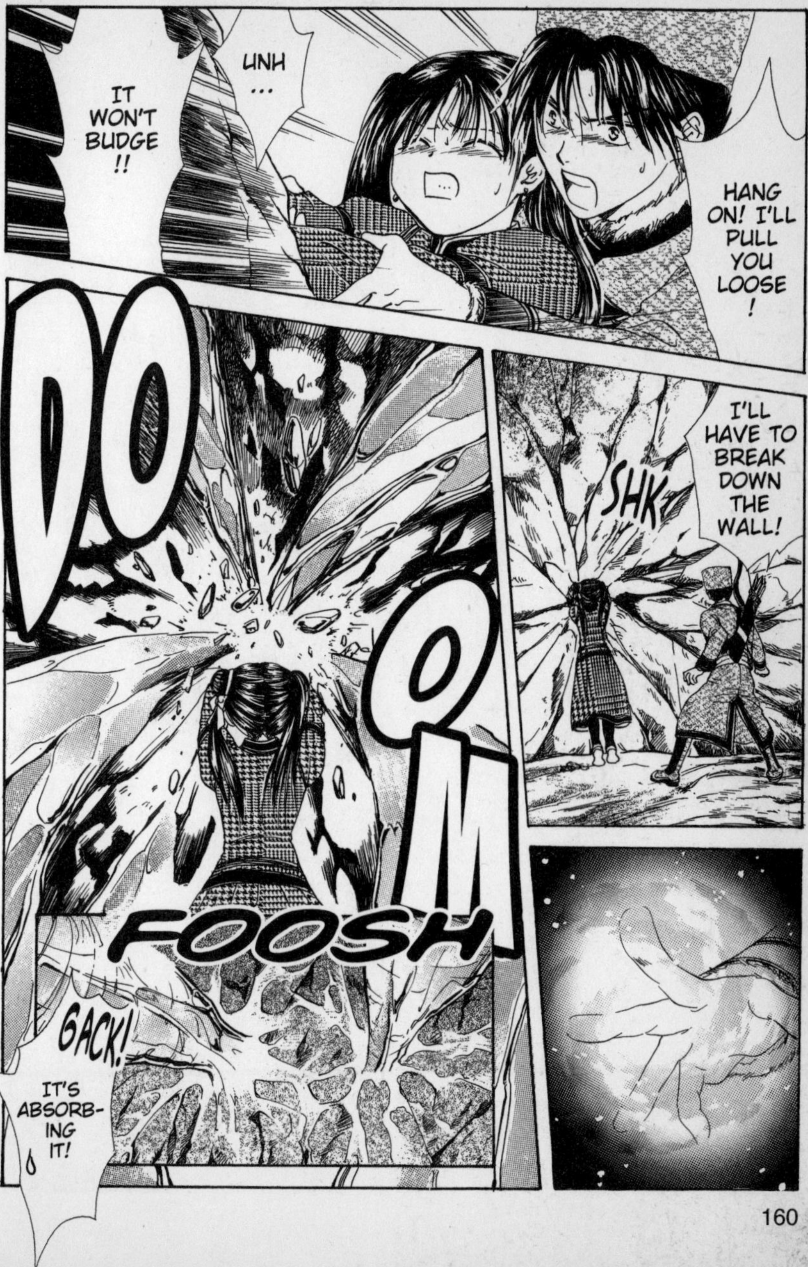
UNH ...
IT WON'T BUDGE !!
...
HANG ON! I'LL PULL YOU LOOSE !
I'LL HAVE TO BREAK DOWN THE WALL!
SHK
DOOM
FOOSH
GACK!
IT'S ABSORB-ING IT!

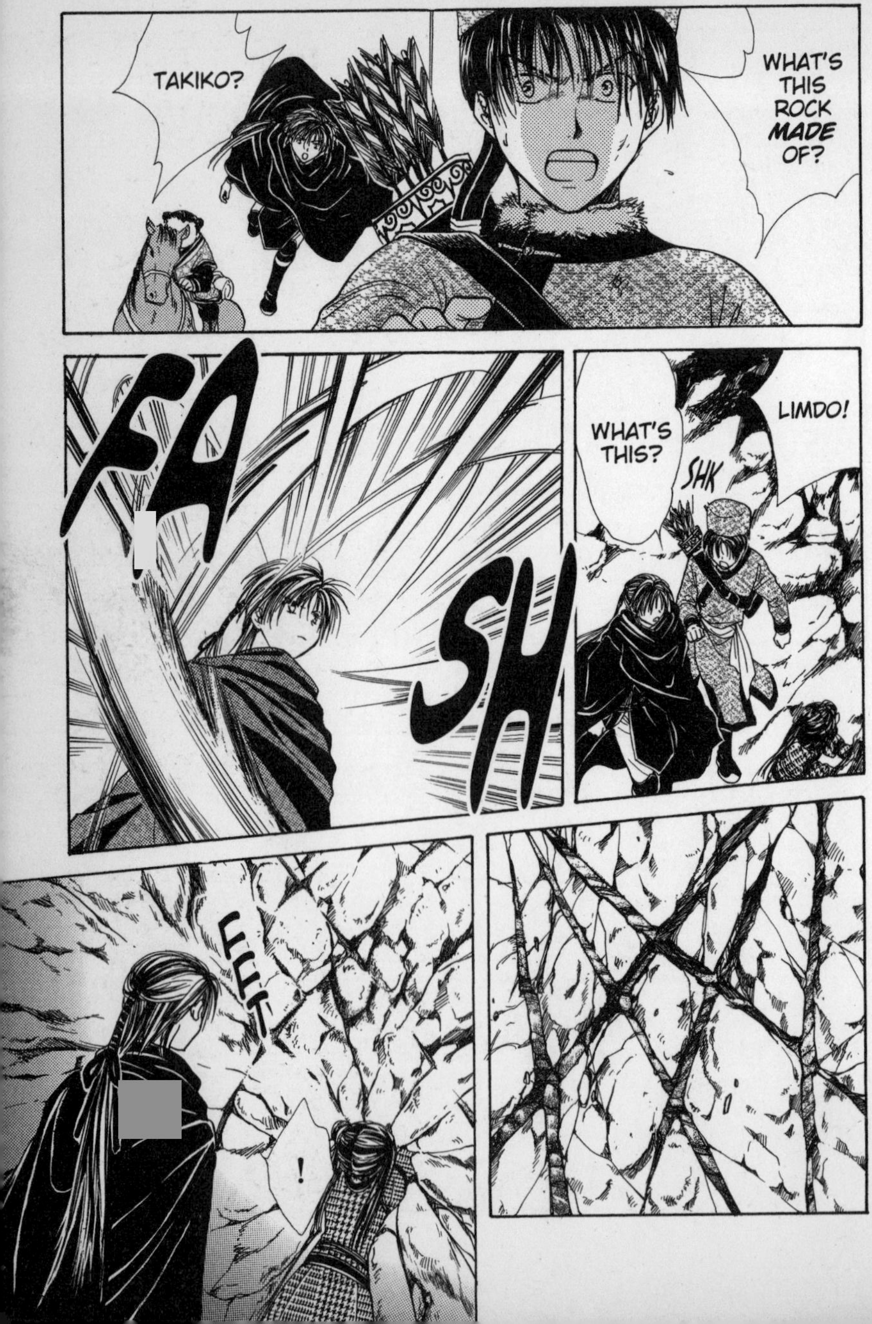
WHAT'S THIS ROCK MADE OF?
TAKIKO?
LIMDO!
WHAT'S THIS?
SHK
FA
SH
FFT
!

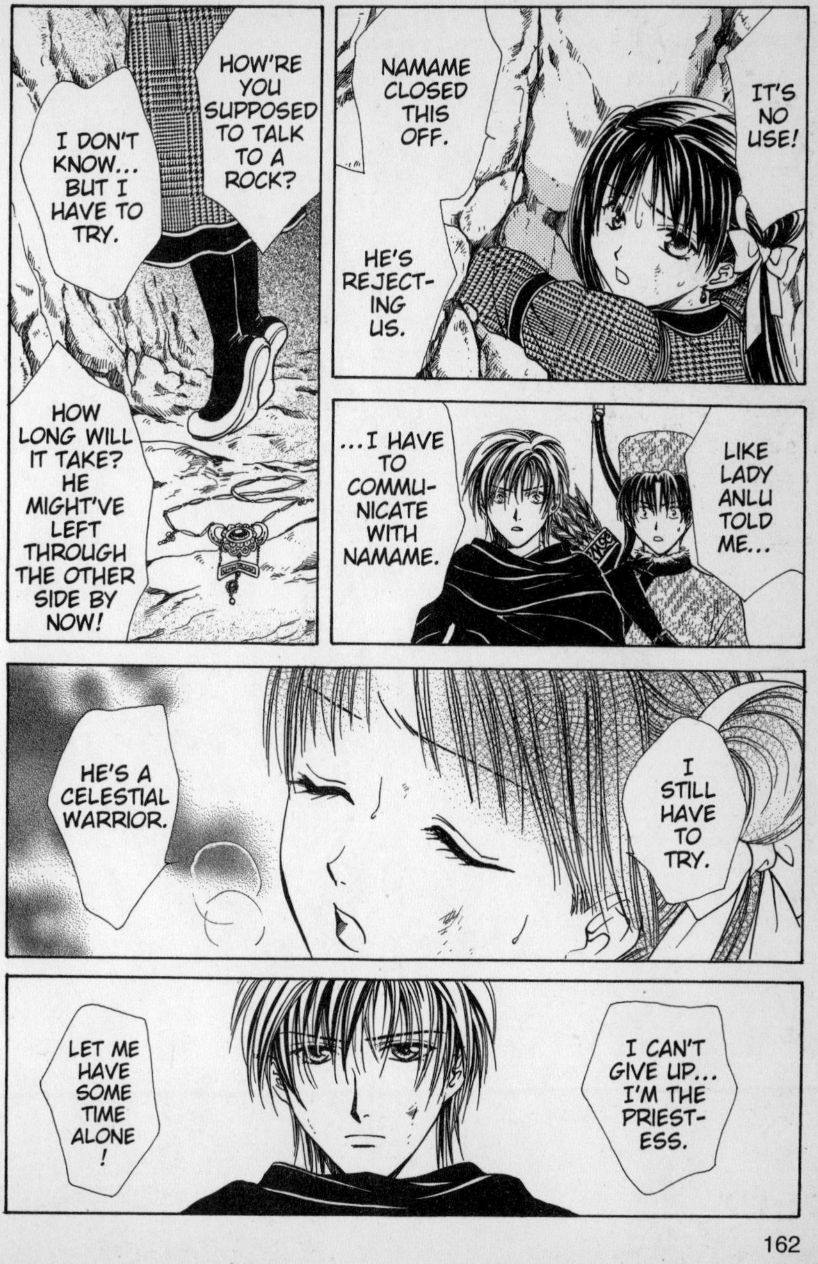
IT'S NO USE!
NAMAME CLOSED THIS OFF.
HE'S REJECTING US.
LIKE LADY ANLU TOLD ME...
...I HAVE TO COMMUNICATE WITH NAMAME.
HOW'RE YOU SUPPOSED TO TALK TO A ROCK?
I DON'T KNOW... BUT I HAVE TO TRY.
HOW LONG WILL IT TAKE? HE MIGHT'VE LEFT THROUGH THE OTHER SIDE BY NOW!
I STILL HAVE TO TRY.
HE'S A CELESTIAL WARRIOR.
I CAN'T GIVE UP... I'M THE PRIEST-ESS.
LET ME HAVE SOME TIME ALONE!

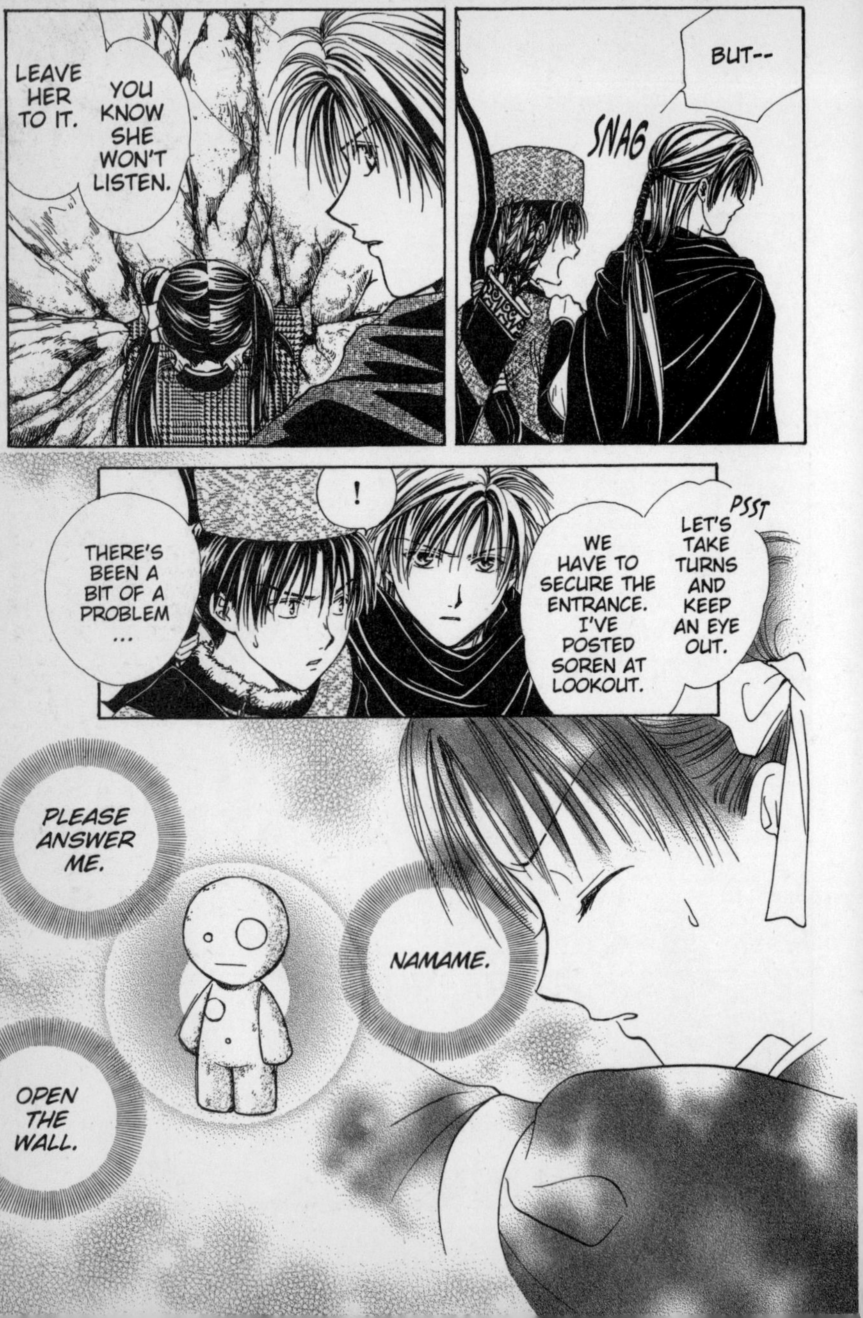
BUT--
SNAG
YOU KNOW SHE WON'T LISTEN.
LEAVE HER TO IT.
PSST
LET'S TAKE TURNS AND KEEP AN EYE OUT.
WE HAVE TO SECURE THE ENTRANCE. I'VE POSTED SOREN AT LOOKOUT.
!
THERE'S BEEN A BIT OF A PROBLEM ...
NAMAME.
PLEASE ANSWER ME.
OPEN THE WALL.

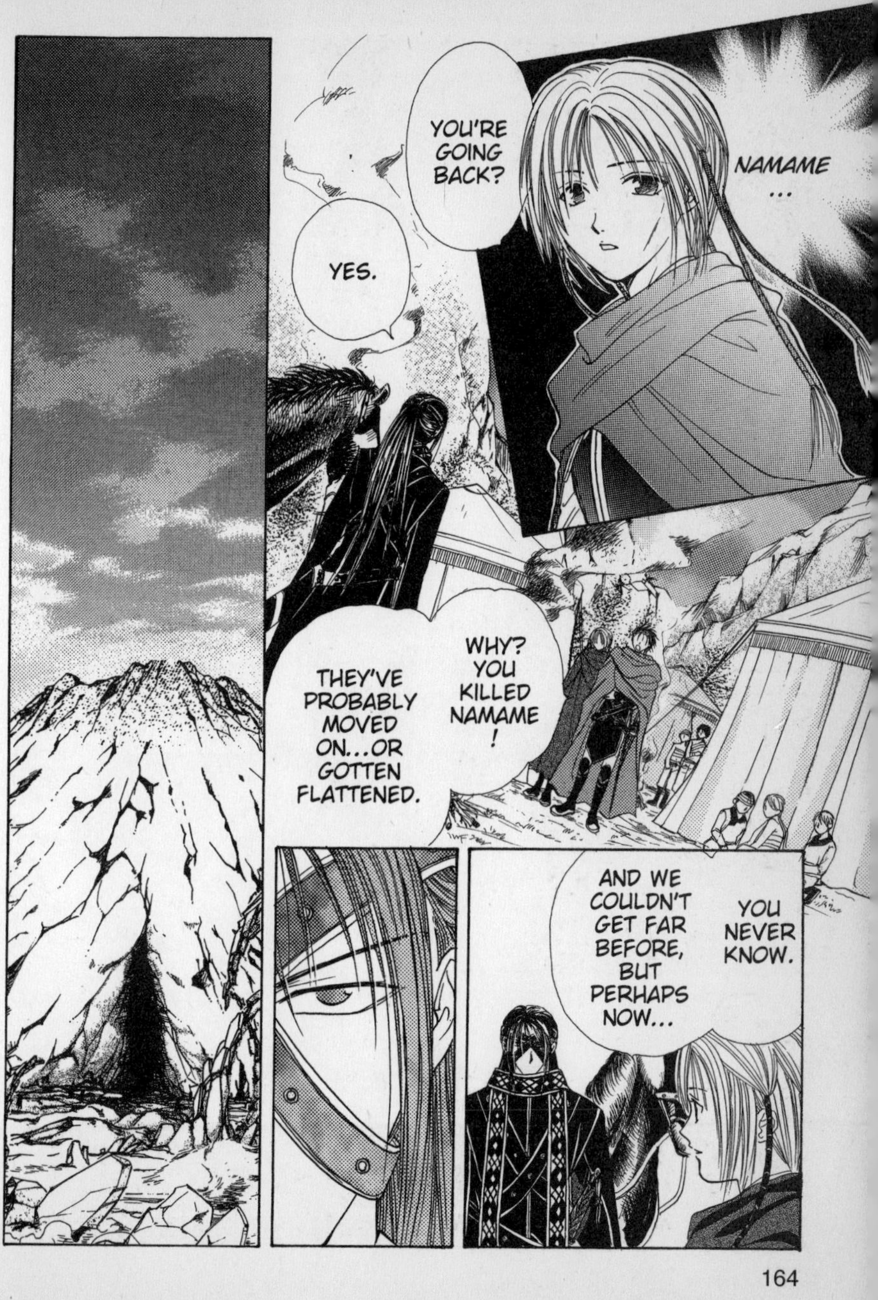
NAMAME ...
YOU'RE GOING BACK?
YES.
WHY? YOU KILLED NAMAME!
THEY'VE PROBABLY MOVED ON...OR GOTTEN FLATTENED.
YOU NEVER KNOW.
AND WE COULDN'T GET FAR BEFORE, BUT PERHAPS NOW...

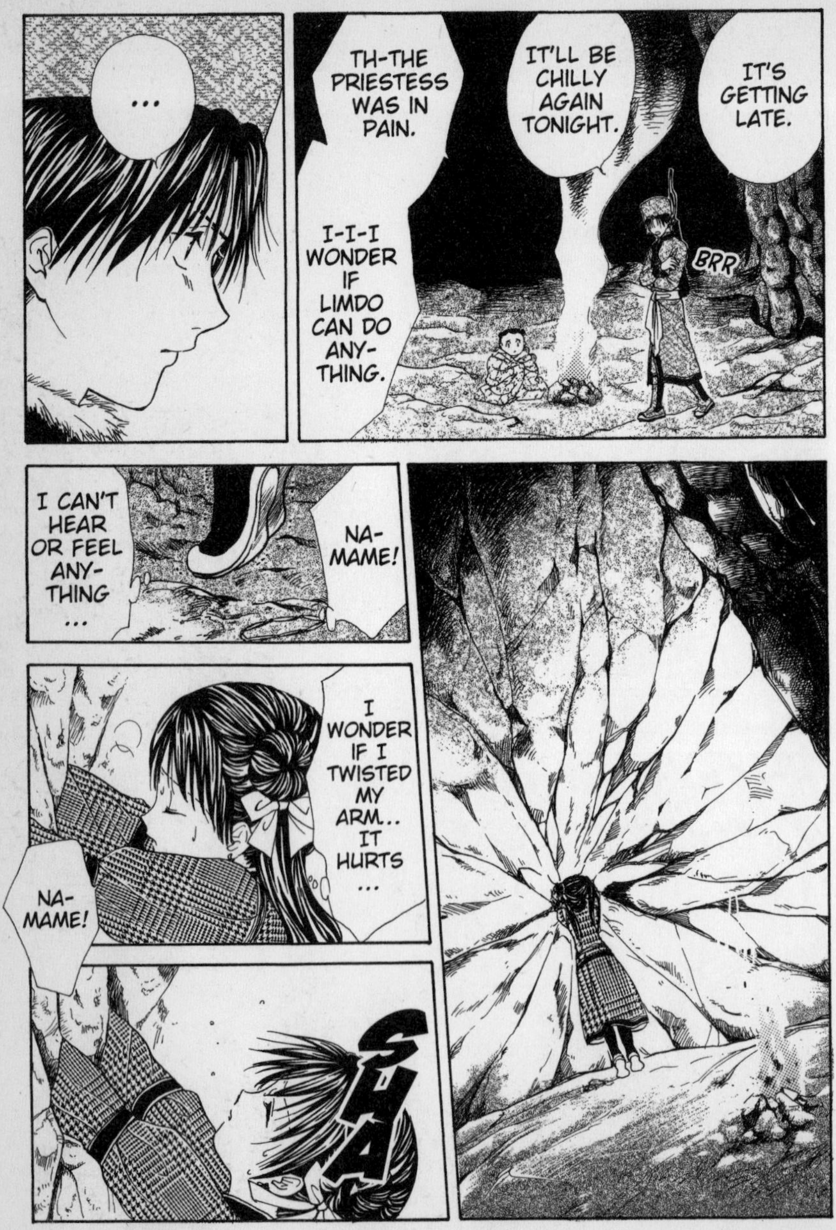
IT'S GETTING LATE.
IT'LL BE CHILLY AGAIN TONIGHT.
BRR
TH-THE PRIESTESS WAS IN PAIN.
I-I-I WONDER IF LIMDO CAN DO ANY-THING.
...
NA-MAME!
I CAN'T HEAR OR FEEL ANY-THING ...
I WONDER IF I TWISTED MY ARM... IT HURTS ...
NA-MAME!
SHA

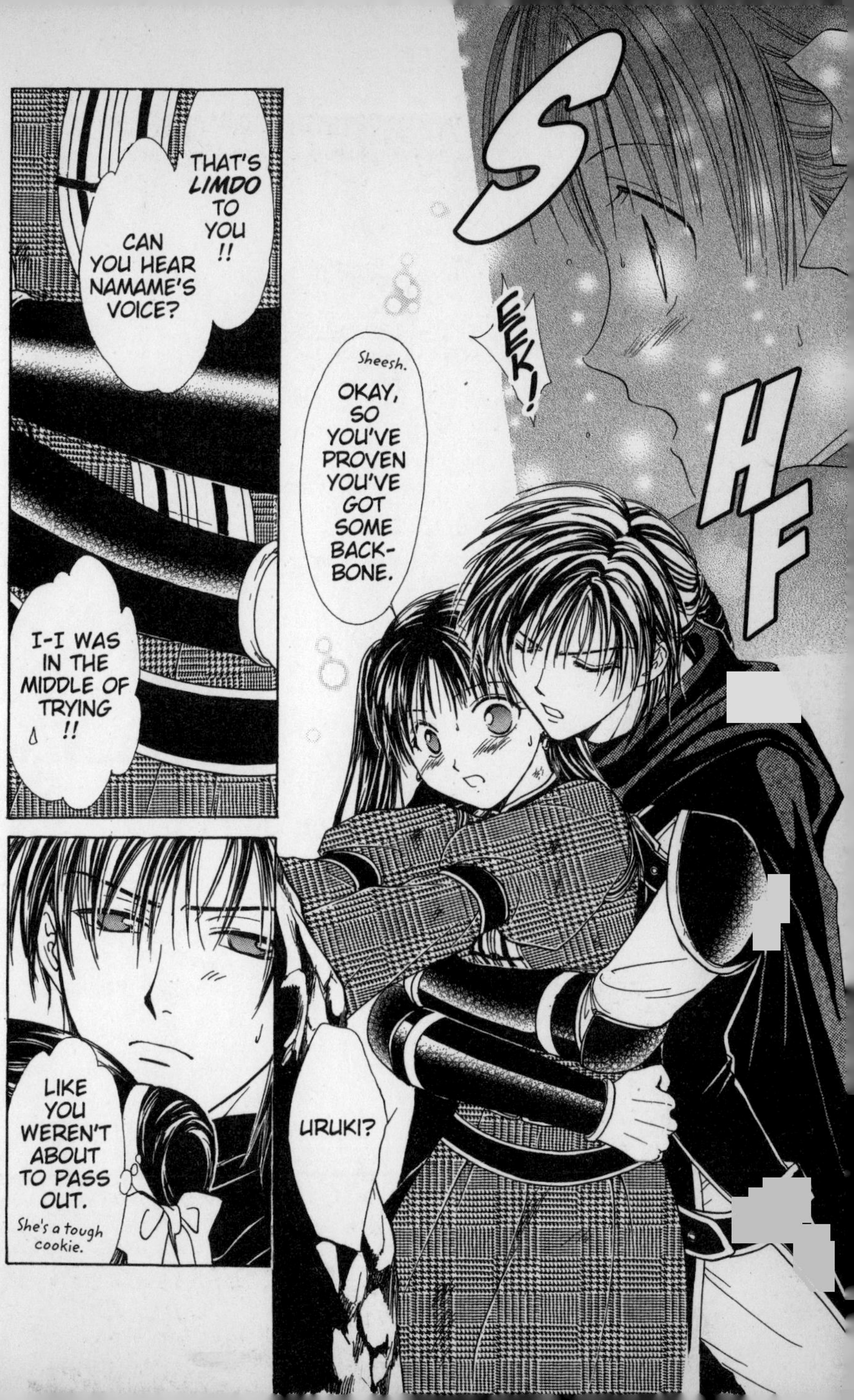
S
EEK!
HF
Sheesh.
OKAY, SO YOU'VE PROVEN YOU'VE GOT SOME BACK-BONE.
URUKI?
THAT'S LIMDO TO YOU!!
CAN YOU HEAR NAMAME'S VOICE?
I-I WAS IN THE MIDDLE OF TRYING!!
LIKE YOU WEREN'T ABOUT TO PASS OUT.
She's a tough cookie.

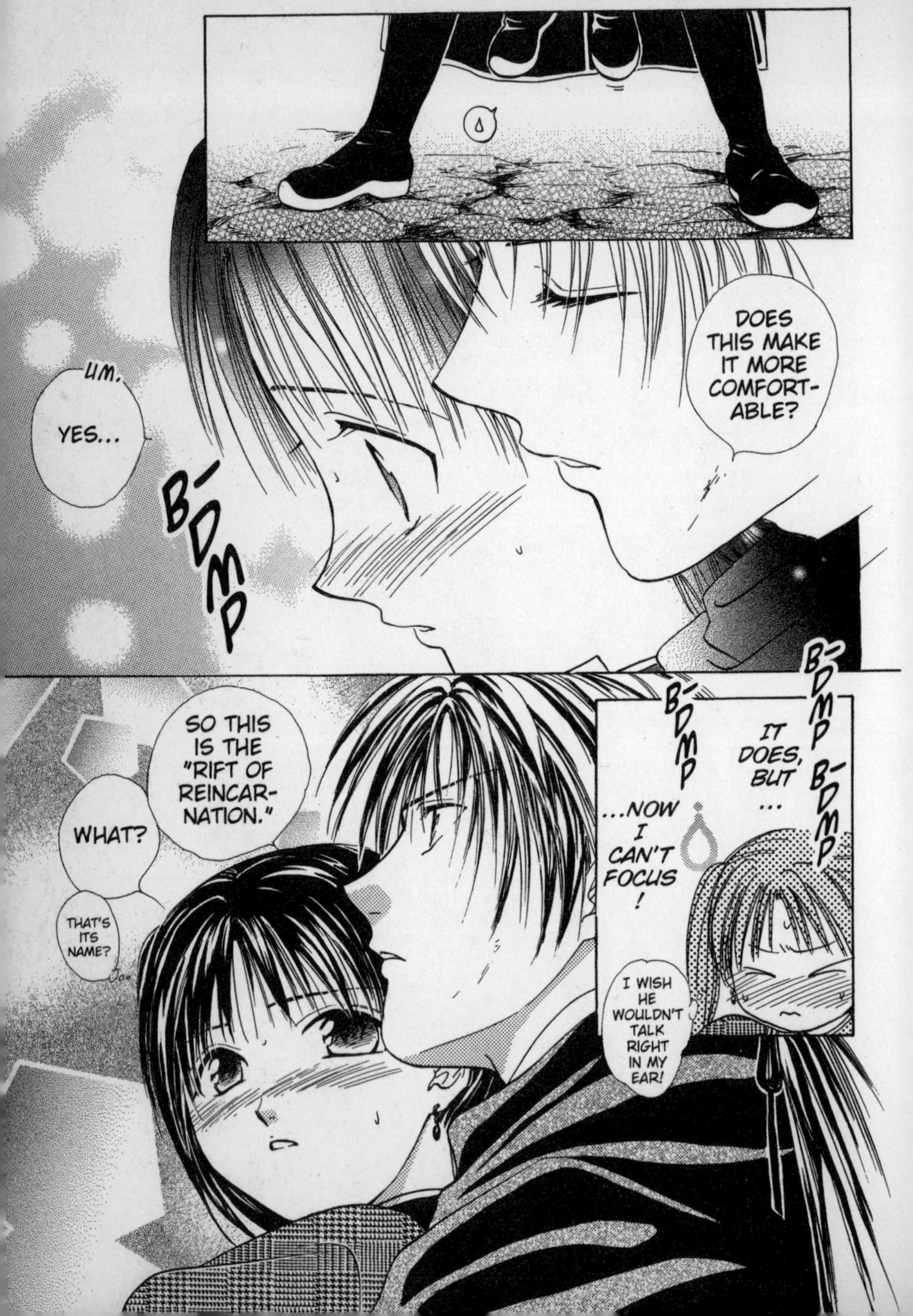
DOES THIS MAKE IT MORE COMFORT-ABLE?
B-DMP
UM.
YES...
B-DMP B-DMP
IT DOES, BUT ...
B-DMP
...NOW I CAN'T FOCUS!
I WISH HE WOULDN'T TALK RIGHT IN MY EAR!
SO THIS IS THE "RIFT OF REINCAR-NATION."
WHAT?
THAT'S ITS NAME?

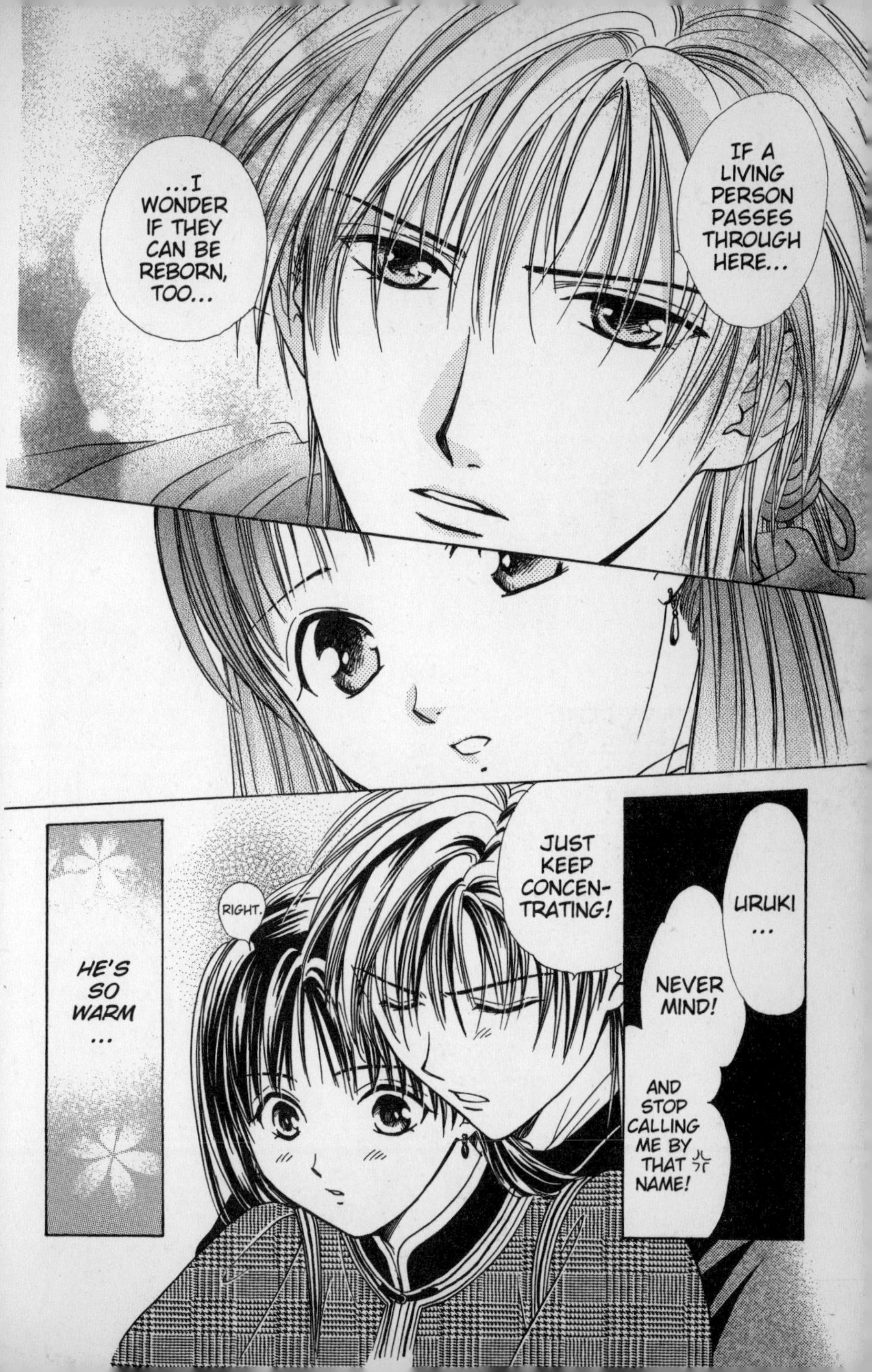
IF A LIVING PERSON PASSES THROUGH HERE...
...I WONDER IF THEY CAN BE REBORN, TOO...
URUKI ...
NEVER MIND!
AND STOP CALLING ME BY THAT NAME!
JUST KEEP CONCENTRATING!
RIGHT.
HE'S SO WARM ...

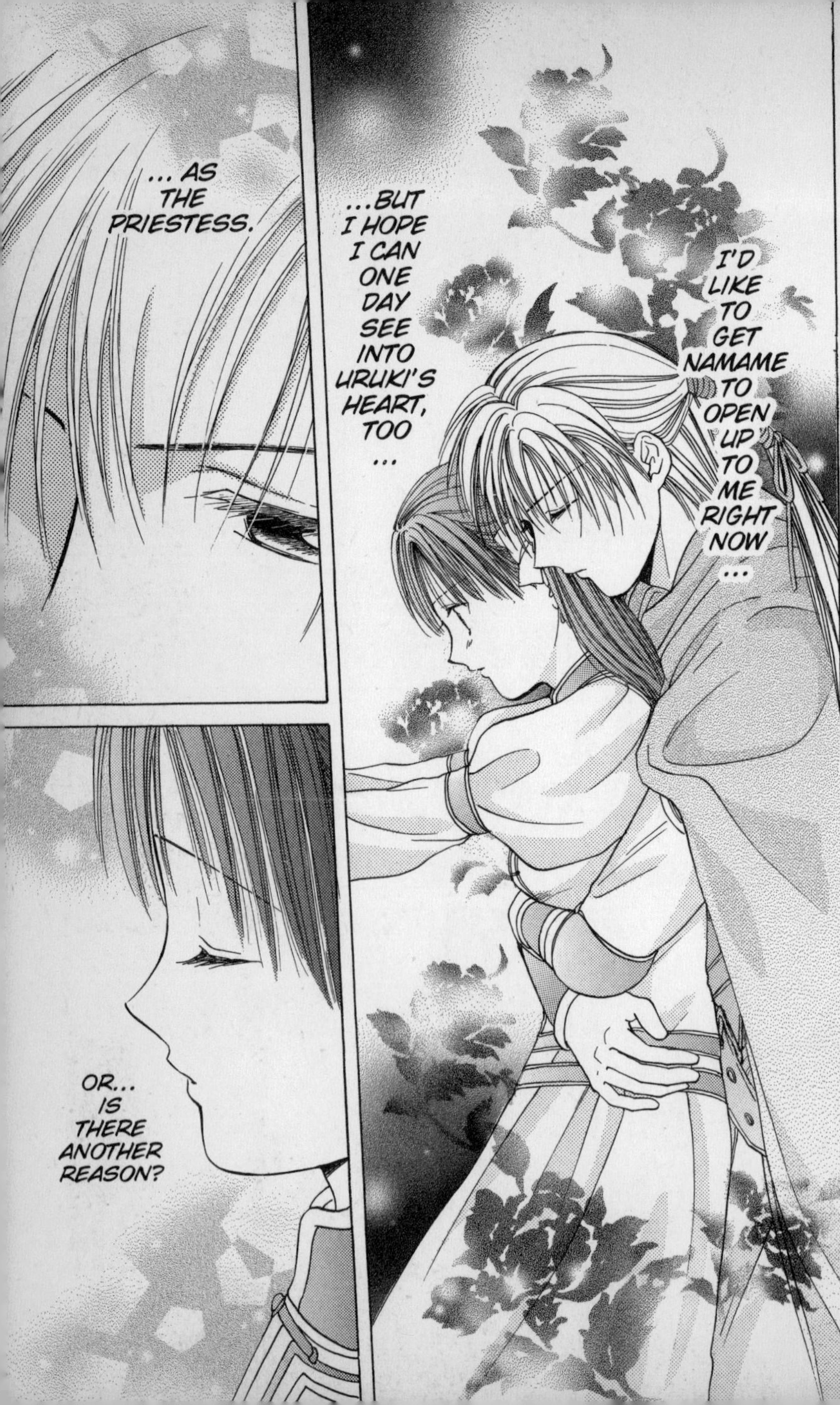
I'D LIKE TO GET NAMAME TO OPEN UP TO ME RIGHT NOW...
...BUT I HOPE I CAN ONE DAY SEE INTO URUKI'S HEART, TOO...
...AS THE PRIESTESS.
OR... IS THERE ANOTHER REASON?

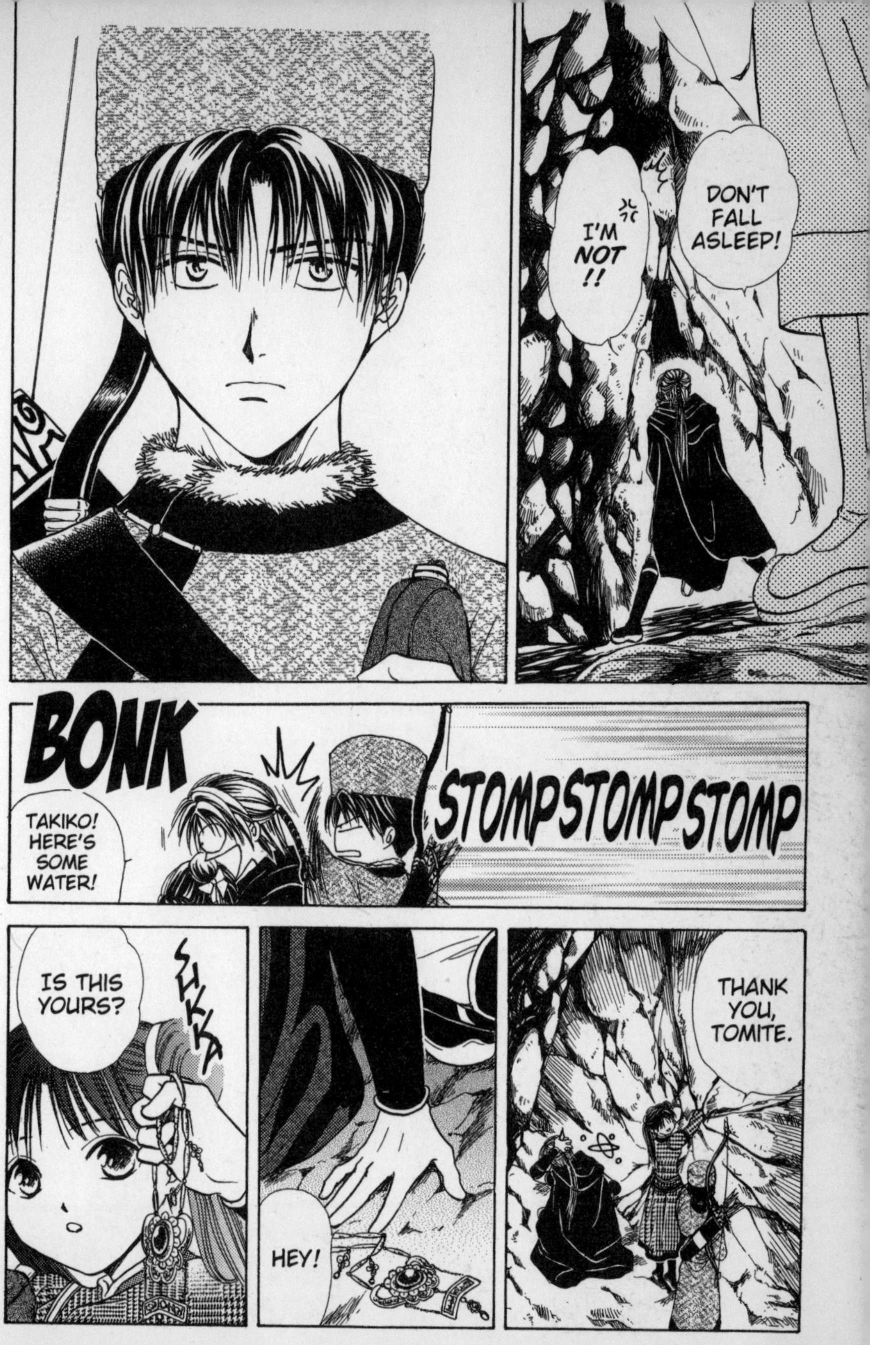
DON'T FALL ASLEEP!
I'M NOT!!
STOMPSTOMPSTOMP
BONK
TAKIKO! HERE'S SOME WATER!
THANK YOU, TOMITE.
HEY!
IS THIS YOURS?
SHKKA

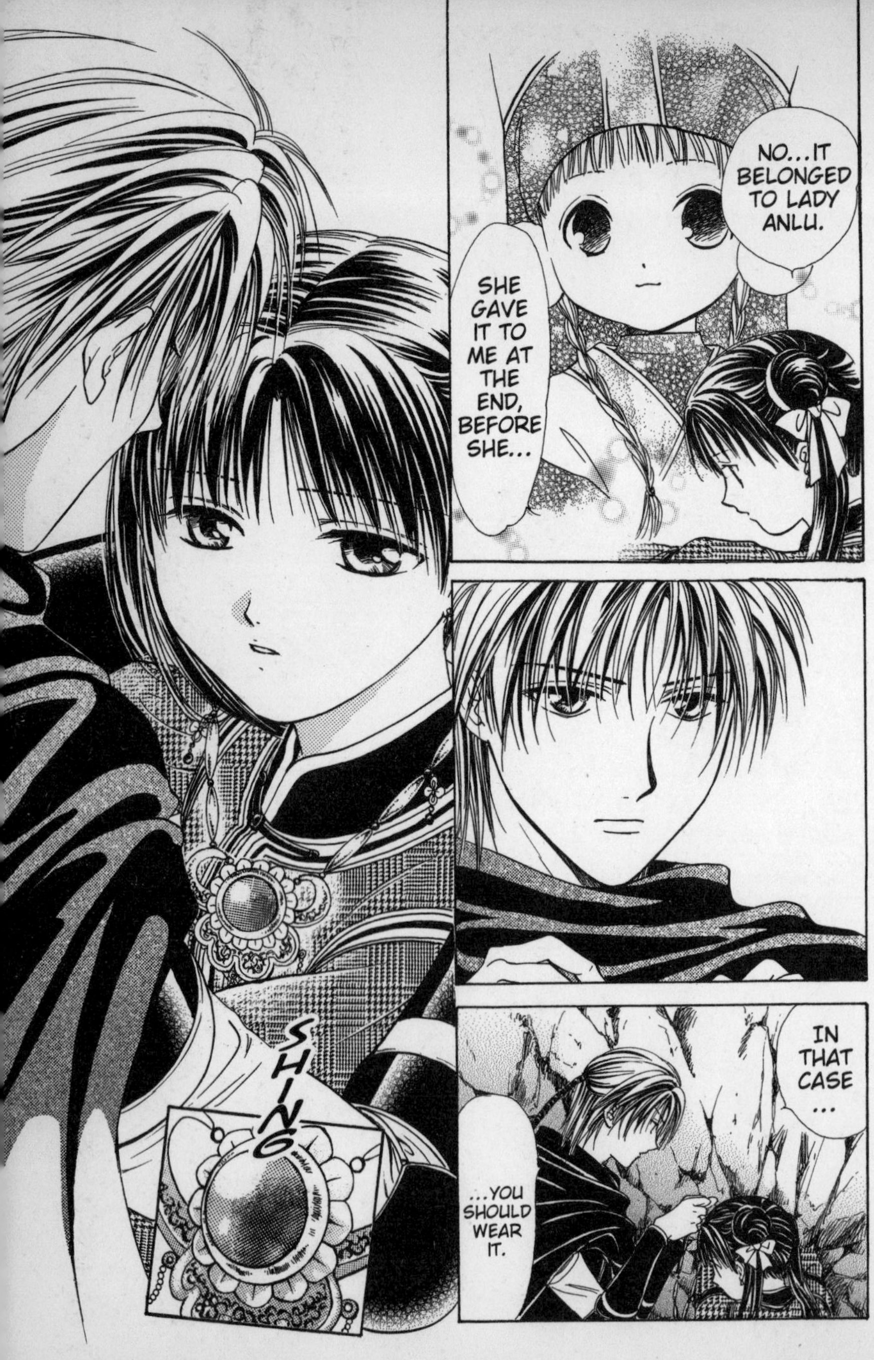
NO...IT BELONGED TO LADY ANLU.
SHE GAVE IT TO ME AT THE END, BEFORE SHE...
IN THAT CASE...
...YOU SHOULD WEAR IT.
SHING

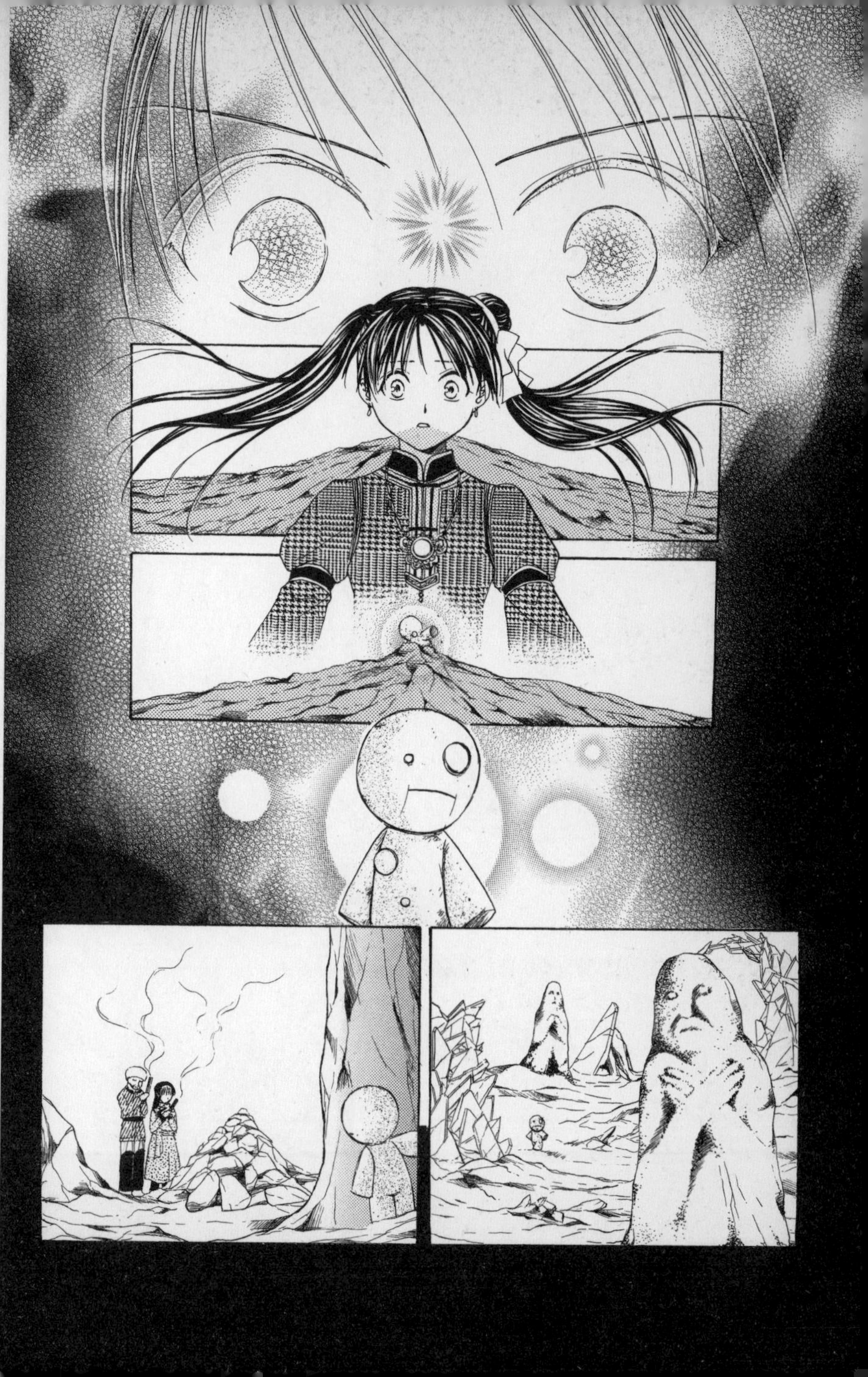

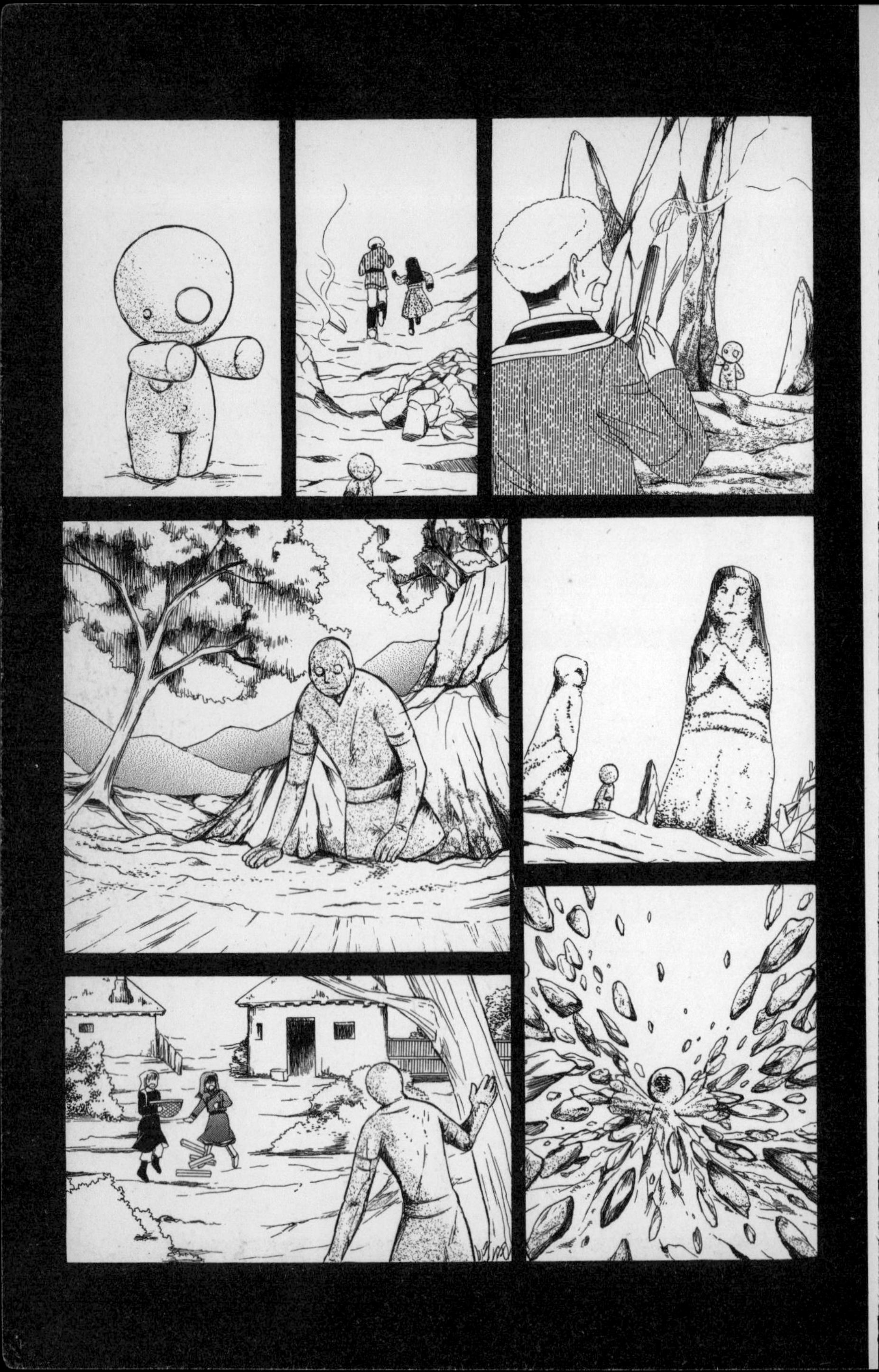

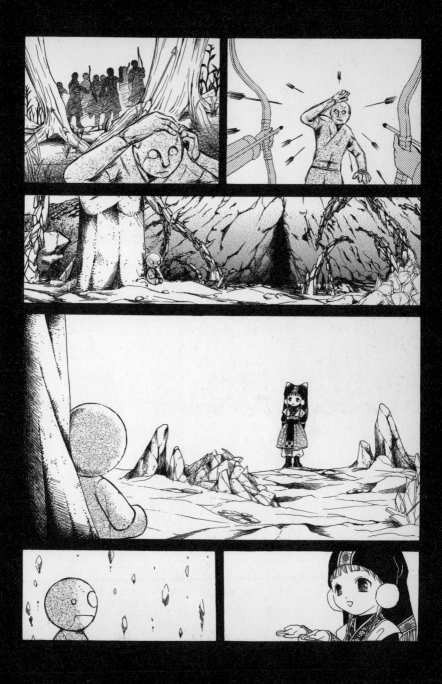

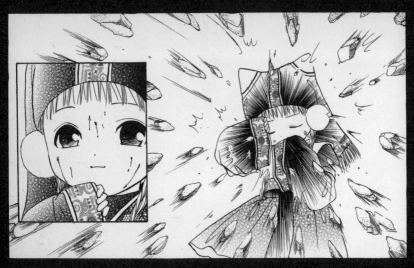

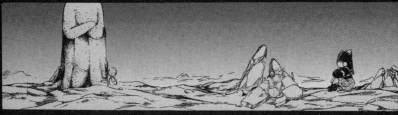

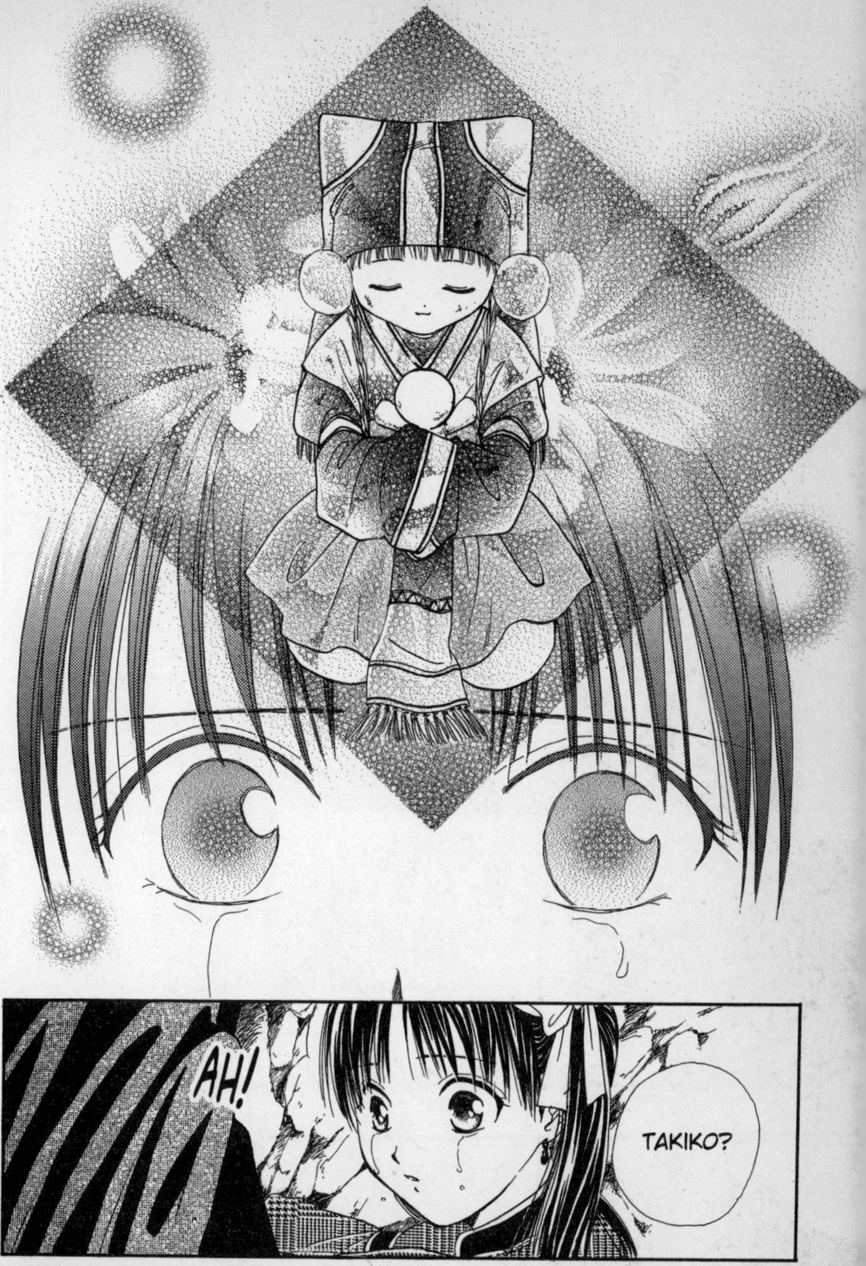
TAKIKO?
AH!

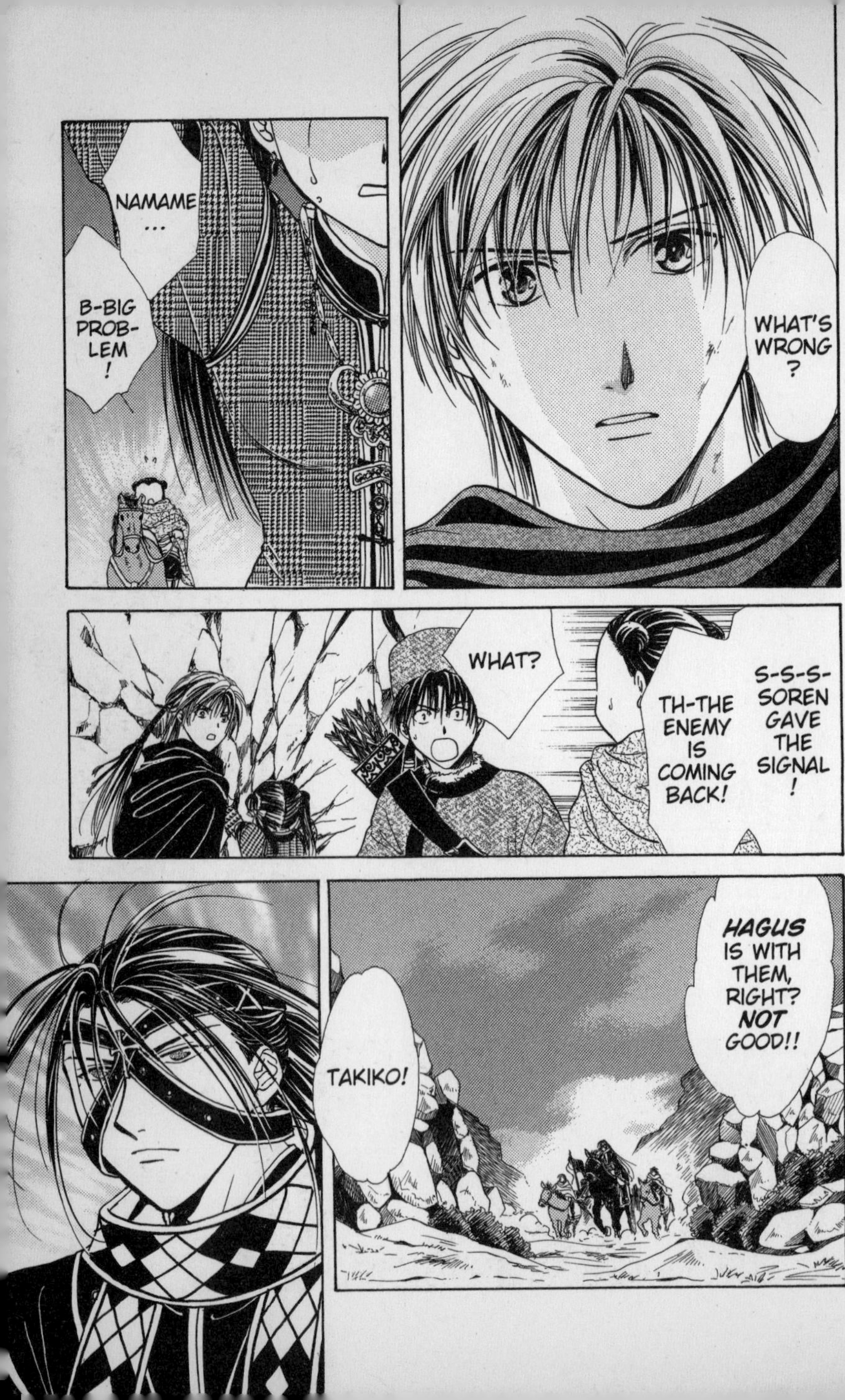
WHAT'S WRONG?
NAMAME ...
B-BIG PROBLEM!
S-S-S-SOREN GAVE THE SIGNAL!
TH-THE ENEMY IS COMING BACK!
WHAT?
HAGUS IS WITH THEM, RIGHT? *NOT* GOOD!!
TAKIKO!

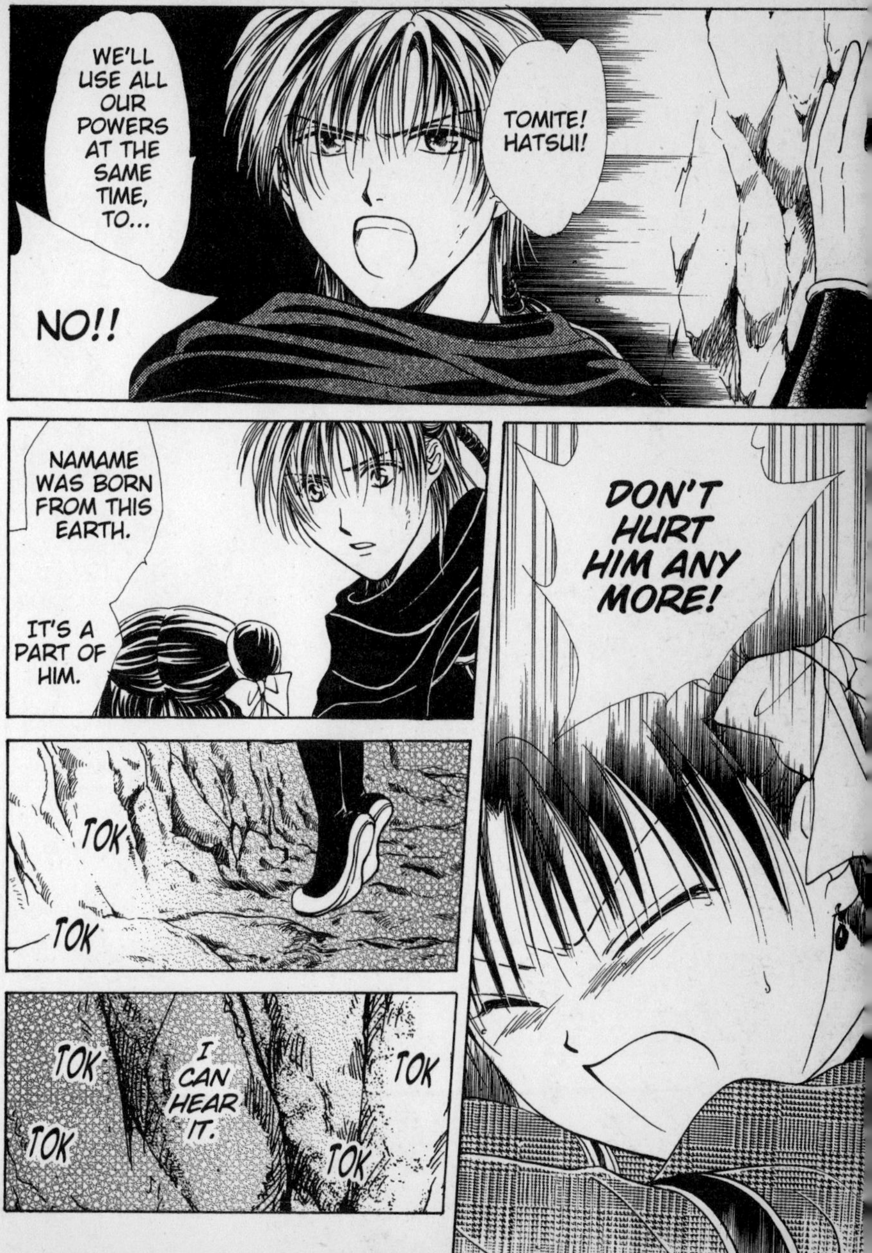
TOMITE! HATSUI!
WE'LL USE ALL OUR POWERS AT THE SAME TIME, TO...
NO!!
DON'T HURT HIM ANY MORE!
NAMAME WAS BORN FROM THIS EARTH.
IT'S A PART OF HIM.
TOK
TOK
TOK
I CAN HEAR IT.
TOK
TOK
TOK

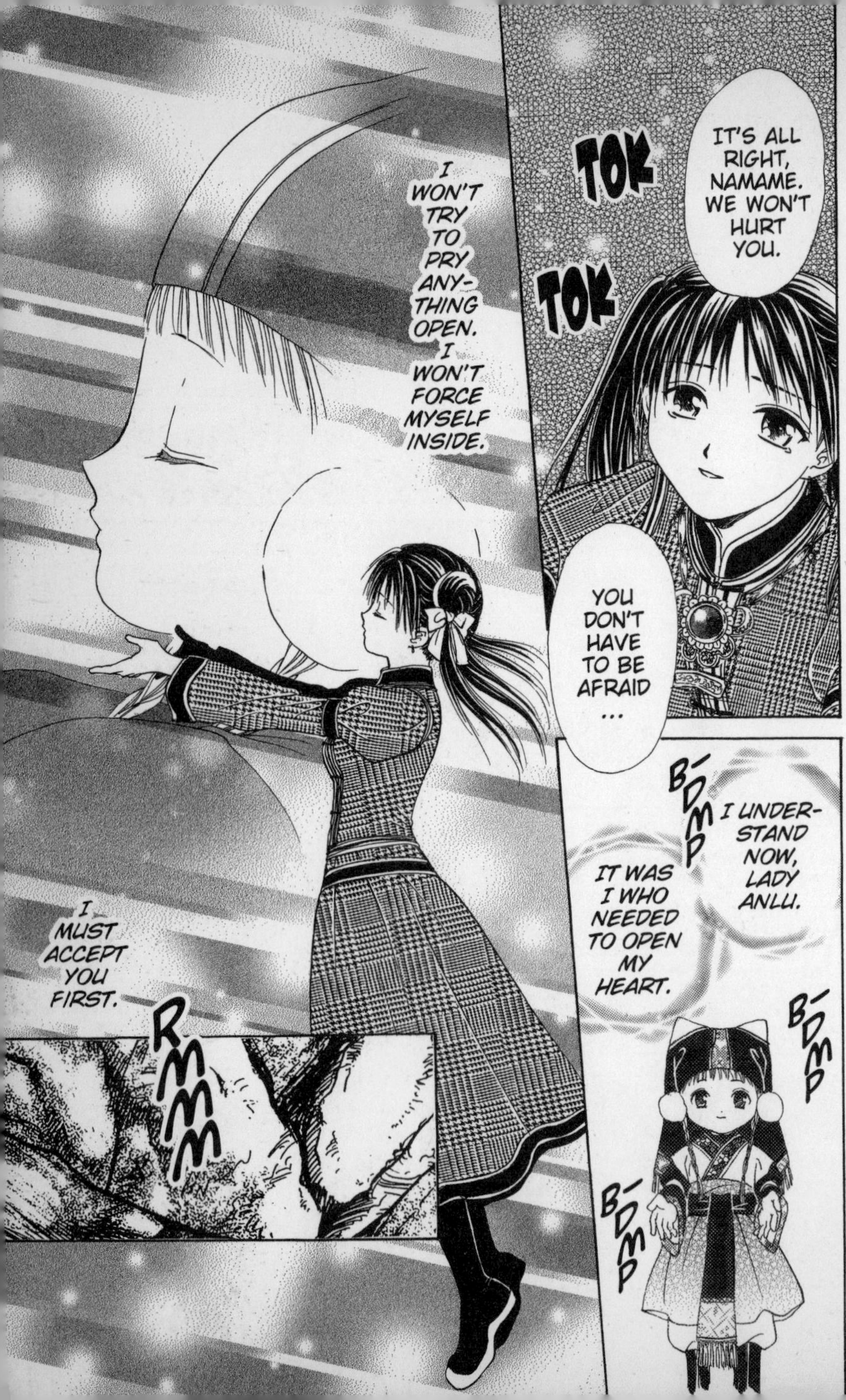
TOK
TOK
IT'S ALL RIGHT, NAMAME. WE WON'T HURT YOU.
YOU DON'T HAVE TO BE AFRAID...
B-DMP
I UNDERSTAND NOW, LADY ANLU.
IT WAS I WHO NEEDED TO OPEN MY HEART.
B-DMP
B-DMP
I WON'T TRY TO PRY ANYTHING OPEN. I WON'T FORCE MYSELF INSIDE.
I MUST ACCEPT YOU FIRST.
RMMMM

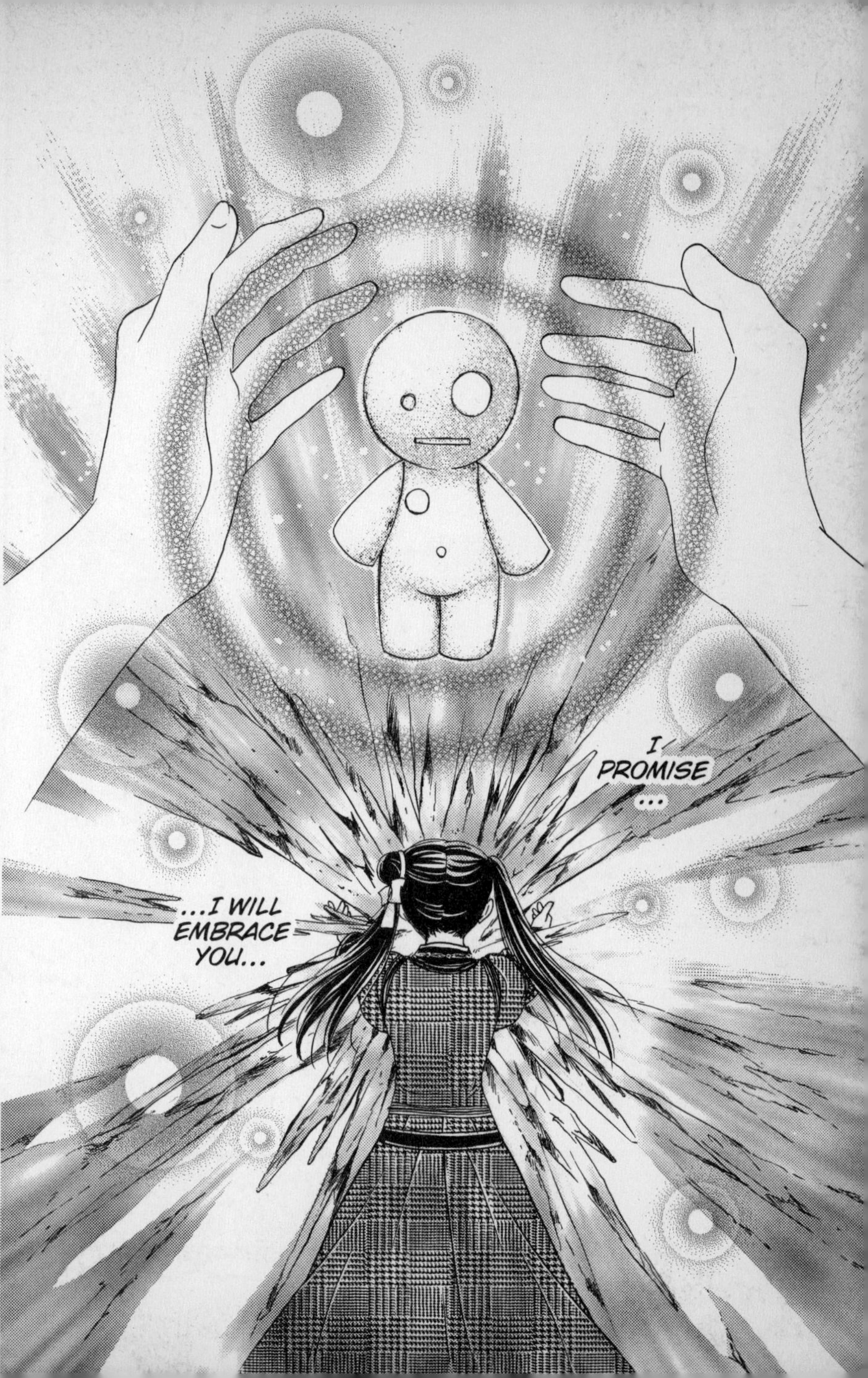
I PROMISE ...
...I WILL EMBRACE YOU...

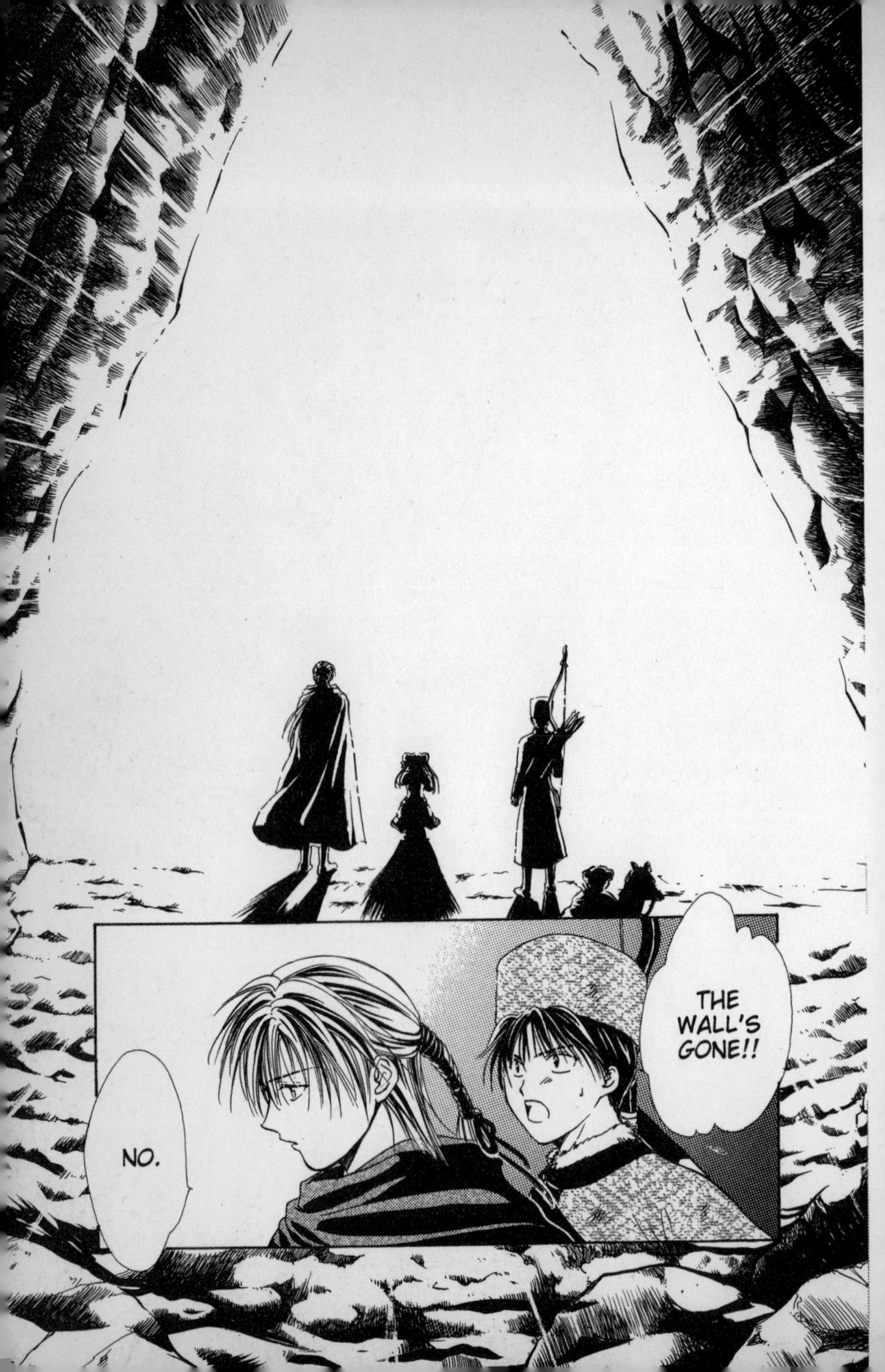
THE WALL'S GONE!!
NO.

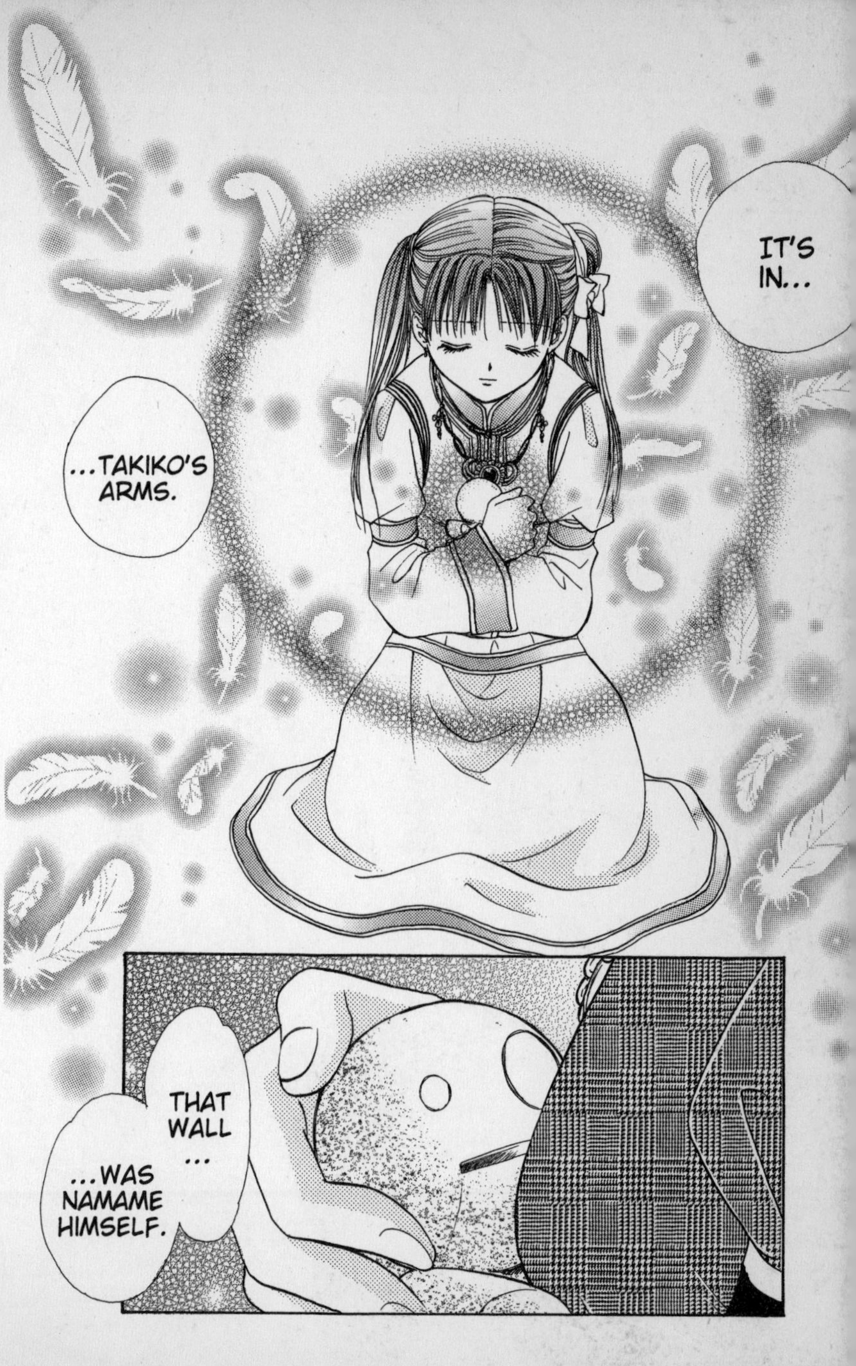
IT'S IN...
...TAKIKO'S ARMS.
THAT WALL ...
...WAS NAMAME HIMSELF.

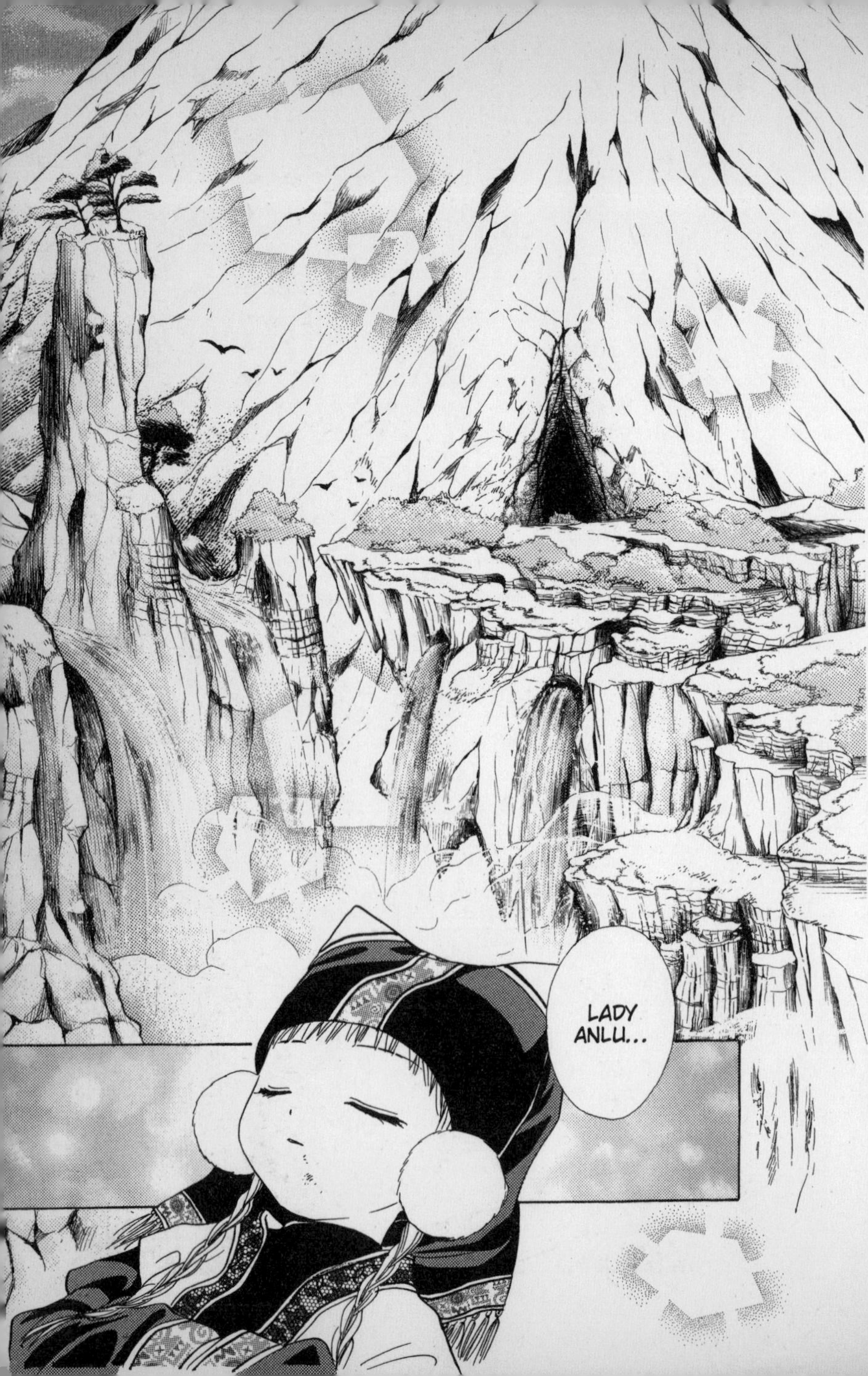
LADY ANLU...

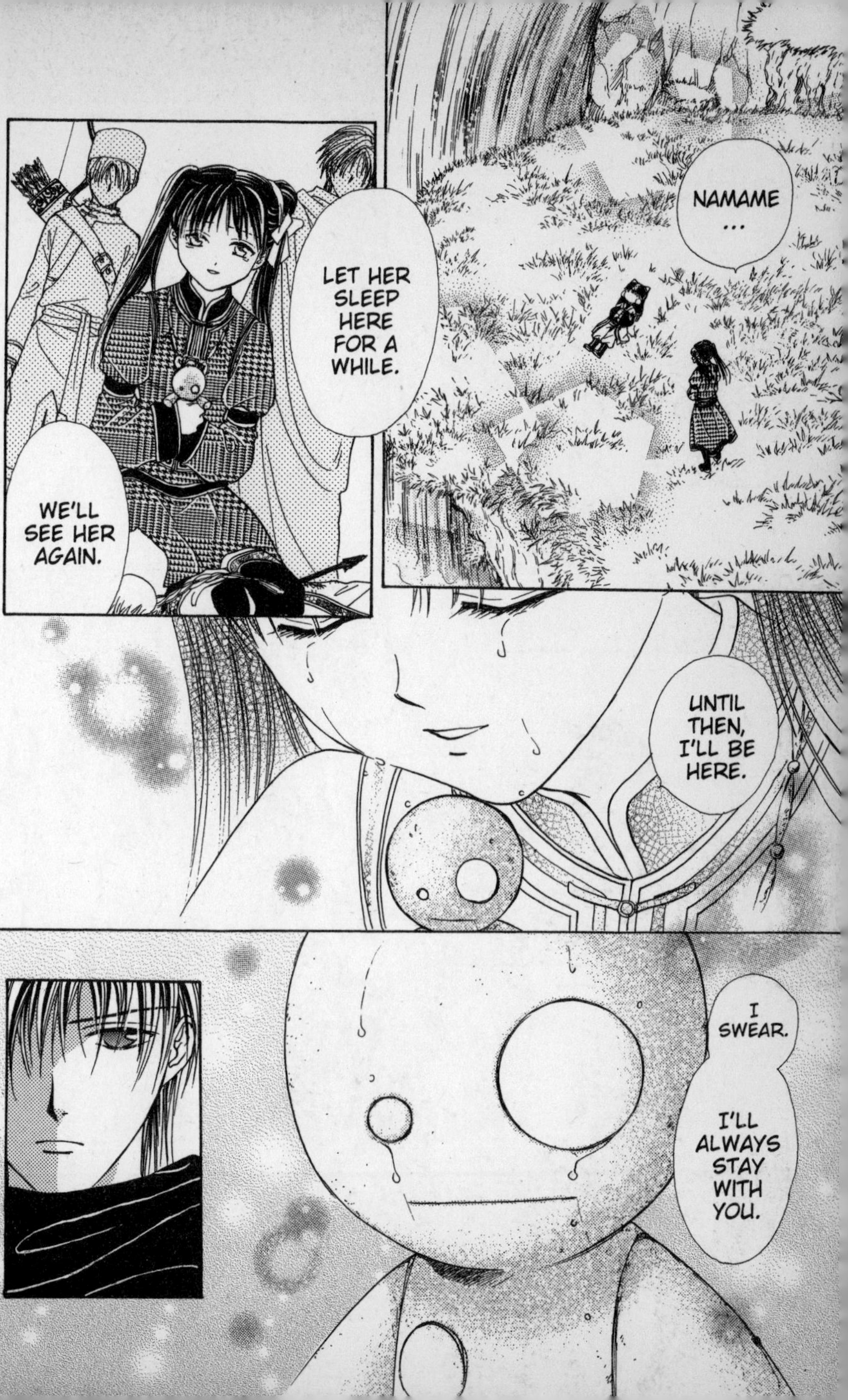
NAMAME ...
LET HER SLEEP HERE FOR A WHILE.
WE'LL SEE HER AGAIN.
UNTIL THEN, I'LL BE HERE.
I SWEAR.
I'LL ALWAYS STAY WITH YOU.

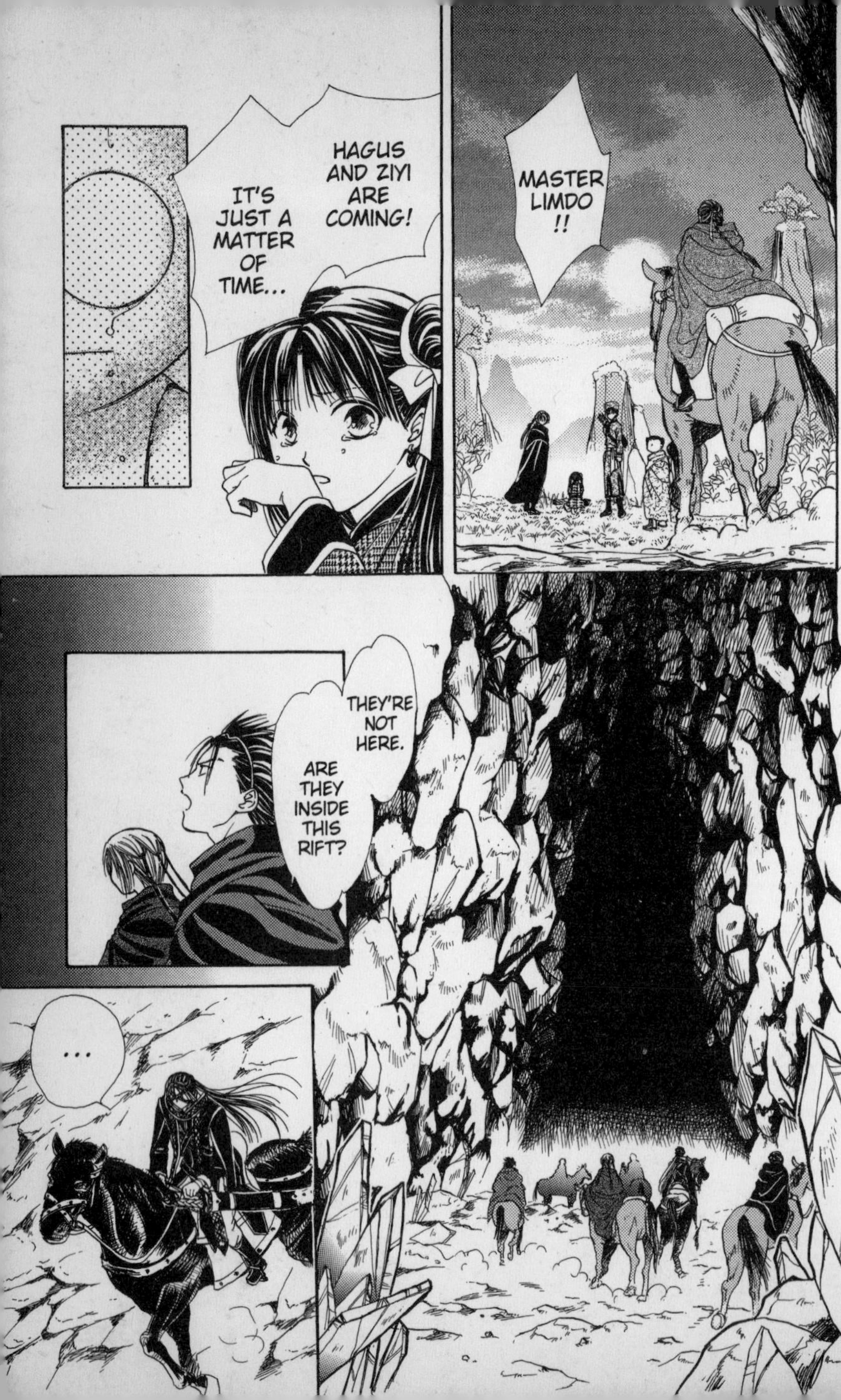
MASTER LIMDO !!
HAGUS AND ZIYI ARE COMING!
IT'S JUST A MATTER OF TIME...
THEY'RE NOT HERE.
ARE THEY INSIDE THIS RIFT?
...

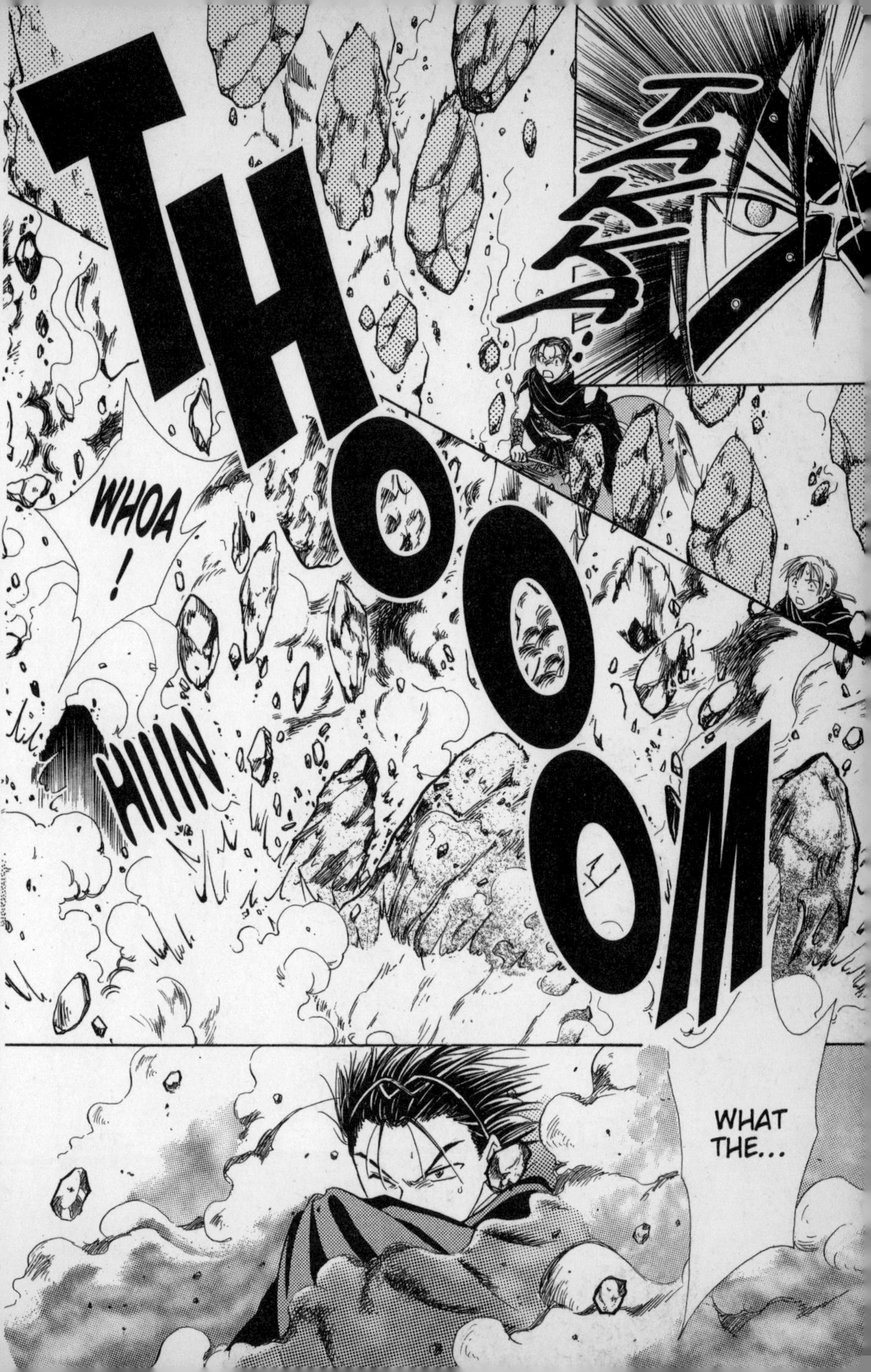
THOOOM
WHOA !
HIIIN
WHAT THE...

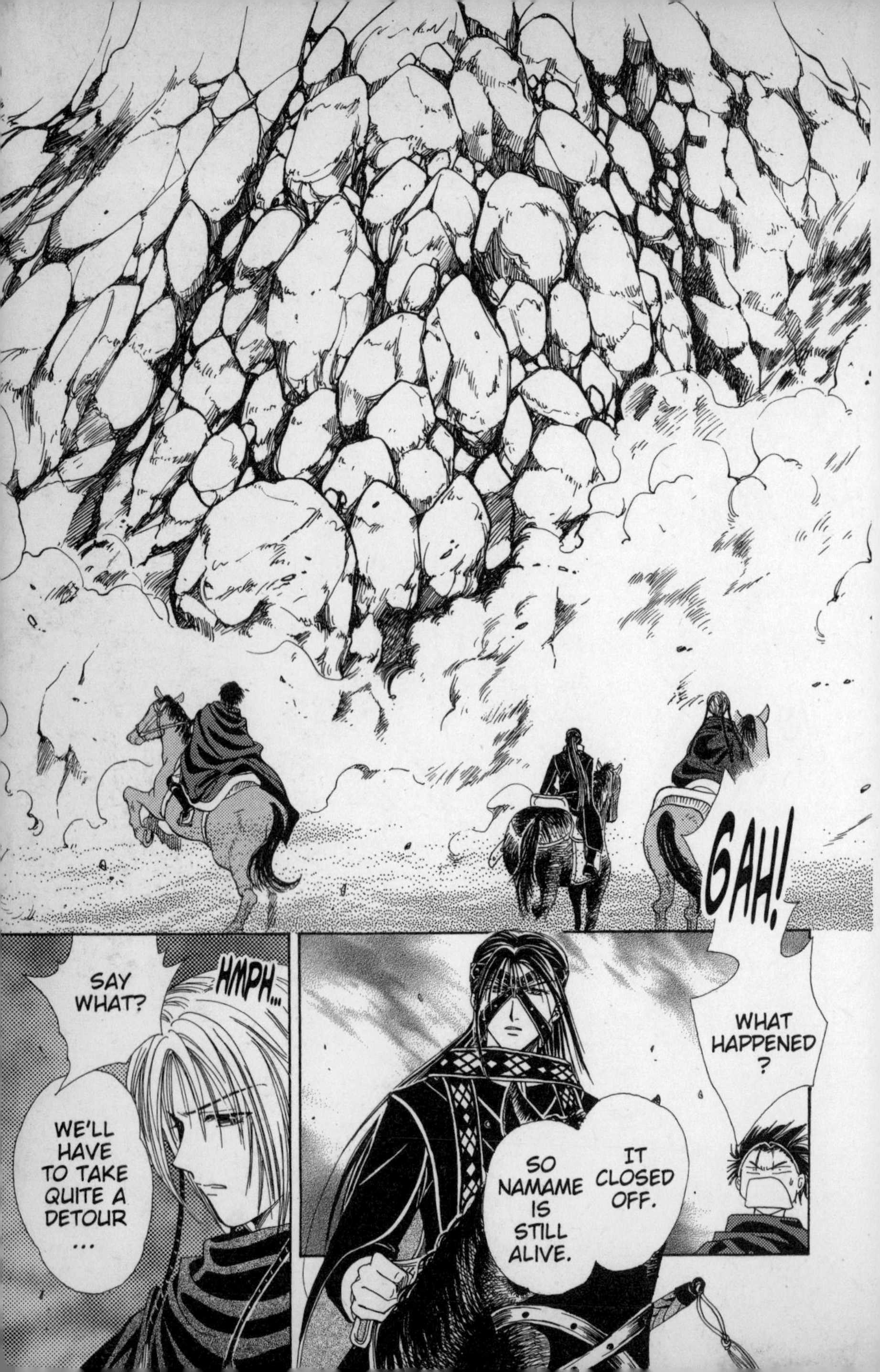
GAH!
WHAT HAPPENED?
IT CLOSED OFF.
SO NAMAME IS STILL ALIVE.
HMPH...
SAY WHAT?
WE'LL HAVE TO TAKE QUITE A DETOUR...

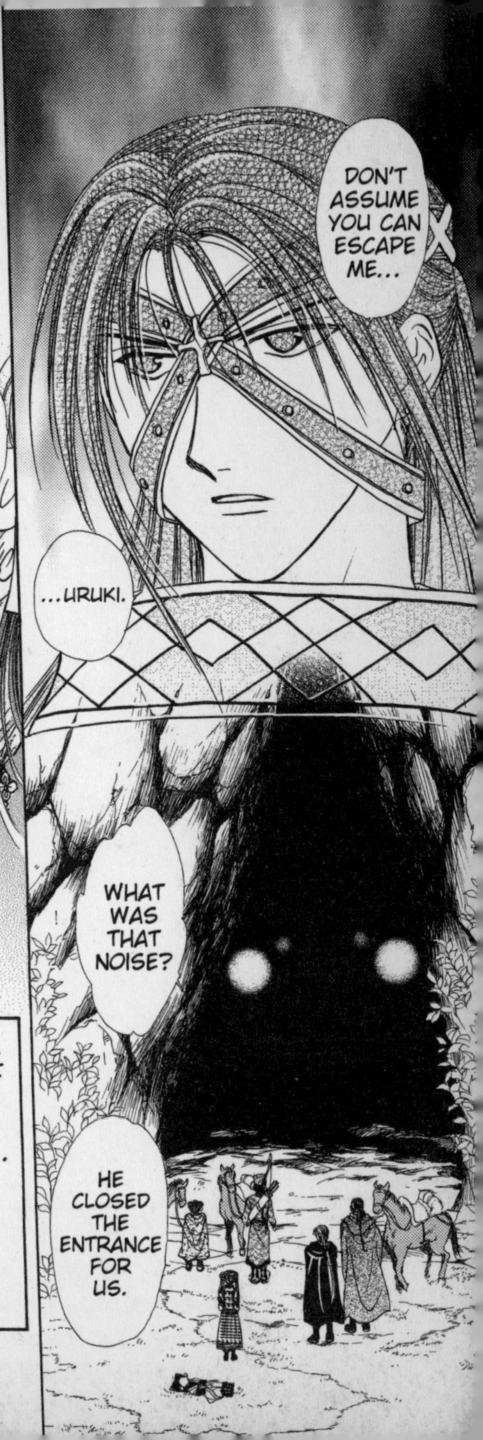
DON'T ASSUME YOU CAN ESCAPE ME...
...URUKI.
WHAT WAS THAT NOISE?
HE CLOSED THE ENTRANCE FOR US.

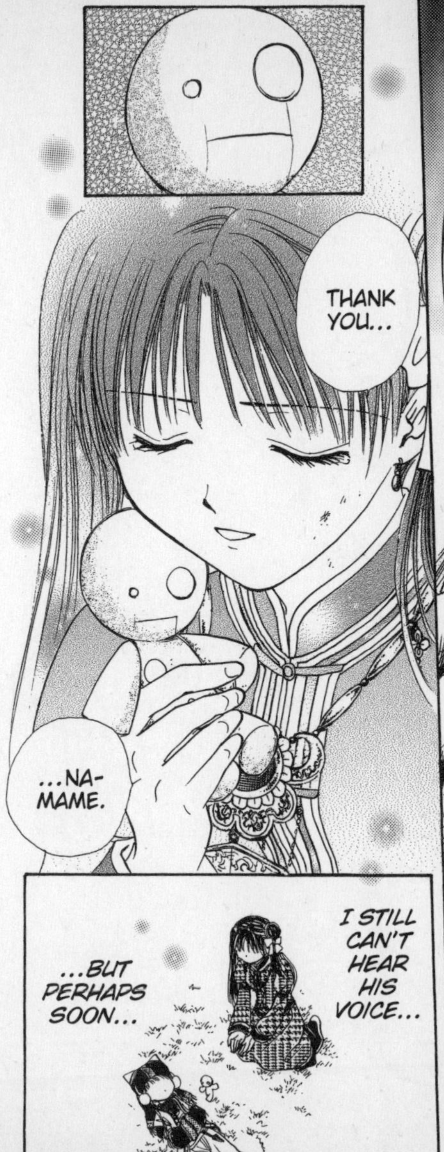
THANK YOU...
...NA-MAME.
I STILL CAN'T HEAR HIS VOICE...
...BUT PERHAPS SOON...

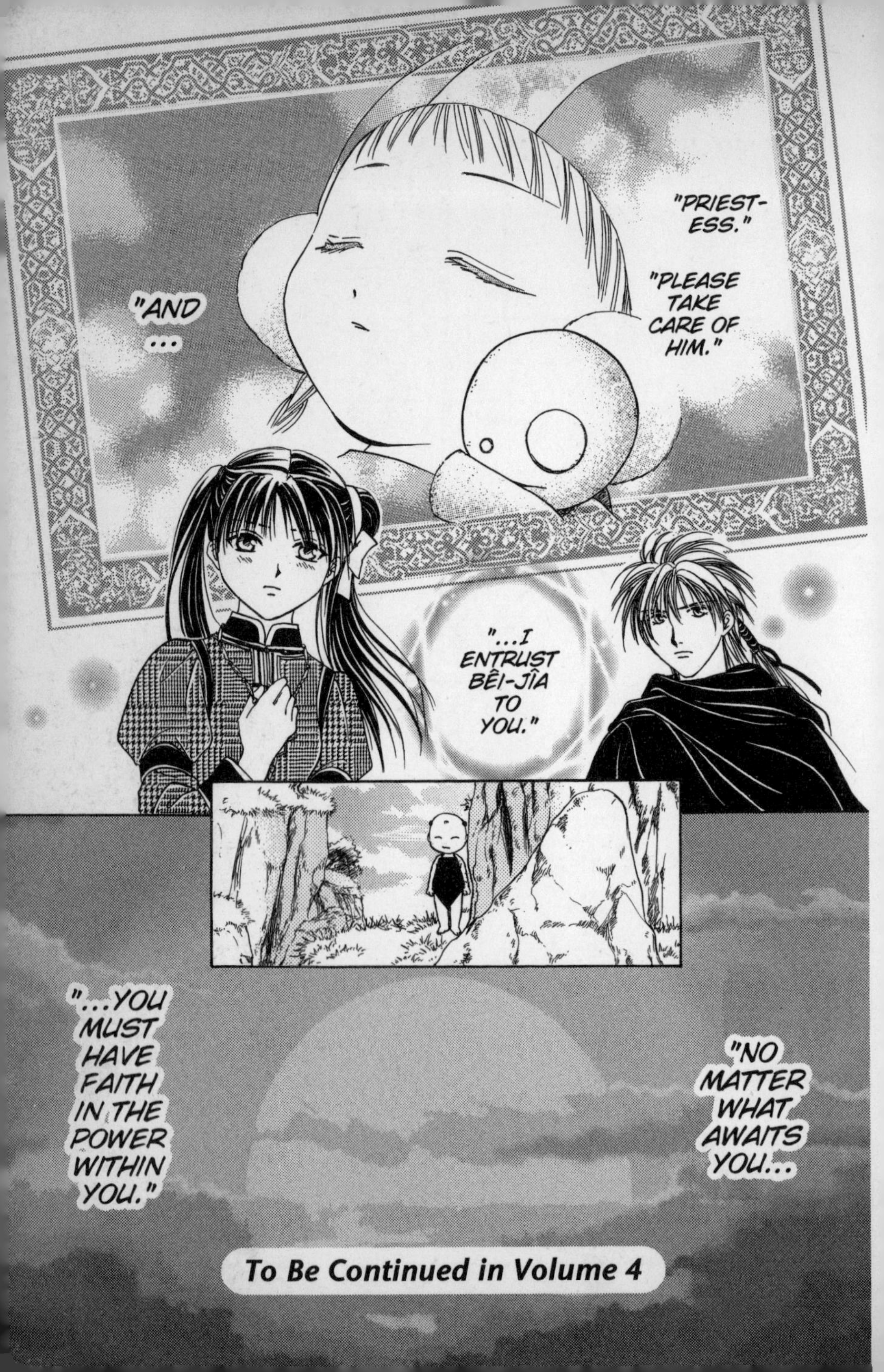
"PRIEST-ESS."
"PLEASE TAKE CARE OF HIM."
"AND ...
"...I ENTRUST BÊI-JÎA TO YOU."
"NO MATTER WHAT AWAITS YOU...
"...YOU MUST HAVE FAITH IN THE POWER WITHIN YOU."
To Be Continued in Volume 4

Yuu Watase was born on March 5 in a town near Osaka, Japan, and she was raised there before moving to Tokyo to follow her dream of creating manga. In the decade since her debut short story, *Pajama De Ojama (An Intrusion in Pajamas)*, she has produced more than 50 compiled volumes of short stories and continuing series. Her latest work, *Absolute Boyfriend*, was serialized in Japan in the anthology magazine *Shôjo Comic* and is currently being serialized in English in *Shojo Beat* magazine. Watase's other beloved series, *Alice 19th, Imadoki!,* and *Ceres: Celestial Legend,* are now available in North America in English editions published by VIZ Media.

Fushigi Yûgi:
Genbu Kaiden Vol. 3

The Shojo Beat Manga Edition

STORY AND ART BY
YUU WATASE

Translation/Lillian Olsen
Touch-up Art & Lettering/Rina Mapa
Design/Amy Martin
Editors/Ian Robertson and Shaenon K. Garrity

Editor in Chief, Books/Alvin Lu
Editor in Chief, Magazines/Marc Weidenbaum
VP of Publishing Licensing/Rika Inouye
VP of Sales/Gonzalo Ferreyra
Sr. VP of Marketing/Liza Coppola
Publisher/Hyoe Narita

© 2004 Yuu WATASE/Shogakukan Inc.
First published by Shogakukan Inc. in Japan as "Fushigi Yugi Genbukaiden."
All rights reserved. The stories, characters and incidents mentioned in this
publication are entirely fictional.

Printed in Canada

Published by VIZ Media, LLC
P.O. Box 77010
San Francisco, CA 94107

Shojo Beat Manga Edition
10 9 8 7 6 5 4 3 2
First printing, February 2006
Second printing, March 2008

www.viz.com

store.viz.com

Thank you for reading the
Fushigi Yûgi: Genbu Kaiden,
Volume 3 manga.
Please turn to the back and
enjoy a special excerpt of the
Kamikaze Girls novel,
written by Novala Takemoto.

"Hey girlie, my name's Shirayuri. Would Miz Momoko be around at home?"

If that was an attempt at polite language, it was a shambles. But anyway, being the "girlie" addressed, I said yes. Oh dear, this was that Ichiko Shirayuri who really wanted Versace no matter what! From the clumsy style of her letter I had assumed she would be about thirteen years old, but there was no question now that she was a bona-fide high-schooler, about the same age as I. It would seem the awkwardness of her letter derived not from childishness but from simple ignorance, or should I say, stupidity. As I fidgeted in the garden, thinking what a pain it was to get involved with someone of this sort, the *sukeban* spoke again.

"So could you conduct me over to Miz Momoko if you will?"

To this, I answered nervously, "Um, I'm Momoko, actually."

You should have seen her face when she heard that. She twisted her mouth and widened her eyes, and her expression could have been taken as wanting to pick a fight, or being really sad and about to burst into tears, either way.   TO BE CONTINUED...

The *Kamikaze Girls* full-length novel will be available soon from VIZ Media at bookstores near you!

something sporting so many decorations both in front and back actually run? Just the accessories alone look pretty heavy—is what I thought as I gazed upon the chopper from a distance, giving it minus a thousand style points for the garish bad taste of its color scheme and utterly nonexistent sense of design. I mean to say, an ordinary motorcycle would probably be fine with all those embellishments so long as it had enough horsepower, but the bike in front of my eyes was, in spite of all the gnarly remodeling, a scooter. No matter how you looked at it, it was a plain old 50cc scooter.

This freakish scooter stopped blasting its horn when it realized I was there. And then, the person who had been doing the blasting, namely the person who had been riding the bike, got off of it and started walking toward me. The person had straight bleached-blond hair down to her shoulders, wore blue eye shadow and bright red lipstick, and had on a navy-blue school uniform comprised of a short jacket and a very long skirt with a prodigious number of pleats, which dragged on the ground. On her feet were—well, it would sound good to call them "mules," but actually they were cheap purple slip-on sandals of the type moms wear when going out to the neighborhood supermarket, and their sparkles glinted in the sun. *Wow, a* sukeban, *and a super old-school one too…Who knew bad girls wearing outfits like this still existed? Hand it to Ibaraki—this place is deep. If a curator for a natural history museum saw her, she'd immediately be captured and exhibited next to a stegosaur skeleton in the Fossils section.* As I was thinking this and watching her approach with some trepidation because, let's face it, people like that are kinda scary, the *sukeban* yelled out to me in a loud voice.

heard the noisy cacophony of an engine, probably from the motorcycle of a passing Yanki. The loud vrooming sound gradually got louder, and then it stopped. Just when I thought it was finally quiet again, the earsplitting sound of those horns that Yanki like to put on their bikes and cars, arranged to play the *Godfather* theme, rang out: *parara rararara rararaaraa*!! *parara rararara rararararaa*!!!! It was blasted out repeatedly, over and over. The source of the sound seemed to be right in front of our house, or at least very close to it, so I ventured out into the yard. The most outrageous motorcycle was parked out front.

In front of the handlebars towered an indescribably strange sunshade-type thing, fixed willy-nilly without any thought of balance, and painted with the Rising Sun. The seat had a backrest, which stretched so high skyward that if Giant Baba stood behind it, his head probably wouldn't show over the top. The seat itself was leopard-print. And the sunshade and backrest were not the only elongated features: behind the backrest were attached what would be called "tail fins" on a car, I believe, like super-long fake nails only a thousand times larger, and these too spread upward, reaching about as high as the seat and painted a camouflage pattern. The muffler was twisted, turned out, and extended, and again, pointed up. This muffler, while oddly shaped, was an ordinary metallic silver color, but the rest of the body was painted shocking pink all over, and overlaid with glitter. This was obviously a hot rod belonging to a Yanki, or more specifically, a Zokki—a member of a Bosozoku biker gang. I had seen bikes of this sort in Amagasaki and here in Ibaraki, but this was my first experience of seeing one this crazily souped-up from right up close. *Could* of which was that she lived in Shimotsuma too, so would it be all right if she came by sometime to see the merchandise for herself? Well, if she was just a middle schooler, I didn't see any problem with inviting her to the house. I called the cell phone number given in her letter and arranged to have her come over after lunch that Saturday.

School ended at noon on Saturday, and I went straight home because that girl was coming over. Even though she was younger than me, it would be our first meeting and moreover, she was going to be buying clothes from me. Thinking it would be rude to greet her without being dressed at least somewhat properly, I decided to wear my white rose-patterned lace blouse with a black velvet knee-length skirt that's decorated in front with ladder lace and all kinds of other white lace, while the back is like curtains that are closed at the top and draped back at the sides, and where the velvet would ordinarily fall—namely the middle of the hips—layers of tulle peek out like bustles. On my head I perched a large white ribbon made to be worn like a headdress, and then I went to the room where all the bogus Versace was stored to arrange everything, sorting it into piles by type while I waited.

We had agreed to meet at one thirty, but she didn't appear. Maybe she was lost? Perhaps my directions had been inadequate. I'd told her to go just a little bit east on Route 131 where it intersects Route 249, and take the first left, which is a narrow road—it was an ordinary farmhouse with rice paddies in front, and she'd see it right after she turned. Maybe that wasn't detailed enough? But there was nothing around the house, so how else could I explain how to get here? As I sat there waiting, I suddenly

Kamikaze Girls depicts the unusual friendship between a bored girl stuck in rural Japan who fantasizes about 18th century France and a spunky biker girl. Please enjoy this excerpt from the novel that inspired the manga and popular movie, both available from VIZ Media.

In the end, I decided to contact only the girl from Ibaraki, who happened to live in Shimotsuma too and was named Ichiko Shirayuri. "Miz Ryugasaki. Pleeze let me buy your Versace stuff. I don't have much money so I can't pay you a whole lot, but I really want some Versace no matter what, so I beg you wherefore pleeze." The writing was printed out in block letters, *please* was spelled "pleeze," and the ending had the mysterious, nonsensical clause, "so I beg you wherefore pleeze." I suppose she meant "so I beg you therefore please," which *still* wouldn't make much sense. But how was I to answer a request couched in the interrogative form of "wherefore please"? Guessing that the writer was maybe in the first year of middle school, I sent her the following answer: "Dear Miss Shirayuri, Thank you for your letter. Regarding the merchandise, I have a considerable variety of items in large quantities. If you would kindly inform me what sort of things you desire, I will select suitable items and send you another letter detailing their color, design, shape, and other particulars. As for the price, I am open to negotiation. However, as I stated in my ad, all of the Versace items I have are counterfeits, and I request your understanding of this point." Wondering if I had used too many big words and complicated sentence structures—did she even know what "particulars" and "negotiation" meant?— I sent off the letter anyway. I received an answer right away, the gist

FREE PREVIEW

Kamikaze Girls

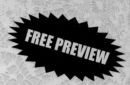

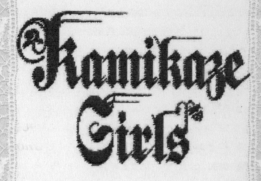

Novala Takemoto

Translated by
Akemi Wegmüller

WELCOME TO THE EXCITING NEW WORLD
OF VIZ MEDIA FICTION!

What you hold in your hands is a sneak preview of a bold step in publishing: America's No.1 manga publisher, VIZ Media, is proud to debut its fiction line, featuring the very best in new writing from Japan!

Our debut titles include *Fullmetal Alchemist: Land of Sand*, a spin-off based on the smash-success manga and anime; *Socrates in Love*, a stirring love story and the all-time best-selling novel in Japan; and *Ghost in the Shell 2: Innocence, After the Long Goodbye*, a powerful vision of the future set in the world of Mamoru Oshii's hit anime film.

Forthcoming titles include *Steamboy*, a novelization of the latest epic from anime auteur, Katsuhiro Otomo (director of *Akira*), and *Kamikaze Girls*, the Japanese cult classic exploring Japan's outré "Goth Lolita" subculture.

In 2004, VIZ released its first foray into fiction, the surprise best seller, *Battle Royale*, which demonstrated that there was a hungry audience for new fiction from Japan.

Now with the *Shojo Beat* fiction imprint, we hope you'll discover that when it comes to the exploding universe of Japanese pop culture, manga is just the beginning!

Tell us what you think about Shojo Beat Manga!

Our survey is now available online. Go to:

shojobeat.com/mangasurvey

Help us make our product offerings better!